# *Managing for Profits*

## A Guide for the Growing Business

# *Managing for Profits*

# A Guide for the Growing Business

**Curtis E. Tate, Jr.**
*Department of Management*
*College of Business Administration*
*The University of Georgia*

**Leon C. Megginson**
*Department of Management*
*College of Business Administration*
*University of Southern Alabama*

**Charles R. Scott, Jr.**
*Department of Management Science*
*College of Business Administration*
*University of Alabama*

**Lyle R. Trueblood**
*Department of Management & Marketing*
*College of Business Administration*
*University of Tulsa*

**DOW JONES-IRWIN**
Homewood, Illinois  60430

ISBN 0-87094-322-7
Library of Congress Catalog Card No. 83-72693

*Printed in the United States of America*

1 2 3 4 5 6 7 8 9 0 B 1 0 9 8 7 6 5 4

# Preface

It is the purpose of the authors to present you the reader with information that will facilitate more effective management of your assets. The objective of the text and exhibit materials is to provide you with a comprehensive range of materials that will enable you, as an individual interested in small business and efficient management of your assets, to effectively accomplish these combined objectives.

The experiences of the authors as scholars in the environment of business, entrepreneurship, and small business, and in the hands-on role as active participants in an on-going business, have provided them with the knowledge of what it takes to be effective in business. The historic success of our students and our business clients attest to this fact.

In the preparation of these materials, it has been our intent to recognize the interest and objectives of the more mature reader. In addition, we have wanted to provide materials that would serve the needs and interests of the person who is already operating their own business. We have been concerned for the prospective business person with aspirations to own and operate their own business.

We perceive entrepreneurship and small business as the gateway to our economic future. If that future is to provide us with an income, goods, services, and employment, then, this sector of our society must function dynamically. It is our intent to contribute to the success of these objectives.

Our thanks to Woodrow Stewart, attorney, Telford Law Group, for his counsel and editorial assistance.

Our special thanks to Mary Combs Tate, Jayne Megginson, Addie M. Scott, and Wyn Trueblood for their support.

We wish to express our gratitude to Robert Lee for his assistance in the collection of pertinent data and to Billie Najour for her faithful secretarial assistance in the preparation of the manuscript.

Curtis E. Tate, Jr.
Leon C. Megginson
Charles R. Scott, Jr.
Lyle R. Trueblood

# Contents

*quirements. Decide the Best Arrangement for the Sequence of Operations. Determine the General Layout. Plan the Detailed Layout for Efficiency and Effectiveness. Implementing Plans.*

Promoting Sale of Products and Services: *Advertising. Merchandising. Sales Promotion.*

*Be Timely. Controls Should Not Be Overly Costly. Controls Should Provide the Accuracy Needed. Controls Should Be Quantifiable and Measurable. Controls Should Show Causes When Possible. Controls Should Be Assigned to One Individual.* Causes of Poor Performance. Established Standards of Performance. Obtaining information on Actual Performance: *Indirect Control by Means of Reports. Effective Cost Control.* Comparing Actual Performance with Standards. The Design and Use of Budgets: *Sales Budget. Cash Budget. Credit, Collections, and Accounts Receivable. Other Types of Budgets.*

## Part Five
## Some Special Considerations in Managing an Independent Business   285

*Objectives. Difficulty of Making Rational Decisions. Incompetence of Family Members—or Worse. Lack of Definite Authority. Sharing the Profits. Some Sources of Help.* Some Difficult Problems with Managers: *What to Do with Incompetent Managers. Replacing Key Executives.* Preparing for Your Successor: *Providing Adequate Information. Starting Early. The Moment of Truth.* A Management Audit. Appendix: Inventory of Information Used to Manage and Operate a Company.

# Chapter One

# Independent Business: An Option in Personal Asset Management

## Introduction

Each day's mail makes one aware of the growing emphasis placed on considerations essential to personal asset management. There are a large variety of investment advisory services available to the individual as well as a number of advisory newsletters, financial journals, magazines, and TV business and financial news information programs whose stated intent is to facilitate wiser investment choices among numerous opportunities. It is the purpose of this publication to guide you the reader to understand the role of the independent business in personal asset management. The intent here is to encourage you to obtain a grasp of the opportunities that the independent business affords the owner of assets—recognizing, at the same time, the importance of managing the application of these assets through well-defined methods and procedures aimed toward the achievement of predetermined economic objectives.

The provisions of the Tax Recovery Act of 1981 and the 1982 Tax Law tend to make independent businesses an important investment alternative, even though the 1982 law reduced some of the benefits. Tax benefits have always been a significant consideration when considering the possible opportunities an independent business may afford the investor(s). The *accelerated depreciation allowances* along with the *investment tax credits* make investments

1

in some independent businesses especially attractive. For, in managing your assets, the prime consideration is "What am I going to be able to keep after taxes?"

## Introduction to Independent Business

Independent business by its nature tends to be a personal matter. Its success is determined to a significant extent by the personalities, the degree of self-discipline, the quality of individual commitment, and the strength of personal motivation. The successful independent business person appears to have certain attributes that enable him to function as an individual in an entrepreneurial environment (as oppposed to the so-called organization person who is better suited to the mode of the larger organizational structure). Viewed in this perspective, the independent business seems to be a viable consideration in personal asset management.

### Why the Independent Business?

It is the intent here to create an awareness of the *economic opportunities* that may be generated through the independent business mechanism. Many of the independent business benefit opportunities are not available to the individual(s) working for others or for a larger corporation. There are three important objectives for involvement with an independent business: the preservation of your asset resources; the creation of an economic opportunity that will contribute to the appreciation of the dollar value of your assets; and the provision for growth in the real value of your total assets.

### Contribution of the Independent Business

In today's society, which places so much emphasis on the giant corporation, it is easy to overlook the important contributions regularly made by independent businesses. Nor are we aware of the many economic benefits that are created through these contributions. Recent studies conducted in the United States and Canada have revealed the important role that independent businesses are playing in both nations' economies through the creation of new employment opportunities. Surprising to many people is the fact that independent businesses have created more new jobs than have larger firms.

### Competitive Advantage

Independent businesses are frequently pioneers in the creation of innovative methods and in the development of new products or services. There are times that the larger firm cannot justify the commitment of capital and labor to bring to fruition the production of a low-volume item; whereas the independent business firm may be able to justify the commitment of resources to bring such items to the market place.

It has been observed that in some situations the larger firm may prefer to purchase component items from a smaller firm, recognizing that the smaller firm may be more capital efficient as well as more production efficient. The benefit to the larger firm is the ability to purchase the needed components at less cost than might be possible if the items were produced in-house. In addition, by going outside, the larger firm is not required to make the capital investment an in-house production facility would require.

## What the Independent Business Can Do for You

The discussion that follows indicates the motivational aspects that directly or indirectly influence the effectiveness of your asset management. As you view both the large and small firm, you may become increasingly aware that the independent business provides a better opportunity for you; you can be more independent in your thinking and actions. This environment provides the opportunity to: express your own ideas; do your own thing; be creative and innovative; and finally, *be your own boss*.

### Economic Benefits

Economic benefits that may accrue to you as the owner of an independent business include the following:

1. You may be able to transfer a significant amount of income to an expenditure status. For example, the benefits of a travel allowance and other expense statement items may be utilized, as well as a company car.
2. Owning an independent business may provide possible tax benefits. Two possibilities are:
   a. Tax avoidance—transferring income to an expense status.
   b. Tax deferral—a shift from income tax liability to a capital gains liability or a gift or estate tax liability.
3. You may have an opportunity to increase your capital.
4. The independent business may be the vehicle to increase the net worth of your estate.

However, the independent business cannot do the following:

1. Free you of risk.
2. Assure you of personal security.
3. Free you from decision making.

4. Guarantee you success.
5. Guarantee you wealth.
6. Guarantee you income.
7. Free you of responsibility.
8. Free you of long hours.

## In Conclusion

If you are willing to weigh the positive against the negative, if you are willing to expend the effort, and if you are willing to work the long hours and carefully manage your time, then the odds are in your favor to be successful as an independent business owner. It would appear, based on these facts, that the economic and psychic rewards will justify the risk and effort. All of these things reflect on the effectiveness of your asset management.

# Opportunities for Independent Business

As a person considering the possibilities of entering an independent business, surely you are curious as to the potentials of various types of independent businesses. In the material that follows, an effort will be made to assist you in better understanding the opportunities different independent businesses may present.

### Minimal Capital Businesses

In recent years, with venture capital sources being more difficult to find, people have been encouraged to look for those businesses with minimal capital requirements. For many of these businesses, labor is a substitute for capital. In a number of instances, you might be surprised at the amount of income some of these businesses produce because of their good earning power. Examples are found in Table 1–1. After reviewing this list of examples, you may be able to think of other possibilities.

### Cottage-Type Industries

Another independent business area that appears to offer good possibilities is the *cottage industry* environment. Examples of these businesses are found in Table 1–2. This list is not all-inclusive. You may be able to think of additional business activities to add to Table 1–2.

Many people with full-time employment may be motivated, by interest or by the need for supplemental income, to initiate *part-time* businesses. In some instances, these businesses never become anything but part-time activities. Yet in other instances, they grow

**Table 1–1**
**Businesses with Low Capital Requirements**

Lawn service
Roof and gutter cleaning
Maid service (usually part-time)
Janitorial service
Window washing (homes and retail establishments)
Baby-sitting
Pickup truck for hire
Home repair service
Home remodeling
House sitting
Seamstress/alteration service
Typing service
Other

**Table 1–2**
**Cottage-Type Industries**

Handmade textiles
Canned food items (pickles, relishes, jams, jellies, preserves, etc.)
Baked food items
Handcrafted ceramics
Stained glass
Handcarved wood items
Handcrafted furniture
Other

into successful full-time businesses with continuing growth. An example of the latter from the period of the "Great Depression" is a home bakery that grew into a multimillion dollar business. Other examples of part-time business opportunities are found in Table 1–3. New opportunities continuously occur and may be added to this list of examples.

**Table 1–3**
**Part-Time Businesses**

Basement/garage machine shop
Job print shop (start in home environment)
Home baking
Cake and cookie decorating
Catering service
Part-time delivery service
Home decorating service
Dressmaking
Catering and managing children's parties
Bridal and wedding consultant
Other

Observations and studies of independent business indicate that people enter full-time small business for a variety of reasons. Some are motivated by interest and a strong commitment to a particular business; others are motivated by a strong desire for personal independence and the desire to be their own boss, while others see it as an investment opportunity. Still others are motivated by necessity—that is, the need for a source of personal income to put food on the table, a roof overhead, and clothes on their backs. A list of full-time business examples is found in Table 1–4.

*Table 1–4*
**Full-Time Businesses**

Intensive vegetable production (on small land area)
Florist shop
Growing cut flowers and potted plants
Auto repair
Auto customizing
Small machine shop
Sheet metal shop
Electric motor repair service
Electronic repair service
Instrument repair shop
Musical instrument repair service
Custom-made musical instruments
Small-engine repair service
Plumbing shop and service
Home repair
Home remodeling
Specialty shops:
   Clothing
   Greeting card
   Lighting
   Floor and wall covering
Real estate sales and development
Recording studio
Record store
Movie/video film studio
Movie/video tape store
Travel agency (requires 2 years' experience for
   license)
Manufacturing plant
Financial service
Investment counseling
Small loan company
Security dealer
Day care center:
   Children
   Adults
Other

One of the outstanding examples from Table 1–4 is the intensive production of vegetables. A small land area with the high application of plant food (fertilizer) and irrigation has been profitable for a former student. He was willing to commit himself to the labor demand and is now grossing $800 to $900 per day producing high-quality turnip greens, mustard greens, and collards on three-acre plots. What could you do with several acres of land in your part of the country?

The purpose of this section has been to guide your thinking to an awareness of the large array of independent business opportunities. Like a cafeteria, there is something for everyone; the choice is yours.

### Should You Obtain a Franchise?

There are many franchise possibilities that temptingly beckon the independent business owner. As previously stated, independent business is a very personal matter. Therefore, when considering a franchising possibility, one of the key considerations is how does it fit with you? Before answering this, there is an array of information to be considered.

First, not all franchises are solid, sound investment opportunities. Many times, even those that purport to guarantee your investment are hoaxes or frauds. You need to check with your attorney, CPA, or banker. In addition, you need to check with existing franchisees. Are they happy? Do they try to sell out to you?

Next, you need to consider what a franchise can do for you that you cannot do for yourself. A good franchise has many desirable features to offer:

1. A recognized name and trademark.
2. Frequently, an easily identified building or facade.
3. A recognized product or service.
4. An efficient layout and production system.
5. An efficient management and cost control system.
6. An effective training program for owner-managers and other key personnel.
7. Management assistance.
8. Regular periodic reviews of operations with suggestions for improvements.
9. Monthly operation reports submitted to franchisor for evaluation and returned to franchisee.
10. In some cases, financial assistance to franchisee.

Certainly a key consideration concerning franchising or being independent is the financing. Will it cost more or less to be franchised?

The question, "What can a franchise do for me that I cannot do for myself?" Your answer should give an indication in which direction you should move, franchise or independent. (See Exhibit 1–1 at the end of this chapter.) Greater detail on franchising will be found later in this book.

## Financing Your Own Business

Depending on your personal financial resources, financing could be one of the major obstacles to your entry into business. Since late 1968 or early 1969, the supply of new venture capital has been sharply reduced. Consequently, the demands on personal financial resources for funding a new business have been significantly increased.

Because of the stringency in the supply of new venture capital, one of the first steps you should undertake in planning for a new business is an inventory of your financial resources. The items listed may be used to guide you in the inventory process.

**Inventory List**

1. Cash in bank/savings and loan:
   a. Demand deposit — $_____
   b. Savings account — $_____
2. Security investments:
   a. Stocks — $_____
   b. Bonds — $_____
   c. Certificates of deposit — $_____
   d. Mutual funds — $_____
   e. Other — $_____
3. Equity:
   a. Personal residence — $_____
   b. Rental property — $_____
   c. Commercial/industrial — $_____
   d. Undeveloped property — $_____
4. Cash value of insurance:
   a. Life insurance — $_____
   b. Annuity — $_____
5. Discounted value of trust beneficiary — $_____
6. Discounted value of estate beneficiary — $_____
7. Value of other assets — $_____

Total value of all assets

The next step in this process, a step that should not be omitted, is to determine the amount of investment your new business will require. After you have determined the cash requirements of your potential new business, return to your asset inventory. Will you be able to personally finance 50–60 percent of the new business's initial investment?[1] If not, then you had best look for a compatible partner with such funds or dismiss the idea.

---

[1]Bankers tend to be very rigid in this criteria when lending money for a new business.

Many people have the mistaken idea that the SBA (Small Business Administration) has an abundant supply of money to lend. For many years, the predominant loans funded by the SBA have not been *direct loans* but *guaranteed loans* made by banks or other financial institutions. The credit requirements of the SBA are comparable to those of banks.

In recent years, a frequently used device in funding new businesses has been the limited partnership. This is done with the general partner being a corporation. It is a way for a minority investor to achieve control without being a major investor.

In this limited discussion, an effort has been made to give you a perspective of the possibilities and problems found in financing a new small business. This information is the result of working with a large variety of entrepreneurs interested in establishing new businesses. This will be discussed in more detail later in this book.

## Organizing a Small Business

An area that often appears to be neglected in establishing a new business is that of organization. In this section, the topic will be approached from two points of view: the legal form of organization and a functional structure.

### Legal Organizational Alternatives for the Independent Business

The selection of an appropriate legal form for your independent business is a vital consideration. Because of the direct relationship between legal form and tax consideration, the choice of the right legal form for your independent business will determine the tax liabilities on your assets. The most popular legal forms are:

1. Proprietorship.
2. Partnership.
3. Corporation.
4. Holding company.
5. Trust.

Each of these will be more adequately discussed later in this book.

### Administrative Organization of an Independent Business

Traditionally, when we think of a formal organization structure for a business, it is the larger corporation. However, it is equally important to develop a formal organization for the smaller firm, even for the one-person business. One of the major problems for this type and size of business is the management of time in relationship to activities. To be effective in this environment, there must be a balance between activities in order to accomplish the desired objective. A formal organization chart serves as a mechanism to aid in this balance of activities for an effective use of time.

For the larger independent business having many employees, the formal organization chart facilitates organizational planning the purposes of which are to provide for a division and specialization of labor; to provide for direction and control; to define roles, relationships, communication channels, and responsibility; and to provide management continuity. Another way of looking at the formal organization is the partitioning of the firm's activities into related functional parts.

Administrative organization will be discussed in more detail later in this book.

## Problems Inherent in an Independent Business

The following considerations give some indication of the needs to be met in the operation of an independent business:

1. The need to deal effectively with a sense of enterprise—i.e., the strong desire to use ideas, abilities, ambitions, and creativeness to the greatest degree possible.
2. The need to cope effectively with personal and family situations in a manner that will prevent their disruptive intrusion into the business.
3. The need to manage effectively the use of your time.
4. The need to achieve a quick, positive return of capital.
5. The need to deal effectively with a limited supply of capital.
6. The need to compensate effectively for educational and skill deficiencies.
7. The need to adapt effectively to change.
8. The need to acquire effectively and use market and operating information.
9. The need to utilize effectively human resources.
10. The need to meet the administrative requirements imposed by government regulation.

## Common Problems Observed in the Ongoing Independent Business

The analysis of a broad diverse spectrum of independent businesses has shown two common problem areas. Those areas are concerned with organizational problems and budgeting and control difficulties.

## Organizational Problems

The first area that seems to create a major difficulty is the failure to formally plan and implement effectively an organizational structure. It is the quality of organizational structure that determines management's ability to achieve successfully its objectives. The lack of an effective organizational structure seems to impede effective communication, interfere with role definition, and preclude appropriately defined responsibility and authority. This circumstance seems to create an environment in which there is a lack of understanding of role relationships. The consequence of this situation generally is a business that functions less effectively, resulting in the assets not being managed most advantageously. The organizational structure serves as an effective means to implement the budgetary and control plans.

## Budgetary and Control Difficulties

A second area observed to present difficulties in the independent business is that of budgets and budgetary controls. It is not unusual to discover that many independent business owners or managers are reluctant to become involved in budgets and the related budgetary control, planning, and implementation. All too frequently, the preference of these individuals is to "fly by the seat of the pants" or to depend on the use of that "old gut feeling." In rare instances, some of these people are successful in spite of themselves; or they may experience a "flash in the pan" significant success, after which they discover that it is all downhill from that point on.

As an entrepreneur concerned with managing your assets, you should be interested in using those assets in a manner that will enable you to achieve an optimum level of success. Therefore, you should not be interested in leaving the operation of your business to chance. We would compare the budgetary process with the flight plan a pilot prepares prior to takeoff, and the various budgetary control mechanisms with the instruments on the instrument panel. These provide the pilot with status information as he/she proceeds to a destination. Just as the pilot's major concern is reaching an objective destination, so your major concern is achieving the predetermined objective for your business.

## In Conclusion

The purpose of this discussion has been to sensitize you to the importance of developing formal organizational plans and of preparing an appropriate budget with its accompanying related control mechanism. These activities are interrelated and directly impact on asset management in terms of *asset conservation, asset appreciation,* and *asset growth.* In the final analysis, you are interested in achieving maximum profits.

In later sections of this book, the areas of organizational planning and budgetary planning and controls will be dealt with in greater detail.

## Defining Objectives for Your Business

Someone has said that the difference between the management and the nonmanagement person is the fact that the *management person makes it happen.* In order for you to *effectively* manage your assets, you must first define your objectives in terms of:

1. The kind of business you wish your business to be.
2. The size of business you want.
3. The *markets* you wish to serve.
4. The *products/service* you wish to produce/sell.
5. The *personnel* your business will require.
6. Your before- and after-tax profit objectives.

It is essential for you to make these determinations. As academic as they may seem to you, they are important. If you wish to achieve your objectives, then you need to develop a plan of operations which will enable you to achieve these objectives. This is a part of an *effective asset management* program.

### Identifying the Mission or Missions Needed to Achieve Your Objectives

An analogy from the military may be considered here. Generally, in a military environment, there is a major objective that is comprised of a group of subordinate objectives. It is possible to satisfy the big objective by accomplishing the subordinate objectives, each of which involves a different mission. In carrying out each individual mission, a different mix of resources is required, dependent on the nature of the objective and the kinds of obstacles involved.

In a business environment, you might think of the major objective as the total profit you wish to derive. For the subordinate objectives, you are concerned with the resources that must be assembled in the individual missions, which *combined* with other missions will make possible the achievement of the big objective. In other words, you are concerned with assembling the appropriate mix of assets required to achieve your mission. This, in turn, enables you to attain your profit goals or objectives.

### Strategic Planning for the Mission

For purposes of this discussion, strategy is defined as the devised plan which, when implemented, will facilitate the achievement of a specific objective. Strategic planning is defined as the formulation of a strategy. As you view strategic planning, you may think of it as relating to the external environment of the firm (i.e., being global in nature). No longer is it feasible for the independent business to think of its environment as being local in nature; social, political, and economic events in various areas of the world impact on even the smallest firm. These events have a relationship with the asset management activities of the firm.

## Are You an Independent Business Person?

The material in the previous portion of this chapter has been directed toward stimulating you to think about what is involved in starting and operating an independent business, and the economic opportunities to be found in owning an independent business. It seems appropriate at this point to have you take a comprehensive look at yourself in terms of your abilities, interests, and physical and behavioral characteristics. We suggest that you complete the questionnaire found in Exhibit 1–2 at the end of this chapter. You should do this as objectively and as honestly as possible. On completion, analyze and evaluate the information. For example: If you are not willing to spend more than 40 hours per week, if you are accustomed to being absent from work one day a week or four to five days a month, if you have very narrow work experience, and if you are not willing to make a complete commitment in time and resources, then you are not an independent business person. The questionnaire is a revealing instrument in determining whether individuals have the traits to be independent business persons or organization persons. If you use the questionnaire appropriately, you will better understand yourself and the route to follow.

## How to Start an Independent Business

If after going through the preceding material you have reached the conclusion that entering a small business is for you, then there are some additional procedures to be followed. These procedures have proven to be important to launch successfully a small business endeavor. The procedures are *an economic feasibility study* and *a formal proposal.*

## Summary

In this chapter, there has been an attempt to make you aware of the differentiating characteristics of the independent business, to focus your attention on the purpose of this book, and to alert you to the contributions that independent businesses have made. You have been directed to consider the benefits of having your own independent business. Some of the problem areas associated with the independent business have been identified. An effort has been made to stress the importance of objectives, their role, and their benefits. Tied closely to objectives is the matter of identifying and planning missions. Another related area is that of strategy and strategic planning.

Reflecting on this chapter should help you perceive the many complexities of owning and operating an independent business. There are both challenge and opportunity in owning and operating a small or independent business, if you appropriately manage your assets.

# EXHIBITS

*Exhibit 1-1*
**Evaluating Whether to Be Independent or to Operate a Franchise**

In today's world, perhaps, an individual has more choices than at any other time in history in selecting what kind of entrepreneur he or she would like to be. Basically, the choices fall into two broad categories, with a multiplicity of combinations in each. The two categories are: to be an independent entrepreneur or to be a franchisee. It is the purpose of this questionnaire to aid you in choosing between these two categories.

Indicate your choices by checking *Yes* or *No*.

**My objectives in life**

Check the appropriate boxes.

1. ☐ To make a lot of money.
2. ☐ To be my own boss.
3. ☐ To have a comfortable living.
4. ☐ To have a business of my own that will allow me leisure time.
5. ☐ To work for someone else.
6. To avoid accepting responsibility:
   a. ☐ For providing employment for others.
   b. ☐ For providing products/services to others.
7. ☐ To spend whatever time and effort is necessary to achieve success.

**My present economic status**

8. My net worth is:
   a. Equity value of real estate          $_____
   b. Cash surrender value of life insurance  $_____
   c. Marketable securities               $_____
   d. Savings                            $_____
   e. Other                             $_____
9. My annual income is:
   a. Salary                            $_____
   b. Special income                     $_____
   c. Investment:
      (1) Rental income                 $_____
      (2) Stocks                        $_____
      (3) Bonds                         $_____
          Total investment income       $_____
   d. Interest                          $_____
   e. Annuities                         $_____
   f. Trust                             $_____
   g. Estate                           $_____
   h. Other                            $_____
      Total annual income              $_____
10. My annual financial responsibilities are:
    a. Mortgage payments               $_____
    b. House insurance                 $_____

c. Real and personal property taxes   $_____
d. Car payments                      $_____
e. Life insurance                    $_____
f. Utility bills                     $_____
g. Other loans, principal and interest  $_____
h. Alimony and child support         $_____
i. Children's education expense       $_____
j. Medical/dental expense            $_____
k. Medical insurance                 $_____
l. Household expense                 $_____
m. House/lawn maintenance           $_____
n. Auto expense                     $_____
o. Food                            $_____
p. Business/professional expense      $_____
q. Other                           $_____
   Total annual personal expense     $_____

**Marital status**

11. ☐ Married
12. ☐ Single
13. ☐ Divorced
14. Children?                         ☐ Yes ☐ No
    If yes, their ages are: _____

**My education**

15. Elementary completed               ☐ Yes ☐ No
16. High school:
    ☐ 1 year
    ☐ 2 years
    ☐ 3 years
    ☐ 4 years
17. Technical school                  ☐ Yes ☐ No
    Type of training _____
    _____

18. College:
    ☐ 1 year
    ☐ 2 years
    ☐ 3 years
    ☐ 4 years
    Kind of degree: _____
    Major_____
    Minor _____
    Master's degree_____ Kind _____
    Fields _____
    Other: _____
    _____

## *Exhibit 1–1* (concluded)

**Experience**

(List in order from last to earliest.)

19. Last/current job _____

Employer _____

Title _____

Dates of employment _____ to _____

20. Previous job _____

Employer _____

Title _____

Dates of employment _____ to _____

21. Previous job _____

Employer _____

Title _____

Dates of employment _____ to _____

Identify what ability you gained from each employment situation:

_____

_____

_____

_____

_____

_____

_____

_____

**My capabilities**

Check the appropriate boxes.

22. ☐ Directing the activities of others.

23. ☐ Planning an activity in a manner that takes the lead time, effort, and materials into account.

24. ☐ My ability to serve people in a pleasing manner.

25. ☐ Helping people resolve their personal differences.

26. ☐ Managing money.

27. ☐ Keeping records.

28. ☐ Organizing people, money, machines, and things to produce products/services.

29. ☐ My ability to effectively follow the instructions and directions of others.

30. ☐ To effectively be my own boss.

31. ☐ To be a self-starter.

32. ☐ To take initiative.

33. ☐ To make decisions.

34. ☐ My innovative ability to create new ideas for products and services.

**My inadequacies**

Check the appropriate boxes.

35. ☐ I can't make decisions.

36. ☐ I postpone making decisions.

37. ☐ I try to get others to make decisions for me.

38. ☐ I dislike assuming responsibility.

39. ☐ I avoid responsibilities whenever possible.

40. ☐ I do not handle money well.

41. ☐ I seem unable to keep my checkbook balanced.

42. ☐ I am generally insecure without someone to guide and support me.

**Franchisor system**

Could you accept working within the rigidity of the organizational framework imposed by a franchisor system? This means, can you do it their way?  ☐ Yes ☐ No

**Kind of business**

What kind of business would you be most happy operating as an owner/manager? (Be honest with yourself in answering this question. Be as specific as necessary to provide an adequate description of the business.)

43. Answer: _____

_____

_____

_____

_____

_____

_____

_____

_____

_____

**Review**

Carefully review the answers you have given to the above questions. Be honest and frank with yourself. Do you think you could accomplish your objectives in life and achieve a reasonable level of success and happiness by:

44. Having your own independent business? ☐ Yes ☐ No

45. Owning a franchise?  ☐ Yes ☐ No

46. Working for someone else?  ☐ Yes ☐ No

*Exhibit 1–2*
**Performing a Personal Self-Analysis**

The purpose of this questionnaire is to aid you in analyzing and evaluating your objectives, abilities, interests, health, economic status, and responsibilities in order to determine whether you would be more effective working for someone else or owning your own business.

You should answer each one of these questions *as conscientiously as possible,* so that you will be able to see whether you have the possibilities of succeeding in a small business. Incidentally, we have been able to develop a profile of people who have answered this questionnaire even when they have not answered a given question. In other words, *the missing answers tend to* be as important as the ones included in evaluating your possibilities. When you have finished the form, look at the facts revealed by the answers in order to have an insight into your future.

Please indicate your choice by checking the appropriate space.

1. My objective in life is:
   *a.* To make a lot of money _____
   *b.* To be my own boss _____
   *c.* To have a comfortable living _____
   *d.* To have a business of my own that will allow me leisure time _____
   *e.* To work for someone else _____
   *f.* To avoid accepting responsibility:
      (1) For providing employment for others _____
      (2) For providing products/service to others _____
   *g.* To spend whatever time and effort necessary to achieve success _____

2. My marital status is:
   *a.* Married _____
   *b.* Single _____
   *c.* Divorced _____
   *d.* Children: Yes _____ No _____
            Ages _____
   Given these responsibilities I plan to commit myself to (circle one):
   20    40    60    80    hours per week to the business.

3. My education is:
   *a.* Elementary _____
   *b.* High school:
      1 year _____ 2 years _____ 3 years _____ 4 years _____
   *c.* Technical school _____
      Type of training _____
   *d.* College:
      1 year _____ 2 years _____ 3 years _____ 4 years _____
      Kind of degree: _____
      Major _____ Minor _____

*Exhibit 1–2* (continued)

Master's degree _____ Kind _____
Fields _____  _____  _____
Other _____

4.  My experience is (list in order from latest to earliest):
    a.  Last/current job _____
        Employer _____
        Title _____
        Dates of employment _____ to _____
    b.  Job _____
        Employer _____
        Title _____
        Dates of employment _____ to _____
    c.  Job _____
        Employer _____
        Title _____
        Dates of employment _____ to _____
        Ability I gained from each employment situation:

        _____
        _____
        _____
        _____
        _____

5.  My expertise is:

                                        (check one)
    (List)                     High    Medium    Low

    _____    _____   _____   _____
    _____    _____   _____   _____
    _____    _____   _____   _____
    _____    _____   _____   _____
    _____    _____   _____   _____
    _____    _____   _____   _____
    _____    _____   _____   _____

6.  My hobbies are: _____
    _____
    _____
    _____
    _____

7.  I spend my free time doing: _____
    _____
    _____
    _____
    _____

**Exhibit 1–2** (continued)

8. My capabilities are:
   *a.* Directing the activities of others _____
   *b.* Planning an activity in a manner that takes the least time, effort, and material _____
   *c.* Serving people in a pleasing manner _____
   *d.* Helping people resolve their personal differences _____
   *e.* Managing money _____
   *f.* Keeping records _____
   *g.* Organizing people, money, machines, and things to produce products/services _____
   *h.* Effectively following instructions and directions of others _____
   *i.* Being my own boss _____
   *j.* Being a self-starter _____
   *k.* Taking initiative _____
   *l.* Making decisions _____
   *m.* Creating new ideas for products and services _____
   *n.* Other _____

9. My inadequacies are:
   *a.* I can't make decisions _____
   *b.* I postpone making decisions _____
   *c.* I try to get others to make decisions for me _____
   *d.* I dislike assuming responsibility _____
   *e.* I avoid responsibilities whenever possible _____
   *f.* I do not handle money well _____
   *g.* I seem unable to keep my checkbook balanced _____
   *h.* I am generally insecure without someone to guide and support me _____
   *i.* Other _____

10. Regarding my health:
    *a.* I always feel good _____
    *b.* I can work two jobs without ever getting tired _____
    *c.* I frequently find it difficult to finish the day _____
    *d.* I have a headache: Once a week _____
        Once every two weeks _____
        Once or twice a month _____
        Seldom if ever _____
    *e.* I sleep: 6 hours _____ 7 hours _____ 8 hours _____
        9 hours _____ Less than 6 hours a day _____
    *f.* I have to take some form of medication to sleep: Yes _____
        No _____
    *g.* I have bad dreams: A lot _____ Average _____ Seldom _____
    *h.* I get dizzy: Sometimes _____ Frequently _____ Seldom _____ Never _____
    *i.* I am absent from work:
        (1) One day a week _____
        (2) One day every two weeks _____

*Exhibit 1–2* (continued)

    (3)  One to two days per month ———
    (4)  Four to five days a year ———
    (5)  Rarely ———
  *j.*  My last complete physical was ———
                     (date)
  *k.*  I have these known health problems: ————————————

————————————————————————————————

  *l.*  I have no known health problems ———

11.  My health permits me to (check one):

| | | | |
|---|---|---|---|
| *a.* | Travel a great amount | Yes ——— | No ——— |
| *b.* | Engage in a lot of physical work | Yes ——— | No ——— |
| *c.* | Work long hours | Yes ——— | No ——— |
| *d.* | Function well in tense situations | Yes ——— | No ——— |
| *e.* | Use my eyes extensively | Yes ——— | No ——— |

12.  My health keeps me from: ————————————————

————————————————————————————————

————————————————————————————————

————————————————————————————————

13.  Regarding my present economic status:
    *a.*  My net worth is:
        (1)  Equity value of real estate          $ ———
        (2)  Cash surrender value of life insurance  $ ———
        (3)  Marketable securities         $ ———
        (4)  Savings                $ ———
        (5)  Other                 $ ———
    *b.*  My annual income is:
        (1)  Salary                $ ———
        (2)  Special income         $ ———
        (3)  Investment:
            (*a*)  Rental income      $ ———
            (*b*)  Stocks          $ ———
            (*c*)  Bonds          $ ———
                 Total investment income  $ ———
        (4)  Interest              $ ———
        (5)  Annuities            $ ———
        (6)  Trust               $ ———
        (7)  Estate              $ ———
        (8)  Other               $ ———
                 Total annual income     $ ———
    *c.*  My annual financial responsibilities are:
        (1)  Mortgage payments       $ ———
        (2)  House insurance        $ ———
        (3)  Real and personal property taxes  $ ———

*Exhibit 1-2* (concluded)

|  |  |  |
|---|---|---|
| (4) | Car payments | $ _____ |
| (5) | Life insurance | $ _____ |
| (6) | Utility bills | $ _____ |
| (7) | Other loan repayments | $ _____ |
| (8) | Alimony and child support | $ _____ |
| (9) | Children's education expense | $ _____ |
| (10) | Medical/dental expense | $ _____ |
| (11) | Medical insurance | $ _____ |
| (12) | Household expense | $ _____ |
| (13) | House/lawn maintenance | $ _____ |
| (14) | Auto expense | $ _____ |
| (15) | Food | $ _____ |
| (16) | Business/professional expense | $ _____ |
| (17) | Other | $ _____ |
|  | Total annual personal expense | $ _____ |

14. How much can I afford to risk?   $ _____

15. Considering my responsibilities, my interests, my hobbies, my health, and my economic status, I am willing:

    *a.* To devote _____ hours per week to the business

    *b.* To invest $ _____ in the business

16. What specific kind of business would I be most happy operating as an owner/manager? _____

    _____

    _____

    _____

    _____

    _____

    _____

17. How would I compensate for my inadequacies? _____

    _____

    _____

    _____

    _____

    _____

18. After carefully reviewing the answers I have given to the questions above, being honest and frank with myself, I think that I could accomplish my objectives in life, and achieve a reasonable level of success and happiness by:

    *a.* Having my own independent business _____

    *b.* Working for someone else   _____

# Part 1

# The Independent Business and Its Owner-Manager

About 95 percent of all business enterprises in the United States are classified as small. Because these small businesses are so prevalent and perform such an important function in our economic system, it is desirable to start this book by showing the challenges and opportunities involved in owning/managing one of them. Owners and managers of these independent enterprises usually believe in individual freedom, initiative, and the free enterprise system.[1] Most people consider it important to keep this segment of our business society healthy.

The first thing to do when considering a small business is to decide whether owning or managing such an enterprise is the right course of action for you.

In Chapter 2, we direct your attention toward defining your objectives. In Chapter 3, you are placed in the role of the independent (small) business owner. Then Chapter 4 carries you into planning in the ongoing business.

---

[1]While some make a distinction between a small business and an independent business enterprise, we will use the terms interchangeably.

# Chapter Two

# What Are Your Objectives?

After presenting the challenges afforded by owning and operating a small business, we would like to explore the role you could play as the owner of one of these important units. In this chapter, we discuss (1) some important personal objectives, (2) the objectives of independent businesses, and (3) the importance of meshing these objectives.

## Some Personal Objectives

An occupation represents much more than just a set of skills and functions—it represents a way of life. It largely provides and determines the environment—both physical and psychological—in which the individual lives; it selects and often strengthens the traits that the person most frequently uses. The occupation usually carries with it a status in the community and provides the individual's social roles and patterns for living. Since it largely determines the sorts of persons with whom one spends much of one's life, it greatly influences value judgments and ethical standards. Occupational preference and personality traits are also usually related. Consequently, the ultimate objective in choosing one's occupation should be the satisfaction of individual needs.

### Theoretical Needs

Many efforts have been made to classify and explain human needs. The more popular efforts are presented here as a summary for readers who have studied them elsewhere, or as an introduction for those who have not.

***Maslow's Need Hierarchy.*** Abraham Maslow, a psychologist, said that human needs could be ranked in an ascending order, or hierarchy, from the bottom up.[1] As one need is satisfied, the next-higher need comes into play. The left side of Figure 2–1 shows these needs in a stairway form. Starting with physiological needs such as hunger, one can reach the top need only after satisfying those in between.

***Figure 2–1***
**Comparison of Maslow and Herzberg Models**

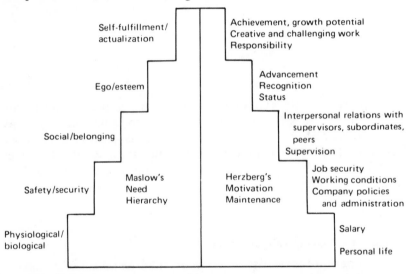

Adapted from Douglas McGregor, *The Human Side of Enterprise* (New York: McGraw Hill, 1960), pp. 36–39; and Frederick Herzberg et al., *The Motivation to Work*, 2d ed. (New York: John Wiley & Sons, 1959).

***Herzberg's Motivators and Maintenance Factors.*** Frederick Herzberg, another psychologist, said there are two sets of factors present in every job situation.[2] One set of factors is necessary in order to maintain a good working relationship but does not moti-

---

[1]Douglas McGregor, *The Human Side of Enterprise* (New York, McGraw-Hill, 1960), pp. 36–39.

[2]Frederick Herzberg, Bernard Mausner, and Barbara Block Syderman, *The Motivation to Work*, 2d ed. (New York: John Wiley & Sons, 1959).

vate the individual to produce at a higher level. The right side of Figure 2–1 shows the lower steps as the factors supporting a good working relationship and employee satisfaction. The upper steps show the motivating factors. These needs or motives primarily pertain to managerial and nonmanagerial employees. They are not necessarily those of owners or entrepreneurs. In fact, they tend not to be. They are included here, though, for your use in evaluating the needs and motives of independent business owners.

## Motives of Independent Business Owners

The above discussion of human needs provides the background for further study. As the owner of an independent business, you have the potential for fulfilling all of these needs through managing your own firm. The manner in which your needs are fulfilled depends upon the knowledge, skills, and personality traits you bring to your business. Your personal objectives express the type of life you wish to lead.

A great deal depends on the type of person you are and your dedication to your business. Owning your own business can be very rewarding in the following ways:

1.  You can make a great deal of money, including certain expense account benefits. Be sure to bear in mind the legality and tax accountability of these!
2.  You can perform a satisfying service to your community.
3.  You can obtain prestige in your community.
4.  You can find the challenges and new experiences many and varied.
5.  You can be proud of what you have built.

In managing something you have built, there is a certain satisfaction that does not come to you from directing a business that others have built. But before you decide upon this course, questions must be answered—if you are to succeed. Ambition, desire, capital, and willingness are not enough. You still need:

1.  Technical and managerial know-how.
2.  Preparation.
3.  Experience.
4.  Ability.
5.  Perseverance.
6.  Willingness to work.
7.  Outgoing personality.
8.  Judgment.
9.  Competitive spirit.
10. Health to use all of these.

Now, one last time—before you consider risking your money, time, and effort to become an entrepreneur—ask yourself the following questions:

1. Am I willing to make the necessary personal and family sacrifices?
2. What is more important—to make a lot of money or to perform a useful service?
3. Do I have the patience and tenacity required for this type of activity?
4. Do I have the skills and knowledge to collect the resources needed; can I convert those resources to goods and services that consumers will want; and can I organize and direct the activities needed to succeed?
5. How much of me do I want to put into the business?
6. How much money do I need to get started, and where do I get it?

Many other questions should be raised, but we will discuss these elsewhere.

## Objectives of an Independent Business

Since the most valid distinction between a smaller independent and a big business is based on the intentions, aims, goals, or objectives of the owner-manager and the firm itself, these factors deserve considerable attention at the very beginning of your interest in an independent business. One of the most important functions you as the owner-manager will perform is setting your goals and objectives. The objectives are the ends toward which all the activities of your organization will be aimed. Essentially, they determine the character of the firm and are the purposes toward which all the activities of your organization—including plans, policies, and programs—will be directed. They are the focal point of all your entrepreneurial functions.

### Difference from Personal Objectives

An important distinction should be made between the objectives of the organization itself and those of its owner(s), managers, and employees. This distinction is important because the two sets of objectives are not necessarily the same. We will now look at some organizational objectives that should be considered along with the personal objectives just mentioned.

For the business itself, there are at least two sets of objectives: the overall enterprise objectives and the subsidiary goals of the individual parts of the organization. Overall objectives should be set, for without them there is the danger that individual goals may not be consistent with each other. The enterprise's objectives give unity of direction to the organization and provide standards by which actions of members of the firm can be measured. Each part of the firm will then set its objectives in order to contribute to the objectives of the enterprise.

Among the overall enterprise objectives that are important for you to consider are those of:

1. Service
2. Profit.
3. Social goals
4. Growth.

These objectives are interrelated, as shown in Figure 2–2. The service objective must be achieved if the profit objective is to be attained. Yet profits must also be used to reach the social and service objectives. Growth depends on attaining profit and social objectives.

**Figure 2–2**
**Interrelationships of a Firm's Objectives**

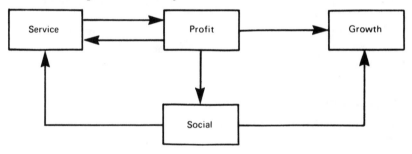

## Service Objective

The overall objective of any business organization must be to perform a useful service for society by producing and distributing goods or services (or the satisfaction associated with them) to the public. Even in a profit-oriented organization, the primary objective is service to the public in the form of producing goods or services at a cost that will ensure a fair price to the consumer and adequate profits to the owners. Thus, the person who aspires to operate an independent business must keep uppermost in mind the necessity for having service as the primary objective—with profit as a natural consequence. If the enterprise ceases to give service, people will not accept the organization, and it will go out of business. Similarly, if profits do not result, the owners will cease operating the firm.

When you make decisions concerning the type of business you desire to establish or enter, the products you offer, and the type(s) of customers you will serve, you will be considering the service objective.

## Profit Objective

A private organization is expected to receive a profit for its operations. In a capitalistic, free-enterprise economy, profit is acceptable and considered to be in the public interest. The profit motive is not always understood, so a word of explanation may be needed by some readers. The production of profits is the reward for taking risks—such as investing your funds in an untried business and trying to anticipate the needs and wants of the public—and profits are required if a private business is to survive. Profits are needed to create new jobs, acquire new facilities, and develop new products or services. The making of profit is fundamental to a capitalistic society. Profits are not self-generating, however; they are residual and come into existence through satisfaction of the demand for a product or service. Products and services must be produced efficiently and effectively.

In summary, profits compensate for your acceptance of business risks and for performance of economic service. They are needed to assure continuity of your business.

## Social Objectives

Your firm also has social objectives pertaining to people in the community other than customers—employees, suppliers, the government, and the community itself. All of these groups should be served effectively. You—as owner—therefore have a social responsibility. You occupy a trusteeship position and should act to protect the interests of your customers, employees, suppliers, and the general public, as well as to make a profit. Your personal moral code should have a sound basis if you are to act fairly and honestly in your relationships with all these groups.

An important social contribution of the small organization is to provide employees with a sense of belonging, identity, and esprit de corps. According to the sales manager of a small distribution company:

> An independent business is both an economic and a social system. There is a sense of belonging that is hard to find in a big company. Also, in a smaller company, the job carries with it a position which gives the person a sense of prestige that he would lose if he went to a larger company.

## Growth Objective

You should be concerned with your firm's growth and select a growth objective early in your career. Some of the questions you need to answer in setting this objective are:

1. Do I seek relative stability or merely survival?
2. Do I seek a rate of profit which is satisfactory, considering my efforts and investment?
3. Do I seek to maximize profits?
4. Will I be satisfied to remain small?
5. Do I want to grow and challenge larger firms?

Walter Barnett is a local contractor specializing in commercial construction.[3] He has had many offers to expand locally, regionally, and even statewide. He has consistently chosen to remain small, bid on the jobs he wants, have few labor problems, earn a comfortable living, and enjoy life. He appears to be succeeding in achieving these objectives.

Ray Williams, who built residential housing, had an excellent reputation for quality at a reasonable price. He received an offer to associate with a firm in an adjoining state, and he accepted. When the economy slackened 18 months later, construction declined, money became tight, and the firm found itself overextended. He is now back working for another contractor.

## Subsidiary Goals

The primary function of the independent business manager is to direct the activities of the business toward attaining its overall objectives. Subsidiary objectives should be set for each functional unit of the organization (such as production, marketing, finance, personnel, and research) to provide guidelines in meeting the overall objectives of the business. In addition, the personal objectives of all individuals performing tasks within each functional unit must be considered and directed toward the organization's overall objective.

This process is not as simple as it may appear, for each level of objectives may consist of several related objectives. In a practical business situation, the attainment of two or more objectives on any given level is often achieved only at the expense of other objectives on the same level or between levels. Consequently, conflict arises between objectives. This conflict must be resolved or minimized if productivity and profitability are to be achieved.

---

[3]The names in these incidents and illustrations are fictitious, although the events are real.

## Meshing of Objectives

A survey of 97 small, owner-managed firms in the San Antonio area revealed a correlation between profitability, customer satisfaction, manager satisfaction, and psychic rewards.[4] It also showed that the chances of success are greatly increased when the objectives of the business—service at a profit—are meshed with the owner's personal objectives. The results of the study indicate that it is possible to integrate multiple objectives into a unified whole.

Questions arise as to whether this integration of objectives can actually be accomplished and to what extent it can be achieved in independent business establishments. An integration of objectives can be accomplished if the emphasis is directed toward optimizing objectives and minimizing company and personal conflicts. Communication plays an important part in the process. The close interpersonal relationships between owners of independent businesses and their subordinates, customers, and others speed up communications and make integration easier.

One thing that may appeal to persons interested in an independent business is to observe the manner and kind of business that seems to come from a simple beginning, yet provides a good income.

> An example of this was Susan Jones's chicken debeaking business. Susan was married to Tim Jones, who at one time was in the poultry supply business. She was a college graduate with a major in home economics and wanted to supplement the family income.
>
> The beaks of young baby chicks have to be trimmed to prevent them from pecking other chicks and injuring them. Susan used a machine that debeaks and cauterizes the cut in a single operation when the chick is five or six days old.
>
> She trained several young women to work with her each day she was in the field. The day normally started for Susan and four to six members of her crew when they climbed into her station wagon about 4 A.M. and departed for the poultry farm to be worked that day. After debeaking 100,000 birds (usually eight hours work), they were finished for the day.
>
> The work was done under terms of a contract with the poultry farmer at a rate of 5 cents per chick. Though the work was not continuous, Susan's income was substantial for the year. Tim Jones took great pride in his wife's business and the income it generated.

## Summary

In this chapter, we have discussed the objectives of independent businesses, some personal objectives of business owners and managers, and the importance of meshing together those objectives.

---

[4]Hal B. Pickle and Brain S. Rungeling, "Empirical Investigation of Entrepreneurial Goals and Customer Satisfaction," *Journal of Business* 46, no. 2 (April 1973), pp. 268–73.

There are at least four important objectives for your independent business. These are service, profit, social goals, and growth. The two overriding objectives are service and profit. A primary objective of your firm should be that of providing a direct service. Profit is your reward for accepting business risks and performing an economic service. Risk is necessary if you are to continue doing those two things.

Next, you must decide upon your own objectives, which motivate you to become an independent business manager. The most important ones are achievement, challenge, stimulation of new experiences, growth and advancement, seeking identity, recognition, and esteem of others. The personal rewards to proprietors of independent businesses are many and varied.

For the most successful operation of an independent business, business objectives must be integrated with your personal objectives.

# Chapter Three

# You Are the Owner of an Independent Business

Earlier, some of the characteristics, advantages, and disadvantages of independent business enterprises were pointed out. Personal and business objectives were looked at in Chapter 2. Now you should look at some unique characteristics of successful independent business managers, at some personal requirements for success in an independent business, and at yourself to see whether you have the characteristics needed for success in managing an independent firm.

As one studies the behavior of people who choose careers in an independent business, one is made acutely aware that all too often failure has resulted from one or more of the following weaknesses:

1. Too much was left to chance.
2. Too many decisions were made by hunch or through intuition.
3. The crucial obstacles went unnoticed.
4. The amounts of time and physical effort demanded of the independent business manager were not recognized and planned for.
5. The amount of capital required was not determined or—as is more often true—was grossly underestimated.

Helping you avoid these pitfalls is what this chapter is all about.

# Characteristics of Successful Independent Business Managers

The skills, abilities, and personal characteristics of owner-managers exert a more powerful influence on the fortunes of small companies than they do on those of large firms. Whether you have these characteristics or not should then weigh heavily in determining whether or not you enter a small firm. Also, the kinds of procedures and methods you adopt in a small firm should be designed not only to offset any personal deficiencies you may have but also to build upon your strengths.

What, then, are the characteristics of successful owners of small enterprises? There are at least five unique characteristics of such individuals, namely:

1. A great sense of independence.
2. A strong sense of enterprise.
3. Motivation as much by personal and family considerations as by professional choices.
4. High valuation of one's own time.
5. Expectation of quick and concrete results.

No individual will have all these characteristics, to be sure; but they are the ones present most frequently in owner-managers of independent firms.

Found in many owner-managers are two characteristics that do not necessarily lead to success: (1) Independent business owners tend to enter the business more by chance than by design, and (2) they may have limited formal education. If there exists a limited formal education, in many instances this is offset by added effort to gather the needed information. Certainly, those businesses with a "high technology orientation," such as those in "Silicon Valley," require a high degree of technical competence.

## A Great Sense of Independence

Successful independent business managers have a highly developed sense of independence; they have a strong desire to be free of outside control, whether this control is financial, governmental, or any other type of restraint on their initiative. They are the unreconstructed rebels of the business world, enjoying the feeling of freedom that comes from being captains of their own fate.

> Robert Smith worked his way through college sweeping floors in a lighting fixture store. Later, he set up a wholesale division for his boss. However, he believed that success depended upon "never working for a company that you can't own," and building a firm of

moderate size that "you can control completely." Seven years ago, at age 23, he borrowed $75,000, purchased some metalworking equipment and set up shop, producing and selling modern lighting fixtures. Now, he sells several million dollars worth of lamps each year.

## A Sense of Enterprise

The managers of independent businesses have a strong sense of enterprise, which gives them a desire to use their ideas, abilities, ambitions, aspirations, and initiatives to the greatest degree possible. They are able to conceive new ideas, plan them, see them carried out, and profit from the results of those plans. This is not always true in a larger organization where different specialists do different phases of the work.

> George Martin was born in Europe under Nazi domination. His goal, from the time he came to the United States at age 16, was to become a millionaire. During college and while in the army, he dabbled in buying and selling securities. This activity provided him with the savings to start a service putting together tax-sheltered investments for wealthy people. At 31 years of age, he attributed his millions to "hard work, intuitive skills, persistence—and luck."

Another aspect of enterprise that is almost always present in independent business owners is their drive for achievement and their willingness to work long, hard hours to reach their goals.

> Dick Crowe, from a middle-class New York neighborhood, worked his way through college doing odd jobs. After graduation, he became a real estate agent and later bought a Weight Watchers franchise. According to his own appraisal, he is totally committed to the firm, works long hours, and doesn't know how to enjoy himself. "I can't relax, for my mind is always working, thinking, calculating."

## Personal and Family Considerations

Independent business managers are probably motivated as much by personal and family considerations as by the profit-making motive. Quite frequently, our students tell us they are returning home to start businesses because that is what their families expect them to do. Even more frequent is the comment that they are going back to run the family businesses rather than go somewhere else and work for another company. In both cases, the persons are doing it from a sense of obligation to the family rather than from the desire for profit.

Other examples are:

A young man resigned a regular commission in the United States Army, where he was quite satisfied to make a career, in order to return to a wholesale distributorship and replace his father, whose health was failing.

Another young man gave up a promising career as a professional personnel administrator in order to replace his father in his family's automobile agency. His father had died, and his mother either had to sell out or get the son to run the firm.

A third man resigned from college in his senior year to run the family-owned, picture-framing business when his father died.

## Perception of the Value of Time

Time is especially valuable to independent business owners because of the many duties they must perform. Managers of large corporations are expected to give a certain percentage of their time to public relations and have someone else perform their duties while they are away. Independent business managers must still perform all the duties even if they engage in outside activities. They are very jealous of their time, and they may appear irritable if someone infringes upon that time.

> Dudley Moore has an insurance agency. He tries very hard to protect his time so as much of it as feasible can be used for his business purposes. For example, even when engaged in nonbusiness activities, he takes steps to conserve his time. He accepts only those positions where his expertise is really needed and he feels he can make a contribution.

## Expectation of Quick Results

Entrepreneurs expect quick and concrete results from an investment, whether it is an investment of time or of capital. They seek a quick turnover of a relatively small amount invested in the firm, rather than engaging in the long-range planning that is common in large businesses.

In general, independent business managers are free and wish to remain free from the artificial conformity required in larger organizations. They are rugged individualists who are willing to take risks and who have the determination and perseverance to capitalize upon those risks.

### Some Other Characteristics of Independent Business Owners

In addition to these characteristics which tend to lead to success, owners of independent businesses tend to enter the business by chance and to have limited formal education.

*Chance versus Design.* Many people have gravitated by chance into a position of ownership or management of an independent firm, rather than having prepared for it by design. This is especially true when they have grown up in the business, have lived with it from day to day, and then one day find themselves in the position of having to take over the business. These are the owners or managers who quite frequently ask for assistance in the form of management training and development. This type of individual differs sharply from those who come to college with the ambition to become professional managers, gearing their programs toward that end.

> Joe Ditta graduated from college in music and sought a career in the music profession. He had worked in the family restaurant while attending school. Soon after he became a professional singer, his father died; he returned home to manage the restaurant for the family.

*Limited Formal Education.* Independent business managers are apt to have only limited formal education. Yet they tend to supplement this learning with informal learning through reading, through "picking the brains" of more learned friends, and through extension and correspondence courses.

## Effects of External Factors

While we accept these characteristics of successful independent business managers, another theory has been developed from several studies at Harvard and MIT.[1] The researchers examined entrepreneurs who were involved in substantial ventures. They found that even though very successful entrepreneurs may ultimately stand apart, at the beginning they are in most respects very much like other ambitious, striving individuals. It was also found that the entrepreneurial interests for those who became independent business managers were a function more of external differences than of internal ones. Their decisions were the result more of practical readiness or financial constraints than of individual psychology or personality.

---

[1] Be sure to read Patrick R. Liles, "Who Are the Entrepreneurs?" *MSU Business Topics* 22, no. 1 (Winter 1974), pp. 5–14.

# Requirements for Success in an Independent Business

Although it is impossible to determine or state all the requirements for success in independent business, at least we know that the following are important:

1. Sensitivity to internal and external changes affecting the business.
2. Ability to react quickly to those changes.
3. Access to accurate and useful operating and marketing information.
4. Effective, but humane, use of human resources.
5. Acquisition of sufficient investment capital, at a reasonable price.
6. Effective handling of government laws, rules, and regulations.

### Understanding the Uniqueness of Independent Business Firms

As the owner-manager of an independent business, you should have a thorough understanding of the peculiarities of a business of your size. You should not seek to duplicate or copy the management techniques of larger firms. Rather, develop your own techniques to meet the needs of your business.

### Adaptability to Change

An important characteristic of independent business enterprises is their vulnerability to technological and environmental changes. Because of the size of these businesses, such changes have a great effect upon their operations and profitability. Yet, independent businesses can have an advantage over larger firms in this respect; they can react faster to change because they have fewer people making decisions. It is extremely important that you be sensitive to the changes taking place both inside and outside your firm and that you be ready to react quickly to these changes.

### Accurate Operating and Marketing Information

Gathering accurate and useful information concerning the operations of your business and its market is extremely important. You must keep informed—on a regular and frequent basis—of the financial position and market position of the business. Analyze this information and develop plans to maintain or improve your position.

### Using Human Resources Effectively

The effective, but humane, use of your human resources is extremely important to an independent business enterprise, because its owner-manager has a closer and more personal association with the employees than occurs in a larger business. These workers can be an economical source of information and ideas, and their productivity can increase greatly, if they are allowed to share ideas with you—and if you are willing to recognize and reward their contributions.

## Obtaining Investment Capital

One of the most difficult problems facing the independent business manager is obtaining sufficient investment capital—at a reasonable price. You can bring in investors, but this reduces control over the firm. Or you can borrow money, creating debt. Or you can plow back your profits into the business. You must be willing and able to delay fulfillment of your desire for dividends in favor of the best long-run interest of the business.

## Handling Government Regulations

You need to be able to handle red tape effectively, for the day when independent business firms enjoyed an exemption from governmental legislation and regulation has passed. It is now even argued that smaller businesses are taxed disproportionately higher than larger businesses. Equal employment opportunity, occupational safety and health, and environmental legislation no longer exempt small business establishments but frequently add tremendously to their costs of operation.

Environmental regulations and compliance directives are of major concern to independent business owners, whose responses are varied and often rebellious.

> An independent sawmill owner had spent 30–40 years of his life in this business. He burned the sawdust and bark in a special incinerator, which emitted smoke. Occasional complaints had never been taken too seriously until a complaint was filed with the Air Pollution Control Section of the Department of Human Resources. This group inspected the premises to determine the validity of the complaint. A directive was issued calling for the installation of new equipment estimated to cost about $40,000.
>
> At this point, the owner, who was 72 years old, picked up his phone and called a son who was also in the lumber business. His terse statement was, "I want you to have this sawmill. I am quitting. I am too old to put up with this environmental stuff. There is no way that I can spend the kind of money they want me to spend."
>
> He quit, and six months later he died.

What can you, as an independent business manager, do about

this government involvement? Several things that you may want to do include:

1. Learn as much as you can about the laws, particularly if it is possible that a law can aid you.
2. Challenge detrimental or harmful laws, either by yourself (perhaps appearing before a congressional independent business committee) or by joining organizations such as the National Federation of Independent Businesses.
3. Become involved in the legal-political system, to elect representatives of your choosing and change the laws.
4. Find a better legal environment, if possible, even if it means moving to a different city, county, or state.
5. Learn to live with the laws, rules, or regulations.

## Increasing Competence and Growing Involvement of Women and Minorities

During recent years, women and minorities have increasingly become involved in small and independent businesses. Various government organizations have helped minorities set up businesses of their own, and the Small Business Administration has several programs to help them.

The same is true of females. According to one estimate, there were around 1 million female-owned businesses in 1977, more than double the number in 1972. According to the director of the American Women's Economic Development Corporation in New York, "The next great group of entrepreneurs will be women."[2] A National Association of Women Business Owners was founded in 1976.

> Susan Sasser and a female partner work 10-hour days in their Washington, D.C., auto repair shop, named Wrenchwoman, Inc. They have found it to be a very stimulating and rewarding business. The success they are achieving in their operation has confirmed that being female imposes no restriction in a business of this kind.[3]

## An Introspective Personal Analysis

Now that you have seen some of the characteristics of successful independent business managers, as well as the personal requirements needed for success in an independent business firm, you should be particularly interested in whether you possess a sufficient number of those characteristics and requirements to be suc-

---

[2]"Starting a Business: Women Show It's Not Just a Man's World," *U.S. News & World Report*, August 29, 1977, p. 55.

[3]Ibid.

cessful. The following personal evaluation should help you decide this important question. (Also, see Exhibit 1–2 at the end of Chapter 1.)

## What Is Your Philosophy of Life?

As shown in Chapter 2, your management philosophy will provide a basis for decision making in your company. In order to manage a firm effectively, you need an ethical value system and some basic principles that you believe in and that you can use as guidelines. Among the more important questions related to this ethical value system are the following:

1.  What are your true motives?
2.  What real objectives do you seek?
3.  What psychological and social relations do you consider to be needed for success?
4.  What general economic atmosphere do you prefer to operate in?

*Need for a Philosophy.*  Everyone has a philosophy, whether it is conscious or unconscious, whether it is well defined or ill defined. If you have and use a conscious and well-formed philosophy of management, many major advantages will be yours. Such a philosophy should:

1.  Help you win effective support and followers. People will know what you stand for and what overall action you are most likely to take. They will know why you act as you do and will therefore have more confidence in your actions.
2.  Provide guidelines and form a foundation for managerial thinking and decision making. Conditions are changing so rapidly that you will face new management challenges to which there are no ready-made solutions. Your guidelines and management philosophy should be especially useful for these challenges.
3.  Supply a framework within which you can improve your thinking abilities. Your thinking process will be directed and stimulated so that you achieve more effective and satisfactory developments.

*Types of Philosophies.*  There are many types of people and an infinite variety of philosophies. However, we limit ourselves to contrasts between two pairs of philosophies: rugged individualism versus group-centered management, and activities-oriented versus results-oriented management.

Characteristics associated with these philosophies vary, but in general the rugged individualist is highly self-reliant and is a decision maker. Most of the strong-willed, powerful industrialists in the 1890s and early 1900s—such as Henry Ford—were guided by this philosophy. On the other hand, many present-day managers believe that the group should be considered in all managerial decisions and actions. These group-centered individuals rely upon planning and decision-making groups, use committees extensively, and consider the many mutual interests of management and other employees.

The activities-oriented manager stresses what must be done, tends to be a "one-person show," prescribes the organization structure, determines the tasks of subordinates, delegates authority, determines the best methods to perform the work, and exercises tight control over employee performance. The results-oriented manager prefers to use the full resources of employees, emphasizes goal setting, assists in achieving goals, wants both management and subordinates to develop self-commitment and self-direction for results, has subordinates play a large part in determining the methods of work, and exercises control by results.

Your philosophy depends upon your personal values, or on what you consider to be right or wrong, good or bad, desirable or not desirable. Based upon your philosophy and value system, your business objectives and policies are formulated.

*Professional versus Personal Approach.* You must consider selection of a business from two viewpoints. These are:

1. An impersonal, professional approach.
2. A personal, moral-ethical approach.

In counseling and consulting with prospective business owners, we have sometimes found it essential to approach the issues from both viewpoints. For example, an individual may come in to discuss the prospects of opening a bar or tavern. Impersonally and professionally, it is pointed out that certain licenses and permits must be obtained. The services of a local attorney may uncover some hidden payments that must be made. The approximate capital investments involved for building, fixtures, and inventory are defined. The consultant may point out certain specific locations that are available and explain why some of them are desirable and other undesirable. Also, the amount of net income that may be anticipated will be stated. From a personal, moral-ethical point of view, one might point out the social implications of this type of business, such as the local tendency to brand the people involved with a stigma. In addition, it might be pointed out that there are certain local ethical sensitivities that might be offended by such businesses. Therefore, it might be best from the personal viewpoint, to avoid those activities that would be in direct conflict with these ethical standards, even though the economic benefits might be substantial.

## What Are Your Mental Attributes?

If you still want to become an entrepreneur, then make a penetrating analysis of your personal attributes in order to determine the type of business that may satisfy your personal objectives and needs. Ask yourself questions such as these about your mental abilities:

1. Am I able to conceptualize my choice of a business; in other words, can I visualize it in its entirety, physically and functionally?
2. Am I able to observe things in perspective?
3. Can I generate ideas in a freewheeling fashion?
4. Can I generate ideas relating to new methods and new products?
5. Am I technically oriented?
6. Can I interpret and translate activities into a technical framework?
7. Am I sensitive to the human factor?
8. Am I sensitive to the feelings, wants, and needs of others?

## What Are Your Attitudes?

If you are still thinking of entering an independent business, make a self-analysis of your personal attitudes in specific areas. Some of these areas are your:

1. Aspiration level.
2. Willingness to accept responsibility.
3. Mental and emotional stability.
4. Commitment to the idea of independent business.
5. Willingness to take risks.
6. Ability to tolerate irregular hours.
7. Self-discipline.
8. Self-confidence.

Are you able to define your aspiration level? Aspiration is the driving or motivational force behind the individual. It is what you want to achieve in life. You may want to express this level in terms of education, marital and parental status, dollars, status in the community, physical or mental labor, service to others, or other achievements.

An excellent student wanted to go into the business of wrapping heating and air-conditioning pipes but did not consider the income from the business to be satisfactory. Consequently, he became a manager in a large business.

The degree to which you are willing to accept responsibility determines the relationship you will have with the public and the customer. So far in your life, have you willingly accepted responsibility? Are you willing to assume responsibility in the future? Are you willing to admit the last error you made? Are you an individual whose attitude toward responsibility is to accept it even though this may mean personal sacrifice? Are you willing to be responsible for the actions of others, even when you have delegated to them the authority to act?

> Faye Fendley, daughter of a poor restaurant owner, dropped out of school at 14; moved to Manhattan, using $300 saved from baby-sitting; worked part-time in a real estate agency; received her own license at 21 and started her own real estate business; married at 23. She was widowed, with three children, at 29. Spurning chances to sell the bakery she and her late husband owned, she assumed the full responsibility for running and expanding the business.

Are you a stable person, or are you a person who is impatient and unwilling to wait for success? If success is not immediate, are you willing to continue to work toward its achievement? Do you seek immediate gratification of your wants, or are you willing to postpone it in order to reinvest in the firm? When given an opportunity that offers a significant potential but may not be readily achievable, many young people tend to grow weary and move to another activity. These people in their limited progression may, on occasion, generate a good income in their chasing after "fast buck" opportunities, but these opportunities may lack stability and security. The successful entrepreneur does not work this way.

> Stan Bernthal, college dropout, worked in a garment factory. In his spare time, he designed clothing for young people out of scraps of material. He and his college roommate organized a firm to provide these good-looking, inexpensive clothes. In spite of initial success, Stan limited himself to $12,000 a year salary until the firm was assured of success.

Are you committed? Commitment is the trait that determines whether an individual will endure the trials, tribulations, and personal and family sacrifices necessary to move ahead toward the achievement of objectives. How committed are you to your idea for the business you have dreamed of? Unless this commitment is firmly implanted, it is suggested that you forego the idea and seek that vocation to which you can be committed.

Do you enjoy taking risks? Are you willing to take the chance of "losing your shirt" to gain other benefits? Or, do you "play it close to your vest" and seek the sure thing in life? It does make a difference.

Can you live with an irregular schedule? Are you willing to

forego regular hours and be worried during your time off? Are you willing to give up your weekends if something goes wrong or it becomes necessary to prepare a proposal for that new contract? Or would you prefer regular hours, holidays, and vacations?

Are you self-disciplined? Are you able to exercise discipline over yourself and your affairs? The old cliché, "Don't take too much out the front door," applied to early business owners. It still applies. It is important that sufficient resources remain in the business to provide working capital and to provide for growth and contingencies.

> A local home-building contractor had a very profitable business. Coming from a low economic background, he began to purchase luxuries he had always wanted for himself and his family. Soon, there were insufficient funds to meet bills, payrolls, taxes, and other business expenses. The end result was bankruptcy.

Are you self-confident? Do you have confidence in yourself, and can you make decisions alone?

If the answers to these questions are yes, or if you feel that you can make them yes at some time in the near future, you may have the qualities that would make an independent business venture a satisfying and rewarding activity.

## Now It Is Decision Time

You are now at the point of deciding whether to go into business or not. As you approach the point of making a decision, you are in a position comparable to an automobile driver approaching a stoplight. Just as the light's control mechanism is outside the influence of the driver, there are factors beyond your control that should influence your decision about entering a business of your own. These include social, economic, cultural, and natural elements. In the same manner as the driver approaching a traffic light must observe its status, so must you be responsive to the environmental factors pertinent to the success or failure of your business. (Again, see Exhibit 1–2 at the end of Chapter 1.)

## Summary

We have tried in this chapter to impress you with some characteristics of successful owner-managers, such as independence, enterprise, motivation, efficient use of time, and opportunism. Also discussed were some personal requirements for a successful small business: sensitivity, ability to react quickly, access to information, skillful use of human resources, economical acquisition of capital, and competent handling of regulations. Finally, a personal analysis program was suggested whereby you may be able to determine whether you have the attitudes required for success in this area.

Before reaching a final decision on what career to follow, you should decide what you want out of life. If your personal objectives and the company objectives are in harmony, you will derive from your business the personal satisfaction you seek.

## Where to Look for Further Information

### Articles

Buchan, P. Bruce. "Corporate Risk Policies." *Management Advisor*, September–October 1973, pp. 45–51.

"For All the Headaches, You Can Still Start Your Own Business." *U.S. News & World Report*, July 26, 1976, pp. 43–46. (Contains an excellent discussion of how five entrepreneurs took the risk of entering a business and how they coped with the problems that arose.)

Henderson, Carter. "What the Future Holds for Small Business." *Nation's Business*, March 1976, pp. 25–28./

Libman, Joan. "Female Entrepreneurs Like Del Goetz Make 'Man's Work' Pay Off." *The Wall Street Journal*, August 22, 1975, p. 1.

Narver, John C., and Preston, Lee E. "The Political Economy of Small Business in the Postindustrial State." *Journal of Contemporary Business*, Spring 1976, reprint.

"Now It's Young People Making Millions." *U.S. News & World Report*, February 25, 1974, pp. 47–50.

Roscow, James P. "Can Entrepreneurship Be Taught?" *MBA*, June-July 1973, pp. 12, 16, 50, 51.

Schreier, James W. "Is the Female Entrepreneur Different?" *MBA*, March 1976, pp. 40–43.

"Small Business, The Maddening Struggle to Survive." *Business Week*, June 30, 1975, pp. 96–104.

"Some Hints on Small Business Company Success." *The Iron Age*, June 1, 1967, p. 25.

### Books

Collins, Orvis F.; Moore, David G.; and Unwalla, Darab B. *The Enterprising Man.* East Lansing, Mich.: Bureau of Business and Economic Research, Graduate School of Business Administration, Michigan State University, 1964.

Finn, Richard P. *Your Fortune in Franchises.* Chicago: Contemporary Books, 1978; *Franchise Opportunities.* Rev. ed. New York: Drake Publishers, 1977.

Moreau, James F. *Effective Small Business Management.* Skokie, Ill.: Rand McNally, 1980.

Peterson, Rein. *Small Business—Building a Balanced Economy.* Erin, Ontario: Press Porcepic, 1977.

Redinbaugh, Larry D., and Neu, Clyde W. *Small Business Management—A Planning Approach.* St. Paul, Minn.: West Publishing, 1980.

# EXHIBITS

## Exhibit 3-1
## Determining the Objectives of Your Company

The purpose of this questionnaire is to aid you in determining the objectives of your firm. These objectives should be set at the beginning of your interest in an independent business.

1. Do you recognize the existence of these two sets of objectives for your firm:
   a. Overall enterprise objectives?    ☐Yes ☐No
   b. Subsidiary goals for the individual parts of the organization?    ☐Yes ☐No

**Overall Enterprise Objectives**

2. Do you intend to consider these objectives:
   a. Service?    ☐Yes ☐No
   b. Profit?    ☐Yes ☐No
   c. Social?    ☐Yes ☐No
   d. Growth?    ☐Yes ☐No

3. Do you concur that the overall objective of any business enterprise is to perform a useful service for society by producing goods or services (satisfactions) and distributing them to the public?    ☐Yes ☐No

4. Do you recognize that profits:
   a. Are the reward for taking risks?    ☐Yes ☐No
   b. Are residual?    ☐Yes ☐No
   c. Come into existence through satisfying the demand for a product or service?    ☐Yes ☐No

5. Do you intend your firm to have social objectives for people in the community other than customers:
   a. Employees?    ☐Yes ☐No
   b. Suppliers?    ☐Yes ☐No
   c. The government?    ☐Yes ☐No
   d. The community itself?    ☐Yes ☐No

6. Do you intend to select a growth objective for your firm:
   a. Seek relative stability or merely survival?    ☐Yes ☐No
   b. Seek a satisfactory rate of profit, considering effort and investment?    ☐Yes ☐No
   c. Seek to maximize profits?    ☐Yes ☐No
   d. Seek to remain small?    ☐Yes ☐No
   e. Seek growth and challenge large firms?    ☐Yes ☐No

**Subsidiary Objectives**

7. Do you intend to set subsidiary objectives for each functional unit of your organization:
   a. Production?    ☐Yes ☐No
   b. Marketing?    ☐Yes ☐No
   c. Finance?    ☐Yes ☐No
   d. Personnel?    ☐Yes ☐No
   e. Research?    ☐Yes ☐No

8. Will you consider the personal objectives of all employees within each functional unit?    ☐Yes ☐No

9. Do you recognize that conflict may arise between objectives; and that if it does, it should be resolved or minimized?    ☐Yes ☐No

10. Are you seeking a meshing of the objectives of your firm—service at a profit—with your personal objectives?    ☐Yes ☐No

11. Are you aiming to achieve a sense of belonging and *esprit de corps* in your firm?    ☐Yes ☐No

**You as Owner-Manager of an Independent Business**

12. Do you recognize that business failures often result from these weaknesses:
   a. Too much left to chance?    ☐Yes ☐No
   b. Crucial obstacles unnoticed through ignorance?    ☐Yes ☐No
   c. Amount of time and physical effort not recognized and planned?    ☐Yes ☐No
   d. Amount of capital either not determined or grossly underestimated?    ☐Yes ☐No
   e. Too many decisions made by hunch or through intuition without adequate background and experience?    ☐Yes ☐No

13. Do you have these characteristics:
   a. A great sense of independence?    ☐Yes ☐No
   b. A strong sense of enterprise?    ☐Yes ☐No
   c. Dominated by personal and family considerations as well as by professional choices?    ☐Yes ☐No
   d. Entered independent business more by chance than design?    ☐Yes ☐No
   e. Jealously guard your time?    ☐Yes ☐No
   f. Limited formal education?    ☐Yes ☐No
   g. Expect quick and concrete results?    ☐Yes ☐No

14. Do you have a strong desire to be independent of outside control?    ☐Yes ☐No

15. Do you desire to use your ideas, abilities, ambitions, aspirations, and initiative to the greatest degree possible?    ☐Yes ☐No

16. Do you have a drive for achievement and a willingness to work long, hard hours to reach your goals?    ☐Yes ☐No

17. Do you appear irritable if someone infringes upon your time?    ☐Yes ☐No

18. Do you supplement your formal learning with informal learning through:
   a. Reading?    ☐Yes ☐No
   b. "Picking your friends' brains?"    ☐Yes ☐No
   c. Courses?    ☐Yes ☐No

19. Do you seek a quick turnover of the amount invested in your firm?    ☐Yes ☐No

# Chapter Four

# Planning in an Ongoing Business

In Chapter 1, the important terms *objectives, missions,* and *strategic planning* were related to asset management. These terms are intimately involved in planning in an ongoing business, the subject of this chapter.

First, let us take an overview of the management process. Assume that you have chosen to manage the independent business rather than to hire a professional manager to run it for you. As the owner-manager, you will need to perform effectively certain basic managerial functions in order to have a profitable firm. These functions are shown in Figure 4–1.

Although these managerial functions are shown separately and in sequence, they are not so neatly separated in the real world of independent business; you often perform them together. For practical purposes, however, we discuss them separately and in the order shown. The planning function is discussed both in this chapter and in the organizing function in Chapters 24 and 25; the others are discussed throughout the text. Planning must be done *both before and after* operations are begun, resulting in two categories: preliminary planning and planning in an ongoing organization.

This chapter covers the need for effective planning for an independent business, some suggestions for making planning more effective, strategic planning, levels and types of planning, and planning the wise use of your time.

*Figure 4–1*

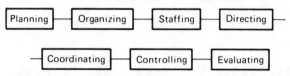

## Need for Effective Planning

Planning is selecting the future courses of action for the firm as a whole and for each department or section. Planning is both the setting of directions and the devising of courses of action to accomplish desired objectives. It can be likened to deciding how much profit is needed and then outlining methods to accomplish that profit.

An early indication of trouble in any firm is that its management performs little or no planning, does not know what is going on, reacts to events as they occur, and is often overoptimistic. Planning is probably the most difficult management function in an independent business because owner-managers are too involved in day-to-day operations, do not see the immediate results from their efforts, and are fearful about the company's future. Other reasons are mentioned later. Yet managers in these firms need to plan thoroughly, because most independent firms:

1. Do not always have sufficient resources to overcome their future problems.
2. Cannot afford to underwrite losses that can occur while adjusting to unexpected changes.

Plans provide courses of action, information to others, bases for changes, and means for delegating work. Before taking action, you need to know where you are going and how to get there. Other people who invest or lend money need to know whether a firm can be successful. Employees are concerned about the direction and activities of a business. Subordinates can assist in planning, particularly in operations and program planning. Your lower-level managers can be personally involved in carrying out the operational plans and programs while you can be free to devote your full attention to executive-level planning. Employees' ideas are often helpful in providing solutions to your firm's problems.

Why, then do so many owner-managers neglect planning—particularly long-range planning? Certain barriers, such as the following, tend to discourage them:

1. Fear—believing that careful thought about their companies' futures will reveal new trouble or problems.

2. Inexactness—believing that planning does not seem worth doing, because things do not work out according to plan.
3. Changeability—complaining that plans change too rapidly to make planning worthwhile.
4. Lack of planning knowledge—finding that it is difficult to state objectives and courses of action on paper.
5. Lack of proper time and place—concentrating on favorite work they like to do, delaying disagreeable jobs, and not delegating.

Planning requires original thinking. Popular programs adopted by others may be used, but usually need to be adapted to your needs. Plans must be tailor-made for each firm.

## Selected Planning Functions and Types of Plans

Table 4–1 shows some of the more important planning functions and types of plans that you—as an independent business owner—will probably have to make. Three components of a strategic plan are development of the firm's mission, objectives, and strategies.

### Mission

The mission is a long-term vision of what your firm is trying to become. It is the unique aim that differentiates your firm from similar firms. Two basic questions that you should answer are: (1) What is my business? (2) What should it be?

Peter Drucker, an eminent management scholar and consultant, believes that the inability to ask and answer these questions has been the greatest cause of business failure. As he states: "It is not only important to *do things right*, but also to *do the right things*."

An example of a mission for an independent life insurance general agency is presented below:

---

John Smith, General Agent
*Mission*

To provide the maximum amount of personal financial security at the lowest possible cost while maintaining the highest quality of personal individualized service.

To serve the financial needs of businesses, individuals, and their families through guaranteed income to meet loss from death or disability, through these policy coverages:

1. Estate tax planning
2. Qualified pension and profit-sharing
3. Group life and health
4. Ordinary life
5. Profit

---

**Table 4–1**
**Planning Functions and Types of Plans**

| *Strategic Planning Functions** | *Examples* |
|---|---|
| **Objectives**<br>Purposes, goals, results of the firm and its parts. | **Financial objectives**<br>Earn a 20 percent return on investment in 1984.<br><br>**Product line**<br>Manufacture and distribute only high-quality, custom-made, special living room and dining room furniture.<br><br>**Personal objectives**<br>Remain independent, bid on jobs I want, have few labor problems, earn a comfortable living, and enjoy life.<br><br>**Market**<br>Confine marketing to Oklahoma, Kansas, Missouri, and Arkansas. |
| **Policies**<br>Guides to action which provide consistency in decision making, particularly in repetitive situations. | **Personnel policy**<br>Promote from within, whereby preference for promotion is given to present employees. |
| **Standards**<br>Values to be used as norms; these are necessary for control because they assist in measurement. | **Time**<br>Replace and aim headlamp of model X automobile, 0.3 hours. |
| **Budgets**<br>Plans of income or outgo, or both—money, sales items, etc. | **Cash budget**<br>Make cash budget to determine effect of renting instead of selling machine. |
| **Procedure**<br>Series of related tasks to be performed in a given sequence, using an established method of performing the work. | **Selection procedure**<br>Complete application, test, interview, investigate, select. |
| **Method**<br>Prescribed manner of performing a given task. A method deals with a task comprising one step of a procedure and specifies how this step is to be performed. | **Task**<br>Pick up phone, greet, state firm's name, ask . . . . etc. |

*Major objectives or goals of defining what business the company is in and the kind of company it is; courses of action to achieve goals.

Three important considerations in formulating your firm's mission are:

**A.** The firm's external environment.
**B.** The firm's internal resources and competitive edge.
**C.** The firm's clients.

*The Firm's Environment.* The external environment—consisting of the economic, technological, social, and political and legal subenvironments and demographic trends—is always present, and you should determine possible opportunities and risks (threats) for your firm. No longer is it feasible for the independent business to think of its environment as being local in nature, for events in various areas of the world impact on it. These events have a relationship with the asset management activities of your firm.

For example, the forecasted decline in the number of college-age individuals during the 1980s should be considered in formulating the mission of a small manufacturer of school equipment or a small textbook publisher. Since changes are ever present in the external environment and either create or destroy strategic opportunities, you should constantly monitor environmental developments.

*The Firm's Internal Resources and Competitive Edge.* The types of resources in your firm are:

1. Human resources—management and nonmanagement—such as production supervisors, sales personnel, financial analysts, engineers, and key operative employees.
2. Physical resources, such as office buildings, manufacturing plants and equipment, warehouses, inventories, and service and distribution facilities.
3. Financial resources, such as cash flow, debt capacity, and new equity availability.
4. Organizational resources, such as quality control systems and short-term cash management systems.
5. Technological capabilites, such as high-quality products, low-cost plants, and high brand loyalty.

The appraisal of these resources is also vital. The two important aspects are their strengths and weaknesses.

Your firm's strengths can become a competitive edge which sets it apart from other firms. Factors that produce a competitive edge are illustrated by creative design talents or other human resource capabilities, location, financial resources, or a distribution network. A proper evaluation of your firm's competitive edge permits you to avoid activities which appear superficially attractive.

*The Firm's Clients.* The needs of your firm's clients are the most significant factor in formulating the mission. The focus of your firm's statement of mission should be external rather than internal. The focus should be on the needs that your firm is seeking to satisfy (external) rather than the physical product or service that it is offering at present (internal). Your firm should be customer oriented, not product oriented. A firm should not define its business in terms of what it is doing at present to fill a need, but rather in terms of the need itself. Examples of needs are: transportation services rather than trucking, containers rather than glass bottles, health care rather than specific drugs, entertainment rather than movies, and personal financial management rather than a particular financial service. A market definition of your firm focuses your attention on the constantly changing market. Your firm should serve the latter by whatever is *required* and *feasible*.

Clear definitions of mission enable you to design results-oriented organizational objectives and strategies.[1]

## Objectives

Based on your firm's current and projected opportunities, you need to formulate its objectives. Objectives are purposes, goals, results of the firm and its parts. They should give direction to your firm. Examples of objectives that you should set for your firm are shown in Table 4–2.

**Table 4–2**
**Firm's Objectives for 1984, 1985, and 1986**

|  | *1984* | *1985* | *1986* |
|---|---|---|---|
| Total net profit (income) after taxes | $_____ | _____ | _____ |
| Return on investment (ROI) | | | |
|   Net income after taxes/total assets | _____ | _____ | _____ |
| Return on equity (ROE) | | | |
|   Net income after taxes/equity | _____ | _____ | _____ |
| Total sales volume (units) | _____ | _____ | _____ |
| Total sales volume | _____ | _____ | _____ |
| Return on sales (ROS) | | | |
|   Net income after taxes/sales | _____ | _____ | _____ |

To attain a _____ percent share of market by the end of 1985.
To have a _____ percent debt-to-equity in the capital structure initially, declining to _____ percent debt-equity at the end of 1986.
To develop a new product by the end of 1986.

As indicated, projections similar to the above should be developed for three years.

---

[1]Ivancevich, Donnelly, and Gibson, *Managing for Performance* (Plano, Tex.: Business Publications, 1980), pp. 60–64.

## Strategic Planning Including Objectives

Your company's strategic plan should be made known to all employees to help them make their own long-range plans and to serve as an inspiration to organizational effort. The poorest part of planning in many independent companies is the setting of overall objectives. Many companies have found programs called management by objective (MBO) very helpful. MBO emphasizes goal orientation—goals are set at all levels and in all parts of an organization. In using MBO, all of your subordinates should be asked to set objectives for themselves, their people, their material, and so forth. You should meet with each of them to reach agreement on those objectives, how they can be accomplished, and how they relate to achieving the overall company objectives. You should also make suggestions for how those objectives can be achieved.

Each subordinate should be provided a continual feedback of the results being attained, and these should be compared with the objectives. You should help each person overcome obstacles that stand in the way of reaching the objectives.

Near the end of the period, each subordinate should prepare a brief statement concerning how the performance compares to the objectives. Each subordinate's report should be reviewed in detail and then discussed. An agreement should be reached on how good performance has been. If the objectives were not achieved, an effort should be made to find out why.

### Strategies

Strategies are the courses of action your firm plans to take. These are actions you believe to be the best means to accomplish your objectives. Examples of strategies that you may set for your firm are presented in Table 4–3.

Other questions that you should answer are: What advantages do my competitors have over my firm? What activities will not be performed if I do not allocate resources to them today? For every product or service or market, if my firm was not in this today, would my firm go into it? If the answer is no, they should be discontinued.

### Planning Policies, Budgets, Standards, Procedures, and Methods

*Policies* are guides to action. They are set so that you can delegate work, and employees will make decisions according to your philosophy and thinking. They are communicated to employees in writing or by actions and/or your decisions.

**Table 4–3[2]**
**Firm's Strategies for 1984, 1985, and 1986**

| Market Segment | 1984 | 1985 | 1986 |
|---|---|---|---|
| Products/services to be sold | | | |
|   Investment required | | | |
|     Total | $_____ | $_____ | $_____ |
|     Individual products | _____ | _____ | _____ |
| Promotion strategy | | | |
|   Investment required | | | |
|     Total | _____ | _____ | _____ |
|     Individual products | _____ | _____ | _____ |
|   Sales and distribution | _____ | _____ | _____ |
|   Advertising | _____ | _____ | _____ |
|   Sales promotion | _____ | _____ | _____ |
| Pricing strategy | | | |
|   Individual products | _____ | _____ | _____ |

*Budgets* set the requirements needed to follow the strategies and to accomplish the goals. For example, a cash budget shows the amounts and times of cash income and outgo. It helps you to determine when and how much to borrow. Chapter 15 includes a more complete discussion of budgets.

*Standards* establish the productivity expected of employees, facilities, and material. Closely related to budgets, they measure rates of performance such as output per employee, percent of good product, and speed at which accounts are collected. They can be used as incentives and give early warning of poor performance.

*Procedures* and *methods* provide employees with instructions for performing work. The network of directives activates employees to do work properly. They are essential for repetitive work.

## Levels and Types of Planning

As far as level of planning is concerned, you should be able to distinguish between executive, operational, and project or program levels of planning. Then you need to determine the appropriate length of the planning period.

### Levels of Planning

Executive-level planning is broad in scope, long-range, and abstract. Strategic planning is performed at this level. It entails selecting the company's objectives and policies, then establishing

---

[2]Adapted from Mark Hanan, *Fast Growth Management* (New York: AMACOM, 1979), p. 22.

programs and procedures for achieving them. This type of planning is neglected by many independent business managers. Too often they are engaged in "fire-fighting," crisis-type management and are so immersed in daily operations and routines that they cannot perform executive-level planning.

Operational planning is limited to separate departmental or functional activities. It tends to be narrow in scope, short-range and concrete. It depends to a considerable extent on prior planning decisions made at the executive level. Often operational plans consist of budgets which are prepared one year in advance with a detailed breakdown by months.

Planning is also concerned with a specific project or program. However, you should recognize that a particular course of action in implementing a project should conform to the overall operations of your company.

### Length of Planning Period

You should be able to differentiate between long-range and short-range planning.

Long-range planning is needed for market development, machine purchase, and product and personnel development. It takes into account trends in income levels, industry developments, growth of population, mobility of people, and how these factors affect product or service usage, market size, business location, production and distribution processes, and operations. The manager of an independent business should forecast whether the volume of sales will be adequate to justify high initial costs of a product.

Short-range planning is more immediate in nature, covering a period of three to six months, a forthcoming season, or—at most— one year. In day-to-day operations, this planning is important because it allows the owner or manager to solve specific problems. Short-range plans should contribute to, and be consistent with, long-range plans. Also, independent companies should probably strive to excel in this type of planning because flexibility is their strong suit. The following case illustrates this point:

> In response to strong competition and reduced profits, a manufacturer, whose background included a career as an outstanding salesman, decided to expand sales.
> *Results:* Sales were increased. The need for working capital to carry inventories and receivables was increased. In negotiations with a lender, the lender wanted a high rate of interest, which practically eliminated the net profit on the increased sales.
> *Failure:* Proper planning was not performed, since functions other than sales—production and financing—were not considered.

*Solution:* The manufacturer posed and answered these questions:

1.  What is the business goal?
2.  Can it be achieved, and if so, how?
3.  What is the future of the business?[3]

An emphasis on short-term planning does not mean that long-range planning can be ignored. The following illustrates this truth:

The management of a consumer durable goods manufacturing company set a goal of industry leadership for its company. A 35 percent share of the market within five years was specified.
*Results:* The company attained only a 15 percent share.
*Cause:* Quality products were priced competitively and marketed aggressively, but were styled above consumer tastes.
*Failure:* Market research was not undertaken to determine consumer tastes.
*Solution:* Replanning of products, which included a market study of potential customers was accomplished.[4]

## Planning to Use Your Time Wisely

Do you know how to use your time wisely? Its proper use can help you to run your business more efficiently. Daily problems tend to keep you from planning properly. It might be revealing for you or your secretary to record how you spend your time during, say, 5-, 10-, or 15-minute intervals for a week. By totaling your time by categories, you may find that you spend too much time on activities such as solving production problems and talking on the telephone and/or to people, while spending too little on more important activities. Having a record of what you do, you may be able to eliminate, combine, and/or reduce activities. Be sure to look at those projects and tasks involving the greatest expenditure of time and the factors responsible for any waste of time.

Some specific methods of saving your valuable time are:

1.  Organizing the work, including delegating to your subordinates as many duties as feasible.
2.  Selecting a competent secretary to sort out unimportant mail, screen incoming calls, and keep a schedule of appointments and activities.
3.  Using dictating equipment.
4.  Adhering to appointment and business conference times.

---

[3]Adapted from Bruce E. DeSpelden, "Management Planning for Sound Growth," *Management Aids Annual No. 9* (Washington, D.C.: Small Business Administration, 1963), pp. 8–15.

[4]Adapted from T. Stanley Gallagher, "Sound Objectives Help Build Profits," *Management Aids Annual No. 11* (Washington, D.C.: Small Business Administration, 1965), pp. 1–7.

5. Preparing an agenda for meetings and confining discussions to only those items on the agenda, making follow-up assignments to specific subordinates.

You should now plan your workday based upon this analysis.

## Summary

In this chapter, we assumed that you would run your business yourself and perform the managerial functions of planning, organizing, staffing, directing, coordinating, controlling, and evaluating.

Planning is selecting the future courses of action for the firm as a whole and for each department within it. This function is probably the most difficult to perform in an independent business. Some barriers to effective planning are fear, inexactness, rapid change, lack of knowledge, and lack of proper time and place. However, these barriers can be partially overcome.

Planning involves the firm's rating the strategic plan, including objectives, strategies, policies, standards, budgets, procedures, and programs. These functions must be integrated and performed at all levels in a firm.

Independent firms are especially adept at doing short-range planning because of their flexibility. They are weak on long-range planning. Also, managers need to plan to use their time wisely.

# Chapter Five

## The Legal Environment of Personnel Relations

This chapter presents some important aspects of personnel relations, with special emphasis on the legal environment. If you follow these personnel policies, and abide by the spirit and letter of the laws, you should have more successful employer-employee relations. You should understand that failure on your part to comply with this legal environment can potentially present you with a series of liability claims. In the interest of protecting your assets from these claims, you want to plan your personnel relations program with a strategy of compliance.

### Complying with Equal Employment Opportunity Laws

All aspects of personnel relations in your business are affected by labor legislation. Some of these laws and their effects on recruiting and selection are now explained in greater detail.

#### Laws Providing Equal Employment Opportunities (EEO)

In 1964, Congress passed the Civil Rights Act. Title VII of this act, as amended by the Equal Employment Opportunities Act of 1972, prohibits discrimination because of race, color, religion, sex, or national origin in hiring, upgrading, and all other conditions of employment. It applies to employers in different ways, as shown in Table 5–1.

As shown in Table 5–1, other groups affected by this type of legislation are older workers, the handicapped, and Vietnam veterans. All of these have special laws, rules, and regulations for their protection, but space permits only some generalizations concerning the most significant ones.

***Some Special Aspects of Sex Discrimination.*** Generally all jobs must be open to both men and women unless the employer can prove that sex is a *bona fide occupational qualification* (BFOQ) necessary to the normal operations of that particular business.

Advertisements cannot be run by a company for "male only" or "female only" employees unless sex can be shown to be a BFOQ. Disqualifying female employees from jobs requiring heavy lifting, night shifts, and dirty work is often illegal unless justification exists for these restrictions. Automatic discharge of pregnant women and refusal to reinstate them after childbirth, requiring retirement at different ages, and not hiring women with small children constitute discrimination.

You must also pay males and females the same rate of pay for performing the same general type of work.

***Some Laws Pertaining to Age.*** The Fair Labor Standards Act and many state statutes prescribe the minimum age for employees. Typically, these laws specify a minimum age of 14–16 years with a higher minimum often set for hazardous occupations. On the other hand, the Age Discrimination in Employment Act says you cannot discriminate against present or potential employees aged 40–69. This includes not only hiring but also retiring and other aspects of employment.

***Some Practical Applications of the Laws.*** In recruiting applicants for employment, companies no longer may be allowed to rely completely on "walk-ins" or word-of-mouth advertising of job openings, especially if their own work force is predominantly of one race. Friends or relatives of present employees cannot be recruited if a company has a disproportionate number of a certain class of employees. A company cannot set hiring standards with respect to test results, high school diplomas, height, arrest records, manner of speech, or appearance if such standards result in discrimination on the basis of race, color, sex, religion, or national origin.

Seniority systems should not result in locking minorities into unskilled and semiskilled jobs without providing them lines of

*Table 5–1*
**Some Legal Influences on Equal Employment Opportunity (EEO) and Affirmative Action (AA)**

| Laws | Coverage | Basic Requirements | Agencies Involved |
|---|---|---|---|
| Title VII of Civil Rights Act, as amended by Equal Employment Opportunity Act. | Employers with 15 or more employees, engaged in interstate commerce; federal service workers; and state and local government workers. | Prohibits employment decisions based on race, color, religion, sex, or national origin; employers must develop affirmative action programs (AAPs) to recruit women and minorities. | Equal Employment Opportunity Commission (EEOC) |
| Executive Order 11246 as amended by Executive Order 11375. | Employers with federal contracts and subcontracts, with 50 or more employees, or with contracts over $50,000. | Requires contractors to take affirmative action, including goals and timetables, to recruit, select, train, utilize, and promote minorities and women. | Office of Federal Contract Compliance Programs (OFCCP), in the Labor Department |
| Age Discrimination in Employment Act. | Employers with 20 or more employees. | Prohibits employment discrimination against employees aged 40 to 70, including mandatory retirement before 70 (or 65 for tenured faculty and highly paid executives). | EEOC |
| Vocational Rehabilitation Act. | Employers with federal contracts of $2,500 or more. | Prohibits discrimination and requires contractor to develop AAPs to recruit and employ handicapped persons. | OFCCP |
| Vietnam-Era Veterans Readjustment Act. | Employers with federal contracts. | Requires contractors to develop AAPs to recruit and employ Vietnam-era veterans. | OFCCP |

Source: L. C. Megginson, *Personnel Management*, 4th ed. (Homewood, Ill.: Richard D. Irwin, 1981), p. 87. Extracted from BNA's Policy and Practice Series, *Fair Employment Practices* (Washington, D.C.: Bureau of National Affairs).

progression to better jobs. Equal opportunity for promotions should be provided. Training and performance appraisals should be conducted on a nondiscriminatory basis. Discrimination should not exist relative to hourly rates and deferred wages, including pensions or other deferred payments. Recreational activities—bowling teams, softball teams, Christmas parties, etc.—should be open to all employees on a nondiscriminatory basis. So far as facilities of a "personal nature" are concerned, an employer should make every "reasonable accommodation" for employees covered by these laws.

In summary, *all employees are entitled to equality in all conditions of employment!* This includes:

| | |
|---|---|
| 1. Hiring. | 9. Paid sick leave time. |
| 2. Layoff. | 10. Paid vacation time. |
| 3. Recall. | 11. Insurance coverage. |
| 4. Discharge. | 12. Training and development |
| 5. Recruitment. | activities. |
| 6. Compensation. | 13. Retirement privileges and |
| 7. Overtime. | pension benefits. |
| 8. Promotional opportunities. | 14. Rest periods, lunch |
| | periods, etc. |

### Enforcing EEO Laws

The Equal Employment Opportunity Commission (EEOC) is the primary enforcing agency. It receives and investigates charges of employment discrimination. In order to stop violations, the commission may take action itself or go to a U.S. district court. The commission promotes *affirmative action programs* (AAPs) to put the principle of equal employment opportunity into practice. In general, AAPs require employers to make concerted efforts to recruit, hire, and promote qualified women, minorities, the handicapped, and veterans through public employment services and at predominantly female and black colleges. Goals must be set up, with timetables, for carrying out these plans. Also, questions and tests must be designed and carried out in such a way as not to prejudice the hiring of one of these groups.

The EEOC and some of the other agencies regulating and enforcing these laws are shown in Table 5–1.

## Outside Assistance Available for Training

There are many outside programs available to help train employees. You can probably use some of the following.

The *National Apprenticeship Act of 1937,* administered by the Bureau of Apprenticeship and Training in the Labor Department, sets policies and standards for apprenticeship programs. Write to this bureau for help in conducting such a program.

All states have *vocational-technical education* programs whereby vocational-technical schools assist firms by conducting regular or special classes. Through such programs, potential employees can become qualified for skilled jobs such as machinist, lathe operator, and power-machine operator.

Another training activity for new employees is the *vocational rehabilitation* programs sponsored by the U.S. Department of Health and Human Resources in cooperation with state governments. These programs provide counseling, medical care, and vocational training for physically and mentally handicapped individuals.

The *Manpower Development and Training Act of 1962* provides a program of federal assistance in training unemployed and underemployed workers. Title V of the *Economic Opportunity* (Antipoverty) *Act of 1964* authorizes state welfare departments to provide training programs for welfare recipients or members of their families.

These last two programs—and many others—were incorporated into the *Comprehensive Employment and Training Act of 1973* during the Nixon administration. It was run by "prime sponsors," most of whom were local governments or community organizations. Yet, in spite of $55 billion spent in the program from 1975 to 1982, only 15 percent of its participants—80,000 workers—obtained jobs in the private sector.[1] Its greatest success was the establishment of *private-industry councils* (PICs) of business and local government leaders. This gave employers a bigger voice in planning and running training programs, which were tailored to local needs.

A new program, the *Job Training Partnership Act,* CETA's successor, went into effect in 1983. Under it, PICs will design and operate training programs funded by federal block grants to the states. At least 70 percent of the funds must go for training and only 15 percent for administration. The other 15 percent may be used for on-the-job training, but none for stipends or wage supplements. About 1 million workers will be trained each year, with the young, poor, long-term jobless, and dislocated workers being special targets. The state governors are responsible for the programs, with occasional reviews by the U.S. Labor Department.

Business groups (such as the Business Round Table, Chamber of Commerce of the United States, Committee for Economic Development, National Alliance of Business, and the National Asso-

---

[1]"Private Jobs Programs: Can They Fill the Gap?" *U.S. News & World Report,* February 21, 1983, p. 68.

ciation of Manufacturers) have agreed to help set up such local programs and obtain participation by local businesses, including small and independent firms.

## Effects of Governmental Factors on Compensation

As with selection and training, there are many state and federal laws, executive orders, rules, and regulations with which your wage policy must comply.

One of the first things you must be concerned with is the Fair Labor Standards Act of 1938 (sometimes called the Wage and Hour Law), which currently requires that you pay your employees a *minimum wage* of $3.35 per hour plus one and one half times their hourly rate for all hours over 40 per week. As these rates are subject to change by action of Congress, you should check with the local Wage and Hour Division of the Department of Labor for the latest figures. While certain managerial and professional personnel as well as students are exempt from the provisions of the act, you should also check with the division for specific details, as they are too numerous and involved to present in a summary such as this.

Efforts are now being made to pass a *teenwage* whereby young people are paid a lower minimum wage than adults during summer vacations. If passed, this should help small firms!

*The Equal Pay Act of 1963* requires you to pay females the same rate you pay males for doing the same "general" type of work. The EEO laws cited in Table 5–1 also require you to pay it for minorities, older workers, handicapped workers, and veterans.

In spite of these laws, there is still a marked difference between male and female salaries. For example, "Women were earning 58 cents for every male's dollar in 1930; in 1980, 50 years later, women are only up to 59 cents."[2] There are many reasons for these lower earnings for women. But the most important reason is probably the fact that for the last decade two out of three new employees were women and they entered the work force at the entry level— at lower salaries. Also, many women are in sex-stereotyped jobs— which pay less than others.

If you have a contract involving federal funds, you may be subject to the Public Construction Act of 1931, the Public Contract Act of 1936, or the Service Contracts Act of 1965. You should check with the Labor Department to see whether you are legally liable under any of these acts. See Table 5–2 for a summary of these laws.

---

[2]Quoted in William Smart, "Sexes: Hormones are Still the Rage," *Washington Post*, November 11, 1982, p. C5.

**Table 5–2**
**Some Legal Influence on Compensation and Hours of Work**

| Laws | Coverage | Basic Requirements | Agencies Involved |
|---|---|---|---|
| Public Construction Act (Davis-Bacon Act) | Employers with federal construction contracts, or subcontracts, of $2,000 or more. | Employers must pay not less than the wages prevailing in the area as determined by the secretary of labor; overtime is to be paid at 1½ times the basic wage for all work over 8 hours per day or 40 hours per week. | Wage and Hour Division of the Labor Department. |
| Public Contracts Act (Walsh-Healy Act) | Employers with federal contracts of $10,000 or more. | Same as above. | Same as above. |
| Fair Labor Standards Act (Wage and Hour Law) | Private employers engaged in interstate commerce, and retailers having annual sales of $325,000; many groups are exempted from overtime requirements. | Employers must pay a minimum of $3.35 per hour; and at the rate of 1½ times the basic rate for work over 40 hours per week; and are limited (by jobs and school status) in employing persons under 18. | Same as above. |
| Equal Pay Act | All employers. | Men and women must receive equal pay for jobs requiring substantially the same skill, effort, responsibility, and working conditions. | EEOC. |
| Service Contracts Act | Employers with contracts to provide services worth $2,500 or more per year to the federal government. | Same as Davis-Bacon. | Same as Davis-Bacon. |

Source: L. C. Megginson, *Personnel Management*, 4th ed. (Homewood, Ill.: Richard D. Irwin, 1981), p. 101. Extracted from BNA's Policy and Practice Series, *Wages and Hours* (Washington, D.C.: Bureau of National Affairs).

# Providing Employee Benefits

Employee benefits, which in general are not taxable income to employees, are growing faster than wages. These benefits, which were originally called *fringe benefits*, can be either legally required or voluntary.

The many voluntary programs take numerous forms and varieties. The most popular ones include (1) pay for time not worked, (2) pay for overtime, holidays, and special events and activities, (3) health and hospital benefits and protection, (4) legal services, (5) educational benefits and scholarships, (6) discounts on purchases of goods and services, and (7) pension and retirement programs. Because of the many changes brought about by the 1981 tax law, more consideration will be given to retirement programs than to the others. This law is forcing independent business people to reconsider all aspects of their benefit programs.

## Retirement Programs

There are two primary types of retirement programs independent businesses can use. First, there are those that the firm pays for and administers until the employee retires. Second, there are *individual retirement accounts* (IRAs), whereby individual employees take part of their regular income and personally put it into brokerage firms, mutual funds, insurance companies, banks, and other thrift institutions. Originally, employees with company-provided retirement programs couldn't have an IRA, but this is no longer true.

*Some Special Considerations in Granting Employee Pensions.* There are at least three types of company-sponsored pension programs you can use for your employees and executives: (1) the *defined-contribution plan*, in which the retirement benefits received depend upon the amount of yearly deposits, (2) *defined-benefit* plan, in which the yearly pension is defined, and (3) *key employee deferred-compensation plan*, in which part of the employees' income is withheld and invested for them until they retire.

Most independent businesses can afford these deferred-compensation programs, which are intended to help attract and hold quality employees. The Internal Revenue Service has approved model plans that contain all the forms and agreements needed to establish a comprehensive, simple, and flexible program. You can choose from a wide variety of plans—from mutual funds, banks, insurance companies, and others—in tailoring a program to your company's needs.

If you desire to give your employees a retirement income based on a fixed-dollar contribution by the company each year, the defined-contribution pension plan is appropriate. Deposits for all employees in the plan must be the same percentage of pay. You should consider this plan only if your company has relatively stable earnings. The ceiling on the amount that can be put in the plan each year is $30,000, or up to 25 percent of the employees' earnings.

Under a defined-benefits pension plan, you can provide your employees with retirement benefits that can be computed at any time. The plan is dependent neither on profits nor on pension fund investments. The top yearly retirement payment that can be made is $90,000 or no more than the individual's average income during the three consecutive years of highest pay.

The Employee Retirement Income Security Act (Pension Reform Law) of 1974 is profoundly affecting small firms; its general provisions are shown in Table 5–3. Because the law proved difficult for many small businesses to conform to, many decided to give up their programs and permit their employees to have their own private retirement programs.

**Table 5–3**
**General Provisions of the Employee Retirement Income Security Act**

| Coverage | Basic Requirements | Agencies Involved |
|---|---|---|
| All employee benefit plans of employers engaged in interstate commerce, with 25 or more employees. | Benefit plans must meet certain minimum standards for employee participation, vesting rights, funding, reporting, and disclosure. Plans must be funded on an actuarially sound basis. Vested benefits are to be insured through Pension Benefit Guaranty Corporation. | Department of Labor Internal Revenue Service Pension Benefit Guaranty Corporation |

Source: Extracted from F. Ray Marshall, Allan G. King, and Vernon M. Briggs, Jr., *Labor Economics*, 4th ed. (Homewood, Ill.: Richard D. Irwin, 1980), especially chap. 17.

Under the key employee deferred-compensation plan, a contract is drawn between you and your employees. The firm agrees to invest annually a specified dollar amount or percent of wages. The firm holds title to these assets until the retirement, disability, or death of the employee, when the benefit becomes payable to the named beneficiary. Congress is now considering taxing these salary-reduction optional retirement plans, as many people are using them for "opting out of the mandatory Social Security system."[3]

*Self-Employed Pension Plan.* If you are a self-employed person, or a partner in a partnership, you can establish a *Keogh Plan.* Starting in 1984, you can set aside 20 percent of your current gross income and invest it for your retirement. Thus, sole proprietorships and partnerships can reap the rewards of pensions offered by corporations, which should slow the movement toward incorporating.

The maximum that can be contributed has been doubled to $30,000 a year. But after 1985, the contributions will be indexed to reflect inflation.[4]

*Individual Retirement Accounts.* Employees can now set up an IRA even if they are covered by a company retirement plan. An individual can deduct up to $2,000 a year ($2,225 if the person's spouse doesn't work) from income subject to income taxes and invest those funds in any account in a financial institution. The return on that investment is not taxed until the person retires, hopefully at a lower tax rate. If the funds, including interest, are withdrawn before age 59½, there is a tax penalty. Also, the funds must begin to be withdrawn in a fixed ratio beginning at age 70½.

The 1981 tax law made it practical for companies to set up payroll-deduction IRAs, deduct the money, and invest it in an account set up in the employees' names. Employees can then transfer the money to other accounts if they choose, but not take it out until age 59½ without penalty.[5]

## Providing Health, Safety, and Security

An aspect of management that is growing in importance to both employees and the public is providing for their health, safety, and security. Of course, it is impossible to provide perfect safety and security. But there are some things that are now expected of all employers.

All employers are now legally required to provide social secur-

---

[3]"Congress Takes Aim at Fringe Benefit Plans that Allow Employees a Choice," *The Wall Street Journal*, March 15, 1983, p. 1.

[4]Leonard Wiener, "New Tax Angles on Your Retirement," *U.S. News & World Report*, October 4, 1982, p. 84.

[5]See Martha Bednary and Robert Wood, "IRAs and SEPs: Retirement Plans Made Easy," *INC* March 1982, pp. 136–39, for an excellent discussion of these retirement plans.

ity, unemployment insurance, workers' compensation, and occupational safety and health for employees and a clean environment for the public. Table 5–4 shows the general requirements of the laws protecting employees. As with other laws mentioned in this book, these are subject to change by the governments involved.

## Social Security

As the owner-manager of an independent business, you are both a taxpayer and a tax collector under the Social Security Act of 1935, as amended. To finance old age, survivors, and disability insurance, you must pay a tax on each employee's earnings and deduct a comparable amount from the employee's salary. As the propor-

**Table 5–4**
**Laws Affecting Employee Health, Safety, and Security**

| Laws | Coverage | Basic Requirements | Agencies Involved |
|---|---|---|---|
| Social Security Act | Employees of private firms, state and local governments, and schools and hospitals. | Disability benefits to disabled workers and their children. Retirement benefits after age 65 (or at reduced rates after 62) to worker and spouse. Survivor's benefits to widow with dependent children under 18, widow over 62, and dependent children under 18. Health insurance for persons over 65 (medicare). Funded by payroll tax on employer, employee, and the self-employed. | Social Security Administration |
| Workers' compensation laws (as passed by each state) | Varies by state; generally, employees of private non-agricultural firms, with work-related accidents or illnesses causing temporary or permanent disabilities, or death. | Income benefits are usually about two thirds of employee's weekly income, plus payments for medical and hospital care and rehabilitation activities; survivor benefits are paid for fatalities; funding is through (1) self-insurance, (2) private insurance carriers, or (3) state insurance systems; in (2) and (3), rates based on employer's experince rating. | Various state agencies |

**Table 5–4 *(concluded)***

| Laws | Coverage | Basic Requirements | Agencies Involved |
|---|---|---|---|
| Occupational Safety and Health Act | Employers engaged in interstate commerce with one or more employees, except those covered by Atomic Energy Act and Federal Mine Safety Act. | Employees must be provided a place of employment free from recognizable hazards that might cause serious illness, injury, or death; employers and employees must comply with the safety and health standards issued by OSHA. | Occupational Safety and Health Administration (OSHA) in the Labor Department. Occupational Safety and Health Review Commission (OSHRC). National Institute for Occupational Safety and Health (NIOSH). |

Source: Extracted from F. Ray Marshall, Allan G. King, and Vernon M. Briggs, Jr., *Labor Economics*, 4th ed. (Homewood, Ill.: Richard D. Irwin, 1980), chap. 17; and Leon C. Megginson, *Personnel Management*. 4th ed. (Homewood, Ill.: Richard D. Irwin, 1961), pp. 98, 104.

tion of the aged in the total population rises, it may be anticipated that both taxes and benefits will increase, even beyond those enacted in 1983.

At present (January 1, 1983), the program is financed by 6.75 percent contributions on the first $35,000 of an employee's income, paid by both the employer and employee. The rate for self-employed individuals is 14 percent, but there are offsetting tax credits of 2.7 percent in 1984, decreasing to 2 percent in 1986.

Table 5–5 shows how the tax rates will increase until 1990 under the present law. The wage base against which the tax is

**Table 5–5**
**Social Security Taxes, 1984–1989**

| Year | Tax Rate for Employer and Employee |
|---|---|
| 1984 | 7.00% |
| 1985 | 7.05 |
| 1986 | 7.15 |
| 1987 | 7.15 |
| 1988 | 7.51 |
| 1989 | 7.51 |
| 1990 | 7.65 |

Source: Social Security Administration

levied is now $35,700 and will rise automatically with the national average wage. *Extreme care should be used in order to keep current on the law and its applications.*

## Unemployment Insurance

An unemployment insurance tax is also provided under the Social Security Act. The state government receives most of this tax. It may be as high as 4.7 percent of the first $8,000 of each employee's pay. If you stabilize employment in your firm, you can have lower rates under merit rating provisions. Maintaining the validity of your tax trust funds is important because of the legal liability associated with them. The amount each unemployed employee receives and the length of time (in weeks) payments are received are set by each state. The federal government does provide assistance in the form of extended payments for 10–16 weeks past the state limit.

## Workers' Compensation[6]

Accidents and occupational diseases are covered under state workers' compensation statutes. You are required to pay insurance premiums either to a state fund or to a private insurance carrier. Funds accumulated in this fashion are used to compensate victims of industrial accidents or occupational illness. Your premiums will be affected by hazards in your company and the effectiveness of your safety program. The amount of payment to employees or their estates is fixed according to the type and extent of injury.

## Occupational Safety and Health

The *Occupational Safety and Health Act* (OSHAct), which created the Occupational Safety and Health Administration (OSHA), was passed in 1970. Its purpose is to assure, so far as possible, safe and healthful working conditions for every employee and to preserve our human resources.

***Employee Rights.*** Employees have these five important rights:

1. If they believe that a violation of job safety or health standards threatens physical harm, they may request an inspection by sending a signed, written notice to OSHA, which is a part of the U.S. Department of Labor. They may not be discharged or discriminated against for filing the complaint.

---

[6]Formerly called workmen's compensation.

2. When the OSHA compliance inspector arrives, usually unannounced, the employees' representative may accompany the inspector on the visit.
3. If the employer is cited by OSHA and protests either the fine or the abatement period, employees may participate at the hearing and object to the length of the abatement period.
4. Concerning exposure to toxic materials or other physically harmful agents, employees may observe the company's monitoring process. If an OSHA standard covers the substance, the workers are entitled to information about the exposure record.
5. The employees' authorized representative may request that the secretary of the Department of Health and Human Services (HHS) determine whether any substance found in the place of employment has potentially toxic effects. If HHS makes this finding, the secretary of labor may institute a procedure to set a safe exposure level for that substance.

*Employer obligations.* Even though many accidents are caused by the employees' own carelessness and lack of safety consciousness, employees usually do not receive citations. Instead, employers are responsible that their employees wear safety equipment. Furthermore, employers are subject to fines for unsafe practices irrespective of whether any accidents actually occur. You should provide safety training for your supervisors and employees and discipline employees for noncompliance with safety work rules. The act has encouraged increased examination and questioning of management's staffing decisions and equipment selection. To illustrate, a union could claim that a crew size is unsafe or that a machine fails to provide a safe workplace.

*Management Rights.* You can request a free health hazard evaluation by the National Institute of Occupational Safety and Health in HHS. Training may be obtained from OSHA and National Safety Council chapters. However, "dry run" inspections are not permitted by OSHA inspectors. If they do inspect you, they are required to inspect fully and, if violations are found, to cite and to fine. Your workers' compensation insurance carrier may be helpful. However, its approval does not guarantee the same from OSHA. You may also obtain useful information from equipment manufacturers, other employers who have had an inspection, trade associations, and your local fire department. You should provide effective coordination among persons responsible for manufacturing, safety, medical care, industrial relations, and so forth.

There is a consultative service, paid for by OSHA, whereby experts can come in if requested to and make recommendations for improving your plant. If you are cited by an inspector on a routine inspection, and correct the violations, these consultants can come in and inspect the improvements. If they meet all inspection requirements, the consultant can give you a certificate of immunity from another inspection for one year.

***Some Improvements in Enforcement.*** There have been many improvements, from management's point of view. For example, businesses with fewer than eight employees are no longer required to maintain injury and illness records. However, these firms must still report fatalities and accidents that hospitalize five or more persons, and small business accident and illness reports are still reflected in BLS statistics.

In 1978, the Supreme Court ruled in the *Barlow* case that the inspectors must present a search warrant if management requests one. Few employers do.

Congress required, in 1979, that OSHA not inspect firms with 10 or fewer employees in "relatively safe" industries. Nearly 80 percent of American firms were exempted under this ruling.

OSHA tries to stretch its limited number of inspectors (around 1,100) by concentrating on workplaces with unsatisfactory records. The order of priority of inspections is: (1) where there is "imminent danger," (2) where an accident has occurred, (3) following up on an employee (or union) complaint, and (4) routine inspections. The last are based on memos from Washington telling which industries have a high injury or illness rate.

The newness of the program and its very nature will keep it in a state of transition for some time. Therefore, you are advised to utilize the resources suggested above, as well as your local chamber of commerce, area planning and development commission, and the office of the Small Business Administration serving your area. Small Business Administration loans could be available to help you meet safety and health standards.

## Environmental Protection

In 1970, the Environmental Protection Agency (EPA) was created under an act of the same title to help protect and improve the quality of the nation's environment. Areas covered are:

1. Solid waste disposal.
2. Clean air.
3. Water resources.
4. Noise.
5. Pesticides.
6. Atomic radiation.

Industrial pollution can be prevented or controlled through the use of waste treatment, process changes, or both. Builders, developers, and contractors—many of them small businesses—can help prevent and control water pollution. Soil erosion, wastes from feedlots, improper or excessive use of pesticides and fertilizers, and careless discarding of trash and junk are among the causes of water pollution. Because of the actions of the agency in requiring pollution control equipment to be installed in marginal plants, many of these plants have closed and employees have lost their jobs.

## Laws Governing Union-Management Relations

You are required by the *National Labor Relations Act of 1935*, as amended by the *Labor-Management Relations Act of 1947* and the *Labor-Management Reporting and Disclosure Act of 1959*, to bargain with the union if a majority of your employees desire unionization. (See Table 5–6 for the provisions of these laws.) You are forbidden to discriminate in any way against your employees for union activity.

The purpose of the act was to facilitate the process of collective bargaining, not necessarily to prevent or settle disputes. Under the act, both you and the union are required to bargain in good faith in order that difficulties may be resolved and an agreement reached.

The National Labor Relations Board (NLRB) serves as a labor court, and its general counsel investigates charges of unfair labor practices, issues complaints, and prosecutes cases. You can appeal a ruling of the board through a circuit court.

Under right-to-work laws in some 20 states, the union shop is outlawed. In the other states, a *union shop* clause provides that employees must join the recognized union within 30 days after being hired.

**When the Union Enters.** If a union does try to organize your firm, there are certain things you can and cannot do. See the appendixes at the end of this chapter for lists of these things.

The purpose of labor unions is to bargain on behalf of their members as a counterbalance to the economic power of the employer. Employees, through their elected representatives, negotiate with the company for wages, fringe benefits, working conditions, and so forth. The union's principal role is collective bargaining.

If your company is unionized, you should be prepared for the possibility that certain difficulties may occur. Many of your actions and statements may be reported to union officials. You may be harassed by the union's filing unfair labor practice charges with

**Table 5–6**
**Some Laws Governing Union-Management Relations**

| Laws | Coverage | Basic Requirements | Agencies Involved |
|------|----------|--------------------|--------------------|
| National Labor Relations Act, as amended (Wagner Act) | Nonmanagerial employees in nonagricultural private firms not covered by the Railway Labor Act, and postal employees. | Employees have right to form or join labor organizations (or to refuse to), to bargain collectively through their representatives, and to engage in other concerted activities such as strikes, picketing, and boycotts; there are unfair labor practices which the employer and the union cannot engage in. | National Labor Relations Board (NLRB) |
| Labor-Management Relations Act, as amended (Taft-Hartley Act) | Same as above | Amended NLRA, permitted states to pass laws prohibiting compulsory union membership; set up methods to deal with strikes affecting national health and safety. | NLRB Federal Mediation and conciliation Service |
| Labor-Management Reporting and Disclosure Act (Landrum-Griffin Act) | Same as above | Amended NLRA and LMRA; guarantees individual rights of union members in dealing with their union; requires financial disclosures by unions. | U.S. Department of Labor |

Source: Extracted from F. Ray Marshall, Allan G. King, and Vernon M. Briggs, Jr., *Labor Economics*, 4th ed. (Homewood, Ill.: Richard D. Irwin, 1980), especially chap. 16, and Leon C. Megginson, *Personnel Management*, 4th ed. (Homewood, Ill.: Richard D. Irwin, 1981), pp. 106–9.

the NLRB. Your best defense is to know your management rights under the prevailing laws.

## Summary

It is the purpose of this chapter to alert you to the various *legal provisions* and *related activities* affecting *personnel relations*. The pertinent laws and regulations concerned with the personnel environment have been summarized. The personnel area has become increasingly significant in terms of the penalties and liability claims that may be imposed for noncompliance. It is hoped that this information will help you avoid these threats to your assets.

## Appendix A: Things You *Can Do* When a Union Tries to Organize Your Company

1. Keep outside organizers off premises.
2. Inform employees from time to time on the benefits they presently enjoy. (Avoid veiled promises or threats.)
3. Inform employees that signing a union authorization card does not mean they must vote for the union if there is an election.
4. Inform employees of the disadvantages of belonging to the union, such as the possibility of strikes, serving in a picket line, dues, fines, assessments, and rule by cliques or one individual.
5. Inform employees that you prefer to deal with them rather than have the union or any other outsider settle grievances.
6. Tell employees what you think about unions and about union policies.
7. Inform employees about any prior experience you have had with unions and whatever you know about the union officials trying to organize them.
8. Inform employees that the law permits you to hire a new employee to replace any employee who goes on strike for economic reasons.
9. Inform employees that no union can obtain more than you as an employer are able to give.
10. Inform employees how their wages and benefits compare with those in unionized or nonunionized concerns where wages are lower and benefits less desirable.
11. Inform employees that the local union probably will be dominated by the international union, and that they, the members, will have little to say in its operations.
12. Inform employees of any untrue or misleading statements made by the organizer. You may give employees corrections of these statements.
13. Inform employees of known racketeering, communist, or other undesirable elements that may be active in the union.
14. Give opinions on union and union leaders, even in derogatory terms.
15. Distribute information about unions such as disclosures of congressional committees.
16. Reply to union attacks on company policies or practices.
17. Give legal position on labor-management matters.

18. Advise employees of their legal rights, provided you do not engage in or finance an employee suit or proceeding.
19. Declare a fixed policy in opposition to compulsory union membershp contracts.
20. Campaign against a union seeking to represent the employees.
21. Insist that no solicitation of membership or discussion of union affairs be conducted during working time.
22. Administer discipline, layoff, and grievance procedures without regard to union membership or nonmembership of the employees involved.
23. Treat both union and nonunion employees alike in making assignments of preferred work or desired overtime.
24. Enforce plant rules impartially, regardless of the employee's membership activity in a union.
25. Tell employees, if they ask, that they are free to join or not to join any organization, so far as their status with the company is concerned.
26. Tell employees that their *personal* and *job* security will be determined by the economic prosperity of the company.

## Appendix B: Things You *Cannot Do* When a Union Tries to Organize

1. Engage in surveillance of employees to determine who and who is not participating in the union program; attend union meetings or engage in any undercover activities for this purpose.
2. Threaten, intimidate, or punish employees who engage in union activity.
3. Request information from employees about union matters, meetings, etc. Employees may, of their own volition, give such information without prompting. You may listen but not ask questions.
4. Prevent employee union representatives from soliciting memberships during nonworking time.
5. Grant wage increases, special concessions, or promises of any kind to keep the union out.
6. Question a prospective employee about his or her affiliation with a labor organization.
7. Threaten to close up or move the plant, curtail operations, or reduce employee benefits.
8. Engage in any discriminatory practices, such as work assignments, overtime, layoffs, promotions, wage increases, or any other actions that could be regarded as preferential treatment for certain employees.

9. Discriminate against union people when disciplining employees for a specific action and permit nonunion employees to go unpunished for the same action.
10. Transfer workers on the basis of teaming up nonunion employees to separate them from union employees.
11. Deviate in any way from company policies for the primary purpose of eliminating a union employee.
12. Intimate, advise, or indicate, in any way, that unionization will force the company to lay off employees, take away company benefits or privileges enjoyed, or make any other changes that could be regarded as a curtailment of privileges.
13. Make statements to the effect that you will not deal with a union.
14. Give any financial support or other assistance to employees who support or oppose the union.
15. Visit the homes of employees to urge them to oppose or reject the union in its campaign.
16. Be a party to any petition or circular against the union or encourage employees to circulate such a petition.
17. Make any promises of promotions, benefits, wage increases, or any other items that would induce employees to oppose the union.
18. Engage in discussions or arguments that may lead to physical encounters with employees over the union question.
19. Use a third party to threaten or coerce a union member, or attempt to influence any employee's vote through this medium.
20. Question employees on whether or not they have or have not affiliated or signed with the union.
21. Use the word *never* in any predictions or attitudes about unions or their promises or demands.
22. Talk about tomorrow. When you give examples or reasons, you can talk about yesterday or today instead of tomorrow, to avoid making a prediction or conviction which may be interpreted as a threat or promise by the union or the NLRB.

## Where to Look for Further Information

Brown, Barry, "Pinpointing Your Personnel Problems." *Personnel Administrator* 24 (January 1979), pp. 26–28.

Chung, Kae H. *Motivational Theories and Practices*. Columbus, Ohio: Grid Publishing, 1977.

Driessnack, Carl H. "Financial Impact of Effective Human Resources Management." *Personnel Administrator* 24 (December 1979), pp. 62–66.

Fels, Lippman G. "15 Questions You Dare Not Ask Job Applicants." *Administrative Management*, 53, no. 6 (June 1974), pp. 20, 21, 80, 82.

Foulkes, Fred K. "The Expanding Role of the Personnel Function." *Harvard Business Review,* 53, no. 2 (March–April 1975), pp. 71–84.

Greenberger, Robert S. "Federal Shift in Hiring Rules Stirs Criticism." *The Wall Street Journal,* March 15, 1983, p. 29.

Harschnek, Robert A., Jr., Donald J. Petersen, and Robert L. Malone. "Which Personnel Department Is Right for You?" *Personnel Administrator* 23 (April 1978), pp. 58–60.

Henderson, J. A. "What the Chief Executive Expects of the Personnel Function." *Personnel Administrator* 22 (May 1977), pp. 40–45.

"How New Tax Laws Benefit Employees." *U.S. News & World Report,* October 19, 1981, p. 80.

Lorber, Lawrence. "Job Segregation and Wage Discrimination under Title VII and the Equal Pay Act." *Personnel Administrator* 25 (May 1980), pp. 31–34.

Megginson, L. C. *Personnel and Human Resources Administration.* 4th ed. Homewood, Ill.: Richard D. Irwin, 1981. This provides a technical, legal, and professional approach to personnel.

"New Tax Angles on Your Retirement." *U.S. News & World Report,* October 4, 1982, p. 84.

"Paying Employees Not to Go to the Doctor." *Business Week,* March 21, 1983, pp. 146–50.

Perham, John. "Latest Corporate Quandary: IRAs." *Dun's Business Month* 119 (February 1982), pp. 64–68.

"Private Jobs Programs: Can They Fill the Gap?" *U.S. News & World Report,* February 21, 1983, pp. 68–69.

Schiavoni, Michael R. "Employee Relations: Where Will It Be in 1985?" *Personnel Administrator* 23 (March 1978), pp. 25–29.

Short, Larry L. "Now You Can Micro-Computerize Your Personnel System." *Personnel Journal 58* (March 1979), pp. 154–56.

"The Widening Choices in IRA Investment." *Business Week,* December 6, 1982, pp. 120–24.

# Exhibits

## Exhibit 5–1
### Evaluating Your Compliance with Equal Employment Opportunity Laws

Title VII of the Civil Rights Act of 1964, the Equal Employment Opportunities Act of 1972, the Age Discrimination in Employment Act of 1967, the Vocational Rehabilitation Act of 1973, and other legislation prohibit you from discriminating against any employee, or prospective employee, because of race, creed, color, sex, or nation of origin; or against 40-64-year-old workers; or against the handicapped.

Are you providing *equal opportunities* for all of them in the following areas:

1. Hiring?                          ☐ Yes ☐ No
2. Layoffs?                         ☐ Yes ☐ No
3. Recalls?                         ☐ Yes ☐ No
4. Discharges?                      ☐ Yes ☐ No
5. Recruitment?                     ☐ Yes ☐ No
6. Compensation?                    ☐ Yes ☐ No
7. Overtime work?                   ☐ Yes ☐ No
8. Promotional opportunities?       ☐ Yes ☐ No
9. Paid sick leave?                 ☐ Yes ☐ No
10. Paid vacation time?             ☐ Yes ☐ No
11. Insurance coverage?             ☐ Yes ☐ No
12. Training and development opportunities?
                                    ☐ Yes ☐ No
13. Retirement privileges and pension benefits?
                                    ☐ Yes ☐ No
14. Rest periods, lunch periods, etc.?   ☐ Yes ☐ No

If you answered no to *any* of these questions, you are *not* in compliance with the laws.

## Exhibit 5–2
### Evaluating Your Compliance with the Occupational Safety and Health Act of 1970

You and your employees have certain rights and responsibilities under this law—if you have one or more employees. See whether you and they are exercising these rights and fulfilling these responsibilities.

**Are you fulfilling your responsibilities?**

1. Are you providing a workplace that is free from health and safety hazards? ☐ Yes ☐ No ☐ Don't know
2. Do you provide safe tools, machines, and equipment for your workers?    ☐ Yes ☐ No ☐ Don't know
3. Do you have equal work standards—as far as health and safety are concerned—for all employees, without regard to race, sex, religion, nation of origin, age, or physical condition?
                                    ☐ Yes ☐ No ☐ Don't know
4. Are you in compliance with *all* the standards, as published in the *Federal Register*?
                                    ☐ Yes ☐ No ☐ Don't know

**Are your employees fulfilling their responsibilities?**

5. Are they complying with *all* health and safety standards?            ☐ Yes ☐ No ☐ Don't know
6. Are they complying with *your* rules, regulations, and orders issued under the law?
                                    ☐ Yes ☐ No ☐ Don't know
7. Are they using the safety equipment issued to them?                    ☐ Yes ☐ No ☐ Don't know

**Are you exercising your rights?**

8. Do (did) you request and receive proper identification of OSHA personnel prior to inspection of your workplace?    ☐ Yes ☐ No ☐ Don't know
9. Are (were) you advised by OSHA personnel of the reason for the inspection? ☐ Yes ☐ No ☐ Don't know
10. Do (did) you participate in the walk-around inspection of the workplace with the compliance officer?
                                    ☐ Yes ☐ No ☐ Don't know
11. Do (did) you participate in the opening and closing conferences with the compliance officer?
                                    ☐ Yes ☐ No ☐ Don't know
12. Have you borrowed money from the Small Business Administration to comply with OSHA standards?
                                    ☐ Yes ☐ No ☐ Don't know

**Are your employees exercising their rights?**

13. Have any of your employees requested a copy of the OSHA standards and other rules from you, the OSHA office, or the Government Printing Office?
                                    ☐ Yes ☐ No ☐ Don't know
14. Have any of your employees requested information from you on:
   a. Safety and health hazards in their work area?
                                    ☐ Yes ☐ No ☐ Don't know
   b. Precautions they need to take to prevent accidents or avoid hazards?
                                    ☐ Yes ☐ No ☐ Don't know
   c. What they must do if they are involved in an accident or are exposed to toxic substances?
                                    ☐ Yes ☐ No ☐ Don't know
15. Have any of your employees requested the OSHA director—in writing—to conduct an inspection because they believed a hazardous condition existed in their workplace? ☐ Yes ☐ No ☐ Don't know
16. Have any of your employees filed a complaint to OSHA—within 30 days—because they believed they had been discriminated against for asserting their rights under this act?    ☐ Yes ☐ No ☐ Don't know

# Part 2

# Producing Your Product or Service

So far, this book has been concerned with planning for and managing the business you have inherited, bought, or organized. Now it is time to look at the process of producing goods or services. This may not be an easy or simple task, for many and diverse activities are required to carry on the production function.

A business must be concerned with determining what products to sell; deciding whether to buy them from someone else or produce them itself; planning, acquiring, laying out, and maintaining the physical facilities required for operations; procuring and producing the right quantity of the right products at the right time and at the right cost; controlling the quality and quantity of inventory; maintaining a work force; and doing all of this as efficiently and economically as possible!

All these activities make the production function interesting, challenging, and rewarding, but also quite frustrating. In order to help you meet this challenge, this part will cover:

1. Changing inputs to outputs, including acquiring physical facilities.
2. Designing and controlling work.
3. Purchasing and controlling materials.

The first of these functions is covered in Chapter 6, the second in Chapter 7, and the third and final one in Chapter 8.

# Chapter Six

## Operations: Converting Inputs to Outputs

All business organizations produce something, either a product or a service. Thus all firms are engaged in some form of operations, which can be called production. Yet the term itself may be misleading, as you will soon see.

In this chapter, we will discuss operations, or converting inputs into outputs. Among the many inputs are personnel, money, machines, materials, and methods. Among the outputs are the product(s) produced and/or service(s) performed for your customers.

An immediate response to the material in this chapter may be that it applies only to a fabricating or manufacturing business. When examined more closely, however, it should become apparent that the principles and procedures detailed here are of such a nature that they are utilized in a broad spectrum of activities, including retailing and services.

### Systems for Converting Inputs to Finished Products

The term *production* often refers to manufacturing, because production methodology was first developed and applied in manufacturing industries. Yet, in reality, production can be defined as the creation of value or wealth by producing goods and services. This definition includes other activities as well as manufacturing. As indicated above, all companies receive inputs and convert them to outputs, as do industrial companies. Managers must have a system to do this. Figure 6–1 shows the transformation or movement of goods for several types of companies. Note that the conversion of the inputs to outputs represents the major activity of the business—the reason for the company's existence—and may be a transforming of form, place, or time.

## Productive Elements

How can the production methods used by industrial firms be applied to all types of small businesses? The processes of changing inputs to outputs have some characteristics that apply to all situations and have the following common elements:

1. Systems of transformation as related to form, place, or time.
2. A sequence of steps or operations to convert the inputs into outputs.
3. Special skills and often tools, machinery, or equipment to make the transformation or conversion.
4. Some time frame in which the work is to be done.
5. Instructions to identify the work to be performed and the units being produced.
6. Standards and maximum rates of input and output.
7. Exceptions and errors that must be handled.

## Productive Elements Applied to Different Industries

Not only do the inputs and outputs within a company have many common characteristics (see Figure 6–2), but the transformation

*Figure 6–1*
**Examples of Production Systems**

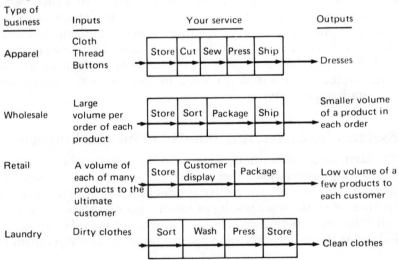

**Figure 6–2**
**Examples of Inputs and Outputs**

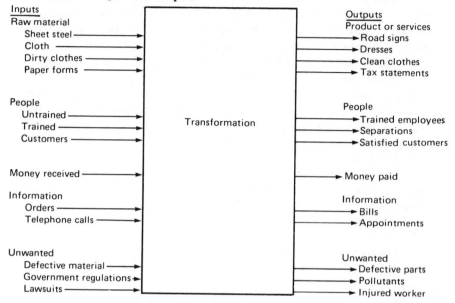

Inputs
Raw material
    Sheet steel
    Cloth
    Dirty clothes
    Paper forms

People
    Untrained
    Trained
    Customers

Money received

Information
    Orders
    Telephone calls

Unwanted
    Defective material
    Government regulations
    Lawsuits

Transformation

Outputs
Product or services
    Road signs
    Dresses
    Clean clothes
    Tax statements

People
    Trained employees
    Separations
    Satisfied customers

Money paid

Information
    Bills
    Appointments

Unwanted
    Defective parts
    Pollutants
    Injured worker

processes within different classifications of businesses have common characteristics. Let us look at some of these different applications to firms in different industries.

**A Manufacturing Company.** To manufacture means to make, or process, a raw material into a finished product. Raw material may be the outputs from other companies (such as synthetic rubber, resistors, or plastic powder), which are changed in form and/or assembled. A series of operations is commonly performed by machines in the conversion process. Formerly, these operations were performed by blue-collar workers using tools and machines. Now, manual labor has largely been replaced by machines, some of which are either automatically controlled or controlled by other machines. These devices can turn out more-uniform products with greater precision, in greater volume, and with less skill required than in manual production.

Manufacturing companies may produce only one standard product, while others, at the other extreme, produce each product to special order, with no product ever being repeated. The former type of process, called continuous production, operates automatically. The production system, once established, keeps performing the same actions. Also, the outputs can be stored with little chance of obsolescence or loss of value because of style or use changes.

Companies producing goods for customers requesting non-standard products must produce these when the customer wants the product. These companies are called job shops—they produce to the customer's order, or by the job. Seasonal and other variations in demand cause production to vary considerably and tend to result in idle time and varying employment levels.

In both processes, planning and controls must be exercised. The product is usually designed by an engineer, who not only executes the design but also converts it into production specifications. The operations to be performed, the machines to use, the needed skills of workers, and the material inputs needed are determined for each product or order. The time to produce is set, and instructions for workers and tools to use are designated. The information is used in performing and checking the work to assure output conformance with specifications. Thus, a key procedure is set to guide and check production.

*A Service Company.* Many independent businesses fall into this category. Cleaning and laundering, insurance, banking, patient processing, consulting, electrical repair, and transportation organizations are examples. The inputs are converted to finished products through one or a series of operations. The required operations are repeated with variations for special orders. Firms of this kind differ from manufacturers in the emphases placed on the design of the system of transformation.

Routing in taxi and trucking companies is similar to that for material in production. Scheduling of patients for doctors, of repairs for plumbers, and of calls for insurance salespeople is important so that the servers' time is used effectively. Proper layout of facilities of banks and automobile garages smoothes the performance of the service. Measurement of performance of people in all types of businesses is needed for control purposes.

The service company usually receives smaller orders or individual customers, with some variation in the input and the desired output. For example, a customer may bring into a laundry different items such as sheets, clothing, rags, and linens. These, in turn, are made from different combinations of white, colored, natural, and synthetic cloth. Emphasis is placed on individual handling and personalized service. These activities result in higher unit costs than for single-product, high-volume processes. Also, the related systems needed to plan, identify, and control are relatively more complex.

These companies fit the job shop classification, but when they are designed properly, they may take on the characteristics of continuous production. In the laundry, for example, all clothing is sorted into different types of cloth. Then each type of cloth follows a set process.

***Wholesalers.*** This group of companies receives large volumes of many items and distributes them in smaller quantities. The transformation process involves converting large packages of like items into large and small packages of a variety of items. The sequence of operations can be planned and controlled in the same manner as for the manufacturing process; but the emphasis is not on transforming by machinery, but on storing, materials handling, and packaging.

***Retailing.*** The process within a store has subprocesses, but the organization includes movements of customers as well as of materials. The primary emphasis is directed toward convenience to the customers and only secondarily toward material flow. The availability and placement of goods in the store and the movement of customers in relation to the goods are important contributors to, or detractors from, the sale of goods.

***Other Types of Companies.*** Many other independent businesses not included in the prior classifications can benefit from the same types of internal analyses as those discussed. Automobile repairing, home building, and accounting firms have similar flows of material, people, or forms.

The set of processes in each organization tends to reflect its reason for existence. For example, materials and parts are converted to finished goods in a manufacturing company; patients are processed through treatments in a hospital; and goods are moved to the proper place, the customer is guided to that place, and the transaction is completed at another point in a self-service store. All other processes, including paperwork, are supportive and designed to assure achieving the objectives of the firm.

## Deciding Whether to Make or Buy

Changing raw material to a finished product that is delivered to the customer is a long process, usually involving many companies performing different productive functions.

### Deciding How Large a Segment

Figure 6–3 shows the sequence of steps raw materials go through to become a finished product for the consumer. One company may

***Figure 6–3***
**The Business Process**

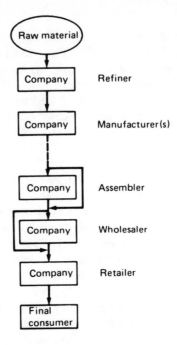

refine the raw materials, several may perform manufacturing processes, another may assemble the parts into finished product, and so on. A given company may perform a large or small part of this process. Fixing the place and the size of the segment is an important decision.

For example, a firm may decide to start a business involving wooden birdhouses. It would probably not grow trees, cut the trees, and saw the trees into wood. But it has those decisions to make. Other decisions which determine the segment are:

1. Buy wood and cut the parts, or buy precut pieces.
2. Assemble the birdhouses, or sell the packaged pieces to be assembled by the customer.
3. Sell to a wholesaler, a retailer, or the final user.

Figure 6–4 illustrates, in chart form, the decisions needed for this relatively simple process.

For best results, you should try to specialize in the segment of the total process where you have the greatest expertise. The advantages of specializing and concentrating in a small area in which the company performs best are:

**Figure 6–4**
**Deciding a Firm's Segment of the Production and Selling Process**

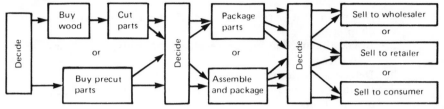

1. Less capital investment is needed for machinery and inventory, and for people with differing capabilities.
2. Management can concentrate better on a small segment.
3. Planning, directing, and controlling are less complex.

The advantages of a larger segment are:

1. More control of the process.
2. Less idle machine and personnel time.
3. Greater potential for growth.

### The Economics of Your Decision

The decision as to what segment to seek is usually based on the economics of the situation. It might be advantageous to make some of the parts you normally buy in order to reduce idle time of the machines and people. You might drop some of the early or late operations instead of buying more machinery when there is not enough capacity. Remember, though, that any additions or reductions must be evaluated from a cost viewpoint and that some of these costs may vary with changes in volume, while others do not.

## Planning Physical Facilities

Having decided on the segment of the total transformation process you wish to perform, you can now begin to plan, obtain, and install the producing unit.

The physical facilities of a company—the building itself, machines and equipment, furniture and fixtures, and others—must be designed to aid the employees in producing the desired product or service at a low cost. The design function includes the layout and selection of machines and equipment and the determination of the features desired in the building. For purposes of discussion, the function is divided into two parts: (1) planning and (2) implementation, which will be discussed later in this chapter.

Good selection and arrangement of physical facilities can pay dividends. Planning physical facilities requires the following steps:

1. Determine the services to be performed (discussed in earlier chapters).
2. Break the production or service into parts, operations, and activities.
3. Determine space requirements.
4. Decide the type of arrangement which is best for the sequence of operations.
5. Determine the general layout, using blocks for sections of the building.
6. Plan the detailed layout that will provide the most effective use of personnel, machines, and materials and provide for customer convenience.

## Determine Your Services

This step was discussed in earlier chapters; in general, the type of business determines what good(s) you need to produce or sell or what service(s) you perform.

## Break the Product or Service into Parts, Operations, and Activities

Assuming you are going to (1) produce a product or (2) sell to customers, you need to break the product down into:

| *Produce* | *Sell* |
|---|---|
| 1. Parts going into it. | 1. Types of goods. |
| 2. Operations needed to produce it. | 2. Operations needed to sell goods. |
| 3. Activities surrounding its production. | 3. Activities servicing sales. |

Identification of parts and products or services provides the detail for planning your physical facilities. You start with output and work backward to inputs. For example, an assembled product is "exploded" to determine the parts needed for assembly. Then, needed operations can be identified.

Operations are the steps or segments of work performed to accomplish the conversion of the inputs into outputs. The segments are often identified by the specialized work of a machine—for example, drilling, typing, or wrapping. The conversion process usually requires a series of operations. Figure 6–5 shows the operations for making metal signs. (The circles indicate operations.)

In a store, operations are the steps taken to complete a sale,

**Figure 6–5**
**Operation Process Chart and Calculations for Making a Typical Metal Sign**

| Operations | Symbols for sequence | Machine | Hours required per machine | Forecast volume per hour | Number of machines needed |
|---|---|---|---|---|---|
| Cut sides | ① | Shear | .12/100 cuts | 500 cuts | 1 |
| Cut corners | ② | Press | .17/100 corners | 600 corners | 2 |
| Punch holes | ③ | Press | .10/100 holes | 500 holes | 1 |
| Wash | ④ | Tank | .005/sign | 300 signs | 10 ft.* |
| Dry | ⑤ | Oven | .01/sign | 300 signs | 15 ft.* |
| Phosphate coat | ⑥ | Tank | .008/sign | 300 signs | 12 ft.* |
| Dry | ⑦ | Oven | .02/sign | 300 signs | 30 ft.* |
| Paint metal | ⑧ | Spray gun | .28/100 signs | 300 signs | 1 |
| Bake | ⑨ | Oven | .10/sign | 300 signs | 150 ft.* |
| Print sign | ⑩ | Silk screen | Varies (see table) | 300 signs | 2 |
| Bake | ⑪ | Oven | .10/100 signs | 300 signs | 1 |
| Box signs | ⑫ | Bench | 1.00/100 signs | 300 signs | 3 workers |

○ = Operation
*Conveyors are used to move signs into, through, and out of tanks and ovens at 10 feet per minute. Tanks and ovens are measured in feet.

such as the steps in the work of a salesperson. Figure 6–6 shows the operations for a customer collecting groceries in a supermarket.

Activities, such as moving materials and displaying goods, are necessary for servicing the production and/or selling operations. Nonactivities, including delays, are caused by imbalance of the times of the operation. Activities and nonactivities may not be identified fully until the final layout planning is performed. Except

**Figure 6–6**
**Operation Process Chart for a Customer in a Supermarket**

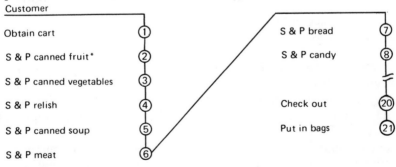

Customer

| Obtain cart | ① | | S & P bread | ⑦ |
| S & P canned fruit* | ② | | S & P candy | ⑧ |
| S & P canned vegetables | ③ | | | |
| S & P relish | ④ | | Check out | ⑳ |
| S & P canned soup | ⑤ | | Put in bags | ㉑ |
| S & P meat | ⑥ | | | |

○ = Operation
*S & P = Select and put in cart

when planned, as in browsing for selling, the number and extent of nonactivities should be minimized.

Sequences of operations may be fixed, as for signmaking shown in Figure 6–5. In stores, sequences may vary as they are designed to maximize sales to customers in a changing environment. The sequence shown in Figure 6–6 changes with each customer.

## Determine Space Requirements

You need to design physical facilities with the capacity to produce and/or sell the planned volume of products or services. Capacity is limited by machines, equipment, people, and space.

Machines are designed to perform specified tasks at certain rates, such as units per hour. People are trained to perform their work according to certain methods. Estimates, or one of several measurement methods (discussed in the next chapter), can be used to determine rates of output of machines and people. Using these rates of output and the planned volume of output, Figure 6–5 shows, for example, that two presses are needed for Operation 2. If one person runs each machine, two people are needed for Operation 2.

The building size for a firm's operations is determined by the space needed for machines, people, aisles, inventory, displays, offices, and service facilities. Space requirements for each of these items can be obtained from published data, measurement, or estimation.

## Decide the Best Arrangement for the Sequence of Operations

In production, you try to obtain the least movement of product and people. Least movement in some stores is desirable; but in others, high customer movement increases sales. However, people and machines should not be idle, and space should be used to greatest advantage. The building can be planned according to either, or a combination of both, of the following two types of layout:

1. Product, or service.
2. Process, or function.

*Product Layout.* The product layout places the machines or serving units in such a way that the products or people move along a line as they pass through the sequence of operations. Assembly lines in the automobile industry are the best-known examples of this type of layout. As the automobile frame moves on a conveyor, the engine, axles, steering mechanism, and other components are added until a finished car comes off the conveyor. A cafeteria line is another example of a product layout. In fact, all layouts should generally conform to this concept, as shown in Figure 6–7.

**Figure 6–7**
**Product Layout**

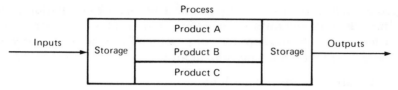

With this type of layout, materials, workers, or customers move forward from operation to operation with little backtracking. A supermarket could set up this type of layout if it knew that a large enough number of customers wanted the same items. If the customers selected purchases according to the order in which the goods are displayed, backtracking is eliminated. The advantages of this type of layout plan include:

1. Specialization of workers and machines.
2. Less inventory.
3. Fewer instructions and controls.
4. Faster movement.
5. Less space for aisles and storage.

***Process Layout.*** The second type of layout, process, is based on keeping the machines and workers busy and thus keeping the idle time to a minimum. Machines performing the same type of work are grouped together, and the same is true of workers with like skills. By grouping the same type of merchandise together, forming a process layout, customers can find and select items they want. Examples of this type of layout include presses grouped together so that each press can keep busy, typists put in an information processing center servicing multiple offices, and toys located together in a store. This type of layout increases the movement of material or people and necessitates higher inventory. The advantages of the process layout include:

1. Its flexibility to take care of change and variety.
2. Its use of general-purpose machines and equipment.
3. Its more efficient use of machines and personnel.
4. Ease in finding and evaluating merchandise.

***Combination Layout.*** Few layout plans are confined to either one type or the other. Instead, they consist of combinations of the two to take advantage of the situation. Idle time created by differing production rates may be more than compensated for by decreased inventory.

Layouts can be planned to move material, people, tools, or

machines. Thus, in some stores, the customers move through self-service lines; in others, the salesperson moves about to bring the goods to the customer. For parts of a physical examination in a clinic, doctors and nurses move to the patient; for other parts, the patient moves from room to room. Some of the factors to be considered in planning for movement are:

1. Size of goods and machines.
2. Safety requirements.
3. Volume of input and output.
4. Type of service.

### Determine the General Layout

The next step is to determine the general layout, using blocks for sections of the layout. A block can be a machine, a group of machines, a group of products on display, or a department. This step is intended to establish the general arrangement of the plant, store, or office before spending much time on details. Estimates are made of the space needed in each block using past layouts; summation of space for machines, people, aisles, and other factors; or the best judgment available.

Figures 6–8 and 6–9 are illustrations of block layouts. In each, dashed lines show space set aside for particular operations and activities to be performed. Similarly, besides the activities directly concerned with the main work of the company, space for mainte-

**Figure 6–8**
**Block Layout of a Fabric Store**

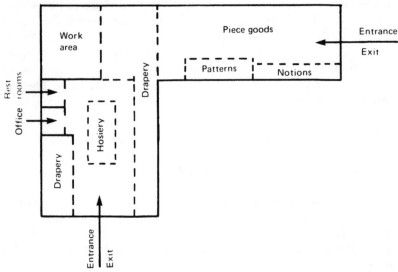

**Figure 6–9**
**Plant Layout for a Metal Sign Company**

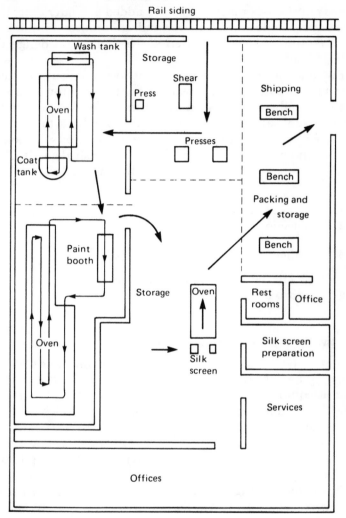

nance, planning, food, personal needs, and other services is provided. Each service should be placed conveniently near the units
that will use it.

If you are replanning the layout of an existing building, or are
planning to move into one, the location of outside walls is predetermined. Figure 6–8 shows an example of this. Also, the size and
shape of the land may be confining.

In planning a new building, on the other hand, you have greater
flexibility. This allows you to design it so that changes can be made

easily in the future. Buildings are usually designed to provide space for several years, while the number of machines planned is for only the near future—as machines can be added at a later date. In most operations, single-story, square, and columnless buildings with movable utility outlets are preferred. The building is designed from the inside out.

Entrance locations are important in the layout, particularly for service establishments. Customers enter downtown stores from the street, and goods usually enter from the back. These entrances may be fixed, setting the flow of goods from back to front. Some producing plants use the same transportation units for delivering supplies and materials as for shipping the finished goods. The flow is thus U-shaped. Other—usually less important—external factors are:

1. Entrances for employees.
2. Connections to utilities.
3. Governmental restrictions.
4. Weather factors.

Included in the layout should be plans for expansion and other future conditions.

### Plan the Detailed Layout for Efficiency and Effectiveness

You must plan in detail the layout of people, machines, and materials if you are to have efficient performance. Each machine and piece of equipment is located and space allocated for its use. As with blocks, templates (or models) of the machines, equipment, and workers help you perform this step. These templates can be moved about to obtain your best plan. Figure 6–9 shows machine locations for the metal sign plant determined by using templates for placing machines.

In manufacturing, many devices are used to move materials. Conveyors, carts, hands, trucks, and cranes are examples. The materials shown in Figure 6–5 could be moved by forklift truck, carts, or overhead and belt conveyors. Notice that, as shown, the conveyor carries the metal plates through washing, drying, coating, and drying, without stopping. Wholesale warehouses are faced with many types of materials-handling problems. The objective is to minimize materials handling and its cost without increasing other costs.

Each operation should be examined to assure easy performance of work. If the worker spends too much time standing, walking, turning, and twisting, the work will take longer and be more tiring. Tools and other items to be used should be located close at hand for quick service. A short study of location of tools in a garage illustrates this point. An understanding of methods study is helpful in planning workers' activities.

Some specifics that should be included in final layout planning are:

1.  Space for movement: Are aisles wide enough for one- or two-way traffic? Is there enough room if a queue forms? Can material be obtained easily, and is space available when the material is waiting? Can shelves be restocked conveniently?
2.  Utilities: Are adequate provisions made for incoming wiring and gas, or for disposal of water at each machine? Will any future moves of utilities be necessary?
3.  Safety: Is equipment using flammable material properly isolated and proper fire protection provided? Are moving parts and machines guarded and the operators protected from accidents?
4.  Working conditions: Does the worker have enough working space and light? Are there provisions for low noise levels, proper temperature, and elimination of objectionable odors? Is the worker safe? Can a worker socialize and take care of personal needs?
5.  Cleanliness and maintenance: Is the layout designed for good housekeeping at low cost? Can machinery, equipment, and the building itself be maintained easily?
6.  Product quality: Are provisions made to protect the product as it moves through the plant or stays in storage?

Although we have been considering manufacturing facilities, many of the same generalizations hold true for retail and wholesale establishments.

## Implementing Plans

The first step in implementing plans is to test them to see whether they are sound. There are many ways this can be done. One method is to have employees—or other persons who can give some experienced opinions—review the plans and make suggestions. Another method is to simulate the process by moving templates or models of the goods or the people through the process so that you can analyze their movements. You might deliberately include some mishaps to see what happens. It might be well to use the processing plans that will be discussed in Chapter 7 to see how the production plan works with the layout.

The actual implementation of your plans will depend on whether this is a brand-new venture, a layout for an existing building, or a rearrangement of an existing layout. Construction of a new building requires further steps in the design of the building and its surroundings. These steps include consideration of at least the following factors:

1. Type and method of construction.
2. Arrangements for parking.
3. Roads and transportation of goods.
4. Landscaping.

The installation of a new or rearranged layout plan requires careful planning and scheduling to minimize delays and costs. Some of the techniques in Chapter 7 will be useful in this planning.

## Summary

This chapter has shown you how to organize your productive system in order to transform your inputs of personnel, money, machines, methods, and materials into the outputs of goods and/or services. Such systems have many common elements, regardless of the type of business involved.

Some illustrative businesses ranging from manufacturing to retailing, and their use of these elements, were discussed. Then, some factors were presented to consider in deciding whether to buy your materials from outside or produce them. The decision should be based upon the relative costs of the alternatives.

After making these decisions, you are able to plan for, purchase, and install your physical facilities. Some principles of laying out facilities for plants and stores were also presented.

# Chapter Seven

# Designing and Controlling Work

So far, you have selected the good(s) and/or service(s) to be produced or performed, estimated what physical facilities will be needed, and decided how those facilities should be laid out. Now, you are ready to start producing the good(s) and/or service(s). This requires that you design work methods, measure work, provide instructions, and direct and control the activities. (Some of these activities have been designed into the systems already described and will be referred to only as the total system is described.)

The planning and control process is, in reality, a total communications system designed to convey to employees the what, how, where, who, when, and why of the work to be done. It is also a check on what has been done to correct and adjust the work and the process, to assure that customers receive good service—in terms of both time and quality.

The specific topics that will be covered in this chapter are:

1. Work design.
2. Work measurement.
3. Planning—the forecast.
4. Planning—converting the sales plan to a production plan.
5. Scheduling—setting the time for the work to be done.
6. Installing an information system to direct activities.
7. Controlling production—quantity and quality.

## Work Design

Chapter 6 showed how to plan the layout of a plant or a store, but the detailed movement of materials and the layout of the workplace were not examined. These topics now need to be studied. For example, in the metal sign plant, are the metal plates properly placed so that the operator cutting the corners has short and easy moves? How many machines can one person operate? Are there new methods of moving materials? The following steps are used in work design and improvement:

1. State the problem.
2. State the function of the work.
3. Collect information.
4. List alternatives.
5. Analyze and select the alternatives.
6. Formulate, review, and test the selected alternative.
7. Install and follow up the new method.

Each of these steps will be discussed briefly.

### State the Problem

As usual, it is best to begin by stating the problem. Why study the work? Is the cost of the work too high? Is the work delaying other activities? Is the quality of the service low? Is the service to customers delayed? The reason(s) for making a study of the work should be clearly understood and stated in order to provide direction.

### State the Function of the Work

Often a given production function appears obvious—for example, sewing a seam, drilling a hole, or selling to a customer. However, you should begin by asking questions. Is this operation necessary? Is it the only alternative? A clear statement of the reason for the operation starts one toward finding the best method to perform the function.

### Collect Information

Collecting information breaks the work into parts and establishes appropriate relationships. The purposes are twofold: training and informing.

The reason for training is to develop the ability to observe work as a series of activities. For example, a description of a machine operation might include statements such as "prepare material," "do the work," and "remove finished product." The term *prepare material* might include reaching for material, selecting material, grasping material, moving material to the machine, and positioning the material. This type of training, combined with the use of some commonsense principles, develops the ability to identify inefficiencies.

The reason for informing is to aid in recording the details of the work for later analysis. Several types of charting procedures are shown in Figures 7–1, 7–2, and 7–3 and are discussed.

Figure 7–1 shows a flow process chart for the first and second operations in making a metal sign, as shown in Figure 6–4. Not only does it show the cutting of sides and corners, but it also adds transportations, delays, and storage. Observe the number of delays and transports that occur for each operation. You want to reduce these because they are costly. Symbols are used to simplify your

**Figure 7–1**
**Flow Process Chart for Making Metal Signs**

| Item description | Operation / Transportation / Inspection / Delay / Storage | Distance in feet | Pick-ups | Lay-downs | Time in min. | Quantity | Why? What? Where? When? Who? How? | Notes |
|---|---|---|---|---|---|---|---|---|
| IN STORAGE AREA | O ⇨ □ D ▽ | | | | | | | |
| TO SHEARS BY CART | O ⇨ □ D ▽ | 15′ | 1 | 2 | | 1 | ✓ ✓ | Fork truck convey |
| IN STACK | O ⇨ □ D ▽ | | | 10 | 1 | | ✓ | |
| CUT SIDES, SHEAR | O ⇨ □ D ▽ | | 1 | 2 | | | | |
| IN STACK | O ⇨ □ D ▽ | | | 10 | 3 | | ✓ | Conveyor-roll to press |
| TO PRESS, CART | O ⇨ □ D ▽ | 10 | 1 | | 6 | | ✓ ✓ | ʺ |
| IN STACK | O ⇨ □ D ▽ | | | 3 | 3 | | | |
| CUT CORNERS, PRESS | O ⇨ □ D ▽ | | 1 | 1 | | 1 | | |

**Figure 7–2**
**Motion Study of Cashier at Checkout Station**

| Left-Hand Description | Activity | Activity | Right-Hand Description |
|---|---|---|---|
| Reach for box | → | D | For reaching |
| Move and turn box | → | D | For moving |
| While reading price | H | D | For reading |
| Push for bagging | → | O | Key in price |
| Reach for bottle | → | D | For reach |
| | etc. | | |

Legend: O = Operation; → = Movement; D = Delay; H = Hold. Note the large percentage of delay.

**Figure 7–3**
**Operator Running an Automatic Printing Machine**

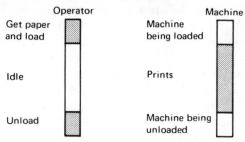

understanding of the process. Data are also collected on methods of movement, distances, time, and quantity.

Figure 7–2 presents a motion study of a simple operation of checking out purchases in a supermarket. Note the items that are repeated many times each day. Use of a foot-operated conveyor reduces or eliminates reach, delay, move, and push. Use of an electronic wand or sensor can make further reductions.

Figure 7–3 shows the relationship between an operator and a machine. The operator loads and unloads the machine, and the machine performs its operations automatically. Note that the idle time for the operator amounts to over half the time.

Figure 7–4 can be used to analyze your decisions involved in getting up in the morning.

### List Alternatives

Listing of alternatives is basic to any type of analysis and is a critical step in decision making. All work and services can be performed in many ways, and products can be made from many different materials. For example, a pencil can be made of wood, metal, or plastic; it can have an eraser and clip, or not have them; and it may be cylindrical or hexagonal. A hole can be punched, drilled, burned, or cut. Products may be sold through a catalogue, a personal-service store, or a self-service store. You should question the whole process, parts of the process, and each individual activity by recording all alternatives. The following questions are helpful:

1. Why is the activity being performed?
2. Can it be eliminated?
3. What and where is the activity, and who is performing it?
4. Can it be combined with another operation or operations?
5. When is the activity performed?
6. Can the work sequence be changed to reduce the volume of work?

**Figure 7–4**
**Computer Diagram on How to Get Up in the Morning**

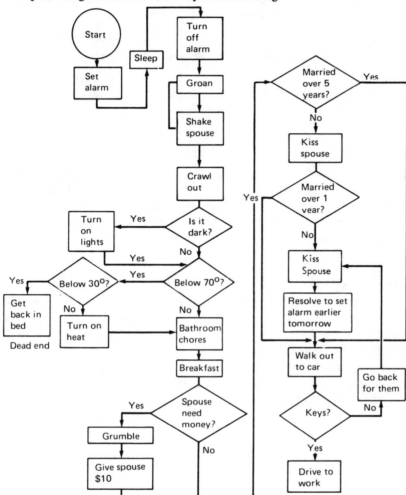

7. How is the activity performed?
8. Can it be simplified?

Can the operator in Figure 7–3 run another machine also? Or inspect? Or perform the next operation? The objective is to remove or simplify as many activities as possible without reducing the quality and quantity of output.

## Analyze and Select Alternatives

This step is the evaluation of the alternatives based on practicality, cost, acceptance by workers, and the effect on output. In a good list of alternatives, a small percentage will be finally acceptable. However, the extra time invested in exploring alternatives improves your chances of finding the best design.

### Formulate, Review, and Test the Selected Alternative

This step converts ideas into reality, checks for any errors or missed possibilities, and makes sure the proposed procedures perform as expected.

### Install and Follow Up the New Method

Installation includes setting up the physical equipment (for example, a foot pedal), gaining acceptance by the people involved with the operation, and training workers. The objective is to establish performance at its optimum level. (See "Implementing Plans" in Chapter 6.)

## Work Measurement

One of the most difficult problems is the measurement of work. We have few precise tools for making these measurements, but rely heavily on the fallible judgment of people to make them. Physical work can be measured more precisely than mental work, but doing so still requires judgment. This section is concerned with measuring the time for doing physical work. Once time standards are set, they can be used to:

1. Determine how many people or machines are needed for a desired output.
2. Estimate the cost of sales and other orders.
3. Determine the standard output for incentive systems.
4. Schedule production.
5. Measure performance.

The time standard for a worker can be divided into (1) the time to do the work and (2) the time for personal needs and irregular activities.

### Time for Work Performance

Methods that can be used to determine the time to perform the work are:

1. Estimates by people experienced in the work.
2. Time study, using a watch or other timing device.
3. Synthesis of the elemental times obtained from tables.

*Time Standards Set by Experienced People.* This is the simplest and least costly method of obtaining a time for work, but it is also the least precise. No breakdown of the work is made, and the standards often include past inefficiencies. Yet, these standards are adequate if the person setting the standards is careful.

*Time Study.* This is probably the best method. However, it has the poorest reputation because time studies have often not been properly done or used. A time study is made by a person—usually an industrial engineer—actually observing the work being done. The observer uses a stopwatch; makes many recordings of the time for each segment of the work; evaluates the workers' performance against the observer's standard of normal speed and effort; adjusts the time values; selects the normal time, using some averaging method; and adds a certain amount of time for personal needs and irregular activities.

*Synthesis of Elemental Times.* This is a pencil-and-paper method based on the accumulation of data from research studies. Tables of manual times have been developed for a wide range of workers' activities, including reaching, moving, grasping, positioning, turning, walking, and bending. A synthetic time can be set for checking out groceries, as shown in Figure 7–2; tables are also available to compute times for machining operations. By analyzing the work into the proper elements, times from the tables can be applied to obtain a normal time for an operation.

### Adding Time for Personal Needs

Personal and irregular time allowances are added to normal time to obtain the total time in which an operation should be performed under "normal" conditions. Allowances for personal needs in time study and synthesis methods include times for use of the rest room, poor working conditions, and fatigue. Tables are available for these times. The time for irregular activities (for example, getting material, receiving instructions, repairing minor breakdowns, and cleanup) can be determined by work sampling or by estimating the frequency and length of time for each type of activity.

Work sampling is based on making a large number of observations at random times. For each observation, you record whether a worker is producing, is idle, or is doing irregular work. The percentage of observations in each category is the estimate of the percentage of the total time the worker spends in that activity.

Work output is usually expressed in standard allowed hours (SAH) per unit of output. Workers on incentive plans, who are paid by the number of units they produce, usually earn 5–30 percent more than their actual hours would indicate on the basis of SAH. Research indicates that the introduction of a good incentive system will increase production by about 30 percent.

## Planning: The Forecast

Sales forecasting and marketing research will be discussed in Chapter 10. Converting those forecasts into a sales plan is the starting point for your production plan. But before the sales plan can be fixed, your production capacity must be checked. The best sales plan from a marketing viewpoint may not be the best plan for the company as a whole. It may require too much overtime, too much idle time, or some combination of the two.

The optimum plan from a production standpoint is to maintain a constant level of production—near capacity for both machine and person—of one product, with inputs arriving as needed and outputs taken by customers as they are completed. This is the ideal situation, and the concept provides the direction toward which you should move.

If the sales plan does not keep production busy, what can be done? Should the company advertise more heavily, reduce prices, or redesign its product to increase the volume? The loss in income from these actions may be more than made up by more efficient operation of the plant. Should another product, or variation of a product, be added to the company's service? Or would this increase the changeover costs and cause such confusion in production that it would cost more than the value received from the added sales?

Maybe the sales plan calls for more output than the capacity of the production process. The excess can be satisfied by expanding the capacity, by producing on overtime, or by subcontracting. However, the extra expense and trouble must be balanced against the benefits.

## Planning: Converting a Sales Plan to a Production Plan

You may have heard that it is impossible to predict the sales of an independent business with any reasonable degree of accuracy. This may be true, but even crude estimates are usually better than none at all. Time is required to purchase, produce, and deliver an item if it is not in stock when the customer orders it. Customers' demands for goods and services vary from period to period for such reasons as changing seasons. Companies must try to have goods available when they are demanded. This requires careful planning.

Planning starts with longer periods and proceeds to the detail of day-to-day operations. Chapter 4 discussed the long-range planning needed to design and install physical facilities. The next step is to plan for the next-shorter period, which may be one year. The sales plan, which is usually done for the year ahead, is broken down into months (or perhaps by quarters for the last six months). The production plan should be prepared for these same periods.

Some alternative production plans (PPs) that may be considered are:

**PP–1.** Produce what is demanded by your customers at the time they need the goods.

**PP–2.** Produce at a constant level equal to the average monthly demand for the year. Inventories will increase when the volume of demand is lower than the production volume, and will decrease when the demand is higher.

**PP–3.** Produce complementary products, which balance out increases and decreases in the volume of demand for individual products. The sum of the monthly demands should result in a constant production level.

**PP–4.** Subcontract production that is in excess of a certain level.

**PP–5.** Decide not to expand production to meet demand.

**PP–6.** Employ special sales inducements, perhaps extra advertising and lower prices, when sales volume is expected to be low.

One of the major causes of predictable variations in demand is the yearly cycle of seasons. Examples include demands for sports equipment, heating and cooling facilities, and landscaping. Alternative production plans using seasonal variations will be discussed in the examples.

Figure 7–5 shows a possible monthly plot of the sales plan for your company for the year ahead. The measure of sales volume can be dollars, standard allowed hours (SAH), tons, or other units—whichever best measures production capacity, inventory level, or sales demand.

**Figure 7–5**
**Sales and Production Plans with Seasonal Changes in Demand**

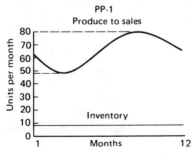
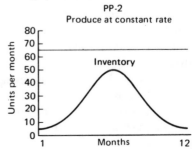

Under Production Plan 1 (*PP–1*), output and sales volume lines are the same, and the inventory of finished goods can be held at a constant minimum level. As plant capacity is large—equaling 80 units—overtime work can be avoided. However, the hiring and layoff of workers is expensive and places a hardship on production workers. Production requires full plant capacity during only a small part of the year, and the plant is idle up to 30 units per month during another part of the year. With the trend to increased fringe benefits, annual wage systems, and severance pay, this type of production plan is becoming outdated.

*PP–2* sets production at a constant level with a heavy buildup of inventory. The advantages of this plan are:

1.  Decrease in capacity needed.
2.  Constant level of personnel, with a minimum of hiring and lay-off costs.
3.  Reduction in paperwork needed in running the production system.

This type of plan is ideal from the production viewpoint.

The major disadvantage of *PP–2* is the large inventory cost, which can bankrupt a company if it is not evaluated carefully (see Chapter 8). Companies ordinarily do not attempt to level production completely but try to find some compromise between PP–1 and *PP–2*. An analysis can be made by finding the minimum-cost plan, using the following formula:

Annual added costs = Inventory costs + Overtime costs
+ Change-in-level costs

Also, many service businesses cannot build inventories. For example, hospitals cannot build inventories of patients. However, hospitals do use appointment systems to move noncritical cases from busy to slack times.

*PP–3* (producing complementary products) might be illustrated by producing, selling, or servicing both furnaces and air conditioners. The furnaces are produced for winter and the air conditioners for summer. If the same machines and skills can be used in producing both products and if the volumes produced and sold can be balanced, the sales and production forces will be kept working at a constant rate the year round. This is one of the reasons many companies have a variety of products in their product lines.

*PP–4* (subcontracting excess production) has several variations. You might make more of the parts yourself during slack periods and subcontract to others during peak periods.

*PP–5* (not expanding production to meet sales) is often rejected without much thought because it means a loss of sales. Many times, however, the costs of expanded capacity and/or overtime exceed the benefits of added sales.

*PP–6* (offering special sales inducements) is a marketing activity that will be covered in Part 3.

After you have established your production, selling, and servicing plans for the year, other plans or budgets can be developed. You can determine, for example, the correct amount of materials, parts, and goods; the employees required; and the financing needed.

## Scheduling: Setting the Time for Work to be Done

We have just discussed the development of the general production plan for a period of one year. This section covers day-to-day scheduling.

As orders are received, they are either filled from inventory or ordered into production. Most companies keep an inventory of standard items in order to give quick service. They stock the items for which they forecast sufficient demand and for which the value of fast service is greater than the added cost of carrying the inventory. When the plant would otherwise be idle, these are the types of items that are produced to stock.

Orders are scheduled into production:

1. On a preplanned schedule.
2. When inventory is reduced to a certain low level.
3. When orders are received and inventory is not available.

The preplanned schedule works best for standard items, the demand for which can be forecast. The number of units in a production order is determined by balancing the costs involved. A large order increases inventory costs per unit; a small order increases the planning, machine setup, handling, and paperwork costs per unit. On the other hand, the order size of special items should be set according to the size of customer orders. (A further consideration of these costs is included with the discussion of purchase order sizes in Chapter 8.)

Schedules set the times to produce specified goods. A company producing the same units continuously can automatically set how many units to produce by setting the total number of operator and machine hours per week. Job shops, on the other hand, must schedule each order. This scheduling can be done by one of the following methods:

1. Sending orders into the shop in sequence. The shop processes the jobs through the operations on a first-come, first-served basis.

2. Setting priorities, and processing orders accordingly. Rush orders have top priority.
3. Using either (1) or (2) for each operation.
4. Setting a specific time for each operation for each job.

Note the following relationships:

| Method | Scheduling Cost | Idle Time | Processing Time | Inventory Level |
|--------|----------------|-----------|-----------------|-----------------|
| 1 | Low | High | High | High |
| 4 | High | Low | Low | Low |

In scheduling operations, an effort should be made to keep inventory as low as practical. Production should be started early on a long-time sequence of operations for a part that is to be assembled to a short-time sequenced part. This can be illustrated by the often used bar, or Gantt, chart shown in Figure 7–6.

**Figure 7–6**
**Scheduling Product AB Using a Gantt Chart**

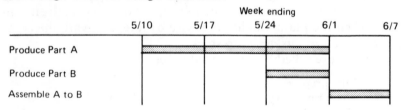

By scheduling Part A to start on May 10 and Part B to start on May 24, the two parts are expected to be completed at the time they are needed for assembly. If the delivery date for the order is June 7, the delivery may be made soon after the work is completed.

A chart has been developed for scheduling networks. Networks are sequences of operations, each of which may be dependent upon the completion of several other activities. This chart, called the critical path method (CPM) or program evaluation and review technique (PERT), is used by many companies in the construction industry. Figure 7–7 shows a chart for the installation of an underground pipe.

Circles represent the start and the end of activities, and lines show activities (the length of the line has no meaning). The times at the circles give the earliest and latest times for the end of the prior operation and the beginning of the next one; the difference is called slack. The circles with zero slack time are on critical path,

**Figure 7–7**
**PERT Chart for Putting in a Pipeline**

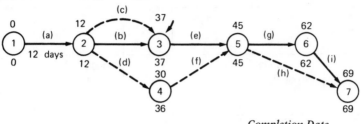

| Legend: | | Days | Completion Date | | Slack |
|---|---|---|---|---|---|
| | | | Earliest | Latest | |
| (a) | Survey ditch | 12 | 12 | 12 | 0 |
| (b) | Dig ditch | 25 | 37 | 37 | 0 |
| (c) | Order and receive rock | 3 | 15 | 37 | 22 |
| (d) | Order and receive pipe and fittings | 18 | 30 | 36 | 6 |
| (e) | Rock ditch | 8 | 45 | 45 | 0 |
| (f) | Assemble valves and fittings | 9 | 39 | 45 | 6 |
| (g) | Lay pipe | 17 | 62 | 62 | 0 |
| (h) | Install fittings | 13 | 58 | 69 | 11 |
| (i) | Cover ditch | 7 | 69 | 69 | 0 |
| | Earliest day estimated to be completed | 12 | | | |
| | Start or end of activity | ○ | | | |
| | Latest day can be completed | 12 | | | |
| | Critical path | (Slack = 0, solid line in chart) | | | |

and the sum for the times for all the activities between those circles determines how long the whole process will take. The times are usually the best estimates of knowledgeable people.

## Installing an Information System to Direct the Activities

Orders received and plans made must be communicated to those doing the work. The information is provided by written or oral instructions, by training workers, and/or by having a fixed flow of material. Each worker must know what and how many items are to be produced, when and where to produce them, and how to perform the job satisfactorily. You should design a simple, yet adequate, system for this in the firm.

The route sheet shown in Figure 7–8 is used in a garment plant and travels with a bundle of cut cloth. This form tells the workers what to sew, the type of operation, the time for the operation, and what the next operation is. The size of the bundle sets the quantity. As each operator completes an operation, the proper tab is clipped to be returned to the office. In a garage, the mechanic receives a

**Figure 7–8**
**Route Sheet Used in Garment Plant**

| | SKIRT | SCH. NO.<br>LOT NO.<br>AMT. | 7732<br>24 | SKIRT | |
|---|---|---|---|---|---|
| | .NR-24-7732<br>Thread bkle. on<br>tab. tack to fnt.<br>* * * * | | | .060-24-7732<br>Reverse | 1:00 |
| 11:00 | .448-24-7732<br>Hem waist and<br>btm. BS | | | .132-24-7732<br>Serge btm. | 3:00 |
| 3:00 | .128-24-7732<br>SS 2d side<br>seam * * * | | | .196-24-7732<br>Serge elastic<br>to waist | 5:00 |
| 4:00 | .164-24-7732<br>SS one side<br>seam T&L | | | 1.134-24-7732<br>Topst. fnt. pleats<br>bste. across top<br>* * | 27:00 |

work order which lists only the operations to perform on an automobile. The simplicity or complexity of the system depends on the needs.

## Controlling Production: Quantity and Quality

Even if the best plans are made, the information is communicated, and the best work is performed, controls are still needed. If adequate control is not exercised over the operations, the process will fail. The principle of exception should be followed. Variations from plans—exceptions—must be reported and checked for corrective action.

Controlling by exceptions involves comparing your plans with the firm's performance. In simple systems, this comparison can be made informally by personally observing the performance. Usually, though, a system of formal checks is needed.

### Quantity Control

Orders may be filed by due dates; work to be completed in each department may be recorded each day; or bar charts or graphs may be used. The record of performance for quantity control is obtained through feedback or by having forms returned with information on work performed. For example, press operators clock their time in and out on the edge of a job envelope carrying instructions; workers in a garment plant clip off pieces of the route sheet and return them pasted on their time tickets; garage mechanics enter their time on the order form.

You need not make changes when performance equals or exceeds your plans. An exception arises when performance does not reach the level desired. Then you decide what to do to improve future performance.

## Quality Control

One example of an important control system is that used for quality control. The methods used in quality control have been developed further than those for other control systems and are used in many other systems, including cost control. The system begins with setting the level of quality desired. The quality level is based on:

1. The value of quality to the customer.
2. The cost of the quality.

Customers want high quality but are often willing to pay only a limited price for a product. Production costs rise rapidly as the demand for quality rises beyond a certain point. Therefore, you should ask the following questions:

1. Who are my customers, and what quality do they want?
2. What quality of product or service can I obtain, and at what costs?

Then you need to establish controls to obtain that quality. Do not try to exceed that level, for your costs will increase and customers may not pay the higher price required. But do not allow quality to fall below that level, for you will lose customers. Design your process so that it will produce products or services within the desired quality range. Then design your quality control system to check performance.

## Control Steps

The steps needed in any system of control are as follows:

1. Set standards for the desired quality range.
2. Measure actual performance.
3. Compare performance with standards.
4. Make corrections when needed.

Standards of quality may be set for dimension, color, strength, content, weight, service, and other characteristics. Some standards may be measured by instruments such as rulers or gauges for length; but color, taste, and other standards must be evaluated by skilled individuals. Measurement may be made by selected people at certain places in the process—usually upon the receipt of material and always before it goes to the customer. You can spot-check (sample), or you can check each item.

Inspection reduces the chances that a poor-quality product will be passed through your process and to your customer. But not all defective work is eliminated by inspection. By recording the number of defective units per 100 units, you can observe the quality performance of the process or person and make needed corrections. The final check might be to keep a record of the number of complaints received per 100 sales made.

## Summary

Planning and controlling a company's internal operations involve the following:

1. Analyzing individual steps of the process to eliminate inefficiencies.
2. Setting time and quality standards.
3. Planning the work and informing the workers.
4. Checking performance.

Some of the techniques for implementing these activities have been presented in this chapter.

# Chapter Eight

## Purchasing and Controlling Materials

It is not unusual to find that the profitability of an independent business depends upon the ability of the owner-manager to exercise effective purchasing and materials control. The absence of know-how in these areas many times is revealed only during the postmortem of the failed business.

Our intent in this chapter is to emphasize the importance of these areas. Another objective is to provide information that leads you to adopt sound procedural practices. The specific topics covered are:

1. Materials (or goods) planning and control.
2. Inventory.
3. Quantities per order.
4. Ordering procedure.
5. Sources of supply.
6. Receiving materials.

### Materials (or Goods) Planning and Control

In the previous chapters, we discussed the flow of materials in a business and the use of inventory to take care of seasonal variations in demand. Now we need to consider the decisions regarding materials planning and control, including:

1. Amount of material needed for the output desired.
2. Amount of inventory and its storage and recording.

3. Quantity and time of order.
4. Vendor relations.
5. Quality of materials and price per unit.
6. Methods of receiving and shipping.
7. Handling of defective materials and stock-outs.

Policies and procedures should be established so that most of these decisions become routine in nature. When exceptions occur, they should be handled by you or someone to whom you delegate the decision. These policies and procedures should minimize the total cost of materials to the company. But remember that total cost includes more than just the price of the materials themselves. It includes costs that are charged to the goods, as well as other costs that are hidden in other expenses—usually in overhead. Overhead consists of expenses that cannot be charged directly to the product or service.

## Materials and Goods Investment

Materials are a form of investment; until they are sold and produce revenue, the money they cost cannot be used for other income-producing purposes. Consequently you want to buy in small quantities and sell rapidly in order to obtain income. But if the quantities you have on hand are to small, you may miss income-producing opportunities and may lose customers. Also, purchasing in small quantities usually results in higher prices. Another problem concerns the controls established to keep losses from theft to a minimum. While increasing controls may reduce the cost from losses, it also increases the control cost. The idea is to find the optimum balance between the two costs.

In materials planning and control, you should recognize that most of your income comes from a small percentage of your products or services, and that some of your materials are of high value and some of lower value. About 80 percent of the average firm's income comes from 20 percent of its products. Materials planning and control should be directed mainly toward the 20 percent. You may want to classify the goods in categories and set a procedure for each category. Thus, for the 20 percent, you may set standards and procedures for each item; for the next, say, 30 percent, you may handle items in groups; and for the last 50 percent, you consider all items as a single group. The percentages given are only guides for consideration. You need to analyze your product line in light of the procedures discussed in the rest of this chapter.

## Value Analysis

Another important area is the study of products and services to determine whether all the particular inputs are needed. This is called value analysis and is based on relating the purpose of each part to its cost or value. It determines the best material or design for each part or input.

## Inventory

The inventory of materials, parts, goods, and supplies represents a high investment in all businesses. Many companies have failed because their inventories tied up too much money or because the items in inventory became obsolete, impaired, or lost. You should have an appropriate set of policies concerning the items to carry in inventory, the level of inventory, and control of the stock.

The purpose of an inventory is to disconnect one segment of a process from another, so that each segment can operate at its optimum level of performance. A process composed of several operations, with inventory between them, might be diagramed as in Figure 8–1. Note that the inventories are shown at different levels at different stages of the process. The level depends on the prior activities of the supplier to, and the user of, the inventory. For example, Operation 1 may have been running recently, and Operation 2 may have been shut down. Also notice that Operation 3 may not have enough material if Operation 2 does not start up soon.

**Figure 8–1**

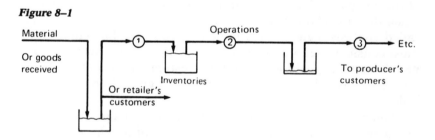

Retailers receive goods, store them, display them for sale, and sell the goods. The level of inventory depends on the amount of goods bought relative to that sold.

### Types of Inventories

Inventories exist in various places in the business and in different stages of production, such as:

1. Purchased materials, parts, and products or goods.
2. Goods in process or between operations.
3. Finished goods at the factory, warehouse, or store.
4. Repair parts for machines or for servicing customers.

5. Supplies for the office, shop, or factory and for packaging.
6. Patterns and tools.

Each of these types of inventory performs basically the same function and can be studied in the same way. Some of the inventories, however, represent a much greater investment, cause more serious trouble if the items are not in stock, and are more costly to restock than others. The amount of attention and time spent on these should be greater than on the others.

On the other hand, businesses are increasingly dependent on machines. New machines are more automatic and integrate larger numbers of operations than in the past. Maintaining inventories of all spare parts needed and not having a spare part when needed can both be costly.

> On Thursday, a belt broke in one of the saws of the Oaks Sawmill. A replacement belt was not in stock, nor did the supplier have one. John Oaks said, "This belt breaks about once a year. It costs only $10, but I cannot have parts in stock for every contingency. We'll be shut down until Monday."

### Determining Economic Inventory Levels

Even a small company may have thousands of items in stock. The total investment should be kept in a proper relation to the finances of the company. This relationship will be discussed in Chapter 12, when the financial analysis of the company is considered. The detailed analysis made to determine the economical inventory level must consider the total inventory so as not to jeopardize the company's financial position. The total investment in inventory should not be so great that it deprives you of enough cash to pay current bills.

Figure 8–2 shows how the number of units of a purchased item varies over a period of time. When a stock of purchased items is received, the inventory increases instantly. The units are removed from inventory as they are demanded. At certain intervals, or when

*Figure 8–2*
**Changing Level of Inventory of an Item**

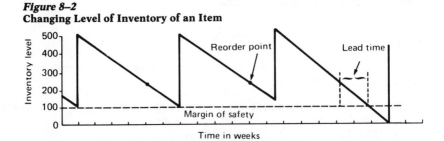

the inventory falls to a given level, a purchase order is sent to the vendor for a certain quantity. The order is received some time later. In the meantime, more units may be drawn from inventory. This cycle is repeated for each item purchased.

Figure 8–2 shows removal of units from inventory as a straight line. This is an approximation, particularly for firms serving the general public. Since demand by customers varies somewhat randomly, approximations must be used.

For items in process and for finished goods, the inventory builds up over a period of time as goods are produced, so the vertical line in Figure 8–2 would be sloping upward to the right. The inventory builds up because the production rate is greater than the demand rate. The following discussion pertains to purchased items; with minor adjustments, it would apply to in-process and finished goods also.

### Determining When to Order

The level of inventory at which an order should be issued is based on:

1. The quantity to be used between the time an order is issued and the time the items are received.
2. The quantity needed to provide a margin of safety.

The time to be allowed (1 above) is determined by the sum of the times for:

1. Order to be processed in your company.
2. Order to be transported to the vendor.
3. Vendor to make and/or package the items.
4. Items to be transported to your company.

The total interval varies from time to time, so a margin of safety is added to determine the quantity at the reorder point. The margin of safety, in turn, depends upon:

1. Variability of the time to obtain the items from the vendor. A higher variability requires a higher margin of safety.
2. Variability of usage.
3. Cost of not having inventory—losses from stock-outs.
4. Cost of carrying inventory, estimated for each item or group of items. These inventory costs include:
   a. Space charges.
   b. Insurance and taxes.
   c. Profits lost because money is tied up in inventory.
   d. Obsolescence of items.
   e. Deterioration.
   f. Theft.

Estimates of the costs of carrying inventory range from 15 percent to over 100 percent of the average inventory investment for a year. Recent high interest rates warrant the use of 30–35 percent values.

The optimum level of inventory at which to order goods can be determined or estimated. It is at that point where the sum of the costs of carrying inventory plus the costs of stocking out are the lowest. Too low a level causes excessive stock-out costs; too high a level causes excessive inventory-carrying costs.

## Quantities per Order

The quantity you include on each order affects the level of inventory and the time between orders. You may place your orders:

1. At certain intervals, such as once a week, month, or quarter, when you order an amount that brings the level of the inventory up to a predetermined standard amount.
2. When the inventory reaches a certain quantity, such as 250 units in Figure 8–2. The quantity ordered is a fixed amount called the economic order quantity (EOQ).
3. When a customer orders special items not in stock.

The quantity to order in items 1 and 2 can be computed or estimated in the same manner, but in 1 it is used only as an expected average. The economic order quantity is determined by balancing:

1. The cost of the order, which includes:
   a. The costs of processing and handling the order.
   b. The costs of the item, realizing that larger orders usually warrant price discounts.
   c. Transportation costs.
2. The inventory-carrying costs.

Figure 8–3 shows the way costs per unit vary as the quantity ordered is changed. The point of lowest cost is the EOQ. This can be found by using a formula[1] or by comparing the unit costs for different order quantities. Note how a discount affects the curve and that quantities in a range near the EOQ have approximately the same low cost.

## Ordering Procedure

Many items can be ordered on a routine basis. The procedure starts with the need as reflected by the reorder point and requires keeping:

1. A perpetual inventory, which records when the inventory has

---

[1]The formula can be found in a production management text.

**Figure 8–3**
**Changes in Purchase Unit Costs**

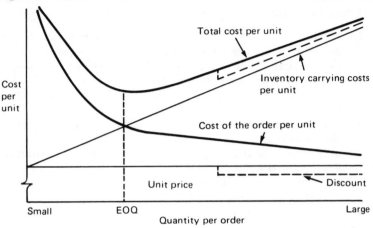

*Economic order quantity.

reached the reorder point. Figure 8–4 shows a perpetual inventory card.

2. Quantities set aside that will not be used without making out a purchase order.
3. A method of calling attention to the need for the order, such as a gauge for a tank of oil.

The amount to reorder is shown on the inventory card or some other form. The vendor and the method of packaging and transporting are also recorded.

## Items Requiring Special Analysis

The major items of purchase require more analysis because their cost and quality can have a greater effect on your company. You,

**Figure 8–4**
**Inventory Record Form**

| Date | Received | | Issued | | Balance |
| | Order no. | Units | Req. no. | Units | on hand |
|---|---|---|---|---|---|
| 7/13 | 3401 | 400 | | | 450 |
| 7/17 | | | 1075 | 10 | 440 |
| 7/22 | | | 1090 | 10 | 430 |
| | | | | | |
| | | | | | |
| | | | | | |

Reorder point: 70 bags      Reorder quantity: 400 bags
Item no.         Description      Unit
315          Zinc oxide (3Z33)     50# bags

or someone else in authority in your firm, should be involved in these purchases. A number of the considerations that require higher-level decisions are:

1. Expected changes in price. Buying later for expected decreases in price, or buying increased quantities for expected inflation in price, can result in savings. However, stock-outs or too heavy inventory costs should be guarded against.
2. Expected changes in demand. Seasonal products fall into this category.
3. Orders for a demand for specialty goods. The quantity ordered should match the amount demanded so that no material is left over. When the quantity of the demand is known, estimates of losses in process are added to the order. When the quantity of the demand is not known, you must depend on the forecasts plus the estimates of losses.
4. Short supply of materials.

Speculative buying should be avoided unless you are in that business. While all business decisions have a certain element of speculation, smaller firms cannot afford to gamble with money required in their businesses.

The procedure for processing a purchase order and receiving the goods is shown in the flowchart in Figure 8–5.

### Placing Responsibility for Ordering

One person should have the responsibility for ordering all materials, but that person should obtain the help of those people knowledgeable in the area where the goods are needed. By having a single person responsible, duplicate orders for the same material are avoided, the specialized skills needed for purchasing are used, and responsibility for improvements in the buying process is localized.

The number of forms needed for obtaining and controlling products and the number of copies of these forms depend on the amount of formality desired. A simple requisition form can be forwarded to the purchasing agent, who in turn reviews the requisitions, issues the purchase order to the vendor, follows up on orders when needed, checks the receipt of the material, takes corrective action when needed, and sees that the material is delivered to the proper place.

## Sources of Supply

Sources from which you obtain inputs are important because:

1. Price of purchased goods is a major cost in your outputs.

**Figure 8–5**
**Purchase Order Procedure**

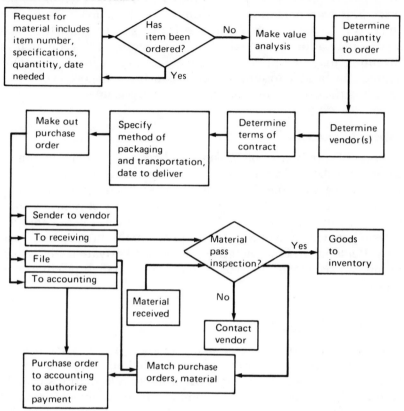

2. Reliability in delivery and quality affects your operations.
3. Vendors can be valuable sources of information.
4. Vendors can provide valuable service.

A smaller company needs to maintain a good image in its dealings with vendors in order to obtain good service.

### Considering Various Aspects of Price

The prices from different vendors are not the same. Higher prices may be charged for:

1. Higher quality.
2. More reliable and faster delivery.
3. Better terms for returning goods.
4. More services, such as in advertising, type of packaging, technical assistance, and information.
5. Better, or delayed, payment plan.

You may be able to purchase an item at a lower price, but the total cost of processing the item may be higher. For example, the price plus transportation cost from a distant source may be less than from a local source, but the faster service from the local source may allow for a reduction in inventory. The reduction in inventory may more than compensate for higher local price. One source may be able to supply a wide assortment of goods you need, reducing the expense of ordering from many sources.

### Types of Sources

Sources of supply may be brokers, jobbers, wholesalers, manufacturers, or others. Each of these sources provides a type of service that may be valuable. For example, the wholesaler stocks many items so as to give fast delivery of a wide variety of items. A manufacturer can ship directly, with no intermediate handler, or through sales representatives or agents who can help the independent business. Regional and national trade shows and private trade associations can keep firms up to date on sources and their products and services.

### Using Few or Many Sources

Should you buy from one or many sources? The argument for a single source is that a closer and more individual relationship can be established. When shortages occur, these relationships usually result in better service than if you have many sources. Discounts may be obtained with larger-volume buying from one source. On the other hand, multiple sources allow you to find the source with a greater variety of goods and, often, better terms. Some companies put out requests for bids, and negotiations result in better arrangements.

You should maintain an ethical relationship with suppliers. Many unethical practices involving gifts, entertainment, misrepresentation, and reciprocity exist and should be guarded against.

## Receiving Materials

The receipt and forwarding of materials to inventory constitute the last step in acquiring inputs. This step is performed to determine that the material is what has been ordered, is in the proper condition, and is the proper quality.

The purchasing agent and the accountant are informed that goods have been received and are ready for processing. A copy of the purchase order and other desired specifications are sent to those receiving the material. The material is checked for damage in transportation; for special characteristics such as color, size, and the item specified; and for the proper quantity and price. Proper receiving procedures can eliminate discrepancies.

Materials can be stored in the containers in which they are received, in separate containers, or by individual item. The receiving agent prepares the material for storing.

## Summary

In this chapter, we have discussed the importance of obtaining the proper materials in the right quantity, of the right quality, at the right time, and for the right price.

In an era of shortages, the success of firms will depend upon their skill—and luck—in finding and acquiring adequate supplies of goods, materials, and supplies. To succeed, you need to manage efficiently and effectively the planning and controlling of materials, inventories, ordering points, sources of supply, and merchandise receiving and storing.

## Where to Look for Further Information

Buffa, E. S. *Modern Production Management.* 5th ed. New York: John Wiley & Sons, 1977.

Dilworth, J. B. *Production and Operations Management.* New York: Random House, 1979.

Hedrick, F. D. *Purchasing Management in the Small Company.* New York: American Management Association, 1971.

"Improving Materials Handling in Small Business." 3d ed. *Small Business Management No. 4.* Washington, D.C.: Small Business Administration, 1969.

Kline, J. B. "Pointers on Scheduling Production." *Management Aids for Small Manufacturers No. 207.* Washington, D.C.: Small Business Administration, 1970.

Mayer, R. R. "The Equipment Replacement Decision." *Management Aids for Small Manufacturers No. 212.* Washington, D.C.: Small Business Administration, 1970.

Miles, L. *Techniques of Value Analysis and Engineering.* 2d ed. New York: McGraw-Hill, 1972.

Moore, F. G. *Production/Operations Management.* 8th ed. Homewood, Ill.: Richard D. Irwin, 1980.

# Exhibits

## *Exhibit 8–1*
## Scheduling Your Process

Proper scheduling of work into production aids in keeping costs down; keeping machines, people, and material busy; and assuring delivery of the product on time.

### General

1. Do you have a procedure for scheduling your products into production?    ☐ Yes ☐ No
2. Are you reasonably satisfied that your company:
   a. Is obtaining about the minimum machine idle time?    ☐ Yes ☐ No
   b. Is obtaining about the minimum human idle time?    ☐ Yes ☐ No
   c. Has the proper inventory?    ☐ Yes ☐ No
   d. Is obtaining the right output?    ☐ Yes ☐ No
   e. Is making deliveries properly?    ☐ Yes ☐ No
   f. Is not losing sales because of time to process orders?    ☐ Yes ☐ No
   g. Has a low scheduling cost?    ☐ Yes ☐ No
   h. Does not have too much overtime?    ☐ Yes ☐ No
3. If the answers to #1 and #2 are yes, you appear to be satisfied with your scheduling. However, you might want to check over the rest of the questionnaire for ideas on improving your scheduling.
4. If any answers in #1 and #2 are no, continue through the questionnaire.

### Scheduling production

5. Is one person responsible for scheduling production?    ☐ Yes ☐ No
6. If yes, is that person:
   a. Qualified by training, aptitude, and desire?    ☐ Yes ☐ No
   b. Properly instructed?    ☐ Yes ☐ No
   c. Given enough time?    ☐ Yes ☐ No
   d. Given proper authority?    ☐ Yes ☐ No
   e. In proper position in organization?    ☐ Yes ☐ No
   f. Informed?    ☐ Yes ☐ No
7. If no,
   a. How many people are involved?    _____
   b. Have you observed losses from conflicts, lack of coordination, etc.?    ☐ Yes ☐ No
   c. Will assignment of scheduling to one person improve the efficiency of the production process?    ☐ Yes ☐ No

### Plant layout

8. Might a change in plant layout help scheduling?    ☐ Yes ☐ No
9. Is your layout of machinery, people, and/or operations proper so that:
   a. Materials movement and bottlenecks are minimized?    ☐ Yes ☐ No
   b. Scheduling is automatic?    ☐ Yes ☐ No
   c. Standard products can flow through with little scheduling and inventory needed?    ☐ Yes ☐ No
10. Scheduling each operation on each order is time-consuming. Can a rearrangement of layout eliminate the need for scheduling some operations?    ☐ Yes ☐ No

### Machine capacity

11. Does the scheduler know the capacity of all machines?    ☐ Yes ☐ No
    Of personnel?    ☐ Yes ☐ No
12. Does the scheduler have standard times for each operation?    ☐ Yes ☐ No
    Can standards be set?    ☐ Yes ☐ No
    Can estimates be developed?    ☐ Yes ☐ No
    ("Standard" times are needed for scheduling.)
13. What is the company's average time from receipt of order to delivery?_____
    What do you estimate is the time needed to satisfy and/or gain customers? _____
    If you are not meeting your estimate,
    a. What portions of the process take the longest time? _____
    _____
    b. Do you believe an improved form of scheduling will reduce the time?    ☐ Yes ☐ No
    Enough to bring the time to a satisfactory lead time?    ☐ Yes ☐ No
    If yes, at a reasonable cost?    ☐ Yes ☐ No

### Scheduling procedure

14. Do you need to schedule each order into production?    ☐ Yes ☐ No
15. How is an order received?
    a. Telephone; written up on a production order (P.O.) form?    ☐
    b. Order form; written up on a P.O. form?    ☐
    c. Salesman's order form; can it be used as a P.O. form?    ☐
    d. Customer interview; written up on P.O. form?    ☐
    e. Other?_____
16. Can origin of order be used as a production order form?    ☐ Yes ☐ No
17. Is enough information included on the P.O. form for the scheduler to process the order?    ☐ Yes ☐ No
    If no, who adds the needed information? _____
    Could information be entered when order is received?    ☐ Yes ☐ No
18. Is delivery time set for most jobs?    ☐ Yes ☐ No
    Have you been meeting delivery dates satisfactorily?    ☐ Yes ☐ No

## Exhibit 8–1 (concluded)

19. After an order is received, is it quickly delivered to the scheduler? □ Yes □ No
    If no, can it be? □ Yes □ No

20. In what order are orders scheduled into production:
    a. First come, first served? □ Yes □ No
    b. Large jobs first and small ones as fillers? □ Yes □ No
    c. Depends on availability of machines? □ Yes □ No
    d. Rush jobs inserted, resulting in delays on other jobs? □ Yes □ No
       Do you have many rush jobs? □ Yes □ No
       If so, can they be eliminated? □ Yes □ No
    e. Other?_____
       _____
       _____

21. Is scheduling primarily:
    a. Loading first machines and order flows through the process, based on shop operating procedure? □ Yes □ No
    b. Loading the busiest (bottleneck) machine and loosely scheduling the rest? □ Yes □ No
    c. Sending the order to each operation as the previous operation is completed and it waits in line for its turn? □ Yes □ No
    d. Scheduling each operation on each machine before sending to the shop? □ Yes □ No
    e. Other?_____

22. Does the scheduler use charts, graphs, etc., which can be helpful in scheduling and in showing the status of orders? □ Yes □ No

23. Do you record the time of an order on each machine? □ Yes □ No

24. Do you collect information to determine whether:
    a. Machines and workers are idle too much of the time? □ Yes □ No
    b. The process is inefficient (actual times exceed the standards)? □ Yes □ No
    c. Quality output of an operation is too low? □ Yes □ No
    d. The order is on schedule? □ Yes □ No
       If the answers to any of the above are no, how do you maintain control of your process? _____
       _____

25. Does your present scheduling procedure result in:
    a. Crowded conditions in the shop due to in-process inventory? □ Yes □ No
       If so, should you decrease the time allowed between operations? □ Yes □ No
    b. High inventories of purchased goods? □ Yes □ No
    c. High finished goods inventory? □ Yes □ No
    d. Delays in process waiting on product from previous operation? □ Yes □ No
       If so, should you increase the time between operations? □ Yes □ No
    e. Many delays caused by breakdown in machines, slow or absent operators, etc.? □ Yes □ No
    f. Rush jobs excessively delaying other jobs or causing idle time? □ Yes □ No
    g. Excessive overtime? □ Yes □ No
    h. Too much time expended correcting for unpredictable events? □ Yes □ No
    i. High-priced machines and labor being idle? □ Yes □ No

*Exhibit 8–2*
## Quality Control

To obtain the desired performance of your company, you need a proper level of product/service quality. Too high a level of quality increases costs and eliminates profits; too low a level of quality decreases sales and eliminates profits. This questionnaire is designed to help you evaluate the level of quality to plan, the method of attaining quality, and the method of checking atainment of that level of quality.

**Quality of product/service**

1.  Do you believe you have a quality problem?
    ☐ Yes ☐ No

2.  How do you determine the level of quality output you should achieve:
    a.  Do your customers provide specifications?
        ☐ Yes ☐ No
    b.  From customer complaints?    ☐ Yes ☐ No
    c.  From industry or government standards?
        ☐ Yes ☐ No
    d.  Do you set your standards based on:
        (1) Your ideas of quality?    ☐ Yes ☐ No
        (2) Your ideas of what the customer wants?
            ☐ Yes ☐ No

3.  Do the customers who buy most of your output want:
    a.  High quality and are willing to pay the prices?
        ☐ Yes ☐ No
    b.  Medium quality and will pay that price?
        ☐ Yes ☐ No
    c.  Lower quality and are price-conscious?
        ☐ Yes ☐ No

4.  Do your customers place most emphasis on:
    ☐ Quality?
    ☐ Cost?
    ☐ Other?

5.  Have you studied the change in cost which would result with a change in quality?    ☐ Yes ☐ No
    a.  Would you have much of a change in cost if you:
        (1) Increased quality?    ☐ Yes ☐ No
        (2) Decreased quality?    ☐ Yes ☐ No
    b.  Would you have much of a change in sales if you:
        (1) Increased quality?    ☐ Yes ☐ No
        (2) Decreased quality?    ☐ Yes ☐ No

6.  How does your quality compare with that of your main competitor? _____
    _____
    _____

    Your price? _____
    _____
    _____

7.  Do you have a formal system of feedback from your customers on the quality of your product/service?
    ☐ Yes ☐ No
    Or, do you just wait for customers' complaints?
    ☐ Yes ☐ No

8.  How many complaints on quality did you have this past year?_____
    How does this compare with earlier years? _____
    _____
    _____

9.  Do you have a policy for the handling of complaints?
    ☐ Yes ☐ No
    If so, what is it? _____
    _____
    _____

10. If you sell some defective output:
    a.  Can it cause an injury to a person?    ☐ Yes ☐ No
    b.  Can it cause a lawsuit?    ☐ Yes ☐ No
    c.  Can the government fine the company?
        ☐ Yes ☐ No

**Product quality**

11. Do you have full-time inspectors?    ☐ Yes ☐ No
    a.  If no, is inspection done by:
        (1) Workers on the job?    ☐ Yes ☐ No
        (2) You?    ☐ Yes ☐ No
    b.  If yes, to whom do the inspectors report? _____

12. Is inspection made:
    a.  Of 100 percent of the product?    ☐ Yes ☐ No
    b.  Using a sampling procedure?    ☐ Yes ☐ No
        _____% range _____ to _____.
        (1) Did you set up the sample plan?    ☐ Yes ☐ No
        (2) Did a consultant set up the sample plan?
            ☐ Yes ☐ No
    c.  By spot checks?    ☐ Yes ☐ No
        On a regular basis?    ☐ Yes ☐ No

13. Has the quality of inspection been checked?
    ☐ Yes ☐ No

14. Are workers trained and able to produce the level of quality desired?    ☐ Yes ☐ No

15. Do you check the quality of purchased items?
    ☐ Yes ☐ No
    a.  Do you have quality standards for purchased items?    ☐ Yes ☐ No
    b.  Are they:
        (1) Recorded?    ☐ Yes ☐ No
        (2) Available to the inspector?    ☐ Yes ☐ No
        (3) Available to the vendor?    ☐ Yes ☐ No

## Exhibit 8–2 *(concluded)*

c. Are the quality standards proper for the product produced? □ Yes □ No
Too high? □ Yes □ No
Too low? □ Yes □ No

d. What percentage do you return for quality reasons? _____%
Are many defects found while processing items? □ Yes □ No

e. Is the check of incoming quality made:
(1) By designated people? □ Yes □ No
(2) By using a designated procedure? □ Yes □ No
(3) By using inspection tools? □ Yes □ No
(4) Of about what percentage of the quantity of an item?
□ 100%?
□ 50%?
□ 10%?
□ 1%?

f. Do you estimate the cost of making a quality check of incoming items? □ Yes □ No

16. Are the proper quality machines being used? □ Yes □ No

17. Do you inspect in-process or finished items? □ Yes □ No

a. Are items inspected at specific points, such as:
(1) After or during setup? □ Yes □ No
(2) Before an expensive operation? □ Yes □ No
(3) Before covering quality inspected? □ Yes □ No
(4) After the operation which produces variable quality? □ Yes □ No
(5) After the last operation? □ Yes □ No
(6) After all operations? □ Yes □ No

b. Do you have recorded standards for inspections? □ Yes □ No

c. Do you have a worker rework poor output:
(1) On his time? □ Yes □ No
(2) On company time? □ Yes □ No

d. Estimate the cost of inspecting in-process items. $_____

e. Estimate the percentage of product below standard which is rejected by inspection? _____

f. What percentage of your output was returned last year for quality reasons? _____%
How does this compare with earlier years?_____

g. How much does it cost to service:
(1) Returned product? $_____
(2) A complaint? $_____

h. What percentage of company cost does it recover from:
(1) Items rejected by the inspector? _____
(2) Items returned from customers? _____

**Service quality**

18. Do you have quality standards for actions of service personnel? □ Yes □ No
Do these include:
□ Attitude toward the customer?
□ Helpfulness to the customer?
□ Appearance?
□ Language?
□ Aggressiveness?
□ Housekeeping?
□ Workmanship?
□ Use of material?
□ _____
□ _____

19. Do you believe that employees know what the quality standards are? □ Yes □ No
Have you had complaints about this? □ Yes □ No

20. How do you check the quality of performance?
a. By continuously observing employees? □ Yes □ No
b. By spot-checking when you can? □ Yes □ No
c. By having supervisors report good and poor performance? □ Yes □ No
d. By customer complaints? □ Yes □ No
e. By use of a sampling plan? □ Yes □ No
f. By spot-checking on a planned basis? □ Yes □ No

21. Estimate the cost of your service quality program. $_____
How much does it cost to service a complaint? $_____

22. How many customer complaints about quality of service have you had this past year? _____
How does this compare with earlier years? _____

**Quality standards**

23. What do you do when an employee does not meet quality standards:
a. For the first time? _____
_____
b. Several more times? _____
_____
c. Continuously? _____
_____

*Exhibit 8–3*
## Planning and Controlling Production

This questionnaire is concerned with strategy planning and controlling production—it is not concerned with the daily operations of your company. How can you make your company more efficient and effective through improved planning and control?

### Your planning activities

1. Have you set aside a set time for planning and thinking about your business?  ☐ Yes ☐ No
   a. Is it enough time?  ☐ Yes ☐ No
   b. Is it interrupted or usurped by pressing daily problems?  ☐ Yes ☐ No
2. Do you spend much time "fighting fires"?  ☐ Yes ☐ No
3. Do you tend to react to situations rather than anticipate situations?  ☐ Yes ☐ No
4. Do you commit yourself to action without a plan?  ☐ Yes ☐ No
5. Do you tend to exploit opportunities rather than create opportunities?  ☐ Yes ☐ No
6. Are employees and outside experts included in the planning process to add a variety of ideas?  ☐ Yes ☐ No

### Long-range production plan

Do you have a three-year production plan?  ☐ Yes ☐ No
If yes, check Worksheet 1 for ideas. If no, complete Worksheet 1, Long-Range Production Plans, using the best information you can obtain.

Review Worksheet 1, Long-Range Production Plans:
7. Will your production plans allow you to meet the goals you set for the company?  ☐ Yes ☐ No
   If no, can you revise your production plans?  ☐ Yes ☐ No
   If no, should you get out of the business?  ☐ Yes ☐ No
   (See Exhibit 71.)
8. Can you take steps to improve the forecast sales?  ☐ Yes ☐ No
9. Is your production capacity adequate for sales forecast?  ☐ Yes ☐ No
   Too large?  ☐ Yes ☐ No

10. Should you consider (in addition to your plans):
    a. Dropping a product/service?  ☐ Yes ☐ No
    b. Adding a product/service?  ☐ Yes ☐ No
    c. Adding or replacing equipment to:
       (1) Decrease the number of employees?  ☐ Yes ☐ No
       (2) Decrease overtime?  ☐ Yes ☐ No
       (3) Reduce costs or increase flexibility?  ☐ Yes ☐ No
    d. Making instead of buying some items?  ☐ Yes ☐ No
    e. Buying instead of making some items?  ☐ Yes ☐ No
    f. Performing more or less operations for customers?  ☐ Yes ☐ No
11. Should you:
    a. Expand space available by:
       (1) Moving to a new building?  ☐ Yes ☐ No
       (2) Adding to the present building?  ☐ Yes ☐ No
       (3) Buying additional space?  ☐ Yes ☐ No
       (4) Renting additional space?  ☐ Yes ☐ No
       (5) Rearranging the layout?  ☐ Yes ☐ No
       (6) Adding or using the second floor? ☐ Yes ☐ No
    b. Add space for employee, customer, or truck parking?  ☐ Yes ☐ No
    c. Reduce space available but not needed by:
       (1) Moving to another building?  ☐ Yes ☐ No
       (2) Reducing inventory?  ☐ Yes ☐ No
       (3) Finding a use for the space?  ☐ Yes ☐ No
    d. Use space more efficiently by:
       (1) Rearranging the layout?  ☐ Yes ☐ No
       (2) Reducing inventory?  ☐ Yes ☐ No
       (3) Changing the type of materials handling used?  ☐ Yes ☐ No
       (4) Changing the flow of product?  ☐ Yes ☐ No
12. Do you plan to hire the skills needed or train employees?  ☐ Yes ☐ No
    Do you have the proper level of training of employees to obtain the production desired?  ☐ Yes ☐ No
13. Do your proposed programs anticipate changes in:
    a. Government regulations?  ☐ Yes ☐ No
    b. Environment requirements?  ☐ Yes ☐ No
    c. Supply of resources?  ☐ Yes ☐ No
    d. Competitor activities, such as in costs and new products/services?  ☐ Yes ☐ No
    e. Technology?  ☐ Yes ☐ No
    f. Customer demands?  ☐ Yes ☐ No
14. Do you believe that you have the proper balance between standard and special-order products/services?  ☐ Yes ☐ No
    Should you increase either?  ☐ Yes ☐ No

*Exhibit 8–3 (continued)*
## Worksheet 1: Long-Range Plans for Production

Period: _____ to _____

| Items You Should Plan | Detail of Items (you pick units you understand— $, lbs., etc.) | | (1) One Year Ahead | (2) Two Years Ahead | (3) Three Years Ahead |
|---|---|---|---|---|---|
| | | From | | | |
| | | To | | | |
| | | Units | | | |
| 1. Sales forecast (list by products, divisions, departments or other) | Total | | | | |
| | | | | | |
| | | | | | |
| | | | | | |
| | | | | | |
| | | | | | |
| 2. Production capacity (list using same divisions as in #1) | Total | | | | |
| | | | | | |
| | | | | | |
| | | | | | |
| | | | | | |
| 3. Volume of production (list using same divisions as in #1) | Total | | | | |
| | | | | | |
| | | | | | |
| | | | | | |
| | | | | | |
| 4. List new products/ services—show volume | | | | | |
| | | | | | |
| | | | | | |
| 5. New or replacement equipment investment | | | | | |
| | | | | | |
| 6. Added space investment | | | | | |
| | | | | | |
| 7. Change in number of employees (list same as in #1) | | | | | |
| | | | | | |
| | | | | | |
| | | | | | |
| | Total production | | | | |

## *Exhibit 8–3 (continued)*

### Worksheet 1 *(concluded)*

**Short-range planning**

Using the first year of Long-Range Production Plans (Worksheet 1), plan your production for each of the quarters and, then, by months for the first quarter (Worksheet 2, Short-Range Production Plans). Use #15 to help determine the production plan.

15. Are you satisfied with last year's production plan?
    □ Yes □ No

16. Do you have seasonal demand?    □ Yes □ No
    If yes,
    a. When production varies up and down with sales, do you need to hire and lay off, pay overtime, and have idle time and other like costs?   □ Yes □ No
    If yes,
    b. Do you produce to customer special order?
       □ Yes □ No
    If yes, you probably cannot inventory these orders to level out seasonal peaks. Do you make any products which can be inventoried?
       □ Yes □ No
    Can parts of products be inventoried?
       □ Yes □ No

17. Which of the following plans might best reduce total costs, satisfy other conditions, and have a good chance of succeeding (you may find that completion of Worksheet 3 will help in ranking)?
    a. Produce at the same level as sales during a time period (month?)       Rank:_____
    b. Produce at a constant level and inventory during low sales period for future high periods.
       Rank:_____
    c. Subcontract or purchase during peak sales periods.       Rank:_____
    d. Add other products/services during slack sales periods.       Rank:_____
    e. Increase marketing effort or give discounts during the slack season to level production.
       Rank:_____
    f. Not sell peak demand sales.    Rank:_____
    To make comparisons in Worksheet 3, certain factors must be developed. (Note: inventory carrying costs for business normally range from 25 percent to 40 percent of average investment.)

18. If you can use a combination of the plans above or some other plan, make a similar analysis of it. For example:
    a. Would it be less expensive to inventory parts before assembly than to inventory finished product?       □ Yes □ No
    b. Can you make parts during slack periods and purchase them during high demand? □ Yes □ No
    c. Does another local company have a countercycle so that employees can work there during your slack period?       □ Yes □ No

19. List other factors you should consider in the above analysis.
    a. _____
    b. _____
    c. _____
    d. _____
    e. _____
    f. _____

**Analysis of Worksheet 2**

20. Are you satisfied with your production plan?
    □ Yes □ No
    If no, go back through the analysis.

21. Have your past forecasts predicted your actual sales reasonably well?       □ Yes □ No
    Have you considered past deviations in your production planning?       □ Yes □ No

22. Have you included items in your short-range plans which pave the way for accomplishing your long-range plans?       □ Yes □ No

23. Will you inform your staff of your plans? □ Yes □ No
    Have you included their ideas in your planning?
       □ Yes □ No

24. Have you made your financial plans to accomplish your production plan?       □ Yes □ No

25. Do you plan to compare your actual performance with your plans?       □ Yes □ No
    Update your plans each month?       □ Yes □ No
    Quarter?       □ Yes □ No
    Year?       □ Yes □ No

**Control**

Plans are most effective when used for control.

26. Do you compare your plans with your actual performance?       □ Yes □ No

27. At the end of the planning month, complete Worksheet 4.

**Evaluation of Worksheet 3**

28. How well did you conform to your plans? _____
    _____

29. Do you need to make changes in your methods of operating?       □ Yes □ No
    If so, list the major changes you should make.
    a. _____
    b. _____
    c. _____
    d. _____

30. Do you need to change your plans for the coming months?       □ Yes □ No
    Year?       □ Yes □ No
    If so, you can revise Worksheets 1 and 2.

*Exhibit 8–3 (continued)*
## Worksheet 2:   Short-Range Production Plans

Period: _____ to _____

| | Items You Should Plan | Detail of Items (you pick units you understand) | Months Ahead | | | Quarters Ahead | | | | |
|---|---|---|---|---|---|---|---|---|---|---|
| | | | 1 | 2 | 3 | 1 | 2 | 3 | 4 | Total |
| | 1. Working days | | | | | | | | | |
| | 2. Present planned number of production workers by department, division, etc. | | | | | | | | | |
| Production plan #1 | 3. Number of man-hours available by department, division, etc. | | | | | | | | | |
| | 4. Forecast of sales by product, department, division, etc. | | | | | | | | | |
| | 5. Number of man-hours needed to produce #4 by same categories as in #3 | | | | | | | | | |
| | 6. Overtime or idle man-hours | | | | | | | | | |

*Exhibit 8–3 (continued)*

**Worksheet 2 *(concluded)***

| | Items You Should Plan | Detail of items (you pick units you understand) | Months Ahead | | | Quarters Ahead | | | | |
|---|---|---|---|---|---|---|---|---|---|---|
| | | | 1 | 2 | 3 | 1 | 2 | 3 | 4 | Total |
| Selected production plan | 7. Production plan output by product, department, division, etc. | | | | | | | | | |
| | | | | | | | | | | |
| | | | | | | | | | | |
| | | | | | | | | | | |
| | | | | | | | | | | |
| | 8. Number of production workers by same categories as in #7 | | | | | | | | | |
| | | | | | | | | | | |
| | | | | | | | | | | |
| | | | | | | | | | | |
| | | | | | | | | | | |
| | 9. Expected loss of employees (gain) | | | | | | | | | |
| | | | | | | | | | | |
| | 10. Number of workers to hire (lay off) | | | | | | | | | |
| | 11. Hours or cost of overtime | | | | | | | | | |
| | 12. Inventory level change (finished goods) | | | | | | | | | |
| | 13. Equipment changes needed | | | | | | | | | |
| | 14. Purchase schedule ($) | | | | | | | | | |
| | 15. Purchase items inventory | | | | | | | | | |
| | 16. Cost of sub-contracted work | | | | | | | | | |
| | 17. Cost of added promotion | | | | | | | | | |
| | 18. Sales discounts planned ($) | | | | | | | | | |

*Exhibit 8–3 (continued)*
### Worksheet 3:  Comparison of Production Plans for Seasonal Sales

| Plan and Factors (estimate as best you can added costs and relative rating)* | Rating (good, satisfactory, etc.) | $ Next Year | Rank |
|---|---|---|---|
| 1. Produce at rate of sales<br> a. Added cost of overtime and idle time | | | |
| b. Added cost of hiring and layoff | | | |
| c. Employee morale | | | |
| d. Customer service | | | |
| e. Chances of success | | | |
| 2. Inventory to maintain constant production<br> a. Cost of carrying added inventory† | | | |
| b. Savings in reduced work force | | | |
| c. Savings in reduced equipment, etc. | | | |
| d. Employee morale | | | |
| e. Customer service | | | |
| f. Chances of success | | | |
| 3. Subcontract during peak period<br> a. Added cost of product/service | | | |
| b. Savings in reduced work force | | | |
| c. Savings in reduced equipment, etc. | | | |
| d. Employee morale | | | |
| e. Customer service (include quality) | | | |
| f. Chances of success | | | |
| 4. Add other products/services<br> a. Cost of added facilities | | | |
| b. Cost of added workers | | | |
| c. Added net profit from product/service | | | |
| d. Employee morale | | | |
| e. Customer service | | | |
| f. Chances of success | | | |
| 5. Constant level of production and sales<br> a. Cost of added sales promotion | | | |
| b. Loss in profit from discounts | | | |
| c. Savings in reduced work force | | | |
| d. Savings in reduced equipment, etc. | | | |
| e. Employee morale | | | |
| f. Customer service | | | |
| g. Chances of success | | | |
| 6. Not sell peak demand sales<br> a. Lost profit from decreased sales | | | |
| b. Savings in reduced work force | | | |
| c. Savings in reduced equipment, etc. | | | |
| d. Employee morale | | | |
| e. Customer service | | | |
| f. Chances of success | | | |
| g. Status from smaller size | | | |

* Make a comparison with the present production plan.

† Be sure to inventory the lowest cost item based on the $/man-hour and its inventory carrying cost.

*Exhibit 8–3 (concluded)*

## Worksheet 4:   Comparison of Short-Range Production Plans and Actual

Month_____ or Quarter_____

| No. on Work-sheet 2 | Items Which You Planned | Detail of Items | Planned (Worksheet 2) | Actual | Difference | Action Needed |
|---|---|---|---|---|---|---|
| 7 | Production output by product, depart-ment, division, etc. | | | | | |
| | | | | | | |
| | | | | | | |
| | | | | | | |
| | | | | | | |
| | | | | | | |
| 8 | Number of production workers by same category as in #7 | | | | | |
| | | | | | | |
| | | | | | | |
| | | | | | | |
| | | | | | | |
| | | | | | | |
| 9 | Loss or gain or employees | | | | | |
| 10 | Number of workers hired (laid off) | | | | | |
| 11 | Hours or cost of overtime | | | | | |
| 12 | Inventory level change (finished goods) | | | | | |
| 13 | Equipment changes made | | | | | |
| 14 | Purchases ($) | | | | | |
| 15 | Purchase items inventoried | | | | | |
| 16 | Cost of subcon-tracted work | | | | | |
| 17 | Cost of added promotion | | | | | |
| 18 | Sales discounts ($) | | | | | |

## *Exhibit 8–4*
## Evaluating Your Materials Planning and Control

Materials must be obtained, stored, processed, and delivered to the customer. These activities should be planned and controlled to provide good service at low cost. This checklist provides guides for efficient performance of these activities.

**Materials**

Amount of materials needed for output desired:

1. Do you start with your finished product to determine subassemblies, parts, and materials needed? ☐ Yes ☐ No

2. Do you have standards for losses due to scrap, waste, etc., at each stage of production so as to determine subassemblies, parts, and materials needed as inputs? ☐ Yes ☐ No

3. Do you check the quantities at critical points during processing to ensure the proper quantity of output? ☐ Yes ☐ No

4. Are you often short of materials when an order is being completed? ☐ Yes ☐ No

**Inventory**

Amount of inventory and its storage and records:

5. Who sets the company's planned inventory levels?
_____

6. Are reorder points used? ☐ Yes ☐ No
   If so, are they based on:
   a. Lead times to get items? ☐ Yes ☐ No
   b. A probability of having a certain number of stock-outs? ☐ Yes ☐ No
   c. An estimated cost of stocking out? ☐ Yes ☐ No
   d. A cost of carrying items in inventory? ☐ Yes ☐ No

7. What do you estimate the cost of carrying $1 of inventory for one year to be?
   ☐ $0.10
   ☐ $0.20
   ☐ $0.30
   ☐ $0.40
   ☐ Over $0.40

8. Do you determine economic order quantities (EOQ) for purchases? ☐ Yes ☐ No
   Of major items? ☐ Yes ☐ No
   If no, how do you determine the quantity to purchase on each order of major items? _____
   _____
   _____

9. Do you use inventory to level production when sales are seasonal? ☐ Yes ☐ No
   If so, do you inventory the least costly (carrying cost) items for the amount of production inventoried? ☐ Yes ☐ No

10. What is your inventory turnover per year?_____
    What is your industry's turnover? _____
    Are you better than your industry? ☐ Yes ☐ No

11. What is your stock-out experience for:
    a. Raw materials? ☐ Good ☐ Fair ☐ Poor
    b. Finished goods? ☐ Good ☐ Fair ☐ Poor

12. Can you reduce lead times for getting materials? ☐ Yes ☐ No
    How?_____
    _____
    _____

    Would a change be economical? ☐ Yes ☐ No

13. Is the lead time reliable so that you can reduce your inventory level? ☐ Yes ☐ No

14. Who determines when an item should be reordered?
    _____
    Is the procedure for most items routine? ☐ Yes ☐ No

15. Are reorder points shown on stock record? ☐ Yes ☐ No

16. Are stored incoming and outgoing items separated from items being processed? ☐ Yes ☐ No

17. Are designated places allotted for items which are stored? ☐ Yes ☐ No
    Are they easily identified? ☐ Yes ☐ No

18. Is layout of storeroom such that:
    a. High-use items are near the using point? ☐ Yes ☐ No
    b. Handling is minimized? ☐ Yes ☐ No
    c. Pilferage is kept to a minimum? ☐ Yes ☐ No
    d. Deterioration is minimized? ☐ Yes ☐ No

19. Are items issued only when a properly signed order is received? ☐ Yes ☐ No

20. Are perpetual inventory records kept? ☐ Yes ☐ No

21. Do you use a computer to:
    a. Make up use orders? ☐ Yes ☐ No
    b. Keep inventory records? ☐ Yes ☐ No
    c. Indicate when and how much to order? ☐ Yes ☐ No
    d. Cost materials to orders? ☐ Yes ☐ No
    e. Provide management with vital information on inventories? ☐ Yes ☐ No

22. Do you receive a report on slow-moving, obsolete, and overstocked items? ☐ Yes ☐ No
    What actions have you taken on these items? _____
    _____
    _____

## *Exhibit 8–4 (concluded)*

23. How often do you take a physical inventory?
    - ☐ Monthly
    - ☐ Quarterly
    - ☐ Semiannually
    - ☐ Annually
    - ☐ Other _____
    Have you found large discrepancies?　☐ Yes ☐ No
    If yes, why? _____

    _____

24. Do you use the proper type of materials handling equipment for your storeroom?　☐ Yes ☐ No

25. Do you have proper insurance coverage of inventory?　☐ Yes ☐ No

**Work-in-process**

26. Do you have some incoming materials delivered directly to the first operation?　☐ Yes ☐ No

27. Do you have inventory on the floor which hinders production and materials handling?　☐ Yes ☐ No

28. Are your operations reasonably balanced to keep work-in-process down?　☐ Yes ☐ No

29. Do you have materials in process and in the production area for so long a time that it might be better to move them aside or to storage?　☐ Yes ☐ No

30. Do you have much scrap on the production floor?　☐ Yes ☐ No
    Do you remove this on a regular basis?　☐ Yes ☐ No

31. Are materials properly identified?　☐ Yes ☐ No
    Have you lost some?　☐ Yes ☐ No

32. Do you use materials handling equipment, such as conveyors, for storing work-in-process?　☐ Yes ☐ No

**Service**

Service to your customer through finished goods inventory.

33. Are your lead times competitive?　☐ Yes ☐ No

34. Do your customers know your lead times?　☐ Yes ☐ No

35. Do you inform your customers what your delivery date will be for an order?　☐ Yes ☐ No

36. Do you keep your delivery date promises?　☐ Yes ☐ No
    Percent of the time?　_____%

37. Do you carry finished goods for fast delivery?　☐ Yes ☐ No

38. Do you stock-out of items, causing customer dissatisfaction?　☐ Yes ☐ No
    How often?　_____times per year.

39. Estimate the cost of a stock-out of an item of finished goods.　$_____

40. Do you believe that your customers are satisfied with your delivery time?　☐ Yes ☐ No

## *Exhibit 8–5*
## Auditing Your Inventory

Often, inventory represents a major asset of the company. It is composed of many items which are subject to change in value, deterioration, loss, and theft. This checklist guides you in checking your policies, procedures, valuation, and count.

### Significance of inventories

1. Inventory is approximately what percentage of assets? _____%
   Is the percentage in line with your industry average? ☐ Yes ☐ No

2. What is the average turnover rate of inventory per year? _____
   Is it in line with your industry average? ☐ Yes ☐ No

3. Does inventory:
   a. Use a large amount of space? ☐ Yes ☐ No
   b. Hinder production? ☐ Yes ☐ No
   c. Incur significant handling costs? ☐ Yes ☐ No
   d. Significantly limit your available capital for other purposes? ☐ Yes ☐ No
   e. _____

4. In the past, have you had items "disappear" from inventory? ☐ Yes ☐ No
   If yes, has the loss been significant? ☐ Yes ☐ No

5. Do you feel that the dollar value in your accounting records is a fair value of your actual inventory? ☐ Yes ☐ No
   If no, too high? ☐ Yes ☐ No
   Too low? ☐ Yes ☐ No

6. What is your average cost to carry your inventory per year? $_____
   Is this too large a cost? ☐ Yes ☐ No

### Policies and procedures

7. Do you have a policy regarding:
   a. The valuation of inventory? ☐ Yes ☐ No
   b. The safeguarding of inventory? ☐ Yes ☐ No
   c. Stock-outs of items of inventory? ☐ Yes ☐ No
   d. The quantities to reorder for inventory? ☐ Yes ☐ No
   e. The use of inventory to reduce fluctuations of production? ☐ Yes ☐ No
   f. Obsolete and slow-moving items in inventory? ☐ Yes ☐ No

8. Do you keep a perpetual inventory for:
   a. All items of materials, supplies, etc.? ☐ Yes ☐ No
   b. Major items of inventory? ☐ Yes ☐ No
   c. Finished goods? ☐ Yes ☐ No
   d. Work-in-process? ☐ Yes ☐ No

9. Should perpetual inventory records be:
   a. Eliminated for some items not needing them? ☐ Yes ☐ No
   b. Installed for some items for better control? ☐ Yes ☐ No

10. Are inventory items for which no perpetual inventory record is kept properly controlled? ☐ Yes ☐ No

11. Are some purchased items delivered directly to the place where used (not inventoried)? ☐ Yes ☐ No
    If yes, do they represent a significant expense? ☐ Yes ☐ No
    If yes, is their use properly controlled? ☐ Yes ☐ No

12. Are inventory items:
    a. Properly identified? ☐ Yes ☐ No
    b. Easily identified? ☐ Yes ☐ No
    c. Stored for ease in locating? ☐ Yes ☐ No
    d. Stored to minimize handling costs? ☐ Yes ☐ No

13. Are items issued only on presentation of a properly authorized requisition? ☐ Yes ☐ No

14. Is the amount issued properly controlled? ☐ Yes ☐ No

15. Is the storeroom too crowded? ☐ Yes ☐ No
    If yes, does this cause confusion in performing the total inventory function? ☐ Yes ☐ No

16. Does each location for a specific item have a record:
    a. Identifying the item? ☐ Yes ☐ No
    b. Showing the number in stock? ☐ Yes ☐ No
    c. Showing removal of items? ☐ Yes ☐ No
    d. Showing the reorder point? ☐ Yes ☐ No

17. Do you separate the safety or reorder point stock to call attention to the need to reorder? ☐ Yes ☐ No

18. Do you regularly compare the number of an item in stock with its forecast usage? ☐ Yes ☐ No

19. Do you believe you have much inventory which will not be used within a reasonable time? ☐ Yes ☐ No

20. What action has been taken in the past on obsolete and slow-moving items?_____

### Organization of inventory function

21. Is one person given the authority and responsibility for inventory planning and control? ☐ Yes ☐ No

22. Are there job descriptions for people involved in the inventory function? ☐ Yes ☐ No

23. Are stores people reliable? ☐ Yes ☐ No

24. If more than one person is needed to perform the inventory function, is the work divided to allow specialization? ☐ Yes ☐ No

25. Are workers in inventory management properly trained? ☐ Yes ☐ No

## Exhibit 8–5 *(concluded)*

26. Have inventory personnel reported slow-moving items, obsolete items, and overstock?  ☐ Yes ☐ No

27. Do they or others forecast changes in inventory levels?  ☐ Yes ☐ No

**Physical count**

28. Is a physical count of items taken regularly?  ☐ Yes ☐ No

How often? _____
Is this often enough?  ☐ Yes ☐ No
Too often?  ☐ Yes ☐ No

29. Have your physical counts been reasonably close to your records?  ☐ Yes ☐ No
If no, state why. _____
_____
_____

Would it be economically feasible to take steps to improve the situation?  ☐ Yes ☐ No

30. Who makes adjustments to records when physical counts are different than records?_____

31. Is physical count made by:
a. Inventory personnel?  ☐ Yes ☐ No
b. Other personnel?  ☐ Yes ☐ No

32. Are written instructions on counting procedure used?  ☐ Yes ☐ No

**Valuation of inventory**

33. Is an item issued from inventory costed out on:
a. A first-in-first-out (fifo) basis?  ☐ Yes ☐ No
b. A last-in-first-out (lifo) basis?  ☐ Yes ☐ No
c. An average price basis?  ☐ Yes ☐ No
d. Another basis? _____

34. Does the book value of inventory fairly represent the company's inventory?  ☐ Yes ☐ No

## Exhibit 8–6
## Purchasing

Purchased items represent a major cost in most companies. This questionnaire is designed to help you review your policies, procedures, and practices with the goal of assuring availability of proper amounts of material, reducing costs, and maintaining proper quality.

**Items to purchase**

1. List purchase items or classes of items which account for 60 to 80 percent of the dollar value of your purchases:

| Item or Class of Items | Purchase Value/Mo. | Number of Suppliers | How Often Ordered? | Special or Standard Items |
|---|---|---|---|---|
| | $ | | | |
| | | | | |
| | | | | |
| | | | | |
| | | | | |
| | | | | |
| | | | | |

2. Have you evaluated your purchase items to determine whether:
   a. All of the items are needed? □ Yes □ No
   b. Less variety can be purchased? □ Yes □ No
   c. Standard instead of special items can be purchased and used at lower cost? □ Yes □ No
   d. The number of suppliers should be increased or decreased? □ Yes □ No
   e. Your sources should be changed to improve costs, delivery, quality, etc.? □ Yes □ No
   f. You are ordering proper quantities at proper time? □ Yes □ No
   g. You should make instead of buy items? □ Yes □ No

3. Does the purchaser work with others in the organization to evaluate possible substitute items? □ Yes □ No
   To evaluate changes in purchased items caused by changes in products made? □ Yes □ No

**Purchasing function**

4. Who has authority to issue a purchase order? _____
_____

5. Who authorizes the issuance of the purchase order?
_____

6. Can orders be issued without authorization? □ Yes □ No
   If yes, what is the dollar limit? $_____

7. From what sources do requests for purchases originate?
   □ Stock clerks
   □ Foreman
   □ Worker
   □ Other (position) _____

8. Does purchaser maintain an up-to-date file of catalogs, price lists, etc.? □ Yes □ No
   Does he/she listen to salesmen and review catalogs, etc., for possible new purchase items? □ Yes □ No
   List several recent changes.
   _____
   _____
   _____

9. Do you have a set of policies for:
   a. The purchasing function? □ Yes □ No
   b. How much to order? □ Yes □ No
      When? □ Yes □ No
   c. Selecting a vendor to whom to issue an order? □ Yes □ No
      If no, how is a vendor selected? _____
      _____
   d. Selecting the method of delivery of purchased items? □ Yes □ No
      If yes, what is the method? _____
      _____
   e. Acceptance of gifts? □ Yes □ No

10. Do you have control procedures for the purchasing function, such as making different people responsible for different steps of a purchase transaction? □ Yes □ No

11. Are purchase procedures standardized? □ Yes □ No

12. Does purchaser coordinate with those who are in charge of inventory, storage, and production planning with regard to reorder points, quantities to order, inventory controls, etc.? □ Yes □ No

## *Exhibit 8–6 (concluded)*

13. Is information made available by purchasing of total dollars of purchases with details for management's evaluation in decision making?    ☐ Yes ☐ No

14. Does purchaser have any voice in selection of material, supplies, specifications, etc.?    ☐ Yes ☐ No

15. Is there an approved vendor list for major items?
☐ Yes ☐ No
Is it adequate to prevent work stoppages?
☐ Yes ☐ No

16. Do you issue requests for bids for materials?
☐ Yes ☐ No
If so, is this advantageous?    ☐ Yes ☐ No

17. Does purchaser keep in contact with professional organizations?    ☐ Yes ☐ No

**Purchasing procedure**

18. Do purchase transactions originate from requisitions?    ☐ Yes ☐ No
If no, what is the originating source? _____

19. Are standard purchase order forms used?
☐ Yes ☐ No
Are they prenumbered?    ☐ Yes ☐ No

20. Do the purchase order forms provide space for:
a. Information needed?    ☐ Yes ☐ No
b. Only information needed?    ☐ Yes ☐ No
c. Proper authorizations?    ☐ Yes ☐ No

21. Is price included on the purchase order? ☐ Yes ☐ No

22. Are specifications clear so that desired items are received?    ☐ Yes ☐ No

23. Are shipping instructions included?    ☐ Yes ☐ No

24. Are duplicate copies made for:
☐ Accounting?
☐ Filing?
☐ Receiving?
☐ Other? _____

25. Do you batch small orders routinely done?
☐ Yes ☐ No

26. Are orders divided among a number of vendors?
☐ Yes ☐ No
Is this advantageous?    ☐ Yes ☐ No

27. Do you have one delivery point for ease in checking deliveries?    ☐ Yes ☐ No

28. Do you have items delivered to the first operation on them?    ☐ Yes ☐ No
If yes, how is this recorded? _____
_____

29. Do you have an inspection of incoming items?
☐ Yes ☐ No

30. Is the purchase order used to check items received?
☐ Yes ☐ No
Is the purchase order designed for ease in checking?
☐ Yes ☐ No
Is a separate receiving form used?    ☐ Yes ☐ No
Prenumbered?    ☐ Yes ☐ No

31. Does checker need to record count of items received?    ☐ Yes ☐ No
a. Is a copy sent to accounting?    ☐ Yes ☐ No
b. To purchasing?    ☐ Yes ☐ No

32. Is there a standard procedure for returns?
☐ Yes ☐ No

33. Do you contract for items and allow subordinates to order when items are needed?    ☐ Yes ☐ No
If yes, how do you control materials ordered?
_____
_____

**Purchasing evaluation**

34. Is postage metered?    ☐ Yes ☐ No

35. Are "economic order quantities" ordered?
☐ Yes ☐ No

36. Are requisitions generated when "reorder" points are reached?    ☐ Yes ☐ No

37. Are items ordered so that they will arrive at the time when they are needed?    ☐ Yes ☐ No
Are lead times known?    ☐ Yes ☐ No

38. Are many orders marked "rush"?    ☐ Yes ☐ No

39. Is much expediting needed?    ☐ Yes ☐ No

40. Are available quantity discounts taken? ☐ Yes ☐ No

41. Are available cash discounts taken?    ☐ Yes ☐ No
Do you know how many are missed?    ☐ Yes ☐ No

42. Does accounting check invoices against purchase orders (and receiving reports)?    ☐ Yes ☐ No

43. Are competitive prices compared?    ☐ Yes ☐ No

44. Who pays the shipping charge? _____

45. Has an analysis been made of various methods of shipping?    ☐ Yes ☐ No

46. Have major vendors been reviewed as potential customers?    ☐ Yes ☐ No

47. Has the purchaser been evaluated as to performance?    ☐ Yes ☐ No

48. How much does it cost to process an order?
$_____ / order

49. How much time does it take to process order-request to mailing? _____

50. Do you speculate by buying large quantities of items when the price is low?    ☐ Yes ☐ No
If yes, how many months supply do you limit this to?
_____ months
What is the risk to you in terms of dollars lost?
$_____
Is this reasonably safe?    ☐ Yes ☐ No

# Part 3
# Marketing the Product or Service

This book is concerned with strategic and operating plans, including objectives, policies, procedures and methods, and actions compatible with these plans that will provide successful results from effective asset management.

Also, staffing, production, marketing, and financing are essential business functions. Each of them should be performed economically and effectively in order for your independent firm to be successful and achieve effective asset management. The chapters in this part should help you perform the marketing function better.

Marketing involves the distribution of your firm's product or service to your customers in order to satisfy their needs and to accomplish your firm's objectives. It is an essential function because, unless your firm has a market or can develop a market for its product or service, the other business functions (staffing, production, and financing) are futile. The marketing function and the philosophy that underlies its performance are presented in Figure 1.

**Figure 1**
**Schematic of Marketing Function**

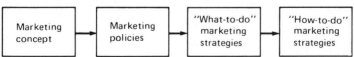

Chapter 9 covers the marketing concept, marketing policies, and ways of developing the "what to do" marketing strategies you plan to use. This chapter is followed by two chapters dealing with the "how to do it" marketing operations. Chapter 10 covers market research, including sales forecasts and pricing and promoting the product or service. In Chapter 11, channels of distribution, use of intermediaries and sales personnel to obtain sales, and personal selling are discussed.

# Chapter Nine

# Developing Marketing Strategies

An area that frequently seems to be neglected by the independent business owner is the marketing activity. Yet, what occurs in the marketplace determines the success or failure of the firm. In this chapter, we have attempted to present in a step-by-step fashion what you must do to succeed in marketing. Attention is focused on the marketing concept, strategic marketing policies, and "what to do" strategies.

The aspects of the marketing concept covered are: determining what customers' needs are and how they can be satisfied, specifying the market to be served (called market segmentation), and deciding the advantage(s) that your company has (called competitive edge). The areas of strategic marketing policies described are: morality and public service, products, markets, profits, personal selling, customer relations, promotion, credit policies, and credit cards.

The chapter concludes with a discussion of the following what-to-do marketing strategies: expanding sales into new markets, increasing penetration into present markets, and making no marketing innovation but rather emphasizing product design and manufacturing innovations.

## The Marketing Concept

The marketing concept is based upon the importance of the customers to a firm. In order to use this approach in a firm, you: (1)

determine what your customers' needs are and how those needs can be satisfied, (2) select the market to serve, and (3) decide what advantage you have that will give you a competitive edge over other firms.

## Learning Customers' Needs

You should learn what customers' likes and dislikes are. The best way to make money is to find out what people want and sell it to them. You should possess an ability to "read" customers—that is, to determine their wants and how they can best be fulfilled. In other words, you should know what "turns them on."

> The owner of a ladies' ready-to-wear store in a rural community had a good business going. She discovered that many of the store's customers lived in a city 50 miles away. Some wondered why people shopped at her store when they could have patronized a store in their own city.
>   *Answer:* She knew her customers by name, understood their needs, and bought with them in mind as individuals. "This dress should please Mrs. Adams." She then called each customer to inform her of the special purchases.[1]

Salespeople should recognize that several people may be involved in a sale. Each person may play only one or a few of the following roles in the purchase decision process. Included are the:

1. User—the person who consumes the product or service.
2. Buyer—the person who actually makes the purchase.
3. Decider—the person who decides what to purchase.
4. Influencer—the person who influences the purchaser.
5. Informer—the person who controls the flow of information.

In a household, different roles in the selection of various products and services are played by the wife, the husband, and the children. Roles are not always easily identified. Likewise, when you sell to a business, identifying who plays what role is difficult.

> A commercial photographer complained about the difficulty in locating, in companies, the persons who needed and decided on his services.

> A company had captured about 80 percent of the local market for trophies. The reason appeared to be the owner's ability to maintain contact with personnel in athletic programs and to anticipate their requirements. He had been a professional baseball player of considerable standing.

---

[1]Irving Schwartz, "Personal Qualities Needed to Manage a Store," *Small Marketers Aids No. 145* (Washington, D.C.: Small Business Administration, 1970).

Salespeople should identify the roles and then the specific needs of customers.

## Meeting Customers' Needs

The underlying principle of the marketing concept as it applies to your business is that the firm should seek to meet the needs of customers—at a profit. Customers' needs are the firm's primary focus, and your resources should be organized to satisfy those needs. The marketing concept should guide the attitudes of all employees in your firm. Employees should be encouraged to stimulate and satisfy the wants and needs of customers. But you should sell customers only as much as they need and can afford. An "oversold" customer will not be a repeat.

Encourage salespeople to build personal followings among customers. One retail salesperson wrote 20 letters each day to build a following. Each letter described new stock that would appeal to the personal preference of the customer.

You should have a policy whereby sales personnel give the benefit of the doubt to customers who return merchandise.

> When the new owner of a men's clothing store checked the records, he found that the last purchase made by one of his close friends had occurred more than six years before. He asked the friend why. The latter replied that the previous owner had refused to make an adjustment on a tuxedo that did not fit.
>
> This policy probably lost the store about $2,000 at retail because the customer would probably have bought about 15 suits plus accessories during that period of time. The new owner assured the friend that he would make future adjustments when needed. He regained a customer.[2]

You should do little favors for customers; they like your thoughtfulness more than any gift, although people dislike receiving big favors that they cannot repay. Make them feel that you are interested in them. Give them the kind of service that they will remember and discuss with others. Customers want a business to be helpful.

In the following examples, the marketing concept was not followed by the salespeople involved.[3]

> The customer asked for a certain kind of fishing rod in a sporting equipment store. The salesman replied, "Sorry, we don't carry that brand," and did not offer to show the store's own brand to the cus-

---

[2]Ibid.

[3]Kenneth Grubb, "Are Your Salespeople Missing Opportunities?" *Small Marketers Aids No. 95* (Washington, D.C.: Small Business Administration, 1970).

tomer. The store's brand had features which the competing brand did not have, and it cost no more. But the customer never knew it unless he heard about it elsewhere.

In an appliance store, the salesman's facial expression said, "Make up your mind," as he waited for a customer to decide which washing machine she liked best. His "message" reached her; she did not buy a washer. He said, "I know she must have thought I had all day to wait on her." He did not know that she planned to buy a dryer also.

**Be Conscious of Your Image.** Rate your business periodically in order to determine what kind of image it has. You can do this by trying to think about the firm as customers view it. Looking at the firm from their standpoint, ask yourself:

1. Is my firm doing all that it can to be customer oriented?
2. Can customers find what they want when they want it and where they want it, at a competitive price?
3. Do my employees and I make sure that customers leave with their needs satisfied and with a feeling toward our company that will bring them back again?
4. Are we servicing customers whose needs match our product or service?
5. Are we conveying the relation of our product or service to customers' requirements?

**Be Aware of Consumerism.** In recent years, the consumer movement has been prodding and forcing business to improve the quality of and knowledge about its products and services. In particular, the movement's major concerns are the rights of consumers to safe products, to be informed, to be able to choose, and to be heard. The movement is forcing business to be responsible for assuring that the public gets a square deal.

Consumerism recognizes that the many customers are small economic units, act independently, and are amateurs. They are at a disadvantage. The movement provides a concerted force—in the form of publicity, regulations, and lawsuits—to correct poor performance of business. Without this movement, business finds the social responsibility goals hard to measure compared to the economic ones. Thus, economic goals tend to dominate.

Business can improve the situation by establishing positive programs, such as obtaining more information from consumers, training employees to inform the public better, placing increased emphasis on safety in design of products, and maintaining greater flexibility to meet needs of customers. Specific examples of actions to take are: being truthful in advertising, making clear statements of terms of warranties and sale, and performing proper tests on products.

***Look for Danger Signals.*** If you are interested in the marketing concept, you will look for these danger signals:

1. Many customers walk out of your store without buying.
2. Many of them no longer visit the store.
3. Customers are not urged to buy additional items or "trade up" to more expensive items.
4. Traffic (pedestrian and vehicle) in front of your store has fallen off.
5. Customers are returning more merchandise than they should.
6. Company's sales are down this month compared to the same month last year, and sales for the year to date are down from the same period last year.
7. Employees are slow in greeting customers.
8. Employees appear indifferent and make customers wait unnecessarily.
9. Employees' personal appearance is not neat.
10. Salespeople lack knowledge of the store's merchandise.
11. The number of mistakes made by your employees is increasing.
12. Because of high prices, you have the reputation of being greedy.
13. The better employees leave for jobs with competitors.

All of these signals are evidence that a store is not following the marketing concept.

## Market Segmentation

Your firm should specify what market it is attempting to serve. Market segmentation is the grouping of customers according to similarity of needs, characteristics, or requirements. A product or service that fulfills the needs and wants of a specifically defined group of people is preferable to that which is a compromise to suit widely divergent tastes. A marketing segment should be defined in terms of various characteristics such as economic status, age, education, occupation, and location. Your best opportunity is to identify a segment that is not well served by other firms.

In determining your segment of the market, there are some fundamental questions you should consider, such as:

1. What is my place in industry, and how can I find my competitive niche?
2. Am I known for my quality or for my price?
3. If I sell industrial products, do I sell to more than one customer?
4. What image do the customers and the public have of my firm?
5. I serve only a limited number of customers. Why?

A common error found in many retailing firms is "straddling the market," or attempting to sell both high-quality and low-quality goods. (Even Sears Roebuck & Co. had difficulty when it tried to change its quality level several years ago.) As a result, the retailer is carrying a limited inventory of everything but does not have a good selection of anything.

In summary, you should clearly perceive the share of the market—or the percentage of total market—that your firm can actually obtain. This perception is possible only when you have clearly defined your market in specific terms.

## Competitive Edge

In order for a firm to be successful, it should seek a competitive edge. All firms need some reason for being: something that is desirable from the customers' viewpoint, that sets them apart from and gives them an advantage over their competition. You should know who your competitors are and how they operate. You should be stressing quality, reliability, integrity, and service rather than lower prices.

The competitive edge should be realistic. To determine whether it is realistic in your firm, you should answer these questions:

1. Is the competitive edge based on fact?
2. Do I know specifically what products/services customers are seeking?
3. Do I have an edge that is sufficiently important to entice customers away from their present sources of supply?
4. Have I used market research to make this determination?
5. Is the competitive edge compatible with the firm's capabilities and constraints?
6. Does the firm have the necessary resources—for example, personnel—to accomplish its goals?
7. Is the competitive edge based on conditions that are likely to change rapidly? That is, am I conscious of, and oriented toward, the future?

One independent retailer determined that her store's competitive edge consisted of these characteristics: friendly service, including greeting regular customers by name; personal attention; prompt assistance; familiarity with products; special ordering; and flexibility of credit terms.

An independent manufacturer determined that his firm's competitive edge consisted of: research on how its customers used its products, promotion to dealers and customers, and packaging the products to assist dealers in selling them.

Management should focus on earning profits instead of on increasing the volume of sales. You should increase sales only after considering added costs, adequacy of capital, position of competition, and so forth. Expenses incurred in achieving the increased volume may exceed the revenues achieved and result in losses. You can literally "sell yourself into bankruptcy." Sales increases should not far exceed the company's well-rounded growth in vital areas such as working capital and productive capacity.

## Marketing Policies

Managers should formulate marketing policies for certain areas, including:

1. Morality and public service.
2. Products.
3. Markets.
4. Profits.
5. Personal selling.
6. Customer relations.
7. Promotion.
8. Credit policies.
9. Use of credit cards.
10. Installment plans.

### Morality and Public Service

Policies on morality and public service consist of general statements expressing management's desire to be honest in its dealing with the public and its customers. To illustrate, the importance of policies prohibiting collusion with competitors became evident when executives of some turbine-generator suppliers were found guilty of market and price collusion in the 1950s.

### Products

A product line is defined as a group of products that have similar physical characteristics and uses. For example, the general product lines of a camera shop are photographic equipment, supplies, and services; the specific lines are cameras, film, projectors, lenses, darkroom supplies, and film developing and printing services. Product mix refers to all the products and services offered by a firm.

The number of product lines offered by an independent firm is called breadth. If, say, a bookstore carried only books, it's breadth is narrow. On the other hand, if the bookstore carried books, maps, calendars, records, magazines, stationery, and cards, its breadth is wide. Depth within the product line pertains to the assortment of models offered. For example, the product line of books can be classified into reference books, fiction, mysteries, children's books, etc.[4]

Considering the terms, *product line, product mix, breadth* of product lines, and *depth* within the product line, it is evident that policies are essential for these areas in independent firms. Policies on products will determine the direction in which the firm may grow in the future, and they may keep your firm from "running off in all directions." If you are an independent manufacturer, you should generally restrict your lines to custom, special-purpose, low-volume products rather than high-volume, assembly-line products where big companies have the advantages. If you have an independent department store, you may deal in either low-quality, low-price goods or high-quality, high-price goods. If you are a retailer, you may specialize in either soft goods or durable goods.

The independent firm often finds its most effective competitive weapon in the field of product strategy. It may concentrate upon a narrow product line, develop a highly specialized product or service, or provide a product-service "package" containing an unusual amount of service. Competitors' products, prices, and services should be studied to determine whether your company can do better in some way.

## Markets

Market policies are designed to clarify what geographic areas you wish to serve and other market characteristics appropriate for your firm. Perhaps you desire to remain simply a local business. You may decide to market only consumer, industrial, or defense goods. You may decide to sell only at retail, at wholesale, or to manufacturers.

## Profits

Profit policies may require that a sufficiently large sales volume goal be specified to obtain a certain dollar profit. Or profit as a percentage of sales may be specified, which calls for low marketing costs.

---

[4]CRC Education and Human Development, Inc., *Something Ventured, Something Gained,* vol. 2 (Washington, D.C.: U.S. Government Printing Office, 1979), II–T–52.

## Personal Selling

Personal selling policies may range from those guiding the structure of the sales department to those covering the sales representatives' behavior. For example, there could be a policy stating that only one representative of the company may call upon an account. You may not permit hard selling. Other sales policies may relate to sales representatives' qualifications and compensation and to constraints on the sales manager's authority. (See Chapter 10.)

## Customer Relations

The company's relationship with customers may be illustrated with this question: Should there be a policy that "the customer is always right"? Should the owner of the men's clothing store cited earlier limit the size and type of adjustments the store will make?

## Promotion

The pattern of a firm's advertisements may reveal the company's promotion policies. You should follow a policy of tasteful advertising at all times. You may restrict promotion to trade shows, industrial publications, or some other advertising medium. (See Chapter 10.)

## Credit Policies

Your policy on credit for customers may be to use one of the following plans:

1. Sell for cash only.
2. Sell for cash but honor checks.
3. Sell for cash and extend credit.
4. Sell for cash and accept credit cards.
5. Sell for cash and use installment plans.

A "cash only" policy is the least expensive plan. Cash flow tends to be high, records are minimized, and there are no bad debts. But sales are not stimulated by this plan. People do not like to carry large sums of money, and many like to buy ahead of payment.

The acceptance of checks for payment adds a stimulus for people to buy. It has a low recording cost and low bad-debt losses. But you must install a proper procedure to be followed for honoring any check.

In order to stimulate sales, you can provide credit for the customers. One method of doing this is to extend your own credit.

This plan allows you to select your customers, includes customers without other means of obtaining credit, and eliminates fees to finance companies. To minimize bad debts, however, you must investigate the customers' ability to pay and their credit ratings.

Even more important, retailers lose far more from slow accounts than from bad debts. Costs related to slow accounts are the most important item in the total cost of doing credit business. Some adverse effects of slow-paying charge accounts are:

1. Increased bad-debt losses.
2. Increased bookkeeping and collection expenses.
3. Increased interest expense due to greater capital requirements.
4. Reduction of capital turnover and profit.
5. Loss of business because slow payers tend to transfer their patronage elsewhere.

The longer a charge account goes unpaid, the more difficult it is to collect (see Chapter 15).

Typical problems that face owners of retail and service firms when they get involved in the overextension or unwise extension of credit are presented below:

Martin's Restaurant, a new business, was located in an area where many families and individuals were receiving public assistance, and its owner-manager gave credit freely. Within the first few weeks of operation, the firm had accounts receivable of $250, more than one fourth of its total capital.

Recognizing his predicament too late, the owner declared: "I have been unable to make enough money to pay my bills. I cannot pay my bills if my customers do not pay me. If some money is not received from them soon, I will have to close the restaurant."

The restaurant closed less than one year after it was established.

Mr. Neely and his wife had invested almost $6,000 of their savings in a venture. They paid $4,000 cash for equipment and allocated the balance for working capital needs.

Sales increased during each of the 13 months they had been in business, and all bills had been paid. Much capital, however, was tied up in accounts receivable that could not be collected. The trouble was that Mr. Neely was soft-hearted. He stated: "I do not want to extend credit to anyone, but the problem is to tell that to my customers so their business will not be lost." The owners stopped giving credit altogether, but the firm's gross profits dropped by almost one half. Mr. Neely was so discouraged that he sold the firm for only $2,500.[5]

[5]*Records and Credit in Profitable Management, Administrative Management Course* (Washington, D.C.: Small Business Administration), pp. 27–28.

The following steps are recommended to reduce losses from bad debts and slow payments:

1. Before giving credit, carefully check applicant's potential to be a good credit risk.
2. Set definite charge limits for each customer.
3. Set specific repayment requirements.
4. Keep accurate, complete records.
5. Send statements at regular intervals.
6. Watch and follow up past-due accounts.
7. Take legal steps when necessary.

### Use of Credit Cards

In order to stimulate sales, retailers should seriously consider the use of credit cards. Their objectives are to attain more rapid completion of credit sales, reduce customer waiting time and inconvenience, and eliminate certain record-keeping costs.

Credit cards (such as Visa, Mastercard, and American Express) have become important in generating sales. Merchants report sales, sales returns and allowances, and other credits; banks charge and credit deposit accounts. Retailers pay a joining fee, a fee on sales made, and other fees.

Some other advantages are (1) no bad-debt losses, (2) no collection problems, and (3) no personnel, equipment, or space requirements for servicing accounts receivable.

### Installment Plans

The use of installment plans can also benefit you—particularly for high-cost items. These plans usually include a down payment, regular weekly or monthly payments, and interest charges on the balance. These plans can be handled by you or by a finance company. The advantages and disadvantages of using installment plans are the same as for credit plans, but may represent larger amounts of money. These plans should be examined relative to a company's marketing plans. Are they consistent with your marketing strategies?

## Approaches to Marketing Strategy—What to Do

Marketing strategy relates to how to meet the needs of the market better than your competitors. There are really two problems involved: determining the available strategies and choosing the one to be used by your firm.

---

**158** *Chapter 9*

## Determining Available Marketing Strategies

In determining the available marketing strategies, you should take this approach:[6]

1. Analyze present and future market situations.
2. Shape product to fit the market.
3. Evaluate the company's resources.
4. Keep informed about competitors.

***Analyzing Present and Future Market Situations.*** You should determine the opportunities that lie in present and future market situations, as well as problems and adverse trends in the environment that will affect your company.

Market size and growth are vital. Growth rate potential should be forecast as accurately as possible. For example, a new business should have a market growing at the rate of at least 15–20 percent per year. Factors that affect this growth, such as actions of the federal government, should be evaluated. Your market segments should then be determined.

Relevant questions covered earlier are: Who are my customers? What are their needs? You should understand your customers' buying process. Concerning consumer products, for example, this process consists of need, awareness, trial, and repurchase. You should determine which stage(s) of the process you will address and how to address it.

***Shaping Product to Fit Market.*** You should be concerned with shaping your products to fit the markets and with finding markets that fit your products. You may decide on a market niche that is too small to interest large companies.

An independent company manufactured and sold truck springs.
*Problem:* Competition with larger companies was severe.
*Solution:* The company started manufacturing and selling springs for swimming pool diving boards.

Another market is for products that offer unique features that differentiate them from competitors' products.

A calculator manufacturer produced and sold calculators that met the needs of scientists more effectively than competitors' simpler models.

***Evaluating Company Resources.*** Your strengths, as well as limitations, should be determined in an overall fashion and at each

---

[6]Donald M. Dible, *Winning the Money Game* (Santa Clara, Calif.: Entrepreneur Press, 1975), pp. 114–15.

stage of the selling process. You should be realistic about financial, cost, competitive, and timing pressures. Your successes and failures should be understood. Why were you successful? Failures should be viewed as important learning experiences. You should understand your strategy. What do you want to accomplish? What are your market-share objectives?

*Understanding Competitors.* You should understand competitors as well as you understand yourself, and keep informed about their activities. What are their strengths, limitations, pressures, costs, profitability, market strategies, and corporate strategies?

## Determining Corporate Marketing Strategy

Next you should identify the strategy to use. Are you pioneering? Do you desire to be a leader in market share? Are you a follower? Such strategy should be written and used by all managers in sales, advertising, production, and finance.

In order to obtain a competitive edge, your company must innovate in product design, marketing, or manufacturing. You may find it necessary to adopt developments made by others in two of these areas while you innovate in the third. You should determine which of these three what-to-do marketing strategies to follow:

1. Expand sales to reach new classes of customers.
2. Increase penetration in existing market segments.
3. Make no marketing innovations, but copy new marketing techniques and attempt to hold the present market share by product design and manufacturing innovations.

*Expanding Sales into New Markets.* To reach markets, you may consider these possibilities:

1. Add related products, models, or services within your product or service line.
2. Add products or services unrelated to the present line.
3. Find new applications in new markets for your products or services.
4. Add customized products, perhaps upgrading from low-quality to medium-quality goods.

In introducing new and improved products, recognize their relationship to the existing product line, established channels of distribution, cost of development and introduction, personnel and facilities, competition, and market acceptance.

The new and improved products should be consistent with the existing product line. Otherwise, costly changes in manufacturing methods, channels of distribution, advertising, and personal selling may be necessary.

Significant capital layouts may be involved for design and development, personnel and facilities, market research, advertising and sales promotion, patents, and equipment and tooling. Profits may not be realized for one to three years on the sale of the new product, and financing should be adequate to cover this period.

Competition should not be too severe. A rule of thumb is that new products can be introduced successfully only if a 5 percent share of the total market can be obtained. An independent firm may compete effectively with (1) a nonstandard product, either a higher-priced product or an economy model, (2) fast deliveries or short production runs of special items, or (3) high quality that makes the product superior to products offered by competitors.

The following example pertains to the acquisition of a product or product line to certain specifications.

> The management of a precision metal stamping and machine shop selling to the defense and aerospace industries wanted to acquire a product or product line that met the following specifications:
>
> *Market*—the product is one of use by industrial or commercial firms of a specific industry, but not by the government or general public except incidentally.
>
> *Product*—the product sought is one of which 60 percent of the total direct manufacturing cost consists of metal-stamping and/or machining processes.
>
> *Price range*—the price range is open, but preferably should be $300–400.
>
> *Volume*—the volume is open but preferably should produce $200,000 in sales in the first year with potential sales of $1–2 million annually.
>
> *Finance*—capital of $50,000 in addition to present plant capacity is available for manufacturing a new product.
>
> *Type of acquisition*—royalties are preferred to a patent, although purchase of a patent, joint venture, merger, or purchase of a company outright will also be considered.[7]

You should carefully consider diversification or product line expansion. Advantages may be:

1. Increased profits.
2. Contribution to long-range growth.
3. Stabilization of product, employment, and payrolls.
4. Filling out a product line.
5. Lowering of administrative overhead cost per unit.

---

[7]John B. Lang, "Finding a new Product for Your Company," *Management Aids for Small Manufacturers No. 216* (Washington, D.C.: Small Business Administration, 1972).

Availability of necessary facilities and skills is a relevant factor. Diversification costs may exceed increased sales.

*Increasing Penetration of Present Market.* Perhaps you have been selling replacement parts primarily, but are attempting to expand by selling to original-equipment manufacturers. Or you may reduce the variety of products and models in order to produce substantial operating economies.

*Make No Marketing Innovations.* The strategy of retaining current marketing practices without trying to innovate is particularly suitable for your firm if its strength lies in its technical competence. In retailing, it is often advisable for store managers to follow this strategy.

Over the long range, your firm may follow one strategy for several years with the intent to change after certain marketing goals have been achieved.

## Summary

In this chapter, an attempt has been made to guide you through considerations essential to the development of marketing concepts. The chapter has indicated the kinds of information you should obtain for the development of your marketing concepts.

We have discussed, also, the analytical steps necessary to the collection of foundation information. Then, in the remainder of the chapter, an effort will be made to alert you to the many facets you need to consider in the formulation of your marketing strategies.

# Exhibits

*Exhibit 9–1*
**Studying the Market for Your Business**

1. Have you determined the relationship of population to your proposed business: ☐ Yes ☐ No
   a. Age, and age distribution? ☐ Yes ☐ No
   b. Sex, race, education, occupation, and other characteristics? ☐ Yes ☐ No
   c. Employment patterns? ☐ Yes ☐ No
   d. Size of population and trends in population characteristics? ☐ Yes ☐ No
2. Have you determined the size and distribution of income within the population: ☐ Yes ☐ No
   a. Personal income? ☐ Yes ☐ No
   b. Business sales and income? ☐ Yes ☐ No
3. Have you determined whether the sales volume for this kind of business is:
   a. Growing? ☐ Yes ☐ No
   b. Stable? ☐ Yes ☐ No
   c. Declining? ☐ Yes ☐ No
4. Have you determined the number and size of your competitors? ☐ Yes ☐ No
5. Have you determined the success rate of your competitors? ☐ Yes ☐ No
6. Have you determined what kind of technology is being applied by firms in your industry? ☐ Yes ☐ No
7. Have you determined the geographic boundaries of your company's market area? ☐ Yes ☐ No
8. Based upon your knowledge of potential customers, have you estimated the products that they might purchase? ☐ Yes ☐ No
9. Have you ascertained the number of similar businesses that have been liquidated or merged with a competitor? ☐ Yes ☐ No
10. Have you computed the volume of sales needed to give you a satisfactory return? ☐ Yes ☐ No
11. Have you determined a "ball park" figure for your company's total sales volume and share of the market? ☐ Yes ☐ No
12. In considering capital requirements and your expected profits after taxes, have you estimated the rate of return on investment and on sales? ☐ Yes ☐ No
13. Have you compared the rate of return for your business with that of alternative investment opportunities with a comparable degree of risk? ☐ Yes ☐ No

**Planning Your Approach to the Market**

The purpose of this part of the questionnaire is to aid you in considering important marketing factors prior to opening your business.

**Building an image**

14. Marketing concept:
    a. Do you plan to use the marketing concept in your company? ☐ Yes ☐ No
    b. How important will your customers be to your company?

    _____

    _____

    _____

    _____

    _____

**Exhibit 9–1 (continued)**

15. Do you intend to determine what your customers' needs are and how those needs can be satisfied? ☐ Yes ☐ No
16. Do you intend to have your employees adhere to the marketing concept? ☐ Yes ☐ No
17. Have you defined your market segment in terms of these characteristics:
  a. Economic status? ☐ Yes ☐ No
  b. Age? ☐ Yes ☐ No
  c. Education? ☐ Yes ☐ No
  d. Occupation? ☐ Yes ☐ No
  e. Location? ☐ Yes ☐ No
18. Have you decided what advantage will give your firm a competitive edge over other firms:
  a. Quality of product? ☐ Yes ☐ No
  b. Innovative product design? ☐ Yes ☐ No
  c. Service related to product? ☐ Yes ☐ No
  d. Price? ☐ Yes ☐ No
  e. Reliability, integrity? ☐ Yes ☐ No
19. Do you intend for your firm to have a customer-oriented image? ☐ Yes ☐ No

**Strategic marketing policies**
20. Do you intend to formulate these strategic marketing policies:
  a. Morality and public service? ☐ Yes ☐ No
  b. Products? ☐ Yes ☐ No
  c. Markets? ☐ Yes ☐ No
  d. Profits? ☐ Yes ☐ No
  e. Personal selling? ☐ Yes ☐ No
  f. Customer relations? ☐ Yes ☐ No
  g. Promotion? ☐ Yes ☐ No
  h. Credit plans? ☐ Yes ☐ No
  i. Use of credit cards? ☐ Yes ☐ No
21. Do you intend your firm to be honest in dealing with the public and your customers? ☐ Yes ☐ No
22. If you are a manufacturer, do you intend to restrict your products to custom, special-purpose, low-volume products? ☐ Yes ☐ No
23. Do you intend to:
  a. Remain only a local business? ☐ Yes ☐ No
  b. Market in your state or region, or nationally or internationally? ☐ Yes ☐ No
  c. Market only consumer or industrial or defense goods? ☐ Yes ☐ No
24. Have you specified sales goals which will provide your firm with:
  a. A sufficiently large sales volume? ☐ Yes ☐ No
  b. Your desired dollar profit? ☐ Yes ☐ No
25. Do you intend to have a policy stating that only one representative of your company may call upon an account? ☐ Yes ☐ No
26. Do you intend to have a policy that your customers are always right? ☐ Yes ☐ No
27. Do you intend to follow a policy of tasteful advertising? ☐ Yes ☐ No
28. Do you intend to:
  a. Provide credit for your customers? ☐ Yes ☐ No
  b. Use credit cards? ☐ Yes ☐ No

*Exhibit 9–1 (concluded)*

**Channels of distribution**

29.  Have you considered carefully the nature of your business
     and the economic characteristics of the industry in
     determining your channels of distribution?                    ☐ Yes    ☐ No
30.  Which channels do you intend to use:
     a.  Direct sales to customers?                                 ☐ Yes    ☐ No
     b.  Manufacturers' agents?                                     ☐ Yes    ☐ No
     c.  Independent retail outlets?                                ☐ Yes    ☐ No
     d.  Your own retail outlets?                                   ☐ Yes    ☐ No
     e.  Wholesalers?                                               ☐ Yes    ☐ No

**Pricing**

31.  Do you intend the focus of your business to be on
     service—not on price?                                         ☐ Yes    ☐ No
32.  In pricing your good or service, do you intend to consider
     all the cost factors and then add an additional percentage
     to provide you with your desired profit?                      ☐ Yes    ☐ No

**Exhibit 9–2**
**Marketing Function: Evaluation and Planning**

Determining whether you are using the market concept properly and the appropriate marketing strategy; and evaluating your market research, sales forecasting, and sales planning.

The purpose of this questionnaire is to enable you to determine whether your firm is adhering to the marketing concept and the appropriate marketing strategy, and is evaluating your market research, sales forecasting, and sales planning.

**Meeting customers' needs**

1. Have you and your employees learned your customers' likes and made your customers feel that you are interested in them? ☐ Yes ☐ No
2. Do you give your customers extra service? ☐ Yes ☐ No
3. Are you are expert on your products, and do you tell the truth about them to your customers? ☐ Yes ☐ No
4. Do you sell your customers only as much as they can afford? ☐ Yes ☐ No
5. Do you encourage your salespeople to build personal followings among their customers? ☐ Yes ☐ No
6. Have you informed your salespersons to give the benefit of the doubt to customers who return merchandise? ☐ Yes ☐ No
7. By putting yourself in your customers' shoes, do you rate your business at least quarterly and determine what kind of image your firm has? ☐ Yes ☐ No
   a. Is your firm customer-oriented? ☐ Yes ☐ No
   b. Can the customer find what he wants, when he wants it, at an appropriate price? ☐ Yes ☐ No
   c. Does your customer leave with his needs satisfied and with a feeling that he will return? ☐ Yes ☐ No
8. Do you and your employees perform little favors for your customers? ☐ Yes ☐ No
9. Do any of the following danger signals, which indicate that your store is not following the marketing concept, exist in your business:
   a. Many customers walk out of your store without buying? ☐ Yes ☐ No
   b. Many former customers no longer visit the store? ☐ Yes ☐ No
   c. Customers are not urged to buy additional or more expensive items? ☐ Yes ☐ No
   d. Traffic (pedestrian and vehicle) for your store has declined? ☐ Yes ☐ No
   e. Merchandise returns are higher than they should be? ☐ Yes ☐ No
   f. Your company's sales have declined? ☐ Yes ☐ No
   g. Your employees are slow in greeting customers? ☐ Yes ☐ No
   h. Your employees appear indifferent and make customers wait unnecessarily? ☐ Yes ☐ No
   i. Your employees' personal appearance is not neat? ☐ Yes ☐ No
   j. Your salespeople lack knowledge of the merchandise? ☐ Yes ☐ No
   k. Employees' mistakes are increasing? ☐ Yes ☐ No
   l. The "mantle of greed" is evidenced through the raising of prices? ☐ Yes ☐ No
   m. Your better-qualified employees leave to work for competitors? ☐ Yes ☐ No

**Market segmentation**

10. Does your product or service:
    a. Fulfill the needs of the specially defined group of people? ☐ Yes ☐ No
    b. Represent a compromise to suit widely diverse tastes? ☐ Yes ☐ No

*Exhibit 9–2 (continued)*

11. Have you identified a market segment which is not well
    served by other firms?                                      ☐ Yes    ☐ No
12. Have you posed these questions:
    a.  Is my firm known for:
        (1) Quality?                                            ☐ Yes    ☐ No
        (2) Price?                                              ☐ Yes    ☐ No
    b.  If my firm sells industrial products, does it sell to
        more than one customer?                                ☐ Yes    ☐ No
    c.  My firm has only a limited number of customers.
        Why?

    _____

    _____

    _____

13. Is my retailing firm "straddling the market" by
    attempting to sell both high-quality and low-quality
    goods?                                                      ☐ Yes    ☐ No

**Competitive edge**
14. Check the characteristics that your firm stresses:
    ☐ Quality
    ☐ Reliability and integrity
    ☐ Service
    ☐ Lower prices
15. Is your competitive edge realistic? Review the
    characteristics:
    a.  Is the "edge" based on facts?                           ☐ Yes    ☐ No
    b.  Do you know specifically what your customers are
        seeking?                                               ☐ Yes    ☐ No
    c.  Does the edge entice the customer away from his
        present source of supply?                              ☐ Yes    ☐ No
    d.  Has market research been used in determining edge?     ☐ Yes    ☐ No
    e.  Is the edge based on conditions that are likely to
        change rapidly?                                        ☐ Yes    ☐ No
16. Does your firm focus on earning profits instead of
    increasing the volume of sales?                            ☐ Yes    ☐ No

**Market Strategy—What to do**
    The purpose of this part of the questionnaire is to enable you and your
management to determine the appropriate "what to do" marketing strategy for
your company.
17. Check which what-to-do marketing strategies your com-
    pany is following:
    ☐ Expand sales into new classes of customers.
    ☐ Increase penetration in market segments correspond-
      ing to existing customers.
    ☐ Make no marketing innovations, but copy new market-
      ing techniques and engage in product design and man-
      ufacturing innovations.
18. To reach new markets, have you considered these
    possibilities:
    a.  Develop additional related products or models within
        your product line?                                    ☐ Yes    ☐ No
    b.  Develop completely new products unrelated to your
        present line?                                          ☐ Yes    ☐ No
    c.  Find new applications in new markets for your product? ☐ Yes    ☐ No
    d.  Develop customized products or upgrade from low-
        quality to medium-quality goods?                      ☐ Yes    ☐ No

*Exhibit 9–2 (continued)*

19. In introducing new and improved products, do you recognize these factors:
    a. Existing product line and established channels of distribution? ☐ Yes ☐ No
    b. Cost of development and introduction? ☐ Yes ☐ No
    c. Personnel? ☐ Yes ☐ No
    d. Facilities? ☐ Yes ☐ No
    e. Competition and market acceptance? ☐ Yes ☐ No
20. Is your company trying to compete with:
    a. A nonstandard product, either high-priced or an economy model? ☐ Yes ☐ No
    b. Fast deliveries? ☐ Yes ☐ No
    c. Short production runs of special items? ☐ Yes ☐ No
    d. High-quality product superior to comparable products of competitors? ☐ Yes ☐ No
21. Has your company engaged in diversification of its product line? ☐ Yes ☐ No
22. Is your company increasing its penetration of the present market:
    a. By expanding its sales to original-equipment manufacturers from selling replacement parts? ☐ Yes ☐ No
    b. By reducing the variety of products and models and realizing operating economies? ☐ Yes ☐ No
23. If your company's strength lies in its technical competence, are you adopting current marketing practices? ☐ Yes ☐ No

**Evaluating Your Market Research, Sales Forecasting, and Sales Planning**
The purpose of this part of the questionnaire is to enable your management to determine whether your company's market research, sales forecasting, and sales planning functions are being performed economically and effectively.

**Market research**
24. Is the market research function being performed in your company? ☐ Yes ☐ No
25. Is your firm using market research to:
    a. Identify customers for your products or services and determine their needs? ☐ Yes ☐ No
    b. Evaluate sales potential for your industry and your firm? ☐ Yes ☐ No
    c. Select the most appropriate channels of distribution? ☐ Yes ☐ No
    d. Evaluate your advertising efficiency? ☐ Yes ☐ No
26. Are your market research studies directed toward the measurement of:
    a. Population? ☐ Yes ☐ No
    b. Income level? ☐ Yes ☐ No
    c. Purchasing power? ☐ Yes ☐ No
    d. Other indexes of sales potential in your trading area? ☐ Yes ☐ No
27. Are these secondary sources of published data used:
    a. Government publications, such as *Survey of Current Business*? ☐ Yes ☐ No
    b. Trade association reports? ☐ Yes ☐ No
    c. Chamber of commerce studies? ☐ Yes ☐ No
    d. University research publications? ☐ Yes ☐ No
    e. Trade journals? ☐ Yes ☐ No
    f. Newspapers? ☐ Yes ☐ No
28. Do you use U.S. Bureau of the Census data broken down by county and SMSA and for SIC codes? ☐ Yes ☐ No

*Exhibit 9–2 (continued)*

29. Do you use primary sources of published data, such as U.S. census reports? ☐ Yes ☐ No
30. Do you use your firm's records in performing research? ☐ Yes ☐ No
31. Do you use external data obtained from your:
    a. Dealers? ☐ Yes ☐ No
    b. Customers? ☐ Yes ☐ No
    c. Competitors? ☐ Yes ☐ No
32. Is your company engaged in sales forecasting and in measuring your company's potential market in units and dollars? ☐ Yes ☐ No
33. Are your sales quotas providing targets for your:
    a. Firm? ☐ Yes ☐ No
    b. Individual salespersons? ☐ Yes ☐ No
    c. Departments? ☐ Yes ☐ No
    d. Sales territories? ☐ Yes ☐ No
34. In deriving sales quotas, are you using:
    a. Market sampling studies and a study of census data? ☐ Yes ☐ No
    b. Salespersons' knowledge obtained through customer contracts? ☐ Yes ☐ No
    c. Mail questionnaires to companies? ☐ Yes ☐ No
    d. Interviews with your customers and distributors? ☐ Yes ☐ No
    e. Direct data concerning competitors? ☐ Yes ☐ No
    f. Estimates of volume of business by:
       (1) Relating sales of your merchandise to other merchandise sold in conjunction with your merchandise? ☐ Yes ☐ No
       (2) Relating known national data to known local data? ☐ Yes ☐ No
    g. Statistical analysis and projection based on past sales, as are reflected in your firm's records? ☐ Yes ☐ No
35. Has your company obtained:
    a. The services of a market research consultant? ☐ Yes ☐ No
    b. Assistance from:
       (1) Trade associations? ☐ Yes ☐ No
       (2) Local chambers of commerce? ☐ Yes ☐ No
       (3) Banks? ☐ Yes ☐ No
       (4) Field offices of the U.S. Department of Commerce? ☐ Yes ☐ No
       (5) Field offices of the U.S. Small Business Administration? ☐ Yes ☐ No
       (6) Small Business Development Center. ☐ Yes ☐ No
36. Has your company engaged in cooperative research with other small companies concerning:
    a. Evaluations of traffic flow? ☐ Yes ☐ No
    b. Parking availability? ☐ Yes ☐ No
37. Does your firm closely follow market changes due to shifts in:
    a. The composition of your customers? ☐ Yes ☐ No
    b. The values and preferences of your customers? ☐ Yes ☐ No
    c. The locations of your customers? ☐ Yes ☐ No
38. Do you specify the objectives of each market research project? ☐ Yes ☐ No
39. Do you make market tests before introducing new products? ☐ Yes ☐ No

*Exhibit 9–2 (concluded)*
**Sales planning**
40. Prior to fixing your sales plan, do you check your
    production capacity?                                    □ Yes   □ No
41. If your sales plan does not keep production busy, what
    should you do:
    a. Advertise more heavily?                              □ Yes   □ No
    b. Reduce prices?                                       □ Yes   □ No
    c. Redesign your products to increase the volume?       □ Yes   □ No
    d. Add another product, or a variation of a product, to
       the company's line?                                  □ Yes   □ No
42. If your sales plan calls for more output than the capacity
    of the production process, what should you do:
    a. Expand the capacity?                                 □ Yes   □ No
    b. Produce on overtime?                                 □ Yes   □ No
    c. Subcontract?                                         □ Yes   □ No

# Chapter Ten

# Market Research, Sales Forecasting, Pricing, and Promoting

It is not unusual to find people who, when thinking of independent businesses and their role in the marketplace, think of market research and sales forcasting as having little or no value. Such people think of these activities as applying to large firms and as being too time consuming and too complex to be used by the smaller firms.

> At a university small-business seminar, a marketing professor emphasized the importance of market research in small businesses. Afterward, a panel member, an owner-manager of a wholesaling firm that sold farm equipment and supplies, stated that market research was not relevant to a small business. Later, this panel member told the participants that he visited dealers to learn their needs for shovels and other items before ordering these items for his stock. He did not realize it, but he was performing research.

Our experience with various types of businesses seems to refute the idea that independent business does not need research. Determining the nature of the market, its location, its potential volume, and the most effective procedure for its penetration are essential elements to all firms. The quality of this endeavor plays a significant role in product design, packaging, displaying, advertising, sales, and—as a result—in the degree of success achieved as measured in dollars of sales and of profit.

**170**

The intent of this chapter is to present some of the marketing means, or the "how to do it" strategies. The means strategies covered are:

1. Market research.
2. Sales forecasting.
3. Pricing the product or service.
4. Promoting the sale of products and services.

## Market Research

Market research consists of the gathering, recording, and analyzing of data about problems related to the marketing of goods and services. It provides a basis for effective decisions by managers of marketing. Market research consists of the following steps:

1. Recognition of a problem.
2. Preliminary investigation and planning.
3. Gathering factual information.
4. Classifying and interpreting the information.
5. Reaching a conclusion.

The real nature of the situation facing your firm should be determined by a careful analysis of the factors involved. A problem creates the need for information. Your next step is to review the facts already known, perhaps through discussions with people inside or outside your firm or by reading trade publications. Once the facts are gathered, their significance, interrelationships, and implications for your firm should be determined.

Market research is beneficial to you at several points in your firm's life:

1. Before beginning or buying a firm. You should define whether the location, product or service, surrounding population, and image of the firm are compatible with each other.
2. After beginning a firm. You should determine:
   a. Where to grow—New or different products or services; expansion at original location, opening additional locations, and extension of hours.
   b. Where to cut back—what products or services or other operations are unprofitable.
   c. Where to change emphasis—change locations, products or services, advertising and promotion strategy, channels of distribution.[1]

[1]CRC Education and Human Development, Inc., *Something Ventured, Something Gained*, vol. 2 (Washington, D.C.: U.S. Government Printing Office, 1979), II–T–45.

## Areas of Market Research

Areas of market research that you should consider are: identification of customers for the firm's products or services and determination of their needs, evaluation of sales potential for your industry and your firm, selection of the most appropriate channel of distribution, and evaluation of advertising efficiency.

Market research studies may be directed toward measuring population, income level, purchasing power, and other indexes of sales potential in your trading area. The establishment of accurate sales quotas and measurements of effectiveness in selling depend upon the determination of sales potential.

The following example shows the importance of researching the customers for a company's products:

> The manager of a customer durables manufacturing firm set a goal of industry leadership and a target share of the market to be obtained within a certain period of time.
>
> *Problem:* The company did not attain the desired share of the market. The product line was styled above mass tastes. The designer was designing the product line for department store buyers (prestige stores, at that), but three fourths of the product was being sold through furniture stores. The manager realized that he had failed to research the customer adequately.
>
> *Solution:* The manager then arranged for market research, which indicated that many furniture store buyers were seeking products styled quite differently.[2]

## Methods of Collecting Market Data

There are many ways of collecting market data.

> The manager of a sporting goods store asked a Small Business Institute team whether to add handmade and custom knives to the company's product line. Although the team had limited financial resources available, it came up with the following findings.
>
> Two new books and the first issue of an annual publication on these types of knives had been published recently. A knife collector's club existed. The average national cutlery purchase per person was over $100; many surgeons and dentists bought $500 worth of custom knives per doctor a year. A wide spectrum of custom knives was being bought as rapidly as the knives were produced.
>
> The team located a company, about 100 miles away, whose founder was generally acknowledged to be the United States' foremost authority on knives. This firm supplied a large range of different types of knives and served as a knife appraiser and consultant.

---

[2]T. Stanley Gallagher, "Sound Objectives Help Build Profits," *Management Aids for Small Manufacturers No. 11* (Washington, D.C.: Small Business Administration, 1965).

The founder maintained that certain types of knives would complement those already in the store. The team also obtained an attractive dealer discount schedule and price list.

On the basis of the above information, the manager decided to stock these knives in the store.

The methods independent businesses most commonly use to collect data include:

1. Personal contact with customers.
2. Personal contact surveys.
3. Questionnaire surveys.
4. Search of published and unpublished data.
5. Statistical analyses and projections.
6. "Top-down" market research.

***Personal Contact with Customers.*** Contacts with customers may be formal or informal. Observant employees collect information each day in stores in their contacts with customers. Channels of communication can be designed to convey significant information to people responsible for marketing. Salespersons can be given forms to complete and return to their managers.

Many small book publishers use a report form which a sales representative completes after each sales visit and returns to headquarters. The information includes comments by the professor contacted on books, book needs, services provided by the company, and other pertinent data.

***Personal Contact Surveys.*** One method of using personal contacts is selecting a small sample, perhaps 10–15 people, of the consumer or potential consumer population. Interviews are arranged with the people in the sample to obtain answers to prepared questions. Some of these questions may be:

1. Is the firm losing business because of price? Because of the discount schedule?
2. Is something wrong with the products? Are they out of date?
3. Are agents or salespeople not pushing products? Are they making good impressions? Is the advertising program appropriate?
4. Are customers experimenting with processes that may replace the product? Are they likely to shift to in-house manufacturing of the product?

This method may be used by prospective retailers of appliances, radios, stereos, photographic equipment, etc., in deciding where to locate their stores.

***Questionnaire Surveys.*** When information is needed from a large number of respondents, you should consider using telephone and/or mail questionnaires. A questionnaire related to the feasibility of a new car-wash firm might be sent to a sample of the population to elicit information on the profile of respondent, ownership of car, use of car-wash facilities, frequency of washing, and factors influencing choice of car wash.

Sometimes confidential information can be obtained that customers prefer not to give to salespeople. Such information as commission percentages that competitors pay their agents, market shares obtained by competitors, and market potential for products in various geographic areas may be obtained from these mail surveys.

A small company made a product used by meat packing plants.

*Problem:* The manager wanted to determine the sales potential for an area consisting of 300 counties.

*Solution:* From *County Business Patterns* (a series of booklets published by the U.S. Department of Commerce), he determined the total number of meat packing plants and their employment. He mailed questionnaires to these plants. Upon analyzing them, he learned that an average plant bought $200 worth of his product per employee per year. By multiplying the total employment in these plants by $200, he derived the potential annual sales.[3]

**Search of Published and Unpublished Data.** The sources of marketing information consist of (1) secondary sources of published data, (2) primary sources of published data, and (3) primary sources of unpublished data.

*Secondary sources of published data.* Secondary sources contain data originally compiled and published elsewhere. Examples of these sources are:

1. Government publications, such as *Survey of Current Business* and *Statistical Abstract of the United States.*
2. Trade association reports.
3. Chambers of commerce studies.
4. University research publications.
5. Trade journals.
6. Newspapers.
7. Marketing journals.

An independent manufacturer developed a unique electrical interior car warmer. It was completely concealed, required only a thermostatic control switch mounted on the dashboard, and did not have to be removed each spring. The proposed market area was the Edmonton, Canada, trading area as the primary market and

---

[3]Warren R. Dix, "Getting Facts for Better Sales Decisions," *Management Aids for Small Manufacturers No. 12* (Washington, D.C.: Small Business Administration, 1966).

the balance of the Alberta area as the secondary market. (See Table 10–1.)

The number of vehicles owned by Albertans had increased substantially from 579,000 in 1965. In 1976, 133,000 new vehicles were sold in Alberta.

The sales potential was to be calculated after conducting a personal research survey of 700 cars to determine how many had warmers installed.[4]

**Table 10–1**

| Market | Population | Vehicle Registration | |
|--------|-----------|---------------------|-----|
| Primary | 560,000 | Passenger cars | 222,000 |
| | | Trucks | 105,000 |
| Secondary | 1,220,000 | Passenger cars | 484,000 |
| Total | 1,780,000 | Trucks | 229,000 |
| | | | 1,040,000 |
| | | Commercial | 213,000 |
| | | Total | 1,253,000 |

The U.S. Bureau of the Census regularly collects data for many industry groups on the number of industrial establishments, their sales volume, and their number of employees. These data are broken down by county and Standard Metropolitan Statistical Area (SMSA). An SMSA contains one city of 50,000 or more inhabitants, or twin cities with a combined population of that size.

The data are reported for Standard Industrial Classification (SIC) codes, which facilitate firms' research in which sales can be related to their customers' type of activity. The code breakdowns start with broad industrial categories—for example, apparel classifications such as men's, youths', and boys' furnishings, work clothing, and allied garments, and subclassifications such as shirts, collars, night wear, underwear, and neckwear. Many trade associations and other organizations that gather industrial data also use the SIC Code.

The Census Bureau has a Data Users' Service, which furnishes information concerning population patterns, family income, business sales, housing, etc. The bureau updates its information on independent businesses every five years and wants to computerize it.

Metropolitan newspapers often develop important market data,

---

[4]Department of Tourism and Small Business, Government of Alberta, *Marketing for the Small Manufacturer in Alberta*, January 1980, pp. 14–16.

such as purchasing-power information, for their advertising clients. Examples are Scripps-Howard publications and the Memphis Commercial Appeal.

*Primary source of published data.* A primary source of published data consists of the compilation and initial publication of the data. The U.S. Census reports are illustrations.

*Primary sources of unpublished data.* Examples of primary sources of unpublished data are your firm's records and external data obtained from your dealers, customers, and competitors.

*Computerized data bases.* These information sources are available at libraries in major cities on a fee basis. For example, a version of *Standard & Poor's Daily News* and *Cumulative News* (Corporation Records) provides current information on over 9,000 companies in the United States. News about company sales, earnings, dividends, management changes, mergers and acquisitions, and other operations can be found.

To learn about companies' expanding operations, sometimes it is possible to select particular kinds of companies (for instance, electronics firms producing home video cassettes) or specific geographic areas (such as firms moving into a particular state or city). Such information may be beneficial to small retailers, service businesses, wholesalers, and manufacturers.

You should consider the extent and intensity of the competition. One way to determine how much merchandise you and your competitors sell is to use direct data.

The manager of a furniture store obtained information on total furniture sales for County A, and determined that the store accounted for 25 percent of that county's furniture sales. For County A, total furniture sales totaled $3 million, and the store's sales were $750,000.

Alternatively, he could have determined total furniture sales for the county by finding the per-family expenditure for furniture and multiplying it by the estimated number of families in the area. Population data could have been used (e.g., total population divided by three) in estimating the number of families.

If sales data are not available for your type of goods in your market area, you should estimate the volume of business by relating sales of your type of merchandise to other merchandise that is sold in conjunction with yours, or by relating known national data to known local data.

A tire dealer determined that the sales of new cars three years before had a strong effect on present retail tire sales. National sales of replacement tires in any one year were found consistently to represent 10 percent of auto sales three years earlier. Ten percent of the 1978 automobile sales could have been used as market potential for 1981.

***Statistical Analyses and Projections.*** In analyzing a firm's records, statistical analyses and projections based on past sales may be utilized in developing sales quotas. Also, an accounting analysis may be made of the profitability of selling to particular customers or of selling particular products. This study may reveal that sales to certain customers or of certain products are unprofitable. Furthermore, analysis of sales records on profitable credit customers may provide good information for merchandising decisions and sales promotion programs. An analysis of the company's accounts-receivable–aging data—current, 30-day, 60-day, 90-day, and over 90 days—is beneficial.

If your store sells many varieties of products, market share should be measured in total dollar volume rather than in product units sold. You should determine the total sales and the rate of growth for the type of goods offered.

An area with apparel sales of $2 million, $2.2 million, and $2.42 million in three successive years shows a 10 percent annual rate of growth. Other things being equal, it may be expected that these sales will amount to $2.662 million in the fourth year. To match that growth, a store's sales volume should increase by 10 percent; to increase its market share, it would have to grow by more than 10 percent.

***Top-Down Market Research.*** You should not engage in the armchair type of top-down market research exemplified by the following: "Of 40 million home owners in the United States in 1976, 70 percent use power lawn mowers, producing a market of 28 million. My firm is attempting to obtain 5 percent of this market, or sales of 1.4 million mowers." This approach is subject to criticism as being too vague and not dealing with enough detail.

## Overcoming Market Research Difficulties

A major problem associated with market research in independent businesses is that such businesses lack knowledge of research techniques. However, the services of outside experts—such as a market research consulting firm—may be secured. You may obtain the services of an advertising person who is moonlighting. Other possibilities include help from trade associations, local chambers of commerce, banks, and field offices of the U.S. Department of Commerce and the Small Business Administration. You should consider cooperative research—such as evaluations of traffic flow and parking availability—with other independent businesses.

In personal contacts with customers and in surveys, respondents often tell you what they think you want to hear. Some people do not want to hurt your feelings and will not tell you if they think that your company is behind the times or that your competitor's new models give better service.

Through the use of various methods of collecting marketing information, a firm should closely follow market changes due to shifts in the composition of customers, their values and preferences, and their locations. Fad items and services tend to have short life cycles. You should plan to get in and get out within an appropriate time frame in order to optimize profits.[5]

You probably cannot afford all the market research you would like, so projects where the payoff is greatest should be selected. The objectives of each research project should be carefully specified. Selection of research techniques should be based upon cost considerations and the value of the decisions to be made. Market tests should be made before the introduction of new products.

## Sales Forecasting

You should measure the company's potential market in terms of both units and dollars. A sales forecast, both long- and short-range, should be prepared. It is the foundation of budgeting for a firm. Typically it indicates sales during the last planning period, current sales, and future sales (see Table 10–2).

**Table 10–2**
**Miller Wholesale Company:**
**Sales Forecast**

| Products | Sales* |
|---|---|
| Last year: | |
| Groceries | $800,000 |
| Drugs | 500,000 |
| This year: | |
| Groceries | 880,000 |
| Drugs | 550,000 |
| Next year: | |
| Groceries | 970,000 |
| Drugs | 605,000 |

*The Miller Company obtained actual data from its records.

[5]Successful products go through a life cycle. The stages of the cycle are (1) the introductory period, in which there is low customer acceptance; (2) a growth period, in which gains are rapid; (3) maturity, in which sales level off; and (4) decline, in which sales fall. In general, the average life of products is decreasing because of rapid technological development and business change.

A firm's sales quotas can be used in sales forecasting. They can be used to set targets for firms, for salespeople, for departments, or for sales territories. They should be realistic. Market sampling studies, past sales data, and a study of census data may be used in deriving the quotas.

The manufacturer of paneling and room accessories had franchise arrangements with local contractors who used these materials to convert basements into finished rooms.

*Problem:* What new areas would be best for franchises?

*Solution:* From census statistics on housing, he determined (1) the type of houses that predominated in a particular area and (2) whether the houses were built on concrete slabs or with full basements. He eliminated areas where the houses had no basements.

*Another question:* Could people in the particular areas afford to finish off their basements?

*Answer:* To answer this question, he examined census data on family income, number of children, and car ownership—particularly for families that owned more than one car, indicating that they had discretionary income that might be spent for home improvement. He granted franchises in areas that had good market potential.

## Pricing the Product or Service

The importance of pricing is illustrated by the observation that about one half of all the failures in small business can be traced to a product or service that was being sold at the wrong price.[6]

### Relating Price to Costs

The first step in setting prices is having an accurate knowledge of costs. All items should be priced at a level to provide an adequate profit margin. The policy of pricing to cover costs has dangerous long-run implications. In periods of rapid inflation, such as in the early 1980s, costs should be constantly monitored and price changes made to provide for continued profitability.

Independent companies that base their pricing solely on costs, rather than on values as seen by their customers, lose profits. Companies selling to a style-conscious market, or ones that provide a unique service, can set more profitable prices by recognizing the short-lived novelty of their products and the values of their services to their customers.

If a firm has idle facilities, the price may be less than total cost. Provided the price covers the variable costs and makes some con-

---

[6]Theodore Cohn and Roy A. Lindberg, *How Management Is Different in Small Companies* (New York: American Management Association, 1972), p. 24.

tribution toward the fixed costs, this practice may be desirable on a limited basis in order to increase the volume of sales.

A word of caution is appropriate at this point. You should constantly check the package price structure and profits based on units sold.

> A new club lessee of a food-beverage concession decided to adopt a pricing policy of selling food at cost and making profits from the sale of beverages. Overlooked was the fact that significant numbers of customers were either nondrinkers or light drinkers. Therefore, profits were not as anticipated.

### Setting a Price Strategy

Your goal should be to find the price-volume combination that will maximize profits. When setting a price strategy, you should consider these factors:

1.  The customer and the channel of distribution.
2.  Competitive and legal forces.
3.  Annual volume and life-cycle volume.
4.  Opportunities for special market promotions.
5.  Product group prices.

*Price Strategies.* Three pricing strategies are possible:

1.  High-price, or "skimming the cream," strategy. Prices of the product or service are set well above cost of production or purchase.
2.  Low-price, or market-penetration, pricing strategy. Prices are set slightly above cost of production or purchase in order to achieve a high sales volume quickly.
3.  Meet-the-competition, or "me too," pricing strategy. Prices charged by competition are matched.

You should select the pricing strategy that is most closely related to the kind of business you want to create. Skimming-the-cream pricing reflects the uniqueness of a business and its status connotations. Market-penetration pricing is usually used for fad products. Meet-the-competition pricing is not recommended if it has a questionable relationship to profit.

> Independent residential construction firms estimate the total costs of building a house, but modify the price in order to meet market conditions. When business is slack during winters, downward price adjustments are made. Cash sales of a house also result in lower prices compared with complicated financing situations for the buyer.

The product, price, delivery, service, and fulfillment of psychological needs form the total package that the customer buys. A price should be consistent with the product image. As customers often equate the quality of unknown products with price, raising prices may increase sales.

> The owner-manager of a women's clothing store considered her merchandise in the medium-price range. However, the newspaper ads for the store emphasized price and did not mention quality. Customers and potential customers evaluated her store as "cut-rate." She changed the ads to emphasize quality and stylishness, obtained new customers, and increased prices.

***Errors in Setting Prices.*** Independent business owner-managers commonly make two errors in setting prices for their goods or services:

1. Charging less than large businesses and considering themselves price leaders. Due to a relatively small volume of sales, product costs per unit tend to be higher for a smaller than for a larger business. Also, small firms cannot take advantage of large-volume discounts on their purchases.
2. Undercharging during the early period of operation, particularly in firms offering services performed personally by the owner-manager, who mistakenly believes that prices can be raised later as more customers are secured. However, it is easier to lower prices than to raise them.

***Price Cutting.*** Price cutting should be considered a form of sales promotion. You should reduce price whenever the added volume resulting from the reduction produces sufficient sales revenue to offset the added costs. However, if an inelastic demand exists for your product, a lower price will not result in a greater number of units being sold. Your competitors' probable reactions should be considered in determining whether to reduce prices. Independent firms generally should not consider themselves price leaders.

> A business machines retailer had a large stock of old and second-hand equipment taken as trade-ins. He held an auction which cleared the stock, made money, and developed good will. Bargain-hunting customers were now good prospects for the regular machines.

> The owner-manager of an appliance store promoted a new model of an electric range. A newspaper ad offered a range to the person submitting the highest sealed bid, which usually was near wholesale cost. This promotion provided a list of good prospects interested in the new model.

## Other Aspects of Pricing

Markups, price lining, and odd pricing are other aspects of pricing you should consider. In calculating the selling price for a particular product, retailers, wholesalers, and manufacturers should add a markup to the costs of goods sold or manufactured. An initial markup should cover operating—particularly selling—expenses, operating profit, and subsequent price reductions (for example, markdowns and employee discounts). An initial markup may be expressed as a percentage of either the sales price or the product cost. A markup of $8 on a product costing $12, for instance, would produce a selling price of $20. The markup would be 40 percent of the sales price and 66⅔ percent of cost. Although either method is correct, consistency should be followed in the use of the bases. Your business should have effective cost analysis by product in order to price the product effectively. You should recognize that modifications of markup percentages may be needed because of factors such as competitors' prices and the use of loss leaders, or promotional pricing.

Price lining refers to the offering of merchandise at distinct price levels. To illustrate, one group of women's dresses might be sold at $40 each, another at $60 each, and the highest at $80 each. Income level and buying desires of a store's customers are important factors. Advantages of price lining are the simplification of customer choice and the reduction of a store's minimum inventory.

Closely related to price lining is demand-backward pricing, which is also closely related to the law of supply and demand. A manufacturer starts with the retail price of a particular product and then works backward, subtracting the typical margins that channel members expect. This process gives an approximate price that the manufacturer should charge.

This method of pricing is commonly used by independent manufacturers of final consumer goods (such as toys, gifts, and women's and children's clothing and shoes) for which customers spend a specific amount.

Concerning odd pricing, some independent business managers believe customers will react more favorably to prices ending in odd numbers. Prices ending with 95 are common—even for high-priced merchandise.

By adding extra service or warranties, or paying transportation costs, a firm may in effect lower price without incurring the retaliation of lower prices by competitors and thus losing any volume gains that might have been made.

## Promoting Sale of Products and Services

Advertising, merchandising, sales promotion, and publicity should be elements of any promotional strategy. Personal selling is also used, but it is emphasized in Chapter 11. A planned and continuing program of communication with customers and the public should be tailored to a market segment and a target market. It should be used in order to gain a competitive edge. Such communication develops awareness, interest in, and desire for a product or service. Effective promotion can not only replace lost customers but also add new ones and sell more to existing customers.

## Advertising

Advertising is used to inform customers of the availability of your products or services and the uses they can make of them, and to convince customers that your products are superior to your competitors'. It is intended to get your message to a large number of potential customers concurrently and is paid for by the firm.

*Developing Your Advertising Program.* An advertising program should be of a continuous nature. Noncontinuous advertising should be limited to preparing customers to accept a new product, to suggesting to them new uses for established products, and to bringing special sales to their attention. Advertising media should reach, but not overreach, the present or desired market. You should determine whether advertising is to be used to back up your sales representatives or used in place of them. You should make four basic decisions in such a program:

1. How much money should be spent for advertising?
2. What media should be used?
3. What should be said and how should it be said?
4. What are the expected results of the advertising program?

*Advertising Budget.* There is no easy answer concerning how much should be spent on advertising. Factors that affect the amount spent are (1) promotional objectives, (2) target customers, (3) characteristics of the product or service, and (4) the type of business. A number of methods are used for deciding on a budget.

The percentage-of-sales method is probably most prevalent. A percentage of projected sales revenue to be devoted to advertising is determined. Perhaps, in your industry, firms allocate 4 percent of revenue to advertising.

The fixed-dollar-per-unit method uses an absolute advertising dollar amount for each unit of product produced or sold. For example, a retailer of men's clothing allocates $4 for each suit sold. If projected sales are 2,000 suits, the advertising budget would be $8,000.

The above two methods are "formula" in nature and do not consider the goal that advertising should aim for—to boost sales.

Matching the competition's budget is another method. However, it is defensive and assumes that you know what your competitors are spending for advertising and that they know the proper amount to spend.

The how-much-can-I-afford approach is often used. But advertising should lead to sales, and the amount spent on it should be related to the amount of sales desired. Therefore, practically, the amount you decide to spend on advertising should be related to forecasted sales and the objectives of the advertising program. The advertising budget should be based on what you want to achieve, not on what current sales permit.

*Selection of Media.* The suitability of any medium (or combination of media) depends upon these factors:

1. Target market—You should use the media that potential customers pay attention to. Representatives of major media can provide you with profiles of the people who buy their publications or live in their broadcasting area.
2. Cost—Two important dimensions of media cost are absolute cost and relative cost. Absolute cost is the actual expenditure for running an ad. One medium may be less expensive than another in actual cost (such as newspapers compared with television). Relative cost is the relationship between the actual cost and the number of consumers the message reaches. A typical measure is the cost per 1,000 consumers reached.
3. Appropriate media—Some media are preferable to others for the message concerning the product or service. For example, radio carries only sound while newspapers, periodicals (magazines), and television can show color pictures.
4. Availability of media—The local situation may determine the number and kind of media used. Generally, retailers in small communities have fewer options than those in large cities.

*Advertising media.* The list of advertising media offers sufficient flexibility to reach any target market. It includes:

1. Newspaper.
2. Trade periodical.
3. Store sign.
4. Direct mail.
5. Circulars.
6. Yellow Pages in telephone directory.
7. Radio.
8. Television.
9. Outdoor sign.

Display ads in the local newspaper are generally appropriate in towns with total newspaper circulation of 50,000 or less. To investigate the effectiveness of display advertising and what days are the most effective, you should talk with independent business managers who advertise in the local paper. High postage rates are making the use of direct mail questionable except when it is used selectively. Offset and instant printing have simplified the preparation of small quantities of circulars; however, increased printing and distribution costs and the impact of local ordinances are adverse features. Yellow Pages advertising is most effective for special products, services, and repair shops. Radio advertising is effective for independent businesses in some of the less populous parts of the United States. Independent business managers who use radio spots can provide guidance.

> The owner of three laundromats—which were clean, well maintained, and had a few loyal customers—could not increase the volume of sales in one of them.
>
> Advertising practice had been to advertise in newspapers on a one-shot basis every four months at a high expense. Money was wasted because most newspaper readers lived outside the marketing area of the problem unit.
>
> A new advertising plan was tried. Three successive mailings of handbills were sent to potential customers in the immediate vicinity of the problem unit. The desired volume was soon reached.

**Types of Advertising.** The types of advertising are *product* and *institutional.* The first term is self-explanatory, but the latter pertains to the selling of an idea regarding your company. The purpose of institutional advertising is to keep the public conscious of your company and its good reputation. The majority of independent business advertising is of the product type.

*Development of advertising message.* In newspapers, ideas or information you want to convey should be translated into words and symbols relevant to the target market. The development of the message involves formulating what is to be said, how it is to be said, what form it will take, and what its style and design will be. Ads should have characteristics such as (1) a headline that attracts attention, (2) appeals and benefits enticing to readers, (3) offers, and (4) a compelling reason to buy now.

Potential results of an ad are:

1. Your firm is made well known for the quality of its products.
2. People are enticed to come to the store or obtain further information such as a catalog or a brochure.
3. Products are sold immediately to customers who come to the store to buy or who place orders by phone or mail.

Skilled employees of the newspaper publishing company can help when this medium is used. There are also specialists for the other media, including the telephone company and radio or TV stations. You may also get help from an advertising agency or a graphic arts firm.

*When and how to use an advertising agency.* Most independent business owner-managers plan and execute their own advertising programs, particularly when they consider the rather high costs of retaining the services of an advertising agency. This practice is often false economy, however, since significant differences exist between materials prepared by professionals and those prepared by amateurs. Before considering the use of an advertising agency, you should recognize that most of the money spent for advertising goes to newspaper publishers, and that most newspaper advertising is developed by skilled persons within the newspaper organization.

Advertising agencies with experienced specialists service business firms in many different industries. Their functions are (1) performing preliminary studies and analyses; (2) developing, implementing, and evaluating an advertising plan; and (3) following up on the advertising. Examples of preliminary studies and analyses are: determinations of the products' or services' advantages and disadvantages relative to competitors' offerings, analysis of present and potential markets, study of distribution channels, and evaluation of the advertising media. Development of an advertising plan includes designing, writing, and illustrating the advertisements; forwarding them to the media; and related activities. Follow-up includes checking and verifying advertisements, as well as handling billing and paying for them.

An advertising agency will also coordinate its work with your other sales activities to ensure the greatest effect from the advertising. And if you wish, it can also help you (usually for a special fee) in areas such as package design, sales research, sales training, preparations of sales and service literature, designing, merchandising displays, preparation of house organs, and public relations and publicity.

**Measuring the Results of Advertising.** Measuring the results of advertising—by comparing sales with advertising—is important. Assume that you are the owner of a retail firm and desire to determine whether advertising is doing the job that you intend it to do. Divide your advertising into two kinds: immediate-response and attitude advertising. The purpose of immediate-response advertising is to entice the potential customer to buy a particular product from your store within a short period of time—today, tomorrow, the weekend, or next week. This type of advertising should be checked for results daily and at the end of one week, two weeks, and three weeks after its appearance. The carry-over effects of advertising are the reason for checking after the first week.

You should consider using these tests for immediate-response ads:

1. Coupons (especially for foods and drugs) to be brought to your store.
2. Letter or phone requests referring to the ads.
3. Split runs by newspapers.
4. Sales made of the particular item.
5. Checks on store traffic.

Attitude, or image-building, advertising is the type used to keep a store's name and merchandise before the public. You continually remind people about your regular products or services or inform them about new or special policies or services. This type of advertising is more difficult to measure, because you cannot always attribute a specific sale to it. You can measure some attitude advertising, such as a series of ads about your stores' brands, at the end of one month from the ad's appearance or at the end of a campaign.

Record keeping is essential in testing attitude advertising because you want to compare ads and sales for an extended time. You may make your comparisons on a weekly basis.

When ads appear concurrently in different media—newspaper, radio and television, direct mail pieces, handbills—you should try to evaluate the relative effectiveness of each.

You can measure the response to a specific offer appearing in only one medium by measuring the difference between sales during the offer period and normal sales of the product. Tallies on mail and phone orders on a specific offer can also be made. You can compare the effectiveness of one publication with that of another by making a different offer in each publication for a week. Drop the offers for two weeks and then switch each offer into the other publication for a week. Then the results should be compared.

## Merchandising

Merchandising is the promotional effort made for a product or service in retailing firms, especially at the point of purchase. It includes window displays, store banners, shelf stackers, the label and package of the product, product demonstrations, samples, bill stuffers, and sales offering significant discount prices.

It is estimated that an effective window display will produce about one fourth to one half of the store's sales. A few innovations in window displays that have proved to be effective are:

1. Guessing contests—such as predictions of scores of baseball, football, or soccer games used by sporting goods retailers;
2. Use of motion—for instance, a toy and recreational equipment

retailer used an electric train system which was controlled by buttons on the store's exterior near the window.

3. Live models—a small furrier arranged for these models to wear fur coats. A sizable number of fur coats were sold to women who referred to particular models and the coats they modeled.

An independent manufacturer entered a new market and offered its product line in a floor display unit placed in retail stores. Window and counter displays should be changed frequently to help bring the merchandise to customers' attention. Some manufacturers and wholesalers advise on store layouts.

## Sales Promotion

Sales promotion consists of activities that have the purpose of making other sales efforts (such as advertising) more effective. It is composed of consumer promotions, trade promotions, and salesforce promotions. Consumer promotions consists of coupons, discounts, contests, trading stamps, samples, demonstrations, and so forth. Trade promotions include free goods, buying allowances, merchandise allowances, and cooperative advertising. Salesforce promotions consist of benefits—contests, bonuses, extra commissions, and sales rallies—to encourage the salespersons to increase their selling effectiveness and efficiency.

Retailers usually promote the opening of their businesses. A premium (or bonus item) may be given with the purchase of a product. During out-of-season periods, coupons offering a discount may be given to stimulate sales by attracting new customers. These coupons should be consistent with the image of your business. Holidays, store remodeling or expansion, store anniversaries, special purchases, fashion shows, and the presence in the store of a celebrity are other events suitable for promotions.

An independent stationery manufacturer promoted its highest-quality stationery by giving away a premium consisting of a medium-price pen. The promotion was effective due to the tie-in of products which complemented each other.

A tract residential contractor installed attractive curtains in several windows of each unsold home. This promotion resulted in a faster sale of homes at higher prices.

A men's clothing store gave each high school male graduate a souvenir newspaper with his own name printed in the heading. A women's clothing store put on fashion preview shows for female college students and arranged for them to vote on which clothes to stock for the coming season. Both of these clothing stores arranged for local high school and college students to write and sign ads for the stores' clothing.

You should determine whether the sales promotions are really effective or are merely reducing profits. Caution is recommended concerning the use of samples, contests, and trading stamps, for their costs can outweigh their benefits. Specialty advertising and occasional use of premiums are considered favorably as sales promotion tools.

Every promotional activity should integrate or mesh with every other activity. To illustrate, if you are advertising a certain item, reinforce the advertising by devoting window displays, points of purchase, and direct mail to it. Customers need several reminders before they act.

Publicity can be considered free advertising. When your firm or its product becomes newsworthy, it obtains publicity. Many local newspapers are interested in publicizing the opening of a new store or any other business in their area. You should take the initiative by sending a publicity release to a copy editor for possible inclusion in the newspaper. Also, new information about your product or concerning a new service may be interesting to the editor. You may consider arranging for an advertising agency to prepare materials and photographs related to a grand opening. Later, as you and your firm perform various community services, you should attempt to obtain publicity.

## Summary

This chapter has directed you toward an understanding of market research—its methodology, its pertinent data, and its usefulness. An effort has been made to make you aware of the role sales forecasting plays in your business.

This chapter also demonstrates the necessary procedures for the development of pricing and promotion policies and procedures.

# Exhibits

*Exhibit 10–1*
**Evaluating Pricing Policies and Practices, Advertising and Sales Promotions, and Personal Selling Activities**

The purpose of this part of the questionnaire is to help you and your managers to determine whether your pricing policies and practices are appropriate for your firm.

1.  Do you price all items at a level which provides an adequate profit margin? ☐ Yes ☐ No
2.  Do you constantly monitor costs and make price changes to provide for continued profitability, particularly in periods of rapid inflation? ☐ Yes ☐ No
3.  If your firm has idle facilities, do you price in order to cover your variable costs and make some contribution toward the fixed cost? ☐ Yes ☐ No
4.  Is your goal to find the price-volume combination that will maximize profits? ☐ Yes ☐ No
5.  When setting a price strategy, do you consider these factors:
    a.  Customers and channels of distribution? ☐ Yes ☐ No
    b.  Competitive and legal forces? ☐ Yes ☐ No
    c.  Annual volume and life-cycle volume? ☐ Yes ☐ No
    d.  Opportunities for special market promotions? ☐ Yes ☐ No
    e.  Product group prices? ☐ Yes ☐ No
6.  Is your price consistent with the product image? ☐ Yes ☐ No
7.  Since customers often equate the quality of unknown products with price, do you raise prices under this condition? ☐ Yes ☐ No
8.  Do you reduce prices whenever the added volume resulting from the reduction produces sufficient sales revenue to offset the added costs? ☐ Yes ☐ No
9.  In reducing prices, do you consider your competitors' probable reactions? ☐ Yes ☐ No
10. Do you desire your firm to be a price leader? ☐ Yes ☐ No
11. Do your initial markups cover:
    a.  Operations, particularly selling expenses? ☐ Yes ☐ No
    b.  Operating profit? ☐ Yes ☐ No
    c.  Subsequent price reductions? ☐ Yes ☐ No
12. Does your company have effective cost analysis by products in order to price them effectively? ☐ Yes ☐ No
13. Does your company practice price lining? ☐ Yes ☐ No
14. Does your company practice odd pricing? ☐ Yes ☐ No
15. In order to avoid retaliation by competitors, have you tried adding extra service, providing warranties, or paying transportation costs rather than lowering prices? ☐ Yes ☐ No
16. Does your firm provide quality workmanship and efficient service, which are bases for your advertising? ☐ Yes ☐ No
17. Has your firm established an advertising program? ☐ Yes ☐ No
18. Have you considered these determinants of advertising:
    a.  The nature of your business? ☐ Yes ☐ No
    b.  Company's strategic plan? ☐ Yes ☐ No
    c.  Industry practice? ☐ Yes ☐ No
    d.  The media used? ☐ Yes ☐ No
19. Is your advertising program primarily of a continuous nature? ☐ Yes ☐ No
20. Do you use noncontinuous advertising to:
    a.  Prepare your customers to accept a new product? ☐ Yes ☐ No
    b.  Suggest new uses for established products to your customers? ☐ Yes ☐ No
    c.  Bring special sales to your customers' attention? ☐ Yes ☐ No

*Exhibit 10–1 (continued)*

21. Do you use your advertising to pave the way for your sales representative by making your company and product well known? ☐ Yes ☐ No
22. Have you developed an advertising budget showing the outlay of funds for advertising? ☐ Yes ☐ No
23. Do you use standard advertising ratios as guides for your line of business or type of industry? ☐ Yes ☐ No
24. Is your company's advertising set as a percentage of projected sales? ☐ Yes ☐ No
25. Have you decided to spend the major portion of your company's total advertising outlay on one of your products and to give only incidental advertising to others?
26. Do you vary your advertising expenditures seasonally? ☐ Yes ☐ No
27. Is your company's advertising truthful and in good taste? ☐ Yes ☐ No
28. Has your firm obtained assistance from suppliers and trade associations concerning your advertising program? ☐ Yes ☐ No
29. Are you attempting to measure the results of your advertising? ☐ Yes ☐ No
30. Before an advertisement is composed, do you consider what you expect the advertising to do for your firm? ☐ Yes ☐ No
31. In planning your ads, do you use these pointers:
    a. Identify your store completely and clearly? ☐ Yes ☐ No
    b. Select similar illustrations? ☐ Yes ☐ No
    c. Select a printing typeface and stick to it? ☐ Yes ☐ No
    d. Develop easily read copy? ☐ Yes ☐ No
    e. Use coupons for direct mail advertising response? ☐ Yes ☐ No
    f. Get the audience's attention in the first five seconds of a television or radio commercial? ☐ Yes ☐ No
32. Check which of these tests you use for immediate-response ads:
    ☐ Coupons to be returned to your store?
    ☐ Letters or phone requests referring to the ads?
    ☐ Split runs by newspapers?
    ☐ Sales made of the particular item?
    ☐ Checks on store traffic?
33. Do you attempt to evaluate the relative effectiveness of each of your advertising media? ☐ Yes ☐ No

**Sales promotion**
34. Check which of these sales promotion techniques you use:
    ☐ Special displays
    ☐ Premiums
    ☐ Contests
    ☐ Free samples
    ☐ Free introductory services
    ☐ Demonstration products
35. If you are a retailer, are your window and counter displays changed frequently? ☐ Yes ☐ No
36. If you are a manufacturer, are you using trade shows? ☐ Yes ☐ No
37. Are your sales representatives furnished with:
    a. Good sales kits? ☐ Yes ☐ No
    b. Up-to-date promotional materials? ☐ Yes ☐ No
    c. Catalogs? ☐ Yes ☐ No
38. If you are selling two or more products, are you promoting them:
    a. Jointly? ☐ Yes ☐ No
    b. Separately? ☐ Yes ☐ No

*Exhibit 10–1 (continued)*

**Using an advertising agency**

39. Are you aware that most newspaper advertising is developed by creative skills possessed by the newspaper staff?   ☐ Yes   ☐ No

40. Have you considered whether to have an advertising agency:
    a. Study your product or service to determine its advantages and disadvantages relative to that of competitors?   ☐ Yes   ☐ No
    b. Analyze your present and potential markets?   ☐ Yes   ☐ No
    c. Study your distribution channels?   ☐ Yes   ☐ No
    d. Evaluate your advertising media?   ☐ Yes   ☐ No

41. Does your advertising agency coordinate its work with your other sales activities?   ☐ Yes   ☐ No

42. Has your advertising agency assisted you in any of these areas:
    a. Package design?   ☐ Yes   ☐ No
    b. Sales research?   ☐ Yes   ☐ No
    c. Sales training?   ☐ Yes   ☐ No
    d. Preparation of sales and service literature?   ☐ Yes   ☐ No
    e. Design?   ☐ Yes   ☐ No
    f. Merchandising displays?   ☐ Yes   ☐ No
    g. Preparation of house organs?   ☐ Yes   ☐ No
    h. Public relations and publicity?   ☐ Yes   ☐ No

43. In selecting your advertising agency, did you interview several of its clients?   ☐ Yes   ☐ No

44. Did you select an agency which had experience in solving problems typical of those related to your products, markets, or channels?   ☐ Yes   ☐ No

45. Did you carefully evaluate your agency's:
    a. Research?   ☐ Yes   ☐ No
    b. Media?   ☐ Yes   ☐ No
    c. Financial management or cost accounting?   ☐ Yes   ☐ No
    d. Administration or account execution?   ☐ Yes   ☐ No

46. Is your agency free of undue control by anyone:
    a. Advertiser?   ☐ Yes   ☐ No
    b. Medium owner?   ☐ Yes   ☐ No

47. Are the terms of your contract with the agency clearly understood and written?   ☐ Yes   ☐ No

48. Has your firm arranged a minimum fee which compensates the agency for its time and efforts and allows a reasonable profit?   ☐ Yes   ☐ No

49. Does the agency understand your needs and wants?   ☐ Yes   ☐ No

50. Has your firm communicated to the agency:
    a. Product and company information?   ☐ Yes   ☐ No
    b. Company objectives?   ☐ Yes   ☐ No
    c. Company marketing strategies?   ☐ Yes   ☐ No
    d. The role of advertising in your company?   ☐ Yes   ☐ No

51. Is your agency's account team creative and conscientious?   ☐ Yes   ☐ No

52. Do you regularly and systematically review your agency's work with it and tell the agency where it stands?   ☐ Yes   ☐ No

53. If you are a manufacturer, have you decided whether to sell through agent intermediaries?   ☐ Yes   ☐ No

54. Are you aware that agent intermediaries are often effective under these circumstances:
    a. New manufacturer within a local or regional operation and having limited capital?   ☐ Yes   ☐ No
    b. Manufacturer expanding to new markets?   ☐ Yes   ☐ No

*Exhibit 10–1 (concluded)*

| | | | |
|---|---|---|---|
| 55. | Do you have your own sales representatives to sell your highly specialized technical products? | ☐ Yes | ☐ No |
| 56. | Does your sales force have adequate product knowledge? | ☐ Yes | ☐ No |
| 57. | Do your sales representatives adopt the sales approach to the customers' needs and meet their objections? | ☐ Yes | ☐ No |
| 58. | Do your sales representatives possess: | | |
| | a. Enthusiasm? | ☐ Yes | ☐ No |
| | b. Friendliness? | ☐ Yes | ☐ No |
| | c. Persistence? | ☐ Yes | ☐ No |
| 59. | Do you assign your sales representatives: | | |
| | a. To industry customers? | ☐ Yes | ☐ No |
| | b. To government customers? | ☐ Yes | ☐ No |
| | c. To institutional customers? | ☐ Yes | ☐ No |
| | d. By product classification? | ☐ Yes | ☐ No |
| 60. | Do you have a basic sales strategy with these features: | | |
| | a. Number of accounts per representative, and average account size? | ☐ Yes | ☐ No |
| | b. Compensation plan and method of payment of expenses? | ☐ Yes | ☐ No |
| | c. Comparison of costs of obtaining new accounts versus the costs of holding old accounts? | ☐ Yes | ☐ No |
| | d. Use of overlapping exclusive territories? | ☐ Yes | ☐ No |
| | e. Sales representatives who are either specialists or generalists? | ☐ Yes | ☐ No |
| 61. | Do you analyze your sales records to determine which: | | |
| | a. Products should be promoted? | ☐ Yes | ☐ No |
| | b. Products should be carried? | ☐ Yes | ☐ No |
| | c. Products should be dropped? | ☐ Yes | ☐ No |
| | d. Territories are overstaffed or undermanned? | ☐ Yes | ☐ No |
| | e. Customers are profitable? | ☐ Yes | ☐ No |
| 62. | Do you provide for continuous or special training programs for your representatives? | ☐ Yes | ☐ No |
| 63. | Do you hold regularly scheduled meetings with your representatives each year? | ☐ Yes | ☐ No |
| 64. | Do you use contests tied into promotions which stimulate your representatives several times a year? | ☐ Yes | ☐ No |
| 65. | Does your sales organization work closely and cooperatively with the manufacturing department? | ☐ Yes | ☐ No |
| 66. | Do you route your traveling representatives efficiently and make appointments prior to their arrival? | ☐ Yes | ☐ No |
| 67. | Do your sales representatives have high ethical standards? | ☐ Yes | ☐ No |
| 68. | Do you or does one of your managers support a representative when he experiences difficulties in obtaining a big account? | ☐ Yes | ☐ No |
| 69. | Do your long-term sales contracts with customers have protective escalation clauses incorporated into them? | ☐ Yes | ☐ No |

# Chapter Eleven

# Distributing and Selling Products or Services

This chapter on distributing and selling your product or service continues the discussion of the how-to-do-it marketing strategies begun in the previous chapter. It examines the channels of distribution, how to design a channel, and when to change channels. Then it deals with the use of intermediaries to sell your product or service.

In addition to all the efforts spent in market research, sales forecasting, and advertising and sales promotion, someone ultimately must do some personal selling of products or services. Salespeople must be selected and used properly. In retailing, self-service operations reduce the number of salespersons needed.

Personal selling is vital to a firm's success. Analysis of key characteristics of a good salesperson and of steps in the selling process provide guides to effective selling performance.

Finally, sales personnel need to be supported and controlled.

## Determining Channel(s) of Distribution

A marketing channel is the pipeline through which a product flows on its way to the ultimate consumer. The choice of channels of distribution is not a simple one but is important, as shown in these examples:

An independent firm manufactured perishable salads, which were sold direct to retail food stores. The salads required frequent delivery and close control to ensure freshness. The company diversified into two new lines: pickles and jelly. The manager selected the same marketing channel for these lines as for the salads. Because sales increased at the stores, expansion was necessary. As pickles and jelly had a longer shelf life, they could have been put into a separate, less expensive channel of wholesalers and chain warehouses.

A small manufacturer added an infant cereal to its product line and selected its existing marketing channel of drug stores.

> *Problem:* Consumers considered cereal a food item and bought it at food stores.
>
> *Solution:* The manufacturer started using food brokers as a channel.[1]

Some traditional channels of distribution for consumer goods are:

1. Producer → Consumer
2. Producer → Retailer → Consumer
3. Producer → Wholesaler → Retailer → Consumer
4. Producer → Agent → Retailer → Consumer
5. Producer → Agent → Wholesaler → Retailer → Consumer

The third channel is most often used by small manufacturers because they usually need the financial, promotional, and sales resources of large wholesalers. Distribution costs are lowest. However, a disadvantage to the manufacturer is loss of control of marketing, because title to the product passes to the wholesaler. The first channel gives the manufacturer complete control of marketing with potentially high sales volume, but distribution costs are the highest. Thus, in choosing a distribution channel, you make a trade-off between cost and control.

## Design Your Own Channel of Distribution

Channels should be tailor-made to meet the needs of the firm. For example, in order to obtain regional or national coverage of its products, a manufacturer may find it productive to use distributors or manufacturers' agents in conjunction with its own sales force.

*Factors to Consider.* You should establish a distribution plan that includes these factors:

1. Geographical markets and consumer types arrayed in order of importance.

---

[1]Richard M. Clewett, "Checking Your Marketing Channels," *Management Aids for Small Manufacturers No. 9* (Washington, D.C.: Small Business Administration, 1963), p. 38.

2. The coverage plan—whether distribution will be effected through many outlets, selected outlets, or exclusive distributors.
3. The kind and amount of marketing effort expected of each outlet.
4. The kind and amount of marketing effort you will contribute.
5. Policy statements concerning any areas of conflict.
6. Provision for feedback information.
7. Adequate incentives to motivate resellers.

New products commonly require distribution channels different from those needed for products that are well established and widely accepted.

A company started selling its new, high-priced germicidal toilet soap through drugstores and prestige department stores. When consumer acceptance made the soap a staple, the company began to sell it in food stores.[2]

A company may have new markets for its products, and new marketing channels may be required.

A paint manufacturer selected hardware and paint stores, its existing channel of distribution, to distribute a new household floor wax.
   *Problem:* The new product was reaching only a small part of the potential market.
   *Solution:* The manufacturer switched to food stores as the channel.[3]

If you are a manufacturer, your ultimate outlets should be willing to work with you on product promotion. You may arrange cooperative advertising with your dealers to share promotion costs. You should specify, in advance, criteria for selection of outlets and apply them.

Another problem a manufacturer may face is whether to ship directly from the factory or establish regional warehouses. The latter will provide more rapid service, but likely mean higher inventory-carrying costs. However, transhipments between warehouses may permit lower inventories.

***Avoid Multiple Channels.*** Multiple distribution channels sometimes create conflicts. Distribution can be adversely affected unless these conflicts are resolved.

A manufacturer introduced a ladder attachment and selected a large mail-order house as the channel.
   *Problem:* The company was incurring high costs by shipping

---

[2]Ibid.
[3]Ibid.

small quantities to many points. The manufacturer attempted to distribute the attachments through hardware stores.

*Results:* Hardware stores refused to sell the attachments, because the greater discount provided the mail-order house left them unable to compete.

In contrast, the manufacturer of do-it-yourself woodworking equipment selected a large mail-order house as the sole channel for a definite period of time. The manufacturer planned to sell through its customary channels later.[4]

## When to Change Marketing Channels

Changes in buyers' locations may dictate a change in marketing channels, as may changes in concentrations of buyers. Because of the rapid growth of markets in the far West and Southwest, many manufacturers in other parts of the country have stopped using agents and started selling directly to wholesalers and distributors.

The need to change your marketing channels may be revealed through examining the following indicators:

1. Shifting trends in the types of sources from which consumers or users buy.
2. Development of new needs relative to service or parts.
3. Changes in the amount of the distributors' profits.
4. Changes in policies and activities of each type of outlet according to customer types and areas, inventory, promotion, and advertising.
5. Changes in manufacturer's own financial strength, sales volume, or marketing personnel or organization.
6. New objectives concerning customer groups and marketing areas.
7. New products.
8. Changes in competitors' distribution plans.

## Some Techniques for Effective Use of Sales People

A firm's sales force should be organized on the basis of decisions regarding these features:

1. Number of accounts per representative and average account size.
2. Compensation plan—salary, commission, salary plus commission with bonus—and method of payment of expenses.
3. Cost of obtaining new accounts versus the cost of holding old accounts. This comparison determines the amount of time a representative should spend servicing accounts of a certain size.
4. Use of overlapping or exclusive territories.

---

[4]Ibid.

5.  Orientation of sales representatives as specialists in one of your products or lines, or as generalists who will handle your entire line.

Specialists are easier to train and are more effective in their fields. Yet, one generalist representative per customer may be less confusing. A small group of high-quality, highly paid representatives may be preferable to a large number of less-competent representatives. Owner-managers of independent businesses often find that only a few customers account for a major proportion of total sales.

> The owner of a company distributing supplies to an industrial market analyzed the firm's accounts and found that 2 percent of the customers accounted for half the total sales and more than half of the gross profits. More than 90 percent of the customers were small and accounted for less than 10 percent of the sales. An analysis of representatives' call reports showed that they were spending most of their time on the small accounts and that many big accounts with good sales and profit potential were neglected.[5]

Through analysis of sales records, you may find which products should be promoted, which products should be carried even though their profit margin is small, which products should be dropped, which territories are overstaffed or understaffed, and which customers are profitable.

You should provide for continuous or special training programs for your representatives and hold regularly scheduled meetings with them each year. To stimulate representatives several times a year, contests tied into promotions are often desirable. The effectiveness of contests may be improved when the rewards include benefits for the representatives' spouses. A guide for improving a representative's performance is presented in the appendix at the end of this chapter.

## Using Your Own Sales Personnel

### Manufacturing

Having your own sales representatives will require the greatest investment. Yet, in the case of a highly specialized, technical product, this course will probably be most effective.

*Selecting Your Sales Personnel.* One source of good salespersons is those who call upon you. You can look them over and

---

[5]Warren R. Dix, "Getting Facts for Better Sales Decisions," *Management Aids for Small Manufacturers No. 12* (Washington, D.C.: Small Business Administration, 1966).

watch them in action. Another source is the personnel whom sales-people call on.

> Pete Cassity worked as a clerk behind the cigar-candy counter of a high-volume drugstore. He received a bonus of 10 percent of sales price on certain brands of boxed candy. The regional sales manager of an independent chocolate company was so impressed with Pete's sales effort that he hired him as a factory sales representative.

If you advertise for personnel, avoid the "we want" approach. Rather, you should use the "we have an unusual opportunity for" approach. Prospective salespersons want to know how you can fulfill their needs. Since good salespersons are hard to find, you may have to overlook some negative qualities when hiring them. A mutually agreeable probationary period (perhaps six months to a year) should be set.

In evaluating applicants as possible salespersons, you should be wary of the following situations:

1. They have held too many jobs (and may be "floaters").
2. There are gaps in their employment records.
3. They have been involved in recent business failures.
4. They have had no previous sales experience.
5. Their income has not shown any steady advancement.[6]

***Needs for Harmonious Working Relationships.*** Your sales organization should work closely and cooperatively with the manufacturing department. The representatives' delivery promises and production's capabilities and willingness should be matched. There should also be good working relationships between your sales organization and market research.

Your salespersons should assist dealers through rendering advice concerning effective displays, improved store layout, and stocking new products.

You should determine whether your sales organization should place its best representatives in the most lucrative markets, to compete with your top competitors, or seek out untapped markets.

### Retailing

Sales expertise is particularly essential in a retail store. Advertising may entice a customer to come to the store, but it is not usually sufficient to complete a sale. Customers appreciate good selling and dislike poor service. They believe that salespersons should show an interest in them and assist them in their buying. Often,

---

[6]Gardiner G. Greene, *How to Start and Manage Your Own Business* (New York: McGraw-Hill, 1975), pp. 129–31.

when competing stores carry the same merchanise, the expertise of the salespersons is the principal reason why one outsells the other.

In a self-service operation, the customer walks into the retail store and is free to choose any desired product with little or no assistance from clerks. Self-service plays an important role in the marketing of groceries, drugs, hardware, and many other types of goods. It is particularly important in the marketing of staple goods for which customers do not require sales assistance.

Self-service puts the burden of preselling merchandise on the manufacturer because the retail store does little other than display it.

Some retailers have found that, of the shoppers who made unplanned purchases, 80 percent bought products because they saw them displayed. Packaging is also important because it provides sales promotion and protects the merchandise from damage and theft. Self-service reduces retail costs primarily because it results in smaller sales salaries and more effective utilization of store space. However, risks of pilferage, etc., increase.

## Personal Selling

Selling is vital to every firm's success. On the basis of a certain margin on sales, increased sales result in increased gross profits, which can cover greater operating expenses and still permit greater net income. You and your employees (clerks, salespersons, and service people) should be able to sell effectively.

### Key Characteristics of a Good Salesperson

One can conceive of many characteristics of a good salesperson, but here are a few key ones:

1. Effectiveness in speaking and in following the selling process (covered later).
2. Experience in selling for others.
3. Self-confidence.
4. Enthusiasm for the product or services and for selling.
5. Reasonable effort in selling.

### Personal interest

A friendly greeting and courtesy in attempting to determine a customer's needs are essential. The ability to call customers by name and to show a personal interest in them is important. Some customers want assistance in choosing the particular item that is tailor-made to meet their needs. Customers do not want to be high-pressured into making decisions.

Suggestion selling is an effective practice in retail stores. Perhaps a salesperson who has sold a particular item suggests related items the customer may need. Alternatively, a salesperson may bring out the benefits of higher-quality goods and entice the customer to trade up, explain savings gained from the customer's buying larger quantities, or suggest special bargains featured by the store.

### Steps in the Selling Process

As stated earlier, one key characteristic of a good salesperson—whether in retailing, wholesaling, service, or manufacturing, or whether an employee or an agent—is effectiveness in following the selling process. There are some well-defined steps in the selling process, as shown in Figure 11–1. They are prospecting, preapproach, approach, presentation, trial close, answering objections, close, and follow-up.

*Prospecting.* Prospecting involves identifying potential customers. Characteristics of a prospect are: availability of money or credit to buy; for a commercial account, the authority to buy; a use for the product or service. You and your salespersons have several sources for prospects, such as former or present customers, friends, neighbors, other salespersons, and nonsales employees in the company.

A salesperson for an automobile dealership can use the following sources of prospects for a new car: (1) individuals who have recently wrecked their cars, (2) prior customers who own two- or three-year-old cars, (3) garage repair records pertaining to people who have frequent troubles with their present autos, and (4) persons who have recently inherited money or obtained substantial promotions (identified from newspaper articles).

*Preapproach.* A preapproach investigation tries to qualify the prospects on the basis of their financial ability and their authority to buy, and to obtain information that will enable the salespersons to tailor the sales presentation to the prospect. Vital information about the prospect may include age, marital status, children, income, occupation, religion, education, friends, hobbies, political leanings, present buying plans, and attitudes toward the salesperson and products.

**Figure 11–1**
**Steps in the Sales Process**

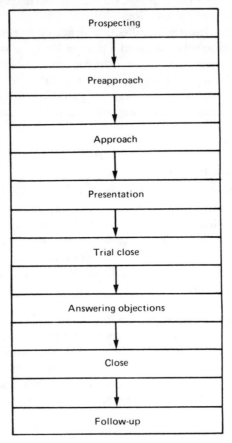

Prospecting

Preapproach

Approach

Presentation

Trial close

Answering objections

Close

Follow-up

**Approach.** The first thing to do is to try to get the prospect's attention and interest. This step is very important because it provides the prospect with the initial impression of the salesperson; that impression affects the prospect's future attitudes. The salesperson's appearance and actions are vital. Important characteristics are neatness, good grooming, greeting of the customer with genuine enthusiasm and courtesy, willing attitude, and interest in the customer's needs and desires.

**Presentation.** A critical step in the selling process is the presentation. You should begin optimistically, assuming that you will be successful. Inform the prospect of how the product or service fills the prospect's wants or needs. Describe the product or service, emphasize its advantages, and give examples of customer satisfaction. Show, tell about, and (depending on the merchandise) let the prospect feel, smell, or operate the product. The benefits of owning, using, and enjoying the merchandise should be stressed through the presentation.

*Trial Close.* A trial closing should be used during the presentation to determine whether the prospect is willing to buy the product or service. For example, an effective salesperson shows the prospect two differently priced home entertainment systems and asks, "Which one do you prefer?" Concerning a lady's blouse, another one will ask, "May I wrap it for you?"

*Answering Objections.* The prospect's objections commonly pertain to product features, cost, need for the product, timing of the purchase, or the company selling the product. These objections should be considered positively because they may show the prospect's interest and desire to obtain answers to questions before buying the product or service. A few typical objections (*O*), and responses (*R*) that may counter them, are:

1. *O:* Business is bad.
   *R:* With this system, your business will improve.
2. *O:* I don't need it now.
   *R:* Yes, but by buying it and working with it now, you'll be ready to use it when you need it.
3. *O:* It costs too much.
   *R:* Let me show you that the payback period is only four months.

*Close.* Another critical point in selling is closing, or asking the prospect for an order. Effective closing techniques used by salespersons are assuming or implying that the sale has been completed, asking the prospect directly, and proposing alternative purchases. One example is the salesperson who gives the customer a choice: "Do you want the coat delivered, or would you like to carry it yourself?" The salesperson may say, "Please check the order and if it's correct, please sign it." A clincher may be necessary, such as a premium for buying now.

A homeowner obtained quotations from three air-conditioning firms on a central heating-cooling unit. She preferred to buy from Firm A because of its reputation and better product. But the price was $500 higher than the other two. When he saw that he was losing the sale, the salesman said, "I was saving this for later, but our price includes complete warranty on parts and labor for five years. You won't have to put out one penny on the unit for five years."
     She gave him the order!

*Follow-up.* Follow-up consists of postsale activities, such as quickly completing the order processing, assuring the customer about the purchase, and checking with the customer to see that the product or service is satisfactory. Repeat customers are the mainstays of most firms, and an effective follow-up contributes toward obtaining and maintaining them. The car salesperson may call the buyer after a few days and ask how he or she likes the car or if it needs any service.[7]

Other useful pointers in increasing personal selling effectiveness are:

1. Break the prospects' preoccupation. Catch their attention!
2. Appeal to their emotions with customer benefits that make their desire grow.
3. Build the value. Show them that the value is far in excess of the investment (cost or price).
4. Ask committing questions that permit the customers to participate in selling themselves.
5. Present proof that builds the customers' confidence and influences their judgment.
6. Close. Show the customers why they should buy today; be ready with clinchers.

In order to improve your selling, at the end of each day review and analyze your sales attempts.

All sales should be recorded. This process gives you an opportunity to get the customers' names (so you can address them by name) and addresses (so you can send direct mail to them), and a series of sales tickets showing their purchases and indicating what they are buying. Numbered sales tickets should be used in order to reduce the possibility of employee dishonesty and to provide a basic business record needed for knowledgeable management and compliance with tax laws.

You should recognize the significance of customer relations—the total experience of customers with the firm. Word-of-mouth advertising results from it.

## Supporting and Controlling Sales Personnel

You should inform your salespersons of good news, such as high earnings or new large orders, prior to making the announcements to other employees. The sales force should also be informed of bad news such as product recalls, production problems, and poor sales and earnings. Also, communicate with them concerning plans for

---

[7]Richard H. Buskirk, *Principles of Marketing*, 4th ed. (Richardson, Tex.: Oak Tree Press, 1976), pp. 582–91.

new or changed products, facilities, or services, because this information can be beneficial in their interactions with customers. Furthermore, send copies of ads and publicity items to them for distribution to customers.

Either you or one of your top executives should support salespersons when they are experiencing difficulties in obtaining a big account. (Preferably, they should initially seek and request your assistance.) You should give them opportunities to be trained and promoted into management positions.

> A small manufacturer emphasized recognition as a tool in motivating his salespersons. He arranged for each member of top management to phone three different salespersons each month to thank them for their sales. This practice brought the managers and salespersons closer together; the latter then phoned the managers when they needed assistance.
>
> This manufacturer also mailed important quotations to his salespersons, in order that they could deliver them to customers and close sales. Furthermore, salespersons were not asked to be "delivery" persons, bad-debt collectors, repairpersons, or clerks. It was recognized that such assignments detracted from their earning commissions.

Rather than looking at details, you should utilize sales reports and stress major facts and trends to check performance. Reports show variances between budgeted and actual sales. You should investigate all excessive deviations upward or downward in order to find their causes. Long-term sales contracts should have protective escalation clauses incorporated into them, particularly under inflationary conditions.

You should check the progress of new salespersons within 90 days. If any are not producing half of what you realistically expected, you should consider terminating them.

To assist your sales manager in managing the sales force effectively, you should consider using the following techniques or forms: job descriptions for salespersons, market evaluation reports, loss-sales reports, product-service reports, and sales-performance evaluations.

## Appendix: Guide for Improving a Sales Representative's Performance[8]

One goal in measuring a representative's performance is to create improvement. The three steps in bringing about improvement are planning, measuring, and correcting.

---

[8]From Raymond O. Loen, "Measuring the Performance of Salesmen," *Management Aids for Small Manufacturers No. 190* (Washington, D.C.: Small Business Administraton, 1972).

## Planning

Get the representative's agreement about goals to be attained or exceeded in the next year:

1. Total profit contribution in dollars.
2. Profit contribution in dollars for each major product line, each major market (by industry or geographical area), and each of 10–20 target accounts (for significant new and additional business).

Get the representative's agreement about expenses for the next year:

1. Total sales expense budget in dollars.
2. Budget for travel, customer entertainment, telephone, and other expenses.

Have the representative plan the number of calls to accounts and prospects during the next year.

## Measuring

Review at least monthly the representative's record for: (1) year-to-date progress toward the 12-month profit-contribution goals, and (2) year-to-date budget compliance.

## Correcting

Meet with the representative if the record shows a shortfall of 10 percent or more from the target. Review the number of calls, plus major accomplishments and problems. In addition, you may need to help the representative in these ways:

1. Give more day-to-day help and direction.
2. Accompany the representative on calls to provide coaching.
3. Conduct regular sales meetings on subjects the representatives want covered.
4. Increase sales promotion.
5. Transfer accounts to other representatives if there is insufficient effort or progress.
6. Establish tighter control over price variances allowed.
7. Increase or reduce selling prices.
8. Add new products or services.
9. Increase the financial incentive.
10. Transfer, replace, or discharge representatives.

## Summary

It has been the purpose of this chapter to make you aware of the alternative possibilities when considering the distribution and selling of your products or services. In order for you to select the appropriate channels of distribution of your product(s) or service(s) you must be able to identify the ultimate customer. In this process you must consider and plan your sales approach.

# Exhibits

*Exhibit 11-1*
**Evaluating Your Channels of Distribution and Logistics, Setting Up Sales Territories**

The purpose of this questionnaire is to enable you and your management to determine whether your channels of distribution and logistics function are economical and effective, and to examine your procedure for setting up territories.

**Channels of distribution and logistics**

1. Do your channels of distribution meet the needs of your firm? ☐ Yes ☐ No
2. Do you use different distribution channels for your new products than for your well-established products? ☐ Yes ☐ No
3. In determining whether changes in marketing channels are necessary, do you examine the following indicators:
   a. Shifts in the types of sources from which consumers buy? ☐ Yes ☐ No
   b. The development of new needs relative to service or parts? ☐ Yes ☐ No
   c. Changes in the amount of the distributors' profits? ☐ Yes ☐ No
   d. Changes in the policies and activities of outlets? ☐ Yes ☐ No
   e. Changes in your organization? ☐ Yes ☐ No
   f. New objectives concerning customers and marketing areas? ☐ Yes ☐ No
   g. New products? ☐ Yes ☐ No
   h. Changes in competitors' distribution plans? ☐ Yes ☐ No
4. Have you established a distribution plan which includes these factors:
   a. Geographic markets and consumer types arranged in order of importance? ☐ Yes ☐ No
   b. Coverage through:
      (1) Many outlets? ☐ Yes ☐ No
      (2) Selected outlets? ☐ Yes ☐ No
      (3) Exclusive distributors? ☐ Yes ☐ No
   c. The kind and amount of marketing effort expected by each outlet? ☐ Yes ☐ No
   d. Policy statements concerning areas of conflict? ☐ Yes ☐ No
   e. Provision for feedback information? ☐ Yes ☐ No
   f. Adequate incentives to motivate resellers? ☐ Yes ☐ No
5. Have you decided whether to ship directly from the factory or to establish regional warehouses? ☐ Yes ☐ No
6. Do your outlets cooperate with you on product promotion and share promotion costs? ☐ Yes ☐ No
7. Have you specified criteria for the selection of outlets and applied them? ☐ Yes ☐ No
8. What are those criteria?

   _____

   _____

   _____

   _____

   _____

9. Are you giving each salesperson clear responsibility for a definite territory? ☐ Yes ☐ No
10. Are all prospective customers with sufficient potential for solicitation visited regularly? ☐ Yes ☐ No

*Exhibit 11–1 (continued)*

11. Is each salesperson assigned a reasonable overall task to perform? ☐ Yes ☐ No
12. Provided that the salesperson works effectively, does he receive a reasonable level of commission income? ☐ Yes ☐ No
13. Has your company assigned sales quotas for each salesperson? ☐ Yes ☐ No
14. Do you compare potential demand with the actual performance of each salesperson, territory by territory, and judge relative performance? ☐ Yes ☐ No
15. Does your company's routing minimize useless travel? ☐ Yes ☐ No
16. Do you have advance knowledge of your salespersons' activities to facilitate the budgeting of sales expense and performance of distribution cost accounting? ☐ Yes ☐ No
17. Are your customer relations improved due to the more regular calls and the attention to customer service your company provides? ☐ Yes ☐ No

**Territories**
18. Check which of these practices your company follows:
   ☐ Permits salespersons to handle a specified list of customers.
   ☐ Makes the salesperson responsible for a particular geographic area.
19. In setting up territories, do you observe these guideposts:
   a. Keep territory size practical? ☐ Yes ☐ No
   b. Plan efficient sales call routes? ☐ Yes ☐ No
   c. Use established geographic boundaries? ☐ Yes ☐ No
   d. Group counties by trading areas? ☐ Yes ☐ No
   e. Design territories for equal potential? ☐ Yes ☐ No
20. In establishing sales territories, do you go through this process:
   a. Secure information on the distribution of sales by counties, states, and trading areas? ☐ Yes ☐ No
      Develop an index of potential demand? ☐ Yes ☐ No
   b. Determine the percentages of potential sales your company can expect to obtain in each territory? ☐ Yes ☐ No
   c. Pinpoint on a map the location of customers and potential customers? ☐ Yes ☐ No
   d. Determine how many calls can be made, on the average, in one day? ☐ Yes ☐ No
   e. Group the customers into logical territories? ☐ Yes ☐ No
   f. Beginning with the city, bring together contiguous counties which constitute complete or partial trading areas? ☐ Yes ☐ No
   g. Recheck each territory in terms of the total business expected and of problems of physical coverage? ☐ Yes ☐ No
21. In order to establish sales territories in a new market, do you make a territorial analysis based on customer information and competitive data? ☐ Yes ☐ No
22. In modifying basic territories, do you consider these factors:
   a. Past sales? ☐ Yes ☐ No
   b. Sales potentials? ☐ Yes ☐ No
   c. Variations in product? ☐ Yes ☐ No
   d. Extent of market development? ☐ Yes ☐ No
   e. Channels of distribution? ☐ Yes ☐ No

*Exhibit 11–1 (concluded)*

     f.  Nature of the work assigned? ☐ Yes ☐ No
     g.  Competition? ☐ Yes ☐ No
     h.  Caliber of salespersons? ☐ Yes ☐ No
     i.  Changes in business conditions? ☐ Yes ☐ No
     j.  Possibilities of specialization? ☐ Yes ☐ No

23. Have you revised any territories for these reasons:
     a.  Shifts in population? ☐ Yes ☐ No
     b.  Changes in competitive pressure? ☐ Yes ☐ No
     c.  Changes in channels of distribution? ☐ Yes ☐ No
     d.  Excessive increase in selling expenses? ☐ Yes ☐ No
     e.  Unacceptable performance by salespersons? ☐ Yes ☐ No
     f.  Many unprofitable accounts solicited? ☐ Yes ☐ No
     g.  Deteriorating competitive position due to lack of product improvement? ☐ Yes ☐ No
     h.  Work loads too heavy on salespersons? ☐ Yes ☐ No

24. When you reduce the size of your sales territories, do you inform your salespersons of the conditions that led to the adjustment? ☐ Yes ☐ No

25. Do you use this procedure for revising territories:
     a.  Develop a list of all desirable present and potential customers? ☐ Yes ☐ No
     b.  Grade accounts for potentiality in purchase? ☐ Yes ☐ No
     c.  Translate potentiality data into call frequencies and develop standards on the number of calls needed for various account sizes? ☐ Yes ☐ No
     d.  Determine number of calls daily for each salesperson? ☐ Yes ☐ No
     e.  Expand or contract territories to fit salespersons' capacities? ☐ Yes ☐ No
     f.  Determine appropriate modes of transportation? ☐ Yes ☐ No
     g.  Determine where salespersons should live? ☐ Yes ☐ No
     h.  Devise various methods of control? ☐ Yes ☐ No

26. Do your salespersons, and possibly consultants, participate in territorial planning efforts? ☐ Yes ☐ No

27. Do you consult your salespersons about their routing patterns? ☐ Yes ☐ No

28. Are reports filed by the salespersons and checked by the sales supervisors? ☐ Yes ☐ No

29. Do you use route sheets which provide the name of the town, the customers to be contacted, and the objective of each visit? ☐ Yes ☐ No

*Exhibit 11–2*
**The marketing Mix, A Sales Analysis**

**Marketing Mix**

The purpose of this questionnaire is to aid you and your management in determining whether your company has the most appropriate marketing mix.

1. Have you developed a marketing mix consisting of these variables:
   a. Product? ☐ Yes ☐ No
   b. Place? ☐ Yes ☐ No
   c. Promotion? ☐ Yes ☐ No
   d. Price? ☐ Yes ☐ No
2. Have you:
   a. Developed the right product for the target market? ☐ Yes ☐ No
   b. Selected the appropriate channels of distribution? ☐ Yes ☐ No
   c. Selected the appropriate methods of promotion in communicating to the target market? ☐ Yes ☐ No
   d. Determined the right price? ☐ Yes ☐ No
3. After developing an integrated marketing strategy, have you checked it by getting affirmative answers to these questions:
   a. Are all marketing activities directed toward selling the same product and product image? ☐ Yes ☐ No
   b. Are trade-offs made so that each activity contributes the same net marginal benefit? ☐ Yes ☐ No
   c. Are programs, budgets, and schedules prepared at regular intervals? ☐ Yes ☐ No

**Sales analysis**

The purpose of this part of the questionnaire is to familiarize you and your sales manager with sales analysis.

**Developing long-range marketing strategy**

4. Have you engaged in sales analysis in order to determine:
   a. Past demand for your company's products or services? ☐ Yes ☐ No
   b. The relative importance of your customers or classes of customers? ☐ Yes ☐ No
   c. Your strengths and weaknesses in specific market areas? ☐ Yes ☐ No
   d. The relative success of your company in exploiting its markets, as compared with that of competitors? ☐ Yes ☐ No

**Developing short-term sales plans**

5. Have you engaged in sales analysis in order to:
   a. Forecast the coming year's sales, establish sales goals, and set efficiency norms? ☐ Yes ☐ No
   b. Point up the need for changes in your sales territories and in the size, dispersion, compensation, and training of your sales force? ☐ Yes ☐ No
   c. Control your sales efforts through appraising performance and comparing actual with planned sales of major product lines or individual products? ☐ Yes ☐ No

**Administering nonmarketing functions**

6. Have you engaged in sales analysis to help you in administering nonmarketing functions, such as:
   a. Production planning? ☐ Yes ☐ No
   b. Inventory control? ☐ Yes ☐ No

*Exhibit 11–2 (concluded)*

| | | | |
|---|---|---|---|
| c. | Purchasing? | ☐ Yes | ☐ No |
| d. | Cash management? | ☐ Yes | ☐ No |
| e. | Research and development? | ☐ Yes | ☐ No |
| f. | Traffic management? | ☐ Yes | ☐ No |
| g. | Facilities planning? | ☐ Yes | ☐ No |

# *Part 4*

## Profit Planning and Control

No business is stronger than its financial strength and vitality. Today, among the greatest requirements for success in smaller businesses are an appreciation of the importance of financial management, an understanding of financial relationships, and the devotion of time, energy, and initiative to these goals. The rewards are worth the effort, ensuring that the firm will not only survive but also will grow and develop.

In this part, you will study the procedures for analyzing and evaluating financial operations and positions in Chapter 12; the "how to" of maintaining adequate and accurate records in Chapter 13; the need for, and methods to use in, planning your profit in Chapter 14; and the procedures for budgeting and maintaining financial control in Chapter 15.

# Chapter Twelve

## Evaluating Financial Position and Operations

The material in this chapter should help you understand better some of the financial aspects of running your own company. Our main purpose is to help you learn how to set up an accounting system for a firm and how to read, evaluate, and interpret the accounts and resulting profit (or loss) figures. A secondary purpose is to serve as a guide in evaluating, or estimating, a firm's financial position. The material should also aid you in determining the value or worth of a firm. Finally, the chapter covers some important ratios that can serve as a guide in forecasting whether you will have successful or unsuccessful operations.

### Changing Status of Financial Position

The operations of a firm result from decisions made by its owner and managers and the activities performed by the employees. As decisions are made and operations occur, the firm's financial position is constantly changing. Cash received for sales increases the bank balance. The balance is decreased by purchases of material, which in turn increase inventory. At the same time, machines are decreasing in value, goods are being processed by employees, and utilities are being used. Consequently, the value of your firm is constantly changing.

Through it all, the important question is whether your company is improving its chances of attaining its objectives. One objective is to make a profit, but there are many problems involved. Some companies have made a profit and still have failed. Profits are not necessarily cash. Profits may be reflected in accounts receivable, and those accounts may not be collectible. Too much money may be tied up in other assets and not available to pay bills.

You may have this trouble with your personal finances. Your salary or income may be adequate to pay for food, clothing, and other operating expenses. However, you may need a new house or car, for which you must make a down payment in the form of cash. If your funds are invested in a fixed asset, they are not available to use to pay bills.

Your firm's accounting records must adequately and accurately reflect the continual changes in its assets, liabilities, income, expenses, and equity. You must make certain that the interrelationships among these accounts remain satisfactory. For example, what amount of cash reduces a firm's income-producing possibilities? An increased investment in building and equipment reduces your ability to pay operating expenses. Increases in liabilities increase your obligations and monthly payments. The continued operation of a company depends upon maintaining the proper balance among its investments, expenses, and income. These subjects are discussed in the balance of this chapter and are divided into two parts:

1. The meaning of each of the accounts and how it affects the company's operations.
2. Methods of evaluating a company's financial condition, and important ratios and their meanings.

We will use The Sample Company as an illustration as we go through the financial analysis.

## Financial Structure of the Firm

The financial structure of a firm is reflected in its assets, liabilities, and equity. These accounts are interrelated and interact with each other. The assets, liabilities, and equity accounts form the financial structure of a company at a point in time, but they tend to change from one period to the next. At regular intervals, a balance sheet is prepared to show the value of the company and how the funds are distributed. See Figure 12–1 for location of the following accounts on the balance sheet.

**Figure 12–1**

THE SAMPLE CO.
Balance Sheet
December 31, 19—

*Assets*

Current assets:
| | | |
|---|---:|---:|
| Cash .............................. | $ 3,527 | |
| Accounts receivable.................. | 30,242 | |
| Inventory .......................... | 40,021 | |
| Prepaid expenses .................... | 523 | |
|    Total current assets .............. | | $74,313 |

Fixed assets:
| | | |
|---|---:|---:|
| Equipment ......................... | 50,250 | |
| Building ........................... | 20,475 | |
| | 70,725 | |
|    Less reserve for depreciation ........ | 8,450 | |
| Net fixed assets ...................... | | 62,275 |
| Total assets .......................... | | $136,588 |

*Liabilities*

Current liabilities:
| | | |
|---|---:|---:|
| Accounts payable .................... | $25,674 | |
| Accrued payables .................... | 1,530 | |
|    Total current liabilities ........... | | $27,204 |
| Long-term liabilities: | | |
| Mortgage payable ................... | | 10,354 |
|    Total liabilities .................. | | $37,558 |

Net worth (equity):
| | | |
|---|---:|---:|
| Capital stock ....................... | $80,000 | |
| Retained earnings ................... | 19,030 | |
|    Total net worth ................ | | 99,030 |
| Total liabilities plus net worth ........ | | $136,588 |

## Assets

Assets are the physical, financial, or other values that a company has, and are divided into current and fixed assets.

*Current Assets.* Current assets are those that turn over—that is, they change from one form to another—within one year. For example, it is expected that accounts receivable will be paid and converted into cash within one year and that inventory will also be converted into sales within that period.

Cash is the first item of current assets. It includes the currency—bills and coins—in the cash register, the deposits in your checking account in the bank, and other noninterest-bearing values that can be converted into cash immediately. When cash is available, you can pay today's bills. It is the most liquid of any of the accounts.

A certain level of cash is necessary to operate a business. However, cash does not produce income. Accumulating too much cash means that the company reduces its income-producing capacity. Yet, you cannot pay bills if you do not have cash. Therefore, a certain level of cash must be maintained, but not too high a level.

Accounts receivable form a current asset that results from giving credit to customers when they buy your goods. Your company may sell entirely on credit, which helps it maintain a level of sales volume. This is a service that customers usually want. While extension of credit implies future payment by the customer, some customers—fortunately, only a few—do not pay their accounts. Care must be exercised to select customers who pay within a reasonable period of time. Policies should be set on the terms of payment and how much credit will be extended.

Credit is a cost to the company. Until the cash is actually received, the money cannot be used for paying expenses or buying other goods. Several means are used to circumvent this, including the following:

1. You may factor your accounts receivable. Under this arrangement, a company sells its accounts receivable and receives cash (less a fee).
2. Your company may honor one or more of the many kinds of credit cards. Under this plan, cash less a 2–6 percent charge is received when a charge slip is deposited with the credit card agency.

Note that both types of transactions make it easier to pay your company's obligations, but they also result in an expense to the company. This expense may be offset by increased sales (or maybe by reducing a loss in sales) and a reduction in the amount of assets needed.

Too large an investment in accounts receivable places the company under considerable financial strain. Investments of financial resources in the company must be increased, and the chance of your incurring a high expense because of bad debts is increased.

Inventory is an asset that provides a buffer between purchase, production, and sale of the product, as discussed in Chapter 8. A company must maintain some level of inventory to serve the customers when they demand or request a product. Some sales are made on the basis of availability. On the other hand, a customer may want a special item and be willing to wait until it is ordered and delivered.

However, there are costs resulting from carrying inventory. Your money is tied up, space is used, products must be maintained and can become obsolete, and so forth. Also, inventory as such is not an income-producing asset. The amount of inventory to carry depends upon a judicious balancing of costs. Too high a level of inventory places a financial burden on the firm.

Other current-asset accounts might include short-term investment, prepaid items, and accrued income. Usually, these are only a small percentage of the current assets and need little attention.

*Fixed Assets.* Buildings, machinery, store fixtures, trucks, and land are included among fixed assets. The company expects to own them for considerable time and writes off part of their cost as a depreciation expense each period.

Different types of fixed assets have different lengths of useful life. Land is not depreciated; buildings are usually depreciated over a period of 20 years; machinery over 5–10 years; and store equipment 2–10 years. The amount of fixed assets should be related to the needs of your company. Idle fixed assets are a financial drain and are avoided when possible.

Some companies find it advantageous to rent fixed assets instead of owning them. A retailer may rent a store to reduce the need to make a large investment. Whether you decide to rent or own your fixed assets will depend on the cost of rental, the per-period cost of owning, the availability of capital, and the freedom to operate.

## Liabilities

A company obtains its funds by borrowing (creating an obligation to pay) and by owner investment. The first results in a liability to pay someone; the second results in owners' equity. The total of the liabilities and the owners' equity always equals the total of the assets. A company is wise to maintain a proper balance between the higher risk of investment by creditors and the investment by owners. The investment by creditors is divided into current liabilities and long-term liabilities.

*Current Liabilities.* Current liabilities are obligations that are paid within one year. They include accounts payable, notes payable, and accrued items (such as payroll), which are services performed for the company but not yet paid.

Accounts payable are usually due within 30–60 days, depending on the credit terms. The delay in required payment is the service a vendor provides to the buyer. A company maintains current assets to pay these accounts. A check should be made to determine whether early payment is beneficial. Some companies offer a cash discount, such as 2 percent if paid within 10 days, for early payment. Maintenance of a high level of accounts payable requires a high level of current assets.

Notes payable, which are written obligations to pay, usually give the company a somewhat longer period before payment is required and usually require payment of interest. An example is a 90-day note.

**Long-Term Liabilities.** Bonds and mortgages are the usual types of long-term liabilities. A company contracts these when it purchases fixed assets when its owners do not have sufficient equity to pay for the assets. Also, long-term loans may be used to supply a base amount of working capital, which is current assets less current liabilities. Smaller businesses use long-term borrowing as a source of funds much less frequently than do large businesses. This type of borrowing requires regular payment of a fixed amount on the principal plus an amount for interest. The necessity of making these payments during slack times increases the risk of being unable to meet other obligations.

### Owners' Equity

Equity is the owners' share of a company after the liabilities are subtracted from the assets. The owners receive income from the profits of the company in the form of dividends or an increase in their share of the company through an increase in the retained earnings. They also absorb losses, which decrease the equity.

**Capital Stock.** Capital stock is the value the owners invest in the company. A share of stock is issued in the form of a certificate and has a stated value on the firm's books. Additional shares can be sold or issued in place of cash dividends.

**Retained Earnings.** Since a company usually does not pay out all its profits in dividends, some earnings are retained as protection for the firm or to provide for its growth. Retained earnings are the accumulation of the profits that are not distributed to the owners in cash dividends. Cash dividends reduce current assets. Many small firms have failed because the owners too quickly paid out the profits as dividends. A long-range plan for retention and distribution of earnings should be established.

## Profit-Making Activities of the Team

The financial structure of a company is changed by its profit-making activities. These activities are reflected in the revenue and expense

*Figure 12–2*

THE SAMPLE CO.
Profit and Loss Statement
January 1 through December 31, 19—

| | | |
|---|---:|---:|
| Net sales | | $231,574 |
| Less cost of goods sold | | 145,631 |
| Gross profit | | $ 85,943 |
| Operating expenses: | | |
| Salaries | $41,569 | |
| Utilities | 3,475 | |
| Depreciation | 5,025 | |
| Rent | 1,000 | |
| Building services | 2,460 | |
| Insurance | 2,000 | |
| Interest | 1,323 | |
| Office and supplies | 2,775 | |
| Sales promotion | 5,500 | |
| Taxes and licenses | 3,240 | |
| Maintenance | 805 | |
| Delivery | 2,924 | |
| Miscellaneous | 875 | |
| Total expenses | | 72,971 |
| Net income before taxes | | $ 12,972 |
| Less income taxes | | 3,242 |
| Net income after taxes | | $ 9,730 |

accounts (Net income = Revenue − Expenses). During a given period, the company performs services for which it receives values. The financial values exchanged are shown by the profit-and-loss statement (see Figure 12–2).

## Revenue and Expenses

Revenue is the return from services performed. Revenue is usually called sales income and is received by the company in the form of cash or credit—an obligation of the customer to pay. Many companies also have other income, such as interest from investments.

Expenses are the costs of performing services. They include materials, wages, insurance, utilities, transportation, depreciation, taxes, supplies, and sales promotion. These items become deductions from the revenue as they are used.

## Profit

Profit is the difference between revenue and expenses. Depending on the type of expenses deducted, profit is often classified as gross, operating, net before taxes, or net after taxes.

The values of these items are related to each other and to the structure of the company. Earlier it was stated that a company has fixed assets that are income producing. Are these assets being used efficiently? To answer the question, the relationship between the volume of sales income and the value of the fixed assets is determined and evaluated.

## Methods of Evaluating the Firm's Financial Condition

Now that we have considered the financial structure and operations of a company, we should consider the methods of evaluating its financial condition.

Look at Figures 12–1 and 12–2, which present the financial statements of The Sample Company. Is the company in a good financial position? In Chapter 14, we will consider a method of analysis called profit planning, which can be used to anticipate the position for the coming year. Now, however, we will evaluate the company on a broader basis. Out of this evaluation, changes can be made that may lead to a strengthening of the company's financial structure and to an improvement in its operations.

The evaluation of a firm's financial condition is based upon establishing relationships between two or more variables. For example, the amount of current assets needed depends on other conditions of a company, such as the size of its current liabilities. So, the current ratio—current assets divided by current liabilities—shows how easily a company can pay its current obligations. Another comparison can be made by subtracting current liabilities from current assets, with the resulting value called working capital. Unfortunately, no standard figures have been determined to be best to use, nor have any been found that can assure success. Yet, a reasonable evaluation is possible and necessary. Two sets of values that can be used for evaluation purposes are:

1. A comparison of the current value of ratios with those of the past.
2. A comparison of the ratios of your firm with other similar ones.

### Values of Each Ratio in the Past

A change in the value of selected ratios for a firm indicates a change in its financial position. For example, suppose the current ratio for The Sample Company has moved gradually from 1.0 to 3.0. The firm apparently has moved to a more liquid position and, therefore, looks good. However, this improvement may be due to keeping old, uncollectible accounts on the books. In this case, the company is not more liquid. While the trend does indicate a change, only in-depth analysis can determine the causes.

## Values of Other Like Companies

Average ratios and ranges of values for the ratios are published for a large variety of small to large companies. Some of these firms will fail, but the averages are ranges that provide a guide to what other companies are doing. Suppose the current ratio of companies with assets of $250,000 or less is found to be 2.3 to 1, while The Sample Company has a ratio of 3.0 to 1. Again, the company's ratio looks good. However, it may be losing income by maintaining too many nonproductive assets in a period of high interest rates.

In the past, a ratio of 2 to 1 has been used as a rule of thumb for the current ratio. However, no one value of a ratio is optimum for all companies.

# Important Ratios and Their Meanings

The ratios and percentages are valuable in answering a number of questions that you may ask yourself about your company. By obtaining answers to these questions, you can make plans to correct deficiencies in the operations and structure of your company. When a ratio is mentioned, look at Figure 12–3 for the method of computation of the ratio. Spaces are provided for you to compute the ratios for The Sample Company, using the data provided in Figures 12–1 and 12–2. Comparable figures for the industry are provided for comparative purposes.

## Are Profits Satisfactory?

Are you making an adequate or reasonable return on your investment? The ratio of net profit to net worth—often called return on investment (ROI)[1]—is used to evaluate this; but several other ratios should be considered to aid in profit planning and to make decisions.

How much return is your company making on its sale dollar? The ratio of net profit to net sales provides this information. Suppose The Sample Company makes four cents per dollar of sales. Is the trend up or down? How does it compare with the experience of similar companies? If it is dropping, why? Your costs may be

---

[1]The term *return on investment* (ROI) may be misleading, since some financial analysts consider ROI as a return on total assets.

*Figure 12–3*
**Ratio Computation Method for Evaluating Financial Position**

| Ratio | Formula | The Sample Company | Industry Average |
|---|---|---|---|
| 1. Net profit to net worth | $\dfrac{\text{Net profit before taxes}}{\text{Net worth}}$ | = _____ | 18.4% |
| 2. Net profit to net sales . | $\dfrac{\text{Net profit before taxes}}{\text{Net sales}}$ | = _____ | 3.1% |
| 3. Net sales to fixed assets ............. | $\dfrac{\text{Net sales}}{\text{Fixed assets}}$ | = _____ | 5.8 |
| 4. Net sales to net worth . | $\dfrac{\text{Net sales}}{\text{Owners' equity}}$ | = _____ | 7.5 |
| 5. Current ratio.......... | $\dfrac{\text{Current assets}}{\text{Current liabilities}}$ | = _____ | 1.3 |
| 6. Acid test .............. | $\dfrac{\text{Current assets} - \text{inventory}}{\text{Current liabilities}}$ | = _____ | 1.0 |
| 7. Receivables to working capital ............. | $\dfrac{\text{Accounts receivable}}{\text{Working capital}}$ | = _____ | 1.2 |
| 8. Inventory to working capital ............. | $\dfrac{\text{Inventory}}{\text{Working capital}}$ | = _____ | 0.4 |
| 9. Collection period...... | $\dfrac{\text{Accounts receivable}}{\text{Average daily credit sales*}}$ | = _____ | 43.0 days |
| 10. Net sales to inventory . | $\dfrac{\text{Net sales}}{\text{Inventory}}$ | = _____ | 22.0 |
| 11. Net sales to working capital ............. | $\dfrac{\text{Net sales}}{\text{Working capital}}$ | = _____ | 10.0 |
| 12. Long-term liabilities to working capital ..... | $\dfrac{\text{Long-term liabilities}}{\text{Working capital}}$ | = _____ | 0.7 |
| 13. Debt to net worth ..... | $\dfrac{\text{Total liabilities}}{\text{Net worth}}$ | = _____ | 1.6 |
| 14. Current liabilities to net worth .............. | $\dfrac{\text{Current liabilities}}{\text{Owners' equity}}$ | = _____ | 1.1 |
| 15. Fixed assets to net worth .............. | $\dfrac{\text{Fixed assets}}{\text{Owners' equity}}$ | = _____ | 1.2 |

*If 80 percent of sales are on credit: Average daily credit sales $= \dfrac{\text{Annual sales}}{365} \times 0.80 = \dfrac{}{365} \times 0.80 =$ _____.

increasing without an increase in price. Your competitors may be keeping their prices lower than yours. You may be trying to obtain a large sales volume at the expense of profit. An increase in sales volume with the same investment and net profit per dollar of sales will increase ROE, but if you reduce the return on a dollar of sales, ROE may decrease.

### Are Assets Productive?

Does your company obtain enough sales from its producing assets? The answer is reflected in the ratio of net sales to fixed assets—fixed assets representing the producing units of the company. This is only a general guide, for so many variables exist (such as leasing instead of owning fixed assets) that the ratio can change with changes in policies. Still, trends and good use of industry data make this a valuable ratio.

Does your company have enough sales for the amount of investment? The ratio of net sales to net worth provides a guide to this evaluation. Note that this ratio can be combined with the profit-to-sales ratio to obtain the ROE.

### Can Firm Pay Its Debts?

Can you pay your current obligations? A number of ratios can be valuable to you. The best known is the current ratio—the ratio of current assets to current liabilities. You may be making a good profit but not be able to pay your debts, for cash does not necessarily increase when you make a profit.

The acid-test ratio—that is, the ratio of current assets minus inventory to current liabilities—is used to make a further check.

Another check is obtained by using working capital, or current assets less current liabilities, as a basis. Working capital is the margin of safety a company has in paying its current liabilities.

The ratios of accounts receivable and inventory to working capital provide an insight into the riskiness of the company's ability to make current payments.

### How Good Are Firm's Assets?

How good are your current assets? Cash in hand is the best current asset. Accounts receivable represent what the company will receive in cash from customers some time in the future. However, the older an account is, the greater the expectation of loss. The collection-period ratio—accounts receivable to average daily credit sales—provides a guide to the quality of your accounts receivable. Suppose The Sample Company has set a 30-day payment period for its customers, and its collection-period ratio is 50 days. Many accounts are less than 30 days old, so many other accounts must be over two months old. Apparently, John Sample is not adequately checking on those to whom he extends credit, he is carrying bad accounts, or he is not exerting enough effort to reduce the slow payments of accounts. Periodically, each account in accounts receivable should be reviewed for its collectibility. A system of control of accounts receivable is discussed in Chapter 15.

Inventories can be evaluated in about the same way as accounts receivable. Goods in inventory become obsolete if not sold within a reasonable time. Therefore, inventory should be turned over during the year. The turnover rate is expressed by the ratio of the net sales to inventory. A company's turnover of inventory six times each year is good if turnover for the industry is five. If your company is turning over its inventory too slowly, you may be keeping obsolete or deteriorating goods. Too high a ratio may result from an inventory so low that it hurts production, or from not providing necessary customer services.

To obtain an idea of the support that a company is receiving from its current assets, the ratio of net sales to working capital is computed. Accounts receivable and inventory should increase with an increase in sales, but not out of proportion. Payroll and other expense increases require a higher level of cash outflow. On the other hand, too low a ratio indicates surplus working capital is available to service the sales.

### How Much Equity Should a Firm Have?

How much equity should your company have? Assets are financed by either equity investments or the creation of liabilities. Retained profits are part of equity and can be used to increase your assets or decrease your liabilities. You can maintain a high level of equity with a relatively low level of risk, or a relatively high level of liabilities with a higher expected return on equity.

Most smaller companies do not like to maintain a large amount of long-term debt. The risk is too great. The common ratios used for checking the company's source-of-funds relationships are:

1. Long-term liabilities to working capital.
2. Debt to net worth.
3. Current liabilities to net worth.
4. Fixed assets to net worth.

If any of these are extremely high, the company is in a risky situation. A bad year decreases the income, but the obligation to pay continues. On the other hand, a very good year results in large returns to owners. Positive financial leverage occurs when you earn more on a loan than it costs to borrow. Current high interest rates tend to discourage borrowing.

### Ratios Are Interrelated

More questions can be asked, and more relationships can be developed to guide you in analyzing your company's financial strengths and weaknesses. Each ratio is an indicator of only part of the firm's position. The ratios overlap because a company is a complex system and a change in the size of one of the accounts, such as cash, affects other values.

The financial ratios for the items on the profit-and-loss statement are usually expressed in percentages of sales. This information is usually hard to obtain from competing firms; when it can be, it can point to any out-of-line costs. High cost of goods sold as a percentage of sales income may indicate a poor choice of vendors, inefficient use of material or labor, or too low a price. A high percentage of salaries may indicate an overstaffing of the company.

## Summary

This chapter has provided a set of tools for analyzing your company's financial condition and operations. The financial structure of your firm is reflected in its assets, liabilities, and equity. It is reported in a balance sheet and is changed by the profit-making activities of the company. The results of these activities are shown in revenue and in many types of expense accounts, which are summarized in an income statement. The profitability of the firm is thus shown. By methodical comparison of various items in these financial statements, the financial condition and potential of your firm can be evaluated. The next chapter presents the accounting system needed to collect the values for the financial statements and their evaluation.

# Chapter Thirteen

# Maintaining Adequate— and Accurate—Records

Have you ever considered how many records you possess or generate? You probably have in your possession a driver's license, credit cards, a social security card, and/or a checkbook.

Without these items, you would be unable to transact much of your business. When you use one of these, records (or entries in the records) are generated. For example, suppose you use a credit card. This generates a sales slip, a bill, and a record of payment. You use the bill to write a check and to deduct the amount from your bank balance. At the same time you keep some information in your head to save time in filling out forms.

While this informal method may be all right for you as an individual, it is not sufficient for you as a business manager. Instead, you need a system of records to aid human memory. A business has a much more extensive set of records than an individual, because it has more transactions and more people are involved.

After finishing State University, Tobe Jackson and his wife decided to use their savings to open an independent trucking firm. Things progressed to the point that he was operating seven tractor-trailer rigs under contract to a major national corporation to haul eggs to New York and/or Chicago. In addition, he had obtained a special certificate to enable him to back-haul other agricultural products.

When Tobe's business became strapped for funds, he felt that if he could just get an SBA loan all would be well. The SBA referred

Tobe to a member of SCORE for counseling. The counselor asked Tobe to bring his most recent balance sheet and profit-and-loss statement.

The debt of $185,000 shown on the statements seemed an awesome sight, especially as the statements were three months old and the income statement revealed a substantial loss on operations. The counselors suggested that Tobe raise the gross contract prices by 10–15 percent and acquire a small computer to expedite accounting procedures. In this way Tobe could obtain current operating cost data and cut costs.

Tobe's response was, "I can't raise my prices, for my customers will give their contracts to someone else and I will be out of business." As Tobe and the counselor parted, it was obvious that Tobe would not raise his prices. Several months later, Tobe was no longer in the trucking business.

## Importance of Record Keeping

You have seen the amount of information needed to make personnel, production, marketing, and financial decisions. Much of the information needed for decision making is carried around in the owner's, manager's, or employees' heads. Certain types of information, however, are more valuable if brought together from a variety of sources, related in a systematic way, kept accurately, recorded permanently, and made available to the people who need them. A procedure is needed to provide the pertinent information in the proper manner.

Accurate and complete accounting information seems to become increasingly important as operations become more complex. We prefer to think of these data as management information. Yet, records still need to be kept in as simple and inexpensive a manner as possible—while providing the required information. How can this be achieved? By knowing what information is needed, by obtaining and storing information with little copying and recording, and by storing information for easy retrieval, you may achieve this.

Historically, accounting data have been developed to satisfy the needs of tax reporting and of reporting the condition of the firm to the owners. The emphasis has been on gathering and using historical data rather than on projective data to be used in the future. Yet, each category has its role. Thus, you need to ask questions such as: What decisions do I need to make? What information do I need to make these decisions? How can I best record and retrieve this information? The answers to these questions should serve as guidelines for establishing an accounting system and for selecting appropriate sets of processing programs and machines.

## What Information is Needed

In determining what information is needed, you should ask: For what purposes do I want the data? The usual answers are:

1. To plan lines of action. Past information can be used for planning the future. For example, plans can be built for the amount of goods to purchase (from sales trends), the number of salespeople to hire (from past sales per salesperson), and the amount of accounts receivable to expect (from past payment experience).
2. To meet obligations. For example, money is borrowed, material is purchased on credit, delivery is promised for a certain day at a certain price, and taxes are due.
3. To control activities. Many activities are routine but vital to the firm and can be checked by a clerk. For example, material ordered has not arrived, inventory has reached zero, losses in supplies are occurring, and too much time is being spent on routine work. By having guidelines and "warning flags," a clerk can perform the control function and save the manager's time.
4. To satisfy the government. For example, the government collects taxes; requires conformance to safety, fair employment, and price control standards; and checks on ethical standards of business practice.
5. To evaluate performance. Evaluation is obtained from review of selected records and reports.

In addition to determining the information needed, you must know how to use it. This involves classifying it into a usable form. The information for accounting purposes was classified in Chapter 12 as follows:

1. Assets.
2. Liabilities.
3. Owners' equity or net worth.
4. Revenue and expenses.
5. Profit.

Many other pieces of information are needed, including economic and market conditions, personnel histories and capabilities, sources of material, and specifications for products. Systems and procedures need to be established to assure the availability of critical information.

### Records of Service to Customers

These transactions provide both the income and an expense of doing business. When you perform a service—such as the sale of a product, repair of an auto, or rental of an apartment—either cash, a check, or a promise to pay is received in exchange for goods and/ or labor. Recording on slips and tapes is used to show the changes in the affected records. For example, the cash sale of a pair of socks increases your cash. Yet, it creates the obligation to pay sales tax and reduces your inventory of socks. See Figure 13–1 for a flowchart of the transfer of data, cash, and goods. A credit slip is used to reverse the above transaction when goods are returned.

**Figure 13–1**
**Accounting for Sales**

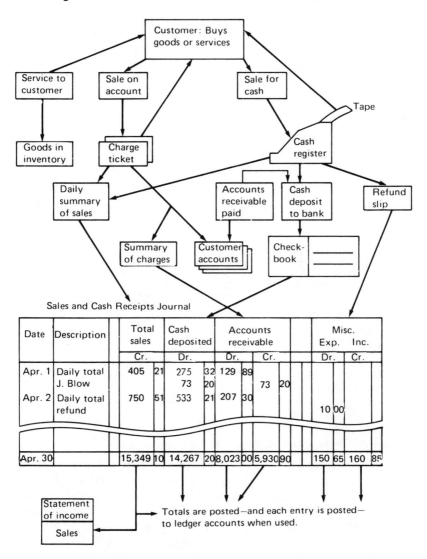

| Date | Description | Total sales | | Cash deposited | | Accounts receivable | | | | Misc. | | | |
|------|-------------|-------------|---|----------------|---|---------------------|---|---|---|-------|---|---|---|
| | | Cr. | | Dr. | | Dr. | | Cr. | | Exp. Dr. | | Inc. Cr. | |
| Apr. 1 | Daily total | 405 | 21 | 275 | 32 | 129 | 89 | | | | | | |
| | J. Blow | | | 73 | 20 | | | 73 | 20 | | | | |
| Apr. 2 | Daily total | 750 | 51 | 533 | 21 | 207 | 30 | | | | | | |
| | refund | | | | | | | | | 10 | 00 | | |
| Apr. 30 | | 15,349 | 10 | 14,267 | 20 | 8,023 | 00 | 5,930 | 90 | 150 | 65 | 160 | 85 |

Totals are posted—and each entry is posted—
to ledger accounts when used.

**Figure 13–2**
**Accounting for Purchases**

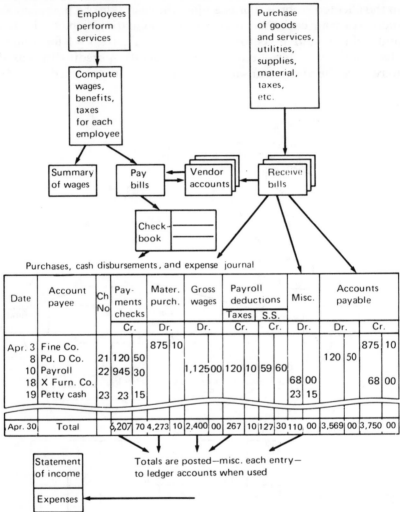

Purchases, cash disbursements, and expense journal

| Date | Account payee | Ch No | Payments checks Cr. | Mater. purch. Dr. | Gross wages Dr. | Taxes Cr. | S.S. Cr. | Misc. Dr. | Accounts payable Dr. | Accounts payable Cr. |
|---|---|---|---|---|---|---|---|---|---|---|
| Apr. 3 | Fine Co. | | | 875 10 | | | | | | 875 10 |
| 8 | Pd. D Co. | 21 | 120 50 | | | | | | 120 50 | |
| 10 | Payroll | 22 | 945 30 | | 1,125 00 | 120 10 | 59 60 | | | |
| 18 | X Furn. Co. | | | | | | | 68 00 | | 68 00 |
| 19 | Petty cash | 23 | 23 15 | | | | | 23 15 | | |
| Apr. 30 | Total | | 6,207 70 | 4,273 10 | 2,400 00 | 267 10 | 127 30 | 110 00 | 3,569 00 | 3,750 00 |

Totals are posted—misc. each entry—
to ledger accounts when used

## Records of Services Performed for You

These transactions originate your expenses of doing business. Materials, parts, and finished products are purchased to be transformed or sold. Employees are paid for work performed. Electricity is consumed, taxes are paid, advertising promotes the products, and supplies are used. Also, the service performed may increase the assets of the company—for example, through the acquisition of equipment and machinery, buildings, and stock. A somewhat different type of service fitting this category is the floating of bonds to obtain cash or credit. All these types of transactions generate obligations and initiate transfers of all data within an accounting system, as shown in Figure 13–1 and Figure 13–2.

### Records for Other Activities

Many matters of a non-accounting nature initiate other records. Sources for these include inquiry letters, agreements on sales, complaints, and implementation of controls over physical units.

## Recording the Information

All transactions involving accounting information must be recorded. Some very small firms use a single-entry system for its simplicity. This type of system records a transaction only in one place: a sale for cash is recorded as cash income. This type of system does not provide much information or control. Your use of a double-entry system of accounting requires that a transaction be entered in two places so that your accounts will be in balance. When a sale is made for cash, income is increased and cash—an asset—is increased by the same amount; inventory of the item is decreased and material expenses increased. When material is purchased on credit, inventory—an asset—is increased and accounts payable—a liability—is increased by a like amount. A machine wears out. So periodically, depreciation is deducted from assets, and expenses are increased by the same amount.

In all of these transactions, notice that the changes are made so that:

$$\text{Assets} + \text{Expenses} = \text{Liabilities} + \text{Equity} + \text{Income}.$$

The amounts of the sums may change, but they change by the same amount.

### How a System Operates

The accounting system starts with tapes or other initial records and includes journals and ledger accounts. The journal is the original book of entry; it records the daily transactions in chronological order. To group like items together, the chronological entries are entered individually or as totals in ledger accounts. A ledger account might be set up for each of the accounts listed in Figure 14–1. The amount of detail depends on the needs of your company and its other records. For example, journals and statements may be used to show the income and expenses, whereas only the profit—the difference between income and expenses—is shown in a ledger account. Under all circumstances, the ledger accounts must balance.

Figures 13–1 and 13–2 diagram the flow of data for some of the more common entries in the accounting records of a small business. The following sections discuss some transactions and entries to help you understand the system of recording information. The month is used for the adjustment time period to emphasize the need for frequent review of the results of your operations. (Some of the formal accounting illustrated may be performed only once a year, often by an accountant. But the examples illustrate the concepts.)

## Sales

The sale of products or the service performed is the source of profit. In every company, a record must be kept of each sale made. An auto repair shop makes a record of the charges to the customer for labor hours and parts used. A sales slip is completed when a radio is sold. The number, type, unit price, and total price of the radio should be entered on the slip. On all items sold, the sales tax must be recorded. Cash sales, when cash registers are available, can be recorded on a tape to be used as the sales slip.

Information on the sales forms is used to accumulate the sales income, to reduce inventory, to make analyses for future plans, and—in the case of a credit sale—to enter in the accounts receivable record for the customer. To eliminate the totaling of sales slips, cash registers that total the daily sales can be used. When many different items and people are involved, the registers can total by variables including type of product, salesperson, or department. Classifications should be aligned with the types of analyses you will make and with the controls to be exercised.

Sales are entered in a sales journal. This shows the daily summary of all sales or of the individual items sold, depending on the detail desired. The sales journal can be multicolumnar paper to record additional information, such as how much was sold for cash (or credit card and account) in each department, how much was sold of each type of product, and how much by each salesperson. If you analyze this sheet, it can provide information on sales trends, where the major volume is, or who is selling the most. Figure 13–1 provides an illustration of a sales and cash receipts journal.

The totals of the columns of the sales journal are transferred to the income statement and/or the sales-income ledger account.

## Cash Income and Outgo

When sales are made, the total of the recordings for cash, credits, and other values must equal the recorded sales income in order to balance the accounts. The accounting for cash is most important, as cash is negotiable anywhere. The recording system for cash should be designed and established with care so as to minimize mishandling and consequent losses.

When sales are made for cash, the goods sold and the cash received should be recorded independently of each other—if possible. Also, in order to maintain control, only certain people should be allowed to handle the cash and only on an individual basis. Each person starts with a standard amount for change, and the cash balance is reconciled each day or more often. The reconciliation makes sure that the cash on hand equals the beginning cash on hand plus cash sales less cash returns.

> A waitress makes out the bill for a customer at a restaurant, and a cashier receives the money. At a gas station, gas pumps record the total gallons pumped, the price, and the total amount of the sale; and the attendant collects the cash. The cash register, placed in view of the customer paying a bill, allows the customer to check the cash recording.

Checks are not as negotiable as cash but are handled with the cash. One extra step is required. To guard against losses from bad checks, a method is established to identify the person presenting the check. Past experience with payment by check often determines the policy to follow. Some companies accept only cash; some require identification such as a driver's license or social security card, the number of which is recorded on the check; and some accept the check without formal identification. A proper balance should be maintained between safeguarding against losses and making the customer feel that a personal service is being performed.

At the end of each day, standard amounts of money are retained to make change the next day, and the rest is deposited in the bank. Deposit slips are forwarded to the bank with the money, and the amount deposited is added to the checkbook stub balance.

Payments are made by check or, for small items, from petty cash. The checkbook can be used as a ledger account by adding bank deposits and deducting each check on the checkbook stubs. Each check is entered in the cash journal to show the account to which it is charged.

It often becomes too expensive to pay small bills by check (for example, payments of $5 and under). A petty cash fund—say, $25 or $50 in cash—can be used to pay these bills. Each payment should be recorded on a form to keep track of the account and the amount paid. The sum of amounts on this record plus the cash in the account should always total the figure set for the size of the fund. Periodically, the fund is replenished by check to the set figure, and the recorded expenditures transferred to the appropriate accounts in the cash journal.

## Accounts Receivable

When customers buy goods using credit cards or open accounts, each sales slip is entered on a customer account record or is filed under the customer's name. These records are details of the accounts receivable account and are totaled periodically to compare with the account. Any differences should be investigated. At the end of each period (usually a month), each customer's account should be totaled and a bill sent to the customer. As payments are received, the amounts of the checks are recorded in each customer's account and totaled for entry in the sales and cash receipts journal. A discussion of the decisions regarding credit is included in Chapter 15.

Periodically, a review of the individual accounts receivable records provides information about the status of the accounts, which ones are slow in paying, and which accounts need follow-up. (The follow-up methods include delinquent notices, personal contact, and use of a collection agency. Some should be written off by charging them to bad debts when they cannot be collected.) Other information can also be obtained, including identification of your large customers, what kinds of items they buy, and who has stopped buying from you.

Credit card sales are totaled by each credit card company and, after service charges are deducted, are processed through the bank. Gross sales are entered as sales income, as are accounts receivable and cash sales; the service charge is charged to that account; and the accounts-receivable or cash account posted, depending on the procedure.

Some transactions—such as installment sales, handling damaged or lost goods, and settling insurance claims on damaged equipment—require more complex accounting procedures than are being presented. For these, we recommend consulting with an accountant or studying an accounting text.

## Accounts Payable

An operating business incurs many obligations for material and equipment purchases, wages, utilities, taxes, and notes payable.

These are reported in a purchase and cash disbursements journal. Almost all purchases are paid by check, and the number of individual payments is relatively small.

Bills and invoices may be filed by date to be paid and, after payment, filed as a history of accounts payable. As each initiating record is received, it is entered in the purchases and cash disbursements journal, as shown in Figure 13–2. Notice the columns used to classify the expenses and the "Miscellaneous" column used for expenses or assets for which there are few bills each month. Columns are used for accounts in which many entries occur during a month. Each month, for example, many purchases are made of a variety of materials, products, parts, and supplies for which one or more columns are provided. Few purchases of office equipment are made in a year, so they are handled in the miscellaneous column. Utilities might warrant a separate column. As a payment is made, the bill is marked and filed, and the amount is entered on the check stub and in the purchases and cash disbursements journal. As with accounts receivable, there are complex transactions about which you should consult an accountant or an accounting book.

### Inventory

One of the troublesome records to keep is that for inventory. The problem of inventory was discussed in Chapter 8. A number of methods are used to assist managers in maintaining records of their stock. All are based on a systematic method of spotting a low-inventory item—that is, there are some methods that help "wave a warning flag" when the inventory is below a predetermined standard. These methods include setting aside the standard amount, setting aside an amount of space, making a regular physical count of the items, and (for bulky material) flashing a light. A business selling a high volume of many items,[1] like a grocery store, depends on visual inspection of the number of items on the shelf by several people, each assigned to certain items. For slower-moving and fewer items, the paperwork is not increased very much by keeping a perpetual inventory record (see Figure 8–4). All the methods require establishing the minimum or standard amount left in inventory before ordering.

A record is made of the sale and the physical movement of an item when it is sold. Recording its removal to expense is handled in two ways. First, for high-volume items, the purchased items are

---

[1]Today, computer-related wands and computer tape cassette machines are frequently used to take physical inventory in groceries and in similar merchandising operations.

charged directly to expense. At the end of the period, the inventory is obtained by a physical count of the items. Holograph scanners at grocery checkouts record sales and make inventory adjustments in the businesses' computer. The inventory value is added to assets and deducted from the expense.

The second method uses perpetual inventory recordings described above, with added columns for dollar values of units. The total cost of units used is the material expense. This method is usually used by manufacturing companies.

*Costing Inventory.* Costs of materials and products used and sold are charged to cost of sales. The prices of these items may change frequently, so the method of charging costs is important when goods are in inventory for more than one period. The most commonly used methods to compute costs charged are:

1. First in–First out (FIFO). This method is like "first come first served." It charges sales with the cost of goods received first; inventory is charged at the cost of goods received last. When prices are rising, this method tends to inflate computed profits.
2. Last in–First out (LIFO). This method is like "last come first served." It charges sales with the last or current cost; inventory is valued at the first or old cost. When prices are rising, this method understates the value of inventory.
3. Average costs. This method averages the price of all items on hand and then charges the average cost to sales. This procedure requires considerable calculating, but the use of a computer makes it feasible.

For tax purposes, the Internal Revenue Service (IRS) requires new businesses to select a method of valuing or costing inventory. From year to year, any changes in methods must be approved by the IRS.

### Expenses

Your business purchases services from other businesses, and these become expenses. Material is transformed and sold, electricity is used, machines decrease in value, and insurance protection elapses. The bases of payments for these costs of doing business vary from daily to over five years, and an item's use may be delayed for years. In order to determine your true profit, income and expenses must be determined for the same period, say for each month.

Many independent businesses compute their profit on a cash basis rather than on an accrual basis. But services are not always performed at the same time as cash payments are received; an example is sales on credit. On an accrual basis, adjustments are made to reflect the income and expenses of services for a given time period. Using the cash basis, items are charged as they are actually paid. The cash basis is used for simplicity and, as will be seen, is not a pure cash procedure. The cash basis assumes that payments and use occur in the same period or that payments do not vary from one period to another. The analysis of the method to choose should balance the validity of the result against the cost of getting a more accurate picture.

*Taxes.* Taxes are discussed separately because of their importance and complexity. An independent firm normally must account for and pay most of the following taxes:

1. Sales.
2. Property.
3. License.
4. Value added.
5. Corporate income.
6. Social Security.
7. Unemployment insurance.
8. Individual income.

Each tax must be computed according to the latest regulations, and these regulations change frequently. Some taxes are costs to the firm; others you are collecting from employees or customers. Some tax expenses may increase if you improperly handle such items as depreciation, inventory, and write-offs of losses. The large number of calculations for payroll, including taxes, makes payroll accounting complex. You are advised to study state and federal tax regulations carefully or to consult with a qualified tax accountant before designing your accounting system and paying the taxes.

*Procedure for Using Accrual Method.* The procedure for obtaining the expenses by the accrual method is:

1. Obtain the values of all assets, payments, and obligations.
2. Determine how much of each has been used during the period.
3. Transfer the used portion to expense, reduce the asset, or increase the obligation.

*Examples of the procedure.* A number of examples of this procedure are on following page. (See Figure 13–3 for sample recordings of each.)

Maintaining the original cost of machinery and equipment in the records is valuable. The cost of using the machine, which is called depreciation, is an estimate, and the reduction in value for depreciation is kept in a separate account called reserve for depreciation.

Many other items of expense and income need the same types of adjustment as just discussed. The main points to determine are: How much of the cost is used up during the period? How much is an asset? How much is a liability? Find the easiest way of assigning the proper values to expenses, income, assets, and liabilities. These records can then be used for analysis and for making reports.

**Figure 13–3**
**Examples of Recordings and Adjustments of Transactions**

1. Receive order for material X, $100, entered when received.
   Used $80 of material X, entered at end of period.

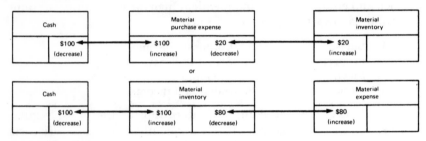

or

2. Paid insurance policy, $75, entered when paid.
   Monthly expense of insurance, $50 (1/12 of annual $600), entered
   at end of period.

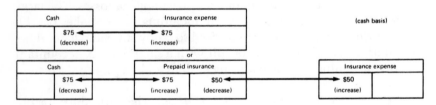

or

3. Paid wages, $4,000 (160 hours x $5.00 per hour x 5 workers) (from
   payroll book). Wages paid for last month's work, $800 (32 hours
   x $5.00 per hour x 5 workers). Work not paid this month, $1,000 (40
   hours x $5.00 x 5 workers).

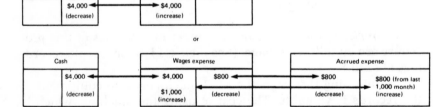

or

4. Have machine which cost $1,300. From machine records, machine
   expense, $20—machine cost, $1,300 less estimated scrap value,
   $100—divided by estimated life, 5 years (60 months).

1. Material for sale in a retail store. The expense of material equals beginning inventory plus purchases minus ending inventory.
2. Insurance. Insurance may be paid monthly, quarterly, or annually for the period ahead. Usually, annual payments reduce the cost, and by spreading the payment of different policies over the year, payment can be distributed to different months. Insurance is usually charged to expenses when paid and, for monthly statements, one twelfth is charged to expenses and the remainder of payments placed in an asset account for prepaid insurance. This adjustment is not necessary when the monthly payment is close to one twelfth the annual cost. The latter is a cash-basis type of accounting.
3. Wages and salaries. These expenses are paid regularly after the employees have performed a service for the business. Since salaries are paid at the end of the month, they are counted as expenses of the month and need no adjustment. When wages are paid every two weeks, the payment is for the past two weeks, which often covers work in the previous month. At the end of the month, wages usually have not been paid for part of the month, and so a liability exists for accrued wages. Adjustments between labor and accrued wages must be made. Subsidiary records are kept to compute the wages, salaries, employee benefits, and company payments for social security and so forth.
4. Machinery, equipment, and buildings. These are used up over a period of years. On a monthly basis, the expense of a machine may be calculated according to the following expression:

$$\frac{\text{Cost of machine} - \text{Sale value at end of expected life}}{\text{Expected life (in months)}}$$

This figure remains constant until the assets are sold, added to, or used up.

## Financial Statements

During each period—on a daily or weekly basis—a check should be made of a few critical accounts, such as sales, for trends and other changes that are occurring. This enables you to anticipate adjustments that may be needed. Shortages or overages of stock may be detected.

Financial statements are prepared from accounting records to aid management in this analysis. They are a profit-and-loss statement and a balance sheet (see Figures 12–1 and 12–2). The accounts are grouped so that a financial analysis can be performed, as discussed in Chapter 14. Profit-and-loss statements should be prepared monthly and balance sheets less often, perhaps semiannually.

Tax reports are completed for the various government divisions many times during the year. These include reports for income, sales, social security, and excise taxes.

## The Role of Computers

Prior discussion has been based on manual and calculator processing of accounting data. However, computers are rapidly taking over the roles of bookkeepers and clerks as computer capabilities expand and costs go down. The use of minicomputers and time-sharing on large systems can provide data more accurately, and in less time, than many manual operations. As your business grows, use of computers can provide many benefits.

### What Is a Computer?

A *computer* is different from a calculator in that its program, rather than a person, directs the processing and in that it can store information or data. Of course, a person needs to activate the computer and insert data. But the total computer system is integrated so that it can receive data, recall previously stored data, call a program, process the data, present results, and store data rapidly, accurately, and without further human help. Computers have the capacity to provide large amounts of information needed for decision making.

Computers receive data, process the data according to instructions and/or programs, and store, print, or display results. The hardware—machines and related equipment—performs the processing. The software includes programs which direct the machines. A large variety of programs are available to direct computers to do a wide variety of processing. Programs designed to perform desired computations may be purchased from computer companies or written by qualified people.

### Use of Computers in Independent Firms

Computers are being used by independent firms for a wide range of purposes. Some of the more frequent uses are for processing data related to sales, cash, payroll, inventory, accounts receivable and payable, and financial analysis. Also, they are used for directing machines (numerical control), collecting and processing data for planning (forecasting), and improving productivity (composing [type], scheduling, and controlling). They are particularly economical for operations that are repeated many times.

***Example of Computer Use.*** To illustrate the use of a computer, let us look at Figure 13–1, "Accounting for Sales." Say a customer buys an item on credit. The salesperson punches in the number of the item and the customer's account number. The computer processes this information, using stored data. The customer's credit is checked. If the sale is accepted, a tape or bill of sale is printed with desired detail and bill total. The item is deducted from inventory, and the amount of sale is stored in the computer. If the inventory of the item drops too low, the computer notes this. At some future time, desired data (such as total and average daily sales, accounts receivable overdue, actual and budgeted expenses, purchases needed, and taxes due) are displayed for analysis and action.

*Computer versus Manual Operations.* The above illustration assumes the use of a fairly comprehensive system for a sale and for processing other data. It may not be economical for a small company to have such a complete system. Therefore, part of the process may be computerized and part manual. On the other hand, added capabilities may be warranted. For example, the use of an electronic wand, holograph scanners and uniform product codes on items reduces the need for punching in information on items sold at checkout stations and when taking physical inventory. You must analyze the costs of the various parts of your systems, using manual and various computer systems, before deciding on the best system for your firm.

### Owning versus Leasing a Computer

The choice of owning or leasing a machine or of having the processing done outside depends on the volume and type of work to be done, personnel, and costs. Computers vary as to types of inputs, logic systems for processing, and outputs. A small computer can be purchased for as little as $2,500. Larger systems cost more but have greater capabilities. The decision on whether to lease depends on the monthly lease cost as compared to purchase and service cost. Also, do you have money available now for the purchase investment?

When changing from manual to computer processing, decisions must be made as to whether a new accounting or other system must be designed and whether standard or specially designed programs are to be used. You should obtain help from technically qualified people such as consultants, accountants, and/or sales representatives in revising or initially installing a system for processing data. Continual review is necessary.

Information that has future use should be properly stored. Critical records should be stored securely (such as in safes) so as not to be lost, stolen, or destroyed. Other information accumulated for daily decision making should be stored for easy and quick access—for example, in the memory system of a computer. Memory systems contain many pieces of data that must be guarded against loss and misuse.

## Job Costs

Not only should you know the costs for a period, but also the cost of units or jobs to determine how profitable each is. Estimates and/ or standards of material, labor, and overhead are used to establish

*Figure 13–4*
**Job-Cost Record**

| DIRECT MATERIALS | | | DIRECT LABOR | | | APPLIED OVERHEAD | | |
|---|---|---|---|---|---|---|---|---|
| DATE | REQ. NO. | AMOUNT | DATE | TIME CARD NO. | AMOUNT | BASIS | RATE | AMOUNT |

JOB COST RECORD

FOR _____ ORDER NO. _____

PRODUCT _____ QUANTITY _____

DATE WANTED _____ DATE STARTED _____ DATE COMPLETED _____

SUMMARY FOR ORDER NO _____

DIRECT MATERIALS _____

DIRECT LABOR _____

APPLIED OVERHEAD _____

TOTAL FACTORY COST _____

FACTORY COST PER UNIT _____

Source: From R. Lee Brummet and Jack C. Robertson, "Cost Accounting for Small Manufacturers." *Small Business Management Series* No. 9, 2d ed. (Washington, D.C.: Small Business Administration, 1972).

planned costs for bidding and pricing of a product. Actual data are collected from material requisitions and time tickets, and costs for a job or product are calculated on a job-cost record (Figure 13–4). Comparison of the planned and actual costs provides a basis for analyses of operations and prices.

## Summary

How we hate to keep records! Yet, record keeping is essential for survival as an independent business or even as an individual, especially at income tax preparation and auditing times.

Considerable detailed, specific, and practical material was furnished in this chapter that should be of help to you in coping with this problem. Specifically, we made suggestions for dealing effectively with (1) deciding what information is needed, (2) locating sources where information can be found, (3) recording information in appropriate places, (4) choosing the processing equipment, and (5) storing information where it can be retrieved when needed.

We also provided tables, figures, journals, and statements to serve as guidelines for you to use in your business.

# Chapter Fourteen

# Planning for a Profit

Profit cannot be left to chance. All too frequently, however, that is what actually occurs. We have observed in the past that even in those rare circumstances where an effort has been made to plan for profit, it has been on a casual basis. It has been assumed that historical relationships are fixed and, therefore, profits will continue.

It is now becoming increasingly important that the independent business owner-manager recognize the need to identify all the cost factors. If profit is to be made, then it becomes essential that each item be broken out and costed with a final increment of profit added.

A recurring problem among independent business owners, as well as others, is the lack of accurate cost information, which usually results in profit of unknown quantity—or even a loss. Also, there is often the illusion that the amount of profit is greater than it really is. Such was the status of things in the two examples that follow:

A phone call from Children's Party Caterer to a consultant on small business set in motion a series of conferences concerning the catering business.

During the first interview, the caterer said she had "around $400 of party materials" in her pantry at home. But, when discussing the amount of time that was involved or the cost of materials used in preparing for each party, she was vague. The consultant gave her a "homework assignment" to determine the time she spent preparing for and giving each party, and the cost of materials. Her homework findings were revealing, if not pleasant. She found she spent 19–20 hours per party; the cost of materials per party ranged from $20 to $25; she had not computed transportation costs or the $5–$6 baby-sitting cost for her two children. Yet, the average fee charged per party ranged from $20 to $25.

When it was suggested that she raise her prices to cover these costs plus a profit, her response was, "People won't pay it." When the consultant responded, "You aren't in the charity business," her exuberant reply was, "Oh! But I like to do it."

For several years, the owner of a compounding company expressed great satisfaction over the profitability of one of his products. His pricing policy was to add 67 percent to raw material costs in order to set the selling price.

When an outside consultant questioned the validity of this practice, the owner became defensive. The matter was discussed periodically over an extended period until a thorough operating-cost analysis was made of that particular product. The facts confirmed that the pricing concept was, in fact, in error. While raw material costs were $1 per pound and the selling price was $1.67, the total cost of the product was $1.83.

All goods and services should be priced for profit. Only in so doing will there be an assurance of profit. This chapter will aid you in planning what profit you desire and determining how to achieve it.

## How to Plan for Profit

When you study the profit-and-loss statement in Figure 12–2 you may tend to read the statement in the following order: "The Sample Company received $231,574 in sales, expended $145,631 for cost of goods sold, had $72,971 of other expenses, and had $12,972 left over as profit." It seems that profit was a "leftover."

Neither you nor Mr. Sample, owner-manager of The Sample Company, can do anything about the past, but you can do something about the future. Since one of your goals is to make a profit, you should plan the operations so that your desired profit is achieved.

### Steps in Profit Planning

The steps you need to take to achieve this goal during the coming year are:

1.  Establish the profit goal.

2.  Determine the planned volume of sales.
3.  Estimate the expenses for the planned volume of sales.
4.  Determine estimated profit based on plans reached in steps 2 and 3.
5.  Compare the estimated profit with the profit goal.

If you are satisfied with the plans, you can stop after completing step 5. However, you may want to check further to determine whether improvements can be made—particularly if you are not happy with the results of step 5. The following steps may help you understand better how certain changes in your business activities may affect your profit. They are:

6.  List possible alternatives that can be used to improve the profit position.
7.  Determine how costs vary with changes in sales volume.
8.  Determine how profits vary with changes in sales volume.
9.  Analyze alternatives from a profit standpoint.
10.  Select an alternative, and finalize and implement the plans.

You should be realistic when going through these steps; otherwise you may not be able to attain the goals. You may feel the future is too uncertain to make such plans, but the greater the uncertainty, the greater the need for planning.

The president of a company said that his forecast was too inaccurate to use, so he had stopped forecasting. The company was not very successful, and he had to sell out.

Recently the owner of a small business complained that she could not forecast next year's revenue within 20 percent of actual sales. However, she continues to forecast and plan, because she needs plans from which to deviate as conditions change.

## An Example of Profit Planning

Using The Sample Company as the example, the following material illustrates the use of the above steps in a company. Details are shown in Figure 14–1.

Place yourself in John Sample's shoes as he plans for the coming year. He should start making his plans several months ahead of the time to put them into effect. In order to present a systematic analysis, we will assume he is planning for the first time. Actually he should be planning for each month at least six months or a year ahead. This can be done by dropping the past month, adjusting the rest of the months in his prior plans, and adding the plans for another month. This planning gives him time to anticipate needed changes and do something about them.

**Figure 14–1**

THE SAMPLE COMPANY
Planning the Profit for the Year, 19—

| Step | Description | Analysis | Comments |
|---|---|---|---|
| 1. | Establish your profit goals | | |
| | Equity invested in company .............. | $ 80,000 | |
| | Retained earnings ....................... | 20,000 | |
| | Owner's equity ......................... | 100,000 | |
| | Return desired ......................... | 20,000 | 20% × $100,000 |
| | Estimated tax on profit ................. | 6,000 | |
| | Profit needed before income taxes ........ | $ 26,000 | |
| 2. | Determine your planned volume of sales | | |
| | Sample's estimate of sales income ........ | $275,000 | |
| 3. | Estimate your expenses for planned volume of sales | | |

| Item of Expense | Actual Last Year | Estimate 19— |
|---|---|---|
| Cost of goods .................................. | $145,631 | $173,300 |
| Salaries ....................................... | 41,569 | 47,000 |
| Utilities ....................................... | 3,475 | 4,000 |
| Depreciation .................................. | 5,025 | 5,000 |
| Rent .......................................... | 1,000 | 1,500 |
| Building services .............................. | 2,460 | 2,600 |
| Insurance ..................................... | 2,000 | 2,300 |
| Interest ....................................... | 1,323 | 1,500 |
| Office expenses ................................ | 2,775 | 3,000 |
| Sales promotion ............................... | 5,500 | 6,100 |
| Taxes and licenses ............................. | 3,240 | 3,600 |
| Maintenance .................................. | 805 | 900 |
| Delivery ...................................... | 2,924 | 3,200 |
| Miscellaneous ................................. | 875 | 1,000 |
| Total .................................... | $218,602 | $255,000 |

| | | |
|---|---|---|
| 4. | Determine your profit based on (2) and (3) plans | |
| | Estimated sales income ........................ | $275,000 |
| | Estimated expenses ........................... | 255,000 |
| | Estimated net profit before taxes .............. | $ 20,000 |
| 5. | Compare your estimated profit with your profit goal | |
| | Estimated profit before taxes ................... | $ 20,000 |
| | Desired profit before taxes ..................... | 26,000 |
| | Difference ................................... | −$ 6,000 |

**Step 1: Establishing the Profit Goal.** Your desired profit must be a specific value that is set as a target. Since you are managing the business, you should be paying yourself a reasonable salary. Also, as the owner, you should receive a return on your investment, including your initial investment plus prior earnings left in the business. In order to determine your desired profit, compare what

you would receive in salary working for someone else, plus the income you would receive if you invested the same amount of money in a savings and loan association, real estate loans, bonds, or stocks.

Each of these investments provides a return with a certain degree of risk—and pleasure. If you could invest at a 12 percent return with little risk, what would you feel the return on your business should be? Peter Drucker states that profits are:

> The "risk premium" covering the cost of staying in business.
> The source of capital to finance the jobs of tomorrow.
> The source of capital for innovation and for growth of the economy.
> Profit planning is necessary. . . . The minimum needed may well turn out to be a good deal higher than the profit goals of many companies, let alone their actual profits.[1]

Originally John Sample invested $80,000 in the company, and he has left about $20,000 of his profits in the business. He made about 10 percent on his investment this past year. He could make about 8 percent if he invested his money in a good grade of bond and about 14 percent on a certificate of deposit. He judges his return has been too low for the risk he is taking and feels that an approximately 20 percent return is reasonable.

In Figure 14–1, step 1, he enters his investment, his desired profit, and his estimate of income taxes (from the past and after consultation with his accountant), and determines he must make $26,000 before taxes, or a 26 percent return on his investment. Having set his goal, he next turns to the task of determining what the profit before taxes will be from his forecast of next year's plans.

***Step 2: Determining the Planned Volume of Sales.*** A forecast of sales for next year is based on your estimate of factors including market conditions, the level of your sales promotion, an estimate of your competitors' activities, and inflation. You can use forecasts of business activity made by business managers, by magazines such as *Business Week*, by government specialists, and by people specializing in forecasting. Talks with your banker, customers, vendors, and others provide added information. John Sample estimates that inflation will be about 10 percent next year.

Sample has been gathering this information and has been watching his company's sales trend. From these, he estimates he can increase his sales about 8 percent. Taking into consideration this increase and inflation, he estimates his sales to be $275,000, which he enters under step 2.

---

[1]Peter F. Drucker, *Management Tasks, Responsibilities, Practices* (New York: Harper & Row, 1974), p. 114.

***Step 3: Estimating Expenses for Planned Volume of Sales.*** To
estimate the expenses for next year, you collect the company's costs
for the past years. Sample has listed these for the past year in step
3. (He also has them for the previous years if he needs to refer to
them.) These expenses must be adjusted for the planned sales volume, for changes in economic conditions (including inflation), for
changes in sales promotion to attain the planned sales, and for
improved methods of production.

Sample figures that about 63 percent of his income is expended
on purchased material and the labor used directly on the goods he
sells. He uses this figure (63 percent), adds a 10 percent increase in
the unit costs for inflation, and enters the result—$173,300—for
cost of goods. He estimates the value of each of the other expenses,
recognizing that some expenses vary directly with volume changes,
others do not change at all, and still others have small changes.
Each figure for expenses is entered in the appropriate place.

***Step 4: Determining Profit from Steps 2 and 3.*** In this step,
John Sample deducts the figure for his total expenses from the
sales income, and adds the total of any other income, such as
interest. He calculates this amount, and finds that his estimated
profit before taxes is $20,000 ($275,000 − $255,000). This amount
is slightly better than the $12,972 made last year (See Figure
12–2). However, he had thought that the increased volume of
sales would increase his profit by a larger amount.

***Step 5: Comparing Estimated Profit with Your Profit Goal.*** John
Sample then compares his estimated profit with his desired profit.
He enters the value for these profits in step 5 and finds that his
plan will result in a profit figure that is $6,000 ($26,000 − $20,000)
lower than his goal. After pondering what he should do, he decides
to follow the rest of the steps.

***Step 6: Listing Possible Alternatives to Improve Profits.*** As
shown in Figure 14–2, step 6, there are many alternatives for improving profits available to Sample. Some of these are:

(1). Increasing the planned volume of units sold through expanding sales promotion, improving the quality of product and/or
service, making the product more available, or finding new
uses for the product.

(2). Increasing or decreasing the planned price of the units. The
best price may not be the planned one. How will price changing affect the profit? What have been the effects of past price
changes? How have customer attitudes and economic status
changed? Which products' prices should be changed?

**(3).** Combining alternatives **(1)** and **(2)**. It has been observed, on occasion, that some small-business owners become too concerned with selling on the basis of price alone. Instead you should price for profit and sell quality, better service, reliability, and integrity. Never be entrapped by the clichés, "I won't be undersold," or "I will meet any price." This economic path is strewn with many failed businesses whose key to failure was this pricing strategy.

***Figure 14–2***
**(continuation of Figure 14–1)**

*Step*
6.    Some alternatives
      *1.*  Increase planned volume of units sold.
      *2.*  Increase or decrease planned price of units.
      *3.*  Decrease planned expenses.
      *4.*  Add other products or services.
      *5.*  Subcontract work.

7.    Determine how costs vary with changes in sales volume

| Item of Expense | Total Estimated Expenses | Fixed Expenses | Variable Expenses |
|---|---|---|---|
| Goods sold .......... | $173,300 | $ | $173,300 |
| Salaries ............. | 47,000 | 25,000 | 22,000 |
| Utilities ............. | 4,000 | 3,000 | 1,000 |
| Depreciation ........ | 5,000 | 5,000 | |
| Rent ................ | 1,500 | 1,500 | |
| Building services ..... | 2,600 | 2,000 | 600 |
| Insurance ........... | 2,300 | 2,300 | |
| Interest ............. | 1,500 | | 1,500 |
| Office expenses ....... | 3,000 | 1,400 | 1,600 |
| Sales promotion ...... | 6,100 | | 6,100 |
| Taxes and licenses .... | 3,600 | 2,500 | 1,100 |
| Maintenance ......... | 900 | 400 | 500 |
| Delivery ............. | 3,200 | | 3,200 |
| Miscellaneous ........ | 1,000 | 1,000 | |
| Total .......... | $255,000 | $44,100 | $210,900 |

8.    Determine how profits vary with changes in sales volume
Total marginal income = Sales income − Variable expenses
= $275,000 − $210,900 = $64,100

Marginal income per dollar of sales income = $64,100 ÷ $275,000
= $0.233/$ of sales income

Estimated costs and profits at various sales volumes:

| Sales Volume | Fixed Costs | Variable Costs | Profit |
|---|---|---|---|
| $175,000 | $44,100 | 0.767 × 175,000 = $134,200 | − $ 3,300 |
| 200,000 | 44,100 | 0.767 × 200,000 = 153,400 | 2,500 |
| 225,000 | 44,100 | 0.767 × 225,000 = 172,600 | 8,300 |
| 250,000 | 44,100 | 0.767 × 250,000 = 191,800 | 14,100 |
| 275,000 | 44,100 | 0.767 × 275,000 = 210,900 | 20,000 |
| 300,000 | 44,100 | 0.767 × 300,000 = 230,100 | 25,800 |

**(4).** Decreasing planned expenses by:
- (1) Establishing a better control system. Money may be lost by having too many people operating the cash register, by poor scheduling, and by having too much money tied up in inventory. Expenses may be reduced if these areas are spotted and controls are established.
- (2) Increasing productivity of people and machines through improving methods, developing proper motivators, and improving the types and use of machinery.
- (3) Redesigning the product. Research is constantly developing new materials, machines, and methods for improving products and reducing costs.

**(5).** Adding other products or services to reduce costs per unit:
- (1) Adding a summer product to a winter line of products.
- (2) Selling, as well as use, parts made on machines with idle capacity.
- (3) Making some customarily purchased parts.

**(6).** Subcontracting work.

Having listed the alternatives that might be available, John Sample needs to evaluate each of them. Some alternatives may not be good choices now. They can be reconsidered later. An understanding of cost and volume relationships is important in evaluating the alternatives.

***Step 7: Determining How Changes in Costs Vary with Sales Volume Changes.*** Sample planned for changes in his expenses with an increase in sales volume, as shown in step 3. He used a simple breakeven chart, which is shown in Figure 14–3. Notice that as the volume of sales changes, the costs of doing business also change. Straight lines are used because costs are estimated and a straight line adequately approximates the costs.

Sample collected the figures for production volume and costs from his records of the past five years. Production figures and costs for items such as direct materials, depreciation, and office supplies are shown in Table 14–1 and are plotted in Figure 14–4. Note that when the cost of direct materials (A) is plotted in the figure, the cost increases in direct proportion to sales volume, starting at zero cost and zero volume. This is to be expected, as amounts of materials used directly in manufacturing the product increase directly as the volume of products increases.

Depreciation (B) is the loss in value of the machinery and equipment as they are used and as they get older. This is similar to the cost of owning your car—its value decreases with time. Businesses usually deduct the estimated resale value of an item from its costs and divide the balance by the life of the item—in years—to obtain its annual depreciation cost. Depreciation is called a fixed cost because its cost per year does not change, regardless of the volume of output, until you buy or sell the fixed asset. Other fixed costs, such as rent, are paid each period.

*Figure 14–3*
**Breakeven Chart, The Sample Company**

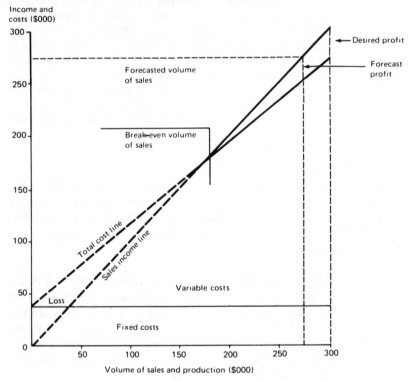

Volume of sales and production ($000)

The office expenses account (C) is shown to illustrate what is called a semivariable expense. When Sample plots this cost, the line starts at about $1,500 at zero sales volume and increases from that amount as the sales volume increases. You can use the graphs to help you in your analysis, but be sure to recognize that:

1.  The relationships exist only within limited changes in sales volume. Very high sales volumes may be obtained only by such measures as extraordinary sales promotions, added fixed costs for machinery, or increases in overtime. Low sales volumes result in extra costs of idle capacity, lost volume discounts, and so forth.
2.  Past relationships may not continue in the future. Inflation or

**Figure 14–4**
**Costs and Volume of Production**

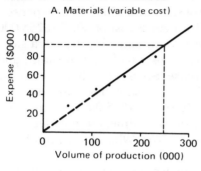

A. Materials (variable cost)

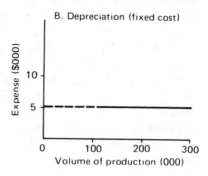

B. Depreciation (fixed cost)

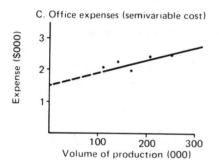

C. Office expenses (semivariable cost)

**Table 14–1**
**Data Collected from The Sample Company Records**

| Year | Production Volume | Direct Materials | Depreciation | Office Supplies |
|---|---|---|---|---|
| 1....... | $110,100 | $ 45,900 | $3,100 | $2,150 |
| 2....... | 139,000 | 52,900 | 3,100 | 2,500 |
| 3....... | 165,200 | 60,700 | 3,800 | 1,900 |
| 4....... | 205,000 | 74,800 | 4,400 | 2,800 |
| 5....... | 231,600 | 85,100 | 5,025 | 2,800 |
| 19—(est.) | 275,000 | 100,000 | 5,000 | 3,000 |

deflation, changing location of customers, new products, and other factors can cause changes in the costs per unit. Sample recognized a possible increase in the cost of goods sold for the next year and upped his budgeted amount for cost of goods.

Sample computed fixed and variable costs for each of his items of expense at his planned volume of sales and entered the figures in step 7 in Figure 14–2.

***Step 8: Determining How Profits Vary with Changes in Sales
Volume.*** How much does profit increase for each dollar of sales?
Mr. Sample planned for $275,000 of sales and $255,000 of expenses.
Therefore, each dollar of sales will incur a cost of $0.93 ($255,000
÷ $275,000). However, if he increases his sales $1, the extra sales
should not cost him $0.93. The fixed costs will stay constant, and
only the variable cost should increase. So his cost should increase
only by the variable portion. For $1 of sales increase, his cost
should increase by only $0.767 ($210,000 ÷ $275,000). His increase
in profit per dollar of increase in sales volume, often called marginal income (MI), is $0.233 ($1 − $0.767). What do you think this
means to Sample?

The marginal income can be determined for each product; it
tells you which product is the most profitable.

***Step 9: Analyzing Alternatives from a Profit Standpoint.*** John
Sample can compute his cost and profit at several sales volumes
in order to get a picture of the related changes in profit. This is
shown in step 8 of Figure 14–2 and is plotted as a graph in Figure
14–3. Note that the sales volume at which the company still makes
no profit is between $175,000 and $200,000. It can make the desired profit only if sales increase to $300,000.

Sample can use the marginal analyses to help him in his decision making, as follows:

1.  How much can he reduce his price for a sale to bring in more
    sales volume? He must not reduce it more than about 23 per-
    cent, for if he does he will be paying out more than the extra
    sales bring in. A reduction in sales price of less than 23 percent
    would contribute to reducing the fixed-cost charges per unit, an
    increase in profits. Sales price is greater than variable unit costs.
2.  Is it profitable to increase his advertising $2,000, which Sample
    estimates would increase his sales $15,000? He should obtain
    additional profits of $3,500 ($0.233 × $15,000) for the $2,000 he
    paid out. This would give him an added profit of $1,500 ($3,500
    − $2,000).
3.  Is it profitable to increase the price 2 percent if he can expect a
    drop of 5 percent in sales? The price increase would result in a
    marginal income (MI) of about $0.253 ($0.233 + $0.02), and the
    profit would change to about $22,000 ($0.253 × 0.95 × $275,000
    − $44,100), which would be better than the present expected
    profit of $20,000.
4.  What would a reduction of 5 percent in this variable cost do to
    profit? The MI should increase to $0.271 ($1 − [$0.767 × 0.95]),
    and the profit at $275,000 sales volume would be $30,400
    ($275,000 × $0.271 − $44,100). This looks very good if the means

can be found to reduce the variable cost without hurting other operations.

5. Which product is the most profitable?

Other alternatives can be evaluated in much the same manner. Having made these economic analyses, Sample is now ready to make his final plan for action.

***Step 10: Selecting, Finalizing, and Implementing the Plans.*** The selection of the plan for action depends on your judgment as to what would be most beneficial to the firm. The results of the analyses made in prior steps provide the economic inputs. These must be evaluated along with your other goals. Cost reduction may result in laying off employees, or in a reduction in service to customers. But lowering prices may satisfy your goal for a larger volume of sales. Higher prices are risky because of competition.

John Sample has just read this book, made the analyses, and studied some other management literature. He believes that he can reduce his cost of goods about 2 percent. Figure 14–5 shows a simplified statement of his planned income and outgo for the next year.

**Figure 14–5**

THE SAMPLE CO.
Planned Profit and Loss Statement
For the Year 19—

| | | |
|---|---|---|
| Sales income ................................... | | $275,000 |
| Less: | | |
|   Cost of goods sold ........................... | $169,800 | |
|   Other expenses ............................... | 81,700 | 251,500 |
| | | |
| Net profit before taxes .......................... | | $ 23,500 |
| Return on investment .......................... | | 23.5% |

# Summary

Profits do not just happen! Planning your operations improves the chances of achieving the profit goals. You can achieve more by knowing your goals, understanding the relationship of the company's sales income to cost, and determining the best operating plan. You should know where your breakeven point is and what the effects of alternative plans might be.

Before making final plans, you need more information about the financial condition of your company. The next chapter provides some more tools for obtaining this information.

# Chapter Fifteen

# Controlling the Financial Structure and Operations of the Firm

The underlying theme of Part 4 to this point has been planning. This chapter relates to control by providing sufficient information for you to understand its nature, its objectives, and its mechanics. Specifically, it is hoped that you will become aware of some of the causes of poor performance, some characteristics of an effective control system, and suggestions for setting up and operating such a system. In addition, the design and use of budgets are discussed.

## What Is Involved in Control?

Profit planning alone is not enough! Instead, after developing plans for generating a profit, you must design an operating system to carry out those plans. Then the system must be controlled to see that the plans are carried out and objectives are reached. This material is designed to help you understand the controls that can be used in a small business.

> A machine shop owner with a reputation as a top-rated, skilled machinist developed a special machine to produce holders for wooden art objects. While there were no comparable American-made machines on the market, there were a number of outstanding machines available from European sources. The machinist arranged to display his machine at a trade show for art dealers in a nearby city.
>
> The reception of this new equipment was good, and he received

orders for 10 machines. Upon returning home he attempted to raise the necessary capital to enable him to produce the machines. After 10 months, he was successful in obtaining financial assistance with the aid of SBA. Four months later, the machines were ready for delivery, but his orders had evaporated, having been filled already by the available European machines. As no advance payment had been received, he found himself with 10 machines and an additional materials inventory of $18–20,000.

If he had obtained advance deposits on the machine orders and made an arrangement to receive in-progress payments, he probably could have filled his contracts on time.

## The Role of Control

The managerial functions are planning, organizing, staffing, directing, coordinating, controlling, and evaluating. As shown in Chapter 4, planning provides the guides and standards used in performing the activities necessary to achieve your company's goals. A system of controls is essential if you are to make actual performance conform to the plans you have made. Any deviation from the plans should point to a need for change—usually in performance, but sometimes in the plans themselves.

Each day, we exercise controls over our activities and also have controls working on us. We control the speed of the car we are driving. Police officers control the traffic flow. Thermostats in our homes keep the temperature within an acceptable range. Controls are everywhere and are established to assure reasonable accomplishment of our objectives.

## Steps in Control

Regardless of where it occurs, the process of control consists of five steps. They are:

1. Setting up standards of performance.
2. Measuring actual performance.
3. Comparing actual performance with the planned performance standards.
4. Determining whether deviations are excessive.
5. Determining the appropriate corrective action required to equalize planned and actual performance.

The steps are performed in all control systems, even though the systems may be quite different. This chapter covers these five steps in detail. The following subjects are discussed:

1. Characteristics of control systems.
2. Causes of poor performance.

3. Establishing standards of performance.
4. Obtaining information on actual performance.
5. Comparing actual performance with standards of performance.
6. The design and use of budgets.


## Characteristics of Control Systems

Almost all control systems have the same characteristics. They should (1) be timely, (2) not be overly costly, (3) provide the accuracy needed, (4) be quantifiable and measurable, (5) show cause-and-effect relationships, and (6) be the responsibility of one individual.


### Controls Should Be Timely

To keep control systems timely, checks should be made frequently and as soon as practical after they are needed. You cannot wait until the end of the year to find out how much sales are and whether they meet your plans. Some stores check their sales daily for indications of whether their performance is meeting expectations. They have many small transactions, and a daily check helps to indicate whether changes are needed. Manufacturers handle fewer transactions on a less-regular basis, so that weekly or monthly checks may be sufficient.

The collection of the totals of an activity, such as sales, takes time. Such data collection has been simplified through the use of cash registers with tapes, minicomputers, and other office machines. A system for fast checks is valuable. The old adage, "It is too late to lock the barn door after the horse has left," applies well to your controls. The machine shop owner cited earlier needed a check on customers before starting to produce the special machines.


### Controls Should Not Be Overly Costly

All controls require the time of a person or of some equipment. Often paperwork is involved. The cost of the control system needs to be balanced against its value. It is not economical "to spend a nickel to save a penny."

Some systems are simple and others are more complex and costly. Therefore you should try to reduce the time of employees, the amount of paperwork, and your time in collecting information. A systematic, simple inspection of what is on the shelves may give enough information for control without having a clerk provide a written or tabulated summary of what has been removed from the shelves. At selected times, extra cost may be justified to provide for more detailed controls.

### Controls Should Provide the Accuracy Needed

Inspection for control of quality can take two forms. It can test every unit of product or only a sample of the units. Statistical techniques can be applied to many areas of control in order to reduce cost and, in many cases, to improve quality. You can periodically check the output per hour of workers, cleanliness of the stock room, and the cost of paper to obtain a good check of performance.

Performance can vary above as well as below standard. Also, part of the variance from standard can be controlled, while part cannot. But, are all corrections justified? The correction of a variation of a few cents in a $10,000 figure may not be desirable or justified, but it may be very significant in a figure of $0.05 per unit.

### Controls Should Be Quantifiable and Measurable

The choice of measuring units for control is vital. Sales can be measured in dollars, pounds, tons, barrels, gallons, grams, kilograms, meters, or other units of product. Which will provide the information needed for control? Which is the least costly? You should choose the unit that will give the needed control for the least cost.

### Controls Should Show Causes When Possible

A report that the costs of a product are higher than past costs may indicate the actual situation but not explain why the higher costs occurred. On the other hand, a report that the cost per unit of purchased goods is higher than planned not only shows the actual situation but also identifies the source of higher costs.

### Controls Should Be Assigned to One Individual

Because you do not have time to control all activities yourself, you need to delegate the authority for those actions to a subordinate. Give that person authority, provide the necessary resources, and then hold the person responsible for accomplishments.

Selected controls that have the above characteristics, and that enable you to meet plans, will be invaluable in managing a business.

## Causes of Poor Performance

Poor performance can result from many factors in a company. A partial list of some of these activities, or nonactivities, would probably include the following:

1. Customer not buying the company's product.
2. Poor scheduling of production or purchases.
3. Theft and/or spoilage of products.
4. Too many employees for the work being performed.
5. Opportunities lost.
6. Too many free services or donations. A company oriented toward research and development was found to be providing customers with special R&D service without reimbursement for the thousands of dollars spent in this manner. This policy was changed, to the company's profit benefit.
7. Having the wrong objective. The president of a TV station authorized items such as the purchase of a fleet of sports cars for key personnel. Subsequent low profits resulted in his dismissal and in the elimination of the expensive items.

## Established Standards of Performance

Standards are used to inform each employee of the level of performance expected and to measure how well he or she does. They are usually stated in terms of units consumed or of price paid or charged. Illustrations of these are standard hours per unit to produce a good or service, miles per gallon of gasoline used, and price per part for purchased goods. These standards are developed from many sources. Some methods of determining values of standard are:

1. Intuition.
2. Past performance.
3. Plans for desired accomplishment.
4. Careful measurement of activities.
5. Comparison with other standards or averages. (See Chapter 7 for a discussion of time standards.)

Once the standards of performance are determined, they should be communicated to the people who are responsible for their performance by means of written policies, rules, procedures, budgets, and statements of standards. Standards are valuable in locating sources of inefficient—as well as efficient—performance.

## Obtaining Information on Actual Performance

Information on actual performance is gained through some form of feedback. It can be obtained by observation, oral reports, written memos or reports, and other methods.

Observation will probably be most satisfying because you are at the scene of action and have direct control over the situation. However, this method is time consuming, and you cannot be in all places at one time. Observation time is justified when your knowledge is needed, when your presence may improve the work, or when you are present for other purposes.

Oral reports are less simple and are time consuming, but they provide two-way communications. They are the most prevalent type of control used in business.

Written memos or reports are prepared when a record is needed and when many facts must be assembled for decision making. These types of feedback are most costly unless the reports are the original records. A good record system (as discussed in Chapter 13) is a valuable aid, and it should be designed to be a source of the reports that will be needed.

### Indirect Control by Means of Reports

The new independent business usually lends itself to the more direct types of control. But indirect controls may be necessary at later stages of growth. Your best means of this indirect control are the reports just mentioned.

Some guidelines for designing reports are as follows:

1. They should cover separate organizational units.
2. They should be designed to be updated as needed.
3. They should be factual and not designed just to make someone look good.
4. They should be designed to indicate actions that have been taken or should be taken.
5. They should be designed to highlight comparisons of performances of various organizational units and/or individuals within your company.

These reports should be given to all executives and supervisors concerned. You should operate on the basis of the exception principle, which requires an immediate investigation of the causes of significant variations, whether favorable or unfavorable. You should arrange for immediate action to prevent a repetition of bad results or to preserve and continue good results.

### Effective Cost Control

Next to providing wanted products, the ability to keep costs low is one of the most important advantages a smaller company can have. In order to do this, an effective cost accounting system and cost-sensitive controls are vital. Smaller companies are usually labor intensive, and labor costs typically represent a significant cost that should be watched and controlled.

## Comparing Actual Performance with Standards

To determine whether any changes are needed, information about actual performance, obtained by feedback, is compared with standards. This procedure may be simple or complex. Most often, you will use simple, informal controls. The measures of performance are carried in your head; you make comparisons as you receive feedback; and you make your decisions accordingly. It must be emphasized, however, that this type of control follows the same steps as the more formal types of control. Examples of the use of standards have been discussed in Chapters 6 through 8 and follow the same pattern as control through the use of budgets. The rest of this chapter will cover the design and use of some budgets that are of most value to independent business firms.

## The design and Use of Budgets

A budget can be defined as an itemized summary of probable expenditures and income for a given period of time, and embodies a systematic plan for meeting expenses. The budget system is based on profit plans for the coming period. As each day, week, or month passes, checks should be made to assure progress toward meeting goals. If actual performance conforms to the budget, the company is meeting its goals. If performance is different, decisions can be made about whether changes are needed. Thus, budgets provide:

1. Guideposts toward achieving goals.
2. Indications of where trouble exists.
3. Planned actions that need to be taken during the year.
4. At planning time, the feasibility of the plans.

An effective budget system includes close controls in the areas in which poor performance most affects your company. Other areas do not warrant such expense for control and may be controlled less often. For example, the cost of goods sold by The Sample Company is planned for 63 percent of the sales dollar, and utilities are 1.5 percent. Cost of goods sold may be divided into material and labor and checked weekly. Utilities might be checked on a monthly basis.

Illustrative budgets presented in this chapter are sales; cash; credit, collections, and accounts receivable; and others.

## Sales Budget

The sales budget is the most basic one; once sales are planned and budgeted, the other budgets can more easily be prepared.

This budget should be the responsibility of a sales manager or you. Let us assume you have a sales manager. The two of you should have worked up the sales plan for the coming year. Now, how much does the sales department need to sell each day? The plan for The Sample Company calls for sales of $275,000 per year. If the firm plans for 203 sales days per year, it must average $1,355 ($275,000 ÷ 203) per sales day. But some days are good days, and some are poor. You may have noticed seasonal, monthly, and even daily patterns in the past. The daily average can be adjusted upward or downward for each day in the week or for the month.

Another method that can be used to figure goals for daily, weekly, or monthly sales is to modify the figures for the past year. If you think the pattern of sales for the coming year will be the same as that of the past year, merely change last year's daily sales by a given percentage. John Sample planned to increase his sales volume by 8 percent, as shown in Chapter 14.

How often should you compare actual sales to the budget? Grocery store managers usually make daily checks, for they find daily sales vary considerably from budget. This is expected, but sales should be within range of the budget, and actual sales should be above the expected figure at least as often as they are below. If they are not, the manager has a warning signal to do a more complete check or perhaps take some corrective action. Weekly, monthly, and year-to-date summaries provide more stable relationships for control.

Companies may check at longer intervals and may use other types of checks. One owner watches the number and size of contracts at the end of each month. Other managers watch the units of product sold—by product line, by customers, and/or by territory. The detail needed for control depends on the nature of the business.

For budgeting purposes, a simple tallying of sales in one column of a control pad, the budget in a second column, and the difference in a third column may be adequate.

## Cash Budget

Cash planning is very important if a company is to meet its payments. Cash planning takes two forms: (1) the daily and weekly cash requirements for the normal operation of the business, and (2) the maintenance of the proper balance for all requirements.

*Planning Cash Status Daily-Weekly.* The first type of planning tends to be routine. For example, the company may have a fairly constant income and outgo, which can be predicted. Policies can thus be established for the level of cash to maintain. Therefore, a procedure should be established to control the level of cash. These routine demands represent a small part of the cash on hand needed and tend to remain fairly constant.

*Planning Cash Status Monthly-Yearly.* The second type of planning requires a budget for, say, each month of the year. Payments for rent, payroll, purchases, and services require a regular outflow of cash. Insurance and taxes may require large payments a number of times each year. A special purchase, such as a truck, will place a heavy demand on cash. It takes planning to have the right amount of cash available when needed.

*Procedure for Cash Planning.* Figure 15–1 shows one form of cash budget for three months ahead. Each month is completed before the next month is shown. Lines 1–3 are completed for estimates of cash to be received. The Sample Company expects to receive 20 percent of its monthly sales in cash. A check of its accounts-receivable budget (presented in the next section) can provide estimates of the cash to be received in January. Other income might come from interest on investments or the sale of surplus equipment.

Expected cash payments, lines 5–12, should include items for which the company pays cash. The Sample Company might list salaries and utilities separately, and combine advertising and selling expenses under sales promotion. Cash is often paid in the month after the service is performed. Examples of this are payments for electricity and for material purchases. Some cash payments can be made at any one of several times. For example, payments on a new insurance policy can be set up to come due when other cash demands are low. The cash budget shows when payment is to be made.

The cash balance on the first of January plus the month's receipts less the month's cash payments provides you with an expected cash balance at the end of January. A negative balance will require an increase in cash receipts, a decrease in payments, or the floating of a loan. A company should have a certain amount of cash to take care of contingencies. Line 17 is used to show the desired amount needed as a minimum balance. Lines 18–22 show an alternative means of maintaining cash balance.

A three-month projection is probably the practical minimum estimation for a cash budget. If sales are seasonal or you expect

*Figure 15–1*

THE SAMPLE COMPANY
Cash Budget Form

CASH BUDGET
For three months, ending March 31, 19—

| | January | | February | | March | |
|---|---|---|---|---|---|---|
| | Budget | Actual | Budget | Actual | Budget | Actual |
| EXPECTED CASH RECEIPTS: | | | | | | |
| 1. Cash sales ......................... | | | | | | |
| 2. Collections on accounts receivable ...... | | | | | | |
| 3. Other income...................... | | | | | | |
| 4. Total cash receipts................... | | | | | | |
| EXPECTED CASH PAYMENTS: | | | | | | |
| 5. Raw materials ..................... | | | | | | |
| 6. Payroll ......................... | | | | | | |
| 7. Other factory expenses (including maintenance) ...................... | | | | | | |
| 8. Advertising....................... | | | | | | |
| 9. Selling expense .................... | | | | | | |
| 10. Administrative expense (including salary of owner-manager) ............. | | | | | | |
| 11. New plant and equipment ........... | | | | | | |
| 12. Other payments (taxes, including estimated income tax; repayment of loans; interest; etc.) ...................... | | | | | | |
| 13. Total cash payments ................ | | | | | | |
| 14. Expected cash balance at beginning of the month ............... | | | | | | |
| 15. Cash increase or decrease (item 4 minus item 13) ........................... | | | | | | |
| 16. Expected cash balance at end of month (item 14 plus item 15) ............... | | | | | | |
| 17. Desired working cash balance ......... | | | | | | |
| 18. Short-term loans needed (item 17 minus item 16, if item 17 is larger) .......... | | | | | | |
| 19. Cash available for dividends, capital cash expenditures, and/or short-term investments (item 16 minus item 17, if item 16 is larger than item 17) ......... | | | | | | |
| CAPITAL CASH: | | | | | | |
| 20. Cash available (item 19 after deducting dividends, etc.) .................... | | | | | | |
| 21. Desired capital cash (item 11, new plant and equipment) ............. | | | | | | |
| 22. Long-term loans needed (item 21 less item 20, if item 21 is larger than item 20) .... ..................... | | | | | | |

[4]Source: J. H. Feller, Jr., "Is Your Cash Supply Adequate?" *Management Aids No 174* (Washington, D.C.: Small Business Administration, 1973).

heavy demands on the cash balance, longer periods may be necessary. Also, as the end of January approaches, your performance should be checked and a month added. In Figure 15–1, the budgets for February and March are reviewed toward the end of January, and April is budgeted.

***Rationale of Cash Budgeting.*** The cash budget is a technique for controlling cash flow so that you can make needed payments and not maintain too high a cash balance. Many independent business people do not recognize the importance of moving money through their system as quickly, effectively, and efficiently as possible. Everything else being equal, the faster you can move your money and turn it over in sales and income, the greater should be your profit.

### Credit, Collections, and Accounts Receivable

As previously stated, the extension of credit increases the potential for sales. In Chapter 12, you may have found that the amount in accounts receivable for The Sample Company was large relative to its credit sales. It is potentially dangerous to wait until the end of the year to find this out. Checks should be made often enough to identify customers who are slow in paying and determine the reason(s) for the slow payments. It is believed that the average retailer loses more from slow accounts than from bad debts.

The best control of losses on accounts receivable starts with their prevention. You will enhance your position if you investigate the customer's ability and willingness to pay and if you provide clear statements of terms. The level of risk is balanced against the gain from giving credit. Then, establish surveillance of past-due accounts each month so that a slow account is followed up promptly. As time passes and an account is not paid, the probability of collection decreases. You can expect to collect only about one quarter of the accounts over two years old and none of the accounts over five years old.

A first check should be made of the total amount of your accounts receivable. Chapter 12 discussed the ratio of the amount of receivables to sales (collection period). It stated that a comparison of your planned figures and the actual amounts indicates whether the situation is satisfactory overall.

Next the accounts can be "aged," which means making a tabulation of the accounts receivable by how long they have been unpaid. Thus The Sample Company's accounts receivable might be something like the following:

| Age of Accounts | Amount |
|---|---|
| 30 days or less | $17,150 |
| 30–60 days | 8,102 |
| 2–6 months | 2,500 |
| 6–12 months | 990 |
| Over one year | 1,500 |
| Total | $31,232 |

What should be done? Particular attention should be given to accounts over 60 days past due, and then to the 30–60-day accounts. Remember that most customers are honest and that you expect them to be willing and able to pay.

Sample's analysis may lead him to write off some accounts as an expense of bad debts and to provide some incentive for earlier payments by slow-paying customers. Bad-debt adjustments should be made at or near the end of the fiscal year. Uncollectible accounts receivable create a misstatement of income, and therefore an unjustified increase in your business income tax liability. Unless there exists a reasonable expectation of collecting the account, a good rule of thumb is to write off all accounts six months old or older at tax time. Sample should examine next year's profit plans for the extra cost of bad debts and for a review of his credit policy.

### Other Types of Budgets

Many other types of budgets can be used to control the activities and investments of a company. Each expense can increase gradually without your noticing the change. Have you noticed how fast the cash in your pockets disappears? You know you need to control this, but it is very hard to do. Some call it being "nickeled and dimed to death." A company has similar problems. Such diverse situations as the following may contribute to this creeping increase in your firm's costs. A clerk is added to take care of the increased paperwork, a solicitor comes in for donations, a big customer wants a special delivery, some of the employees use company stamps for personal letters, and inflation increases costs. While it may be unpleasant to do, these costs must be controlled if the firm is to survive.

Detailed control of inventory has been discussed in Chapter 8. An inventory budget can be established for weekly or monthly checks, based on the level of expected sales. Purchases may be budgeted on the basis of the demand for materials. The budget can then be coordinated with the inventory and cash budgets. Analysis of a similar nature can be performed for other expenses.

Control over current liabilities is tied to expense and cash plans. Fixed assets and long-term liabilities usually change on a fixed basis, except for infrequent changes of equipment and other needs. Capital-stock changes are infrequent, and retained earnings change as a result of the operations of the company. Budgets for fixed items can be maintained through a quarterly set of planned financial statements.

## Summary

Controlling is measuring and correcting actions of subordinates in order to ensure that objectives and plans are achieved. It involves the following steps:

1. Setting up planned standards of performance for all employees.
2. Measuring actual performance.
3. Comparing actual performance with planned performance.
4. Determining whether variations between actual and planned performance are excessive.
5. Taking the appropriate action to bring actual and planned performance together.

Controls in an independent company need to be simple, yet effective. While a smaller firm cannot spend much money for controls, it cannot afford the risks of any out-of-control activity. Therefore, it must establish at least a basic control system.

Direct control by an owner is possible for a very small business. As the company grows, however, the owner must depend increasingly on subordinates and must use policies, rules, procedures, and budgets to help control operations. The owner always uses some type of standards of performance, either formal or informal. Also, as the business grows, more information is recorded rather than being merely remembered. The art is to keep paperwork and cost low and yet maintain effective controls.

# Exhibits

*Exhibit 15–1*
**Maintaining control of Your Cash**

**Cash receipts**

1. Expected cash receipts/day — minimum $_____
   — maximum $_____

2. Persons authorized to receive cash:

| Names or Positions | Number of Persons | Expected Volume/day/person | Amount at Start of day |
|---|---|---|---|
| a. _____ | _____ | $_____ $ | _____ |
| b. _____ | _____ | $_____ $ | _____ |
| c. _____ | _____ | $_____ $ | _____ |

3. Cash is located in:
   a. Locked cash registers?  ☐ Yes ☐ No
      How many? _____
   b. Unlocked cash registers?  ☐ Yes ☐ No
      How many? _____
   c. Money boxes?  ☐ Yes ☐ No
      How many? _____
4. Are checks from customers accepted?  ☐ Yes ☐ No
   If yes,
   a. What identification is required? _____
   _____
   b. Who approves acceptance? _____

**Deposits to bank**

5. Is cash deposited in bank?  ☐ Yes ☐ No
   If no, explain procedure: _____
   _____
   _____

   If yes,
6. Frequency:
   ☐ Once/day?
   ☐ Once/week?
   ☐ Other? Specify _____
7. Timing:
   a. Hour of day _____
   b. Random _____
8. Average amount of deposits:  $_____
9. Persons making deposits:
   a. Names or positions: _____
   _____
   _____
   b. Random person: _____
   _____

10. Route taken to bank:
    a. Fixed  ☐ Yes ☐ No
    b. Variable  ☐ Yes ☐ No

11. Container for cash moved to bank:
    a. Locked bag?  ☐ Yes ☐ No
    b. Unlocked bag?  ☐ Yes ☐ No
    c. Other? Specify _____
12. Bank balance maintained:
    a. Minimum  $_____
    b. Maximum  $_____
13. Type of account: _____

**Cash disbursements**

14. Percent of bills paid by:
    a. Check?  _____%
    b. Cash?  _____%
    c. Other? Specify_____ _____%
15. How many checkbooks?  _____
16. Persons or positions authorizing bills to pay:
    a. _____
    b. _____
    c. _____
17. Persons or positions signing checks:
    a. _____
    b. _____
    c. _____
18. Policy for payment of bills:
    a. Pay to obtain cash discounts?  ☐ Yes ☐ No
    b. Pay near end of credit period?  ☐ Yes ☐ No
    c. Pay on receipt of service?  ☐ Yes ☐ No
    d. Pay at a set time of month?  ☐ Yes ☐ No
    e. Other?_____

**Cash in building**

19. Amount of cash in building overnight:
    a. Petty cash?  $_____
    b. Other? _____  $_____
20. Amount of cash in cash registers during the day:
    a. Start of shift?  $_____
    b. Maximum each register?  $_____
    c. Maximum all registers?  $_____

## *Exhibit 15–1 (concluded)*

21. Method of removing excess cash:
   a. Check registers every _____ hour(s)?
   b. When register operator requests?    □ Yes □ No
   c. Other?_____

22. Retain excess cash until deposited:
   a. In a safe?                          □ Yes □ No
   b. In a money box?                     □ Yes □ No
   c. Other?_____

**Control of cash**

23. Procedure to assure that company receives all cash payments:
   a. Continual observation of cash receipts?
                                          □ Yes □ No
   b. Spot check? Explain: _____
   _____
   c. Sales slips received and reconciled? □ Yes □ No
   d. Two persons involved in each cash receipt?
                                          □ Yes □ No
   e. One person responsible for each cash register?
                                          □ Yes □ No
   f. Other? Explain: _____
   _____
   _____

24. Petty cash:
   a. Maximum disbursement?        $_____
   b. Each disbursement recorded on slip?
                                          □ Yes □ No
   c. Persons authorized to make payments are:
   _____
   _____
   _____
   d. Procedure for reimbursing petty cash is:
   _____
   _____
   e. Petty cash is used to pay: _____
   _____
   _____

25. Procedures (not included above) maintained to discourage theft of cash by outsiders: _____
   _____
   _____
   _____

## Exhibit 15–2
## Evaluating Your Cash Flow

Cash planning to allow you to be able to meet obligations, obtain desired assets, maximize use of cash, and safeguard against reasonable contingencies is essential for a business. This checklist should aid you in your cash planning and procedures.

### Cash planning

1. Do you forecast your cash receipts, disbursements, and balances? ☐ Yes ☐ No
   If yes,
   a. Is the forecast by month? ☐ Yes ☐ No
      Other? ☐ Yes ☐ No
   b. Is the forecast projected ahead a month? ☐ Yes ☐ No
      Quarter? ☐ Yes ☐ No
   c. Is the forecast mental? ☐ Yes ☐ No
      In writing? ☐ Yes ☐ No
2. Do you convert your forecasts to budgets? ☐ Yes ☐ No
   If yes, do you compare your budget with your actual each period (say, monthly)? ☐ Yes ☐ No
   Have the results been reasonably satisfactory? ☐ Yes ☐ No
3. If you have not planned your cash budgets, complete the accompanying worksheet.
4. Do you plan your heavy payments, such as insurance premiums, for times when cash will be most available? ☐ Yes ☐ No
5. Have you compared your book cash balance with your bank balance to determine your float? ☐ Yes ☐ No
6. Have you reviewed your customers' payment habits? ☐ Yes ☐ No
   Have you talked to them about how you can make it easier for them to pay? ☐ Yes ☐ No
7. Do you know which portions of your cash are working cash and which are capital expenditures cash? ☐ Yes ☐ No
8. Do you use your cash forecast to plan your borrowing? ☐ Yes ☐ No
9. When determining the amount to borrow, do you include an amount for contingencies? ☐ Yes ☐ No
10. Do you have a policy on payment of obligations? ☐ Yes ☐ No

### Cash flow

11. Do you feel that you get good use of your cash? ☐ Yes ☐ No
12. What percentage of your assets are cash?
    _____%
    How does this compare with the industry average?

13. Do you place short-term surpluses of cash in short-term investments to receive interest? ☐ Yes ☐ No
14. Do you have larger cash balances than are required for payments of operating expenses and contingencies? ☐ Yes ☐ No
    On the other hand, are you often pressed for cash? ☐ Yes ☐ No
15. Do you pay in time to obtain cash discounts? ☐ Yes ☐ No
    Do you receive a report on cash discounts lost? ☐ Yes ☐ No
16. Do you age your accounts receivable regularly? ☐ Yes ☐ No
    Do you have delinquent accounts which can be collected with a reasonable effort? ☐ Yes ☐ No
17. Do you bill on delivery of products/services? ☐ Yes ☐ No
    If not, reasonably soon after delivery? ☐ Yes ☐ No
18. Do you give cash discounts for early payment? ☐ Yes ☐ No
    Have you found this to be economical? ☐ Yes ☐ No
19. Have you analyzed your inventory for obsolete, slow-moving, and overstocked items? ☐ Yes ☐ No
    Should these items be converted into cash for other uses? ☐ Yes ☐ No
20. Do you have heavy purchased goods, work-in-process, and/or finished goods inventories because of slow processes of production and distribution? ☐ Yes ☐ No
21. Do you have other assets, such as old tools, machines, and jigs for past jobs, which can be economically converted into cash? ☐ Yes ☐ No
22. Do you evaluate your new investments in fixed assets with respect to their demands for cash? ☐ Yes ☐ No
    Your payment schedules? ☐ Yes ☐ No
23. Have you considered renting or leasing fixed assets instead of purchasing? ☐ Yes ☐ No
24. Is it better to use short-term rather than long-term borrowing because of fluctuating cash demands and better knowledge of needs? ☐ Yes ☐ No
25. Do you have such heavy interest payments that you are short of cash? ☐ Yes ☐ No
26. Do you have the proper balance between interest-bearing liabilities and equity? ☐ Yes ☐ No

*Exhibit 15–2 (concluded)*
### Worksheet 1:   Cash Budget Form

| | CASH BUDGET (for three months, ending _____, 19___) | | | | | |
|---|---|---|---|---|---|---|
| | Budget | Actual | Budget | Actual | Budget | Actual |
| **Expected Cash Receipts:** | | | | | | |
| 1.  Cash sales | | | | | | |
| 2.  Collections on accounts receivable | | | | | | |
| 3.  Other income | | | | | | |
| 4.  Total cash receipts | | | | | | |
| **Expected Cash payments:** | | | | | | |
| 5.  Raw materials | | | | | | |
| 6.  Payroll | | | | | | |
| 7.  Other factory expenses (including maintenance) | | | | | | |
| 8.  Advertising | | | | | | |
| 9.  Selling expense | | | | | | |
| 10.  Administrative expense (including salary of owner-manager) | | | | | | |
| 11.  New plant and equipment | | | | | | |
| 12.  Other payments (taxes, including estimated income tax, repayment of loans, interest, etc.) | | | | | | |
| 13.  Total cash payments | | | | | | |
| 14.  Expected cash balance at beginning of the month | | | | | | |
| 15.  Cash increase or decrease (item 4 minus item 13) | | | | | | |
| 16.  Expected cash balance at end of month (item 14 plus item 15) | | | | | | |
| 17.  Desired working cash balance | | | | | | |
| 18.  Short-term loans needed (item 17 minus item 16, if item 17 is larger) | | | | | | |
| 19.  Cash available for dividends, capital cash expenditures, and/or short-term investments (item 16 minus item 17, if item 16 is larger than item 17) | | | | | | |
| **Capital Cash:** | | | | | | |
| 20.  Cash available (item 19 after deducting dividends, etc.) | | | | | | |
| 21.  Desired capital cash (item 11, new plant equipment) | | | | | | |
| 22.  Long-term loans needed (item 21 less item 20, if item 21 is larger than item 20) | | | | | | |

Source: J. H. Feller, Jr., *"Is Your Cash Supply Adequate?" Management Aids No. 174.* (Washington, D.C.: Small Business Administration, 1973).

## Exhibit 15-3
## A Checklist to Help You Plan for Your Profits

You need to plan for profit rather than wait until after actual performance to determine your company's profit. By planning ahead, you can compare actual performance during performance so as to take corrective action early. This checklist carries you through a series of steps to plan for next year.

**Establish your profit goals**

1. What is your company's equity? $_____
2. What is your owner's investment? $_____
3. What are your owner's retained earnings? $_____
4. What rate of return do you desire for the company?

   _____%

   Is this a reasonable return to expect?   ☐ Yes ☐ No

5. What is the desired return (#1 times #2)? $_____
6. Estimate income tax on earnings?   $_____
7. Profit needed before taxes (#5 plus #6)? $_____
8. Have you met this goal in the past?   ☐ Yes ☐ No

**Next year's financial operations**

Plan your next year's preliminary financial operations. (Enter last year's figures to aid in estimating this year's plans.)

9. Estimate your sales income

10. Estimate your expenses for planned volume of sales:

    1. Cost of goods sold _____
    2. Salaries _____
    3. Utilities _____
    4. Depreciation _____
    5. Rent _____
    6. Building services _____
    7. Insurance _____
    8. Interest _____
    9. Office expense _____
    10. Sales promotion _____
    11. Taxes and licenses _____
    12. Maintenance _____
    13. Delivery _____
    14. _____
    15. _____
    16. _____
    17. Total expenses

11. Estimated net profit before taxes

12. Estimated (#11) less desired (#5) net before taxes

13. Are you satisfied with your planned profit?

    ☐ Yes ☐ No

    If yes, you can convert your annual to monthly or quarterly plans for comparison to actual performance for decision making. You may find value in completing the rest of the checklist.

| | Last Year | Planned for This Year |
|---|---|---|
| | $_____ | $_____ |
| | $_____ | $_____ |
| | $_____ | $_____ |

## Exhibit 15–3 (continued)

### Improve your profits

Can you use one or more of the following to improve your profits? (Rank them to aid in selecting the best choices.)

14. Increase sales volume by increasing sales promotion? ☐ Yes ☐ No

15. Increase sales price with little volume drop? ☐ Yes ☐ No

16. Decrease sales price with large volume increase? ☐ Yes ☐ No

17. Increase sales price on some product/service and decrease on others? ☐ Yes ☐ No

18. Reduce some expenses? ☐ Yes ☐ No
    If yes,
    a. By better controls? ☐ Yes ☐ No
    b. By higher productivity? ☐ Yes ☐ No
    c. By better methods? ☐ Yes ☐ No
    d. By new and better machines? ☐ Yes ☐ No
    e. By product redesign? ☐ Yes ☐ No
    f. _____
    g. _____

19. List some of the best prospects for reduced costs with plans for reducing.

    _____
    _____
    _____
    _____
    _____
    _____
    _____

20. Increase sales income by adding other products/services without increasing expenses a comparable amount? ☐ Yes ☐ No
    List some possibilities.

    _____
    _____
    _____
    _____
    _____
    _____
    _____
    _____
    _____
    _____
    _____
    _____
    _____
    _____
    _____
    _____

21. Subcontract some work or products? ☐ Yes ☐ No

### Sales volume

22. Do you know how the company's costs vary with changes in sales volume? ☐ Yes ☐ No
    (Worksheet #1 can be used to estimate how expenses vary with sales volume change.)

23. Do you know the company's break-even volume? ☐ Yes ☐ No

### Evaluation of methods to improve profit

| | Change in Income | Change in Expenses | Net Change |
|---|---|---|---|
| 24. Increase sales income and sales promotion expenses: | $ | $ | $ |
| 25. Increase sales price, decrease sales volume and expenses: | $ | $ | $ |
| 26. Decrease sales price, increase sales volume and expenses: | $ | $ | $ |
| 27. Change price mix: | $ | $ | $ |
| 28. Reduce expenses (usually), added expense: | $ | $ | $ |
| 29. Add other products—added sales income and expenses: | $ | $ | $ |
| 30. Subcontract—change expenses: | $ | $ | $ |

## Exhibit 15–3 (continued)

**Next year's plan**

Select plans for this next year.

31. Will any changes result in a plan to obtain desired profit? □ Yes □ No
    If no, are there other changes which will give desired profit? □ Yes □ No
    Or should you operate this next year with a smaller planned profit and work toward the desired profit in future years? □ Yes □ No
    Or should you sell your business? □ Yes □ No

32. Complete columns (1) and (2) in Worksheet 2.

**Evaluation**

At end of first month or quarter, complete columns (3) and (4) in Worksheet #2.

33. Evaluate performance. _____
    _____

34. List decisions made and actions to take to bring plans and/or performance into line with your desired performance:

    _____
    _____
    _____
    _____
    _____
    _____

**Worksheet 1. Expense Variation with Changes in Sales Volume.**

| Item | Years | | | | | Fixed Expense | Variable/ Unit of ____ |
|---|---|---|---|---|---|---|---|
| | 5 | 4 | 3 | 2 | 1 | | |
| Sales or production level | | | | | | | |
| Expenses: 1a. Material | $ | $ | $ | $ | $ | $ | $ |
| 1b. Labor | | | | | | | |
| 1c. Production overhead | | | | | | | |
| 2. Salaries | | | | | | | |
| 3. Utilities | | | | | | | |
| 4. Depreciation | | | | | | | |
| 5. Rent | | | | | | | |
| 6. Building services | | | | | | | |
| 7. Insurance | | | | | | | |
| 8. Interest | | | | | | | |
| 9. Office expense | | | | | | | |
| 10. Sales promotion | | | | | | | |
| 11. Taxes and licenses | | | | | | | |
| 12. Maintenance | | | | | | | |
| 13. Delivery | | | | | | | |
| 14. | | | | | | | |
| 15. | | | | | | | |
| 16. | | | | | | | |
| 17. Total expenses | $ | $ | $ | $ | $ | $ | $ |

Note: Break-even point = Sales income X (1 minus variable expense rate) — fixed expenses = 0.

_____ X (1 — _____) — _____ = 0

*Exhibit 15–3 (concluded)*
## Worksheet 2:    Financial Plans for Planned Profit

| Item | (1)<br>Plan for<br>19___ | (2)<br>Plan for<br>☐First Month, or ☐Quarter | (3)<br>Actual for | (4)<br>Variance<br>(2) — (3) |
|---|---|---|---|---|
| Sales income | $ | $ | $ | $ |
| Expenses<br>1a.  Material | | | | |
| 1b.  Labor | | | | |
| 1c.  Production overhead | | | | |
| 2.  Salaries | | | | |
| 3.  Utilities | | | | |
| 4.  Depreciation | | | | |
| 5.  Rent | | | | |
| 6.  Building services | | | | |
| 7.  Insurance | | | | |
| 8.  Interest | | | | |
| 9.  Office expense | | | | |
| 10.  Sales promotion | | | | |
| 11.  Taxes and licenses | | | | |
| 12.  Maintenance | | | | |
| 13.  Delivery | | | | |
| 14. | | | | |
| 15. | | | | |
| 16. | | | | |
| 17.  Total expenses | $ | $ | $ | $ |
| Profit before taxes | $ | $ | $ | $ |
| Income taxes | | | | |
| Profit after taxes | $ | $ | $ | $ |

*Exhibit 15—4*
## Determining Whether Full Earning Potential Is Being Exploited

Even though you have considered net income and have calculated net income/sales and net income/equity ratios, have you made a more detailed examination of your business to determine whether its full earning potential is being exploited? The purpose of this questionnaire is to enable you to make this detailed examination.

1. Have you calculated expense ratios and trends and compared them with ratios published by Dun & Bradstreet, trade associations, or other sources?
   □ Yes □ No

2. If you are a manufacturer, have you estimated as carefully as possible the profitability of each product, territory, and customer?   □ Yes □ No

**Product profitability**

3. Have you determined your manufacturing efficiency in producing each product?   □ Yes □ No

4. Have you determined the operating efficiency related to each product?   □ Yes □ No

5. Is the profit margin on each product adequate to justify its retention in the product line?   □ Yes □ No

6. If nominal profits or losses are sustained on one or more of your products, should these products be continued in your line?   □ Yes □ No
   Are they essential to make your "good products go"?
   □ Yes □ No

**Territory profitability**

7. Does your firm have poor customer coverage, indicated by excessive complaints and requests for sales service?   □ Yes □ No

8. Does your firm have insufficient new accounts?
   □ Yes □ No

9. Is your firm unable to present and push new products?   □ Yes □ No

10. Does your firm have excessive variances in selling cost ratios among the field salespersons?
    □ Yes □ No

11. Does your firm have high travel costs in comparison to industry averages?   □ Yes □ No

12. Are some of your salespersons "creaming the market" because their territories are too "rich" for thorough coverage?   □ Yes □ No

13. Is your firm's turnover of salespersons too high, due to excessive time away from home?   □ Yes □ No

14. Does each of your territories have sufficient revenues (or at least potential revenues) to justify the costs (shipping cost, salespersons' expenses, etc.)?
    □ Yes □ No

**Customer profitability**

15. Is your firm characterized by a great number of accounts representing only a small portion of your sales volume? (For example, 80 percent of your accounts represent 20 percent of the sales volume.)
    □ Yes □ No

16. Do you derive sufficient revenues (or at least potential revenues) from each of your customers to justify the costs of serving them?   □ Yes □ No

17. If your firm is nonmanufacturing, have you evaluated the service or selling departments?   □ Yes □ No

**Sales potential and selling methods**

18. Does your firm have:
    a. A saturated market?   □ Yes □ No
    b. An unexploited market?   □ Yes □ No

19. By plotting company and industry sales on a single ratio chart, have you compared your firm's growth with that of the industry?   □ Yes □ No

**Gross profit analysis**

20. Have you examined any unfavorable gross profit trend in your firm?   □ Yes □ No

21. Have you analyzed gross profit variations to determine the reasons for them?   □ Yes □ No

## Exhibit 15–5
## Evaluating Credit and Accounts Receivable

Accounts receivable represents an investment for which you receive no income, may incur losses, and may expand sales. Completion of this checklist should aid you in setting up policies and procedures for credit and accounts receivable which will give you the best balance between gains and losses.

**Present status and policies**

1. My company's balance of accounts receivable is:
   a. Percent of assets?  _____%
      Industry average?  _____%
   b. How many days of sales?  _____
      Industry average?  _____
      (sales/365/accounts receivable)
   c. Increasing?  ☐Yes ☐No
      Decreasing?  ☐Yes ☐No
      About constant?  ☐Yes ☐No

2. My company's bad debts last year were? $_____
   As a percentage of sales?  _____%
   Industry average?  _____%

3. The age of the accounts receivables is as follows:

| Time since Billing: | Dollars | Percent |
|---|---|---|
| 30 Days or Less | $_____ | _____% |
| 31 Days to 60 Days | $_____ | _____% |
| 61 Days to 6 Months | $_____ | _____% |
| 6 Months to 1 Year | $_____ | _____% |
| Over 1 Year | $_____ | _____% |
| Total | $_____ | _____% |

4. My company's policy on credit is:
   a. To sell only for cash?  ☐Yes ☐No
   b. To extend credit?  ☐Yes ☐No
      (1) Percent of sales on credit?  _____%
      (2) Open account?  _____%
      (3) Credit cards?  _____%
      (4) Which credit cards?_____
   c. To accept checks?  ☐Yes ☐No
      Identification needed? _____

5. Terms of credit extended are: _____

6. Are cash discounts given?  ☐Yes ☐No
   If yes, what are the terms? _____

7. Company policy regarding delinquent accounts is: _____

8. What percent of delinquent accounts were collected last year?  _____%

**Control of credit and accounts receivable**

9. Is the extension of credit based on a policy?
   ☐Yes ☐No
   a. Check of customer's background?  ☐Yes ☐No
   b. Credit bureau's research?  ☐Yes ☐No
   c. Credit card?  ☐Yes ☐No
   d. Judgment of a company employee?  ☐Yes ☐No
   e. Signing sales slip?  ☐Yes ☐No
   f. Other? (specify)_____

10. Monthly statements are sent to:
    a. All customers on company books?  ☐Yes ☐No
    b. All customers with a balance due?  ☐Yes ☐No

11. Are credit extension activities separated from sales activities?  ☐Yes ☐No

12. Are bad debts:
    a. Kept so low as to suggest lost sales? ☐Yes ☐No
    b. Too high, indicating a lax credit system?
       ☐Yes ☐No
    c. Properly removed from accounts receivable to expense?  ☐Yes ☐No
    d. Reviewed periodically by a responsible person?
       ☐Yes ☐No
    e. Pursued after writing off?  ☐Yes ☐No

13. Does person who prepares sales invoices have access to cash?  ☐Yes ☐No

14. Does a responsible official:
    a. Authorize extension of credit?  ☐Yes ☐No
    b. Approve returns and allowances?  ☐Yes ☐No
    c. Approve discounts?  ☐Yes ☐No

15. Are the duties of accounts receivable bookkeeper separate from any cash functions?  ☐Yes ☐No

16. Are accounts receivable audited?  ☐Yes ☐No

17. The following actions are taken for accounts the following ages:
    30 days _____
    60 days _____
    90 days _____
    Bad debt _____

18. Do you collect data on credit sales and accounts receivable for decision-making purposes?
    ☐Yes ☐No

## Exhibit 15–5 *(concluded)*

**Procedure for accounts receivable**

19. Does each customer receive a sales slip and/or invoice with the goods/service?  ☐ Yes ☐ No

20. How many copies are made of the sales slip? _____

21. List the places slips go, activities, and forms to which information is copied.

| Place, Function or Department | Activities | Other Forms |
|---|---|---|
| | | |
| | | |
| | | |
| | | |
| | | |

22. Is each customer's account:
   a. Balance kept on one form?  ☐ Yes ☐ No
      (1) Posted by hand?  ☐ Yes ☐ No
      (2) Posted by machine?  ☐ Yes ☐ No
      (3) Posted by other means?  ☐ Yes ☐ No
   b. Balance kept by filing sales slips?  ☐ Yes ☐ No
   c. Balance not kept?  ☐ Yes ☐ No
      Explain _____
   d. Other? (specify)_____

23. Are copies of sales slips sent out with bills?
      ☐ Yes ☐ No

24. Is there a set procedure for handling:
   a. Returned items?  ☐ Yes ☐ No
   b. Defective items?  ☐ Yes ☐ No
   c. COD sales?  ☐ Yes ☐ No
   d Other? (specify)_____

25. Are customers billed:
   a. Once a month?  ☐ Yes ☐ No
      (1) At end of month?  ☐ Yes ☐ No
      (2) On a set schedule during month? ☐ Yes ☐ No
      (3) When time is available?  ☐ Yes ☐ No
   b. On delivery?  ☐ Yes ☐ No
   c. Other? (specify)_____

**Cost of credit and accounts receivable**

26. How much do its credit operations cost the company?  $_____
   a. Cost of credit department or function?  $_____
   b. Cost of bad debts?  $_____
   c. Interest lost on money invested?  $_____

27. How much does it cost to process a bill from updating account to receiving money? (estimate)  $_____

28. How much does a credit card sale cost for service?
      _____%

29. How much does it cost to collect a delinquent account (average)?  $_____

30. How much does it cost to process:
   a. A returned item?  $_____
   b. A defective item?  $_____
      Do you receive any rebates on this item?
      ☐ Yes ☐ No

**Changes**

31. Are you planning to make changes?  ☐ Yes ☐ No
   If yes, list changes and procedure to make changes.

   _____
   _____
   _____
   _____
   _____
   _____
   _____
   _____
   _____

## Exhibit 15–6
## Evaluating Your Credit and Collections

Many firms deal with credit and collections in a haphazard manner. It is the purpose of this questionnaire to aid you in developing a formalized system for choosing credit customers and providing for a regular and orderly collection of your accounts receivable. An often overlooked fact is that capital tied up in accounts receivable has cost. A shorter collection cycle reduces this cost. In addition, uncollectible accounts that are not charged off increase your income tax liability and give an erroneous perspective of your net worth.

1. What is the current status of your accounts receivable:

| Age | $ Amount | % Outstanding A/R |
|---|---|---|
| 30 days or less | | |
| 30-45 days | | |
| 45-60 days | | |
| 60-75 days | | |
| 75-90 days | | |
| 90-120 days | | |
| 120-180 days | | |
| Over 180 days | | |

What is the average current collection cycle (in days)? ⎯⎯⎯⎯

2. What percentage of your assets are in accounts receivable? ⎯⎯⎯⎯%

3. Does there seem to be a tendency for your accounts receivable to be concentrated among a small proportion of your customers? ☐ Yes ☐ No

4. What would happen to your business if you suddenly failed to collect these concentrated accounts:
   a. Nothing? ☐ Yes ☐ No
   b. Activity would be curtailed? ☐ Yes ☐ No
   c. Business would fail? ☐ Yes ☐ No

5. In giving credit to a customer, do you:
   a. Set a dollar limit line of credit? ☐ Yes ☐ No
   b. Leave the amount of credit open? ☐ Yes ☐ No
   c. Give consideration to ability to pay obligation? ☐ Yes ☐ No

6. How do you determine the creditworthiness of a customer:
   a. Depend on personal knowledge of customer's credit history? ☐ Yes ☐ No
   b. Depend on personal ability to judge a person's integrity by appearance? ☐ Yes ☐ No
   c. Check on credit references? ☐ Yes ☐ No
   d. Check with customer's bank? ☐ Yes ☐ No
   e. Request most recent financial statement? ☐ Yes ☐ No
   f. Request bank letter of credit? ☐ Yes ☐ No

g. Obtain credit history report from credit bureau/credit investigating service? ☐ Yes ☐ No
h. Ask to see personal credit cards (consider creditworthy if customer possesses national credit cards)? ☐ Yes ☐ No
i. Generally, extend credit to anyone requesting it? ☐ Yes ☐ No

7. Do you ever review the credit status of each of your customers? ☐ Yes ☐ No
   If yes, how often? ⎯⎯⎯⎯⎯⎯⎯⎯

8. What procedure do you use in collecting your accounts receivable?
   a. Monthly statements? ☐ Yes ☐ No
   b. Send letter at end of 45 days? ☐ Yes ☐ No
   c. Send second letter at end of 60 days? ☐ Yes ☐ No
   d. Make a telephone call after ⎯⎯⎯⎯ days? ☐ Yes ☐ No
   e. Make a second telephone call after ⎯⎯⎯⎯ days? ☐ Yes ☐ No
   f. Make a personal visit after ⎯⎯⎯⎯ days? ☐ Yes ☐ No
   g. Send a strong letter indicating legal/collection agency action after ⎯⎯⎯⎯ days? ☐ Yes ☐ No
   h. Turn account over to lawyer/credit bureau for collection/collection agency after ⎯⎯⎯⎯ days? ☐ Yes ☐ No
   i. Charge account off to bad debts after ⎯⎯⎯⎯ days? ☐ Yes ☐ No
   (Generally, this should be done after six months. This does not mean that you shouldn't continue to try collecting the account.)
   j. Other comments: ⎯⎯⎯⎯⎯⎯⎯⎯
   ⎯⎯⎯⎯⎯⎯⎯⎯⎯⎯⎯⎯⎯⎯⎯⎯
   ⎯⎯⎯⎯⎯⎯⎯⎯⎯⎯⎯⎯⎯⎯⎯⎯
   ⎯⎯⎯⎯⎯⎯⎯⎯⎯⎯⎯⎯⎯⎯⎯⎯
   ⎯⎯⎯⎯⎯⎯⎯⎯⎯⎯⎯⎯⎯⎯⎯⎯
   ⎯⎯⎯⎯⎯⎯⎯⎯⎯⎯⎯⎯⎯⎯⎯⎯

9. Do you have customers whom you are reluctant to press for collection? ☐ Yes ☐ No
   If yes, why? ⎯⎯⎯⎯⎯⎯⎯⎯⎯⎯
   ⎯⎯⎯⎯⎯⎯⎯⎯⎯⎯⎯⎯⎯⎯⎯⎯
   ⎯⎯⎯⎯⎯⎯⎯⎯⎯⎯⎯⎯⎯⎯⎯⎯

10. At what point do you cut off a customer's credit?
    Days ⎯⎯⎯⎯ $⎯⎯⎯⎯
    Other: ⎯⎯⎯⎯⎯⎯⎯⎯⎯⎯
    ⎯⎯⎯⎯⎯⎯⎯⎯⎯⎯⎯⎯⎯⎯⎯⎯
    ⎯⎯⎯⎯⎯⎯⎯⎯⎯⎯⎯⎯⎯⎯⎯⎯

11. When do you go to COD? ⎯⎯⎯⎯⎯⎯
    ⎯⎯⎯⎯⎯⎯⎯⎯⎯⎯⎯⎯⎯⎯⎯⎯
    ⎯⎯⎯⎯⎯⎯⎯⎯⎯⎯⎯⎯⎯⎯⎯⎯

## Exhibit 15–6 (concluded)

12. What percent of your sales are:
    a. Open account? _____ %
    b. National/local credit cards? _____ %
    c. Factored? _____ %
    d. Other? _____ %
       What terms? _____

13. Have you made a cost comparison among the various methods of financing your credit sales?
    ☐ Yes ☐ No

14. What percent of your sales are charged off to bad debts? _____ %

15. How much does it cost you to carry your accounts receivable:
    a. Per week? $_____
    b. Per month? $_____
    c. Per quarter? $_____
    d. Per year? $_____

16. After reviewing the information above concerning your credit experience and your credit policies, what changes do you propose?

_____
_____
_____
_____
_____
_____
_____
_____
_____
_____

Note: It may seem from this credit and collection analysis that the authors are anticredit. Let us assure you that this is not the case. We believe that a sound program of credits and collection will provide expanded sales and profitability. Just remember, however, that a sale is useful only after the cash is in the till.

# *Part 5*

# Some Special Considerations in Managing an Independent Business

Most of the general aspects of managing a smaller, or independent, business have been covered in the preceding parts. However, there are special considerations that need to be viewed. The chapters of this part are intended to provide this information.

Chapter 16 deals with issues of safeguarding your assets. Chapter 17 gives you a perspective relating to the role of tax planning and business activity. Chapter 18 gives you a brief insight into the roles of bankruptcy in business operations. Then, Chapter 19 presents you with the issues and needs in providing for management succession. We have found this to be a topic that the vast majority of business owners do not want to talk about—in fact, they almost always refuse to discuss it. Yet, to be realistic in assuring the continuance of the firm or in providing a going concern for your children to operate, this question must be viewed analytically. The material found in Chapters 17 and 19 should be of additional assistance in dealing with the matter of management succession.

# Chapter Sixteen

# Safeguarding the Firm's Assets

"The number of colleges offering courses in 'security and loss prevention' is soaring, according to the American Society for Industrial Security. There are 30 colleges in the Midwest alone that offer degrees in the field. [This is a tremendous increase] from two nationwide in 1972. Students study such things as accounting, criminal investigation, and computer security."[1] This trend dramatizes the growing need to safeguard your assets.

This chapter deals with the many risks that you face in managing and operating your company. The more common risks that are emphasized are fire hazards; flood, hurricane, and tornado losses; business interruptions; liability; death or other loss of a key executive; business frauds; and crime.

Insurance provides one of the surest and most effective methods of safeguarding yourself against extremely large losses from these risks. In addition there are many security measures you can take that will further reduce your chances—or at least the magnitude—of loss.

The first part of the chapter discusses how you can use insurance to minimize your losses. The second part looks at security systems you might use to deter losses from crime.

---

[1]*The Wall Street Journal*, April 17, 1979, p. 1.

## Safeguarding Your Assets with Insurance

In deciding what to do about business risks, you should ask yourself, Without adequate insurance, what happens to my company if:

1. I die or suddenly become incapacitated?
2. A fire destroys my firm's building and/or inventories?
3. A customer is awarded a liability judgment for an accident?
4. There is pilferage by customers or employees?
5. An employee embezzles company funds?
6. A robber "hits" my firm?
7. A customer is awarded a whopping settlement after bringing a product liability suit?

Often, when such disasters occur in independent companies whose insurance protection is inadequate or nil, the owners are forced out of business or operations are severely restricted. Therefore, you need to understand as much as possible about the nature of insurance and how you can use it for your protection.

### The Nature of Insurance and Its Limitations

Pure risk always exists when the possibility of a loss is present but you do not know the possible extent of the loss. The consequences of a fire, the death of a key employee, or a liability judgment cannot be predicted with any degree of certainty. Yet it is probably impossible to handle the full burden of pure risks through insurance, because the premiums would be so great that they would leave you nothing, or almost nothing, with which to operate your business.

The principal value of insurance is its reduction of pure risk. In buying insurance, you are trading a potentially large but uncertain loss for a small but certain cost (the expenditure for the premium). Briefly, you are trading uncertainty for certainty.

You should not attempt to insure situations that should be handled in other ways, such as:

1. Trivial losses. If the potential loss is trvial, you should not insure against it.
2. Unnecessary coverage. If the insurance premium is a substantial proportion of the value of the property, you should not buy the insurance. For example, if the annual premium for a $50-deductible automobile collision insurance policy is $35 greater than the premium for a $100 deductible, the insured would in effect be paying $35 for $50 additional coverage—70 percent of the possible recovery if a single collision occurred during the policy term.

A well-designed insurance program not only provides for losses but also provides other values, including reduction of worry, freeing funds for investment, loss prevention, and easing of credit.

## Alternatives to Commercial Insurance

Methods other than commercial insurance for dealing with risk include noninsurance, loss prevention, risk transfer, and self-insurance. One or more of these methods, combined with commercial insurance, may reduce your costs related to risks.

Noninsurance is used by most firms, for they must inevitably assume some risks. You should use this method only when the severity of the potential loss is low and when risks are more or less predictable, preventable, or largely reducible.

Loss prevention programs involve reducing the probability of loss. Examples include programs for preventing fire and burglary. Such programs usually result in reductions in insurance premiums.

Risk transfer involves transferring the risk of loss to others, as in leasing an automobile under a contract whereby the lessor buys the accident insurance.

For self-insurance to be considered, you should have adequate finances and broadly diversified risks. Often these requirements cannot be met in independent companies. Self-insurance plans should be actuarially maintained with a cash reserve accumulated to provide for losses.

## Types of Coverage

Some of the major types of insurance you should consider are:

1. Fire.
2. Casualty.
3. General liability.
4. Workers' compensation.
5. Business life.
6. Business continuation life insurance.
7. Fidelity and surety bonds.

The basic fire insurance policy insures you for only fire, lightning, and losses due to temporary removal of goods from your premises because of fire. In most instances, this policy should be supplemented with an extended coverage endorsement that insures against windstorm, hail, explosion, riot, and aircraft, vehicle, and smoke damage. Business interruption coverage should also be provided through an endorsement, because indirect losses are frequently more severe in their eventual cost than are direct losses.

To illustrate, while rebuilding after a fire, you must continue to pay salaries of key employees and expenses such as utilities, interest, and taxes.

Casualty insurance consists of automobile insurance (both collision and public liability) plus general liability, burglary, theft, robbery, plate glass, and health and accident insurance. Automobile liability and physical damage insurance are necessary because firms may be legally liable for the use of trucks and passenger cars in their behalf, even those the company does not own. For example, employees may use their own cars on company business. In case of accident, the employer is liable.

General liability insurance is particularly important because, in conducting your business, you are subject to common and statutory laws governing negligence to customers, employees, and anyone else with whom you do business. One liability judgment could easily result in the liquidation of a business.

Workers' compensation and employer liability insurance are related to common-law requirements that an employer provide employees a safe place to work, hire competent fellow employees, provide safe tools, and warn employees of any existing danger. Damage suits may be brought by employees for failure of employers to perform these duties. State statutes govern the kinds of benefits payable under workers' compensation policies, which typically provide for medical care, lump sums for dismemberment and death, benefits for disablements by occupational disease, and income payments for disabled workers or their dependents.

Business life insurance can be used in several ways in independent firms. A firm can buy, or help buy, group life insurance and health insurance policies for its employees.

Also, business owner's insurance is an important coverage consisting of:

1. Protection of an owner or dependents against losses from premature death, disability, or medical expenses.
2. Provision for the continuation of a business following the premature death of an owner.

Business continuation life insurance, which is related to (2), is used in sole proprietorships, partnerships, and closely-held corporations. Advance planning involves the provision of ample cash and projecting its use. Life insurance often provides the cash, while the trust agreement, coupled with a purchase-and-sale plan, provides for its use. The cash can be used to retire the interest of a partner or to repurchase the stock of a closely held corporation. As for life insurance, partners or stockholders may buy sufficient insurance on each other's life to retire each other's interest in case of death.

Fidelity and surety bonds are issued by insurers that guarantee that your employees and others with whom your company transacts business are honest and will fulfill their contractual obligations. Fidelity bonds are purchased for employees occupying positions that involve the handling of company funds, in order to provide protection against their dishonesty. Surety bonds provide protection against the failure of others to fulfill contractual obligations.

### Guides to Selecting an Insurer

In choosing an insurer, the two most important factors are:

1. Financial characteristics of the insurer and the insurer's flexibility in meeting your requirements.
2. Services rendered by the agent.

***Financial Characteristics and Flexibility of Insurer.*** The major types of insurers are stock companies, mutual companies, reciprocals, and Lloyd's groups. While mutuals and reciprocals are cooperatively organized and sell insurance "at cost," in practice their costs may be no lower than those of profit-making companies. In comparing different types of insurers, you should use the following criteria:

1. Financial stability.
2. Specialization in types of coverage.
3. Flexibility in the offering of coverage.
4. Cost of protection.

Only after you are satisfied with the first, second, and third should you consider the fourth of these criteria.

While you ordinarily rely on your insurance agent to judge the financial stability of insurers, Best's Insurance Reports are reliable sources of financial ratings and analyses of insurers if you want to check for yourself.

Some insurers specialize in certain types of coverage and offer the advantage of greater experience in these lines. For example, Lloyd's groups often underwrite unusual risks that other insurers will not assume.

Some insurers offer great flexibility by tailoring their policies to meet your needs. Tailoring can be accomplished through the insertion of special provisions in the contracts and/or the provision of certain services to meet particular requirements.

In making cost comparisons, you should not confuse the initial premium with the net premium. Some insurers have a lower initial rate (deviated rate), while others have a higher initial rate but pay a dividend to the insured. Valid comparisons of insurance costs are difficult to make, but insurance brokers, independent insurance advisers, or agents may assist you.

***Services Rendered by Agent.*** You should decide which qualifications of agents are most important, and then inquire about agents among business friends and others who have had experience with them. In comparing agents, some of the things to look for are contacts among insurers, professionalism, degree of individual attention, quality of extra services, and help in time of loss.

You should determine whether an agent's contacts among insurers are sufficiently broad to supply all the coverage needed without undue delay and at reasonable cost. Professionalism is indicated by the agent's possession of the Chartered Life Underwriter or Chartered Property and Casualty Underwriter designation. Choose an agent who is willing and able to devote enough time to your individual problems to justify the commission, to survey exposure to loss, to recommend adequate insurance and loss prevention programs, and to offer alternative methods of insurance. The agent should also be known for serving clients well in time of loss. The quality of the agent and the companies represented may be validated by checking with your state's insurance commission.

### Product Liability

In our contemporary legal and societal environment, the liability of the producer or seller of a product or service is increasingly significant. A recent Supreme Court decision holding a manufacturer liable for a piece of equipment sold to the Navy during World War II and subsequently sold to a series of purchasers has reverberated through both business and casualty insurance communities. Premiums for product/service liability coverage are becoming exorbitant. Since many independent business managers and owners are unaware of the potential liability they may incur in offering their products or services, we urge you to give thoughtful consideration to your possible liabilities. Seek the guidance of your attorney and the assistance of your insurance agent or broker to minimize cost and maximize protection from such claims. Since legislative action and court decisions are regularly occurring in this field, we suggest that you stay current on the legal status.

## Safeguarding Your Assets with Security Systems

It is important that independent business owners be aware of crimes that may be committed against their businesses. You are probably aware of incidents of criminal acts that have forced independent—

as well as large—businesses into insolvency. We will cover three areas in this category: armed robbery, pilferage, and white-collar (employee) crimes.

It is our intention to make you aware of the potential dangers and to make suggestions that will help you to minimize the risks involved and to deter those who would harm you. You will note that we say deter, not prevent, for it seems impossible to have a security program that will prevent all criminal acts against your business. All you can hope to do is minimize their occurrence and severity.

## Armed Robbery

*Nature of the Problem.* In recent years, the incidence of armed robbery has increased significantly. A person or persons enter the premises armed and with the intent of obtaining cash as quickly as possible and then departing. Since time is of the essence in these circumstances, locations that afford easy access and relatively secure escape routes seem most vulnerable to being hit. This type of robber usually wants to be in and out of the location in three minutes or less in order to minimize the risk of identification or apprehension. The pressure of the situation tends to make the robber trigger-happy.

We are becoming more aware of areas particularly susceptible to crime. The nature of the crimes seems to fit a pattern—there may be a given neighborhood where armed robbery occurs frequently; there may be another where pilferage is the problem; or there may be an area where both categories are problems. Because of the increasing incidence of this type of problem, you as a business owner need to evaluate a potential site with this problem in mind.

*Preventive Measures.* Several measures can be taken to reduce the chances of being robbed. They include modifying the layout of your store, securing entrances, using security dogs, controlling the handling of cash, and redesigning the surrounding area.

*Modifying store layout.* Location of the cash register or cash is important in preventing armed robbery. If the perpetrators are not able to dash in, scoop up the cash and dash out again within a short time, they are not as likely to attempt the robbery. Visibility from the outside, or being able to see all over the customer area, is also important.

One convenience food chain removed all material from the windows that would impair the view into the store. In addition, it encouraged crowds at all hours by using various gimmicks, and attracted policemen by giving them free coffee. The average annual robbery rate dropped markedly.

*Securing entrances.* Security of entrances and exits is extremely important in preventing robbery. Rear doors should be kept locked and barred. Windows should be kept secure by bars and locks. In high-crime neighborhoods, many businesses have found it advantageous not to use glass in their windows, but to use a tough, shock-resistant, transparent material such as Lexan.[2] Safes are not infallible. Many businesses no longer allow access to the safe's combination by more than one or two people. It is not uncommon for a sign to be posted on the safe, or in its vicinity, advising that the person on duty does not have access to the combination.

*Dogs.* You may obtain security dogs from people who train vicious dogs to respond to command. These animals have been found to be effective deterrents against armed robbers. The animals may be purchased outright or rented. Even if you purchase a dog, it may be advisable to have it periodically run through a refresher course to keep it effective. Health and sanitation regulations, in some jurisdictions, may prevent the use of dogs.

*Controlling the handling of cash.* Daily deposit of cash is highly recommended. Banks and other businesses are rigidly enforcing minimum cash rules for cash drawers. In order to reduce the loss in the event of an armed robbery, some business people have found it desirable to keep only minimum cash on hand and to use safes with unobtrusive hiding places.

> Several businesses have found it advantageous to use lockboxes with a sign posted for all to see: "Notice: Cash in drawer does not exceed $50."
> Other stores use locked cash boxes and accept only correct change or credit cards during certain hours. (The locked cash box usually has an accompanying sign saying that no employee on duty has a key to the box.)

Different people, different vehicles, and different times should be used to make deposits. If easily recognized people use predictable vehicles routinely to make deposits, they invite the would-be robber and make it easier to plan and carry out the robbery.

*Redesigning the surroundings.* Well-lighted parking lots help deter robbers. If possible, try to keep vehicles from parking too

---

[2]A trademarked product of General Electric Co.

near the entrance of your business. Anything that reduces the convenience of access or creates the possibility of a foul-up reduces the probability of armed robbery.

> A convenience food store parking lot had concrete precast bumper blocks so dispersed in the lot that they deterred fast entry and exit from the lot.

It is advisable for some businesses to use video cameras to photograph crime in action from several different camera angles, or to use video cameras tied to TV monitors in a security office.

## Pilferage

*Nature of the Problem.* Pilferage has become a serious problem for businesses, and the reasons are numerous. One is inflation. As incomes have not kept up with rising prices, people resort to pilferage to maintain the standard of living to which they have become accustomed. Many national merchandising businesses add a factor of 2–3 percent pilferage cost to their prices, but even this may not be enough to compensate for the total loss. Another reason is the recent high level of unemployment. In order to survive, some of the unemployed have resorted to pilferage. In other instances, pilferage is a game, a challenge—Can I get away with it?—and unfortunately, in some circumstances, it occurs for peer approval.

*Types of Pilferage.* There are essentially two types of pilfering—that done by outsiders, which is usually called shoplifting, and that done by employees.

Shoplifting may be done by the amateur, the kleptomaniac, or the professional. The amateur may be a thrill seeker who takes an item or two—experimenting to see whether he or she can get away with the act. Or the person may not be able to purchase the item, and desire for it overcomes self-control. The kleptomaniac is the individual with an uncontrollable urge to take things, whether they are needed or not. The professional is a person who may wear specially prepared or large garments to conceal stolen merchandise. Instead of special garments, the thief may carry a large handbag to accommodate the loot. Other professionals may ask you for an empty box, or boxes, which will then be used to facilitate removal of merchandise. Another may walk in with an air of confidence (as if he or she were a delivery person or clerk), pick up merchandise, and proceed out of the store.

> A convenience food store was forced out of business by pilferage losses. Customers concealed prepackaged cheese, luncheon meats, and other high-value items in regular garment pockets and handbags.

A well-known matron was at the checkout counter. Upon inspection, her large purse was found to contain several prepackaged steaks and packages of luncheon meat. The store owner was heard to observe, "I thought she was one of our good customers. She has been coming in here for years. I wonder how much she has taken?"

A man entered a store during the rush hour, picked up a large box, moved to the cartoned-cigarette display, filled the box with cartons of cigarettes, hoisted it on his shoulder, and proceeded to pass through the checkout as if he had an empty box. Suddenly the box separated, and 30 cartons of cigarettes fell to the floor. The culprit departed in haste.

Not easily discouraged, the culprit returned the following day with a well-taped box. Being immediately recognized, he was invited from the premises.

Employee pilferage may range from the act of an individual who takes only one or two small items to raids by groups that remove truckloads of merchandise. An individual employee, operating independently, may steal anything from an inconspicuous item to whatever he or she can get out the door. The culprit may be the person least likely to be suspected of such an act.

A batch mixer in a small baking plant carried away sugar, flour, and shortening in 25-pound metal cans in which other materials were received. Supposedly he was taking some empty cans home.

A fast-food place lost $20,000 worth of raw chicken in a six-month period, not by the piece or even as whole chickens, but by the case—out the back door.

Two or more employees may conspire to cheat their employer by stealing.

Workers loaded material to take to a job site, but no tally sheet identifying the quantity or kind of material was filled out. The trucks were detoured to the site of a side job being done after-hours by the employees, and a portion of the material was unloaded.

Some workers took a special route to a job, stopping at a place where some pipe, rolls of electrical wire, conduit, and electrical switch boxes were left for later retrieval and sale.

Construction materials may be pilfered by either employees or outsiders. A lack of controls, looseness of accountability, and the minimal—or nonexistent—security at many storage yards and job sites lead to this type of pilferage.

A contractor purchased a mobile concrete mixer and sent it to the site of one of his jobs. Those responsible for the mixer left it outside of the fenced-in area that night, and it was stolen. Subsequently, the contractor found that a subordinate had failed to record it for insurance coverage.

Employees sometimes conspire with outsiders to steal from their employer. They may do this in various ways—for example, by charging the outsiders a lower price or by placing additional merchandise in their package.

A service station attendant serviced a friend's car by changing the oil, lubricating it, and putting in $4 worth of gasoline. He charged the friend only $1.

A tire dealer's service attendant sold four first-line tires to a customer for $50 and pocketed the cash.

*Preventive Measures.* Several loss prevention techniques can be used by retail establishments and construction firms.

*Retail merchandising establishment.* These firms have found the following measures effective in reducing pilferage:

1. Wide-angle mirrors and one-way mirrors placed strategically about the store expand the opportunity to observe employee or customer behavior that indicates pilferage.
2. TV cameras are frequently tied to monitors that allow one person to observe a large portion of the store.
3. Electronic noise activators—some visible, some not— attached to the merchandise will activate an alarm if the merchandise is removed from the area without the warning device first being detached.
4. Security guards may also be used. If your business is large enough and if pilferage is sufficiently serious, you may wish to employ a full-time security person or obtain the services of an independent security organization.
5. Security audits are also effective. Unannounced spot checks of cash register activity may be advisable. Check to see if appropriate amounts are rung up. Be sure that correct change is returned and that all items are accounted for by the clerk or cashier.
   a. Unannounced spot checks may be made of employees' packages, car trunks, lunch pails, other personal effects, and rest rooms. Check garbage or waste disposal holding areas for concealed materials that may be removed later.
   b. Visible security surveillance may be used. It is important to observe employees in the normal work activities for indications of criminal acts.
   c. Monthly or quarterly physical inventory checks may be made. In many situations, they serve as a deterrent. On occasion it has been found even more effective to conduct weekly inventory checks.
6. Polygraph tests may be used before and after hiring—if legal

requirements are met. While the use of these tests is questioned by unions and others, many business people believe they serve as an effective deterrent against employee pilferage activities. Some firms require that such a test be taken by all employees periodically. In the event of questionable circumstances, they may be administered as part of an investigation. A word of caution: Before using polygraph tests, you should thoroughly investigate the background of persons or organizations responsible for administering the tests and consult an attorney.

*Construction contractors.* These firms need to take special care to prevent or minimize pilferage. Planning and control are important. You need to develop a schedule of materials needed for each job, including both the correct quantities of materials and the times they will be used on the job. You can then order the appropriate quantities of materials and time the delivery to meet the need. Delivery of material far in advance of need increases the opportunity for loss.

> One contractor found that by running his material inventory down near the end of the week and not replacing it until early Monday morning, he could substantially reduce his losses.

Purchasing procedures may be improved by ordering dimensional lumber and other materials and by determining the exact material requirements as specified in the project plans. These improvements reduce the opportunity for waste in the construction process and make it more difficult for someone to remove material from the job site without detection. It also helps you maintain more effective control over your costs.

Other security measures that you can take, in addition to dogs and security guards discussed earlier, include:

1. Storage yards should be fenced and well-lighted. There should be a cleared area adjacent to the fence on all sides.
2. Locks that are difficult to jimmy seem to provide additional security. A locksmith or a hardware dealer may provide the latest lock systems. No system is foolproof, however, so you may discourage only the amateurs with some of these systems.
3. You need a receiving clerk or some employee who is sufficiently knowledgeable to assume the responsibility for checking materials into the job site. Unfortunately, too many people fail to recognize the importance of this activity and permit it to be dealt with haphazardly. They say, "Put it over there, and when you've finished unloading check back with me." Unannounced rotation of the person responsible for receiving materials may serve as a deterrent to collusion with the delivery person.

## White-Collar (Employee) Crimes

*Nature of Problem.* Another category of serious abuse against business is white-collar crime, especially employee theft, which has been rising rapidly. Such thefts are estimated to amount to $50 billion in 1981.[3] Possibly the take is greater than the totals in other categories. White-collar crimes include the removal of cash; falsification of accounts; fraudulent computer manipulation; bribery of purchasing agents and various other employees; collusions that result in unrecorded transactions; sale of proprietary information; sabotage of new technology, new or old products, or customer relations; and so forth.

Who steals? Investigators say employees who think their income is too low or stagnating steal more often and in greater amounts than other employees. "The most likely employee thieves are young, ambitious clerks and professionals who feel frustrated in their jobs. So concludes a University of Minnesota study of 5,000 workers at stores, hospitals, and electronic manufacturing plants in the Minneapolis area."[4]

*Preventive Measures.* Special measures must be taken to minimize crimes by white-collar personnel.

*Audits.* Purchasing agents may take bribes, not always in cash but in various gratuity forms. Audit of inventory levels and prices on a comparative basis may uncover undesirable circumstances. This kind of detective work requires a much more thorough and detailed audit than is sometimes carried out.

Cashiers and disbursing agents have been known to prepare bogus or forged invoices, purchase orders, receiving reports, and so forth. Spot audits of documents and of actual receiving areas should help in reducing this type of loss.

Computer crimes are increasing in frequency and severity. If you use a computer in your business, you need the services of a CPA firm with computer security expertise.

*Officer adjustments.* Sales adjustments should be handled by an officer of the company. No salesperson should be permitted to make the adjustment, for that practice allows collusion and cash compromises to the customer's and salesperson's advantage. Ap-

---

[3]Paul A. Gigot, "Companies Try Harder to Recover Money Stolen by Their Employees," *The Wall Street Journal*, January 5, 1981, p. 13.

[4]*The Wall Street Journal*, January 6, 1981, p. 1.

propriate reports showing adjustments made on each customer's account should aid in revealing any misdeeds.

*Work habits vigil.* You should be aware of your white-collar employees' work habits. They may all be open and aboveboard, but they deserve being checked. You should ask yourself questions such as: Do they work nights regularly? Do they never take a day off? Do they forego their usual vacation? Standards of living, dress, car, housing, entertainment, and travel that seem to cost more than the employee can afford are often signals of economic misconduct.

*Identification.* Proper identification along with a device that takes pictures of the check and the person cashing it tend to discourage bad-check artists. Your bank may assist you in developing effective identification procedures.

Since credit cards are frequently stolen, you or your cashier should require additional identification. You should be sure that the signature corresponds to the one on the card.

> Recently a professional thief removed a credit card from a home. The card had never been used by the owner, but the thief used it to purchase an airline ticket, some personal items, and a new set of burglar tools. He signed the purchase tickets by crudely printing the name that was on the card. The carelessness in accepting the card needlessly cost the airlines and merchants $750.

As in the case of credit card, be sure to ascertain the validity of trade documents. Each year, millions of dollars are lost by business people through carelessness that allows others to pawn off on them bogus documents. A careful check with the appropriate bank or company prevents many of these losses.

**Insurance.** Fidelity bonding is a form of insurance against employee fraud or theft. The employer pays a premium to an insurance company to assume the risk.

### Document Security

Our recent personal experiences in working with independent businesses—as well as press releases in recent years—have made us aware of the importance of document security. Information is a vital factor in directing and controlling business activities. Its management and maintenance are significant in assuring the continuation of the business. The life of an organization is dependent on the appropriate recording of information and its transmission to the appropriate person. Recorded information can be classified as (1) confidential, or (2) nonconfidential (see Chapter 13).

The proprietary nature of confidential business records and various documents makes essential their protection from unauthorized eyes and hands. The trade secrets and competitive advantage of the firm may be lost if this information passes into the wrong hands. Records with confidential information should be stored in: (1) bank lockboxes, (2) safes, or (3) restricted areas. Only authorized persons should have access to these records.

In designing and maintaining a document security system, it is desirable to make a list of personnel who are authorized to have access to these records and documents. This list should be frequently updated and provided to the person or persons responsible for the document security.

An unbending rule should be that under no circumstance do you permit the removal of this material from the restricted area or from the business premises. Some business owners think they are able to gain an economic advantage by permitting material to be carried to an employee's residence where the employee works on the firm's records after hours when convenient. The opportunity for loss, the opportunity for access by unauthorized persons, and the risk of a claim for adequate compensation makes this practice inadvisable.

## Summary

The design of systems to safeguard assets is very important for a business. Insurance is used to reduce risks. A small but certain cost is substituted for a potentially large but uncertain loss. Commercial insurance and several alternatives can be used to protect a company from losses of physical assets and claims resulting from personal injury. Steps should be taken to select the proper insurer and agent.

Security systems can be used to protect against robbery, pilferage, and white-collar crimes. These systems involve properly designing procedures, installing protection devices, and hiring guards. Confidential documents warrant special attention.

## Where to Look for Further Information

Anthony, R. N., and Reece, James S. *Accounting: Text and Cases.* 6th ed. Homewood, Ill.: Richard D. Irwin, 1979.

Anthony, Robert N., and Welch, Glenn A. *Fundamentals of Management Accounting.* Rev. ed. Homewood, Ill.: Richard D. Irwin, 1977.

Brummet, R. L., and Robertson, J. C. "Cost Accounting for Small Manufacturers." 2d ed. *Small Business Management Series No. 9.* Washington, D.C.: Small Business Administration, 1974.

Crowningshield, Gerald R., and Gorman, Kenneth A. *Cost Accounting: Principles and Managerial Applications.* 4th ed. Boston: Houghton Mifflin, 1979.

Greene, Mark R. "Insurance Checklist for Small Business." *Small Marketers Aids No. 148.* Washington, D.C.: Small Business Administration, 1971.

Gruenwald, A. E., and Nemmers, E. E. *Basic Management Finance.* New York: Holt, Rinehart & Winston, 1970.

Horngren, Charles T. *Cost Accounting: A Manager's Analysis.* 4th ed. Englewood Cliffs, N.J.: Prentice-Hall, 1977.

Katz, G. *Happiness or Misery.* Alexandria, Va.: Overlook, 1971.

Kenney, Donald P. *Minicomputers.* New York: AMACOM, 1973.

Kreutzman, H. C. "Managing for Profits." *Management and Financial Control Series.* Washington, D.C.: Small Business Administration, 1968.

Miller, D. E. *The Meaningful Interpretation of Financial Statements.* Rev. ed. New York: American Management Association, 1979.

# Chapter Seventeen

## Tax Planning and Business Activity

This chapter's purpose is to give you a perspective of tax considerations that influence the plans and choices the business person makes. In order to accomplish our objective and cover the pertinent related topics, it has been necessary to create a lengthy chapter. Hopefully, you will find the material to be of exceptional value. The topics covered in this chapter are:

1. The role of taxes in business finance.
2. Estate taxes.
3. Buy-sell agreements.
4. Profit sharing.
5. Employee stock option plans (ESOPs).
6. Cooperatives.
7. The influence of taxes on operating management's decisions.

The purpose of considering each of these areas is to assure the protection and maximization of assets for both you and your heirs. This is more difficult to accomplish in a closely held business. The problem arises because, in these circumstances, it is frequently difficult to separate the business from personal affairs.

In the preparation of this material, we have tried to focus on the topical tax areas most appropriate to the average business person. An effort has been made to present information with the most practical application. We have relied very heavily on a *tax attorney practitioner,*[1] an individual whose day-to-day activities span a group of diverse businesses. These criteria, we believe, are essential to satisfy the guidance needs of the reader of this material.

## Role of Taxes in Business Finance

We will approach the role of taxes in business finance from these possibilities: financing the new business, financing a relatively new business, or financing an established business that wants to expand its operation.

### Example 1

An existing business may decide to acquire a new line. The existing business is producing Product X and has discovered that a larger company producing Product Y (a low volume, low product item which is not meeting that company's objectives) is available for purchase.

The first guiding principle, if possible, in purchasing another operation is to buy the assets. An exception would be in a case where there exists a substantial net operating loss, but the general rule for the buyer is to purchase only hard assets. The objective is to avoid the purchase of "goodwill" and nondepreciable assets of the corporation. Always try to negotiate the contract so that the total purchase price is based on hard assets only. You should try to avoid "blue sky," the residual beyond the value of the hard assets. In the event the purchase price will exceed the hard assets, the buyer should attempt to negotiate an agreement that the seller will not compete with the purchaser and charge as much of the margin as possible to the covenant not to compete. In order for this agreement to be legally binding, the time and area covered must be reasonable in nature.

If the so-called blue sky is covered by a noncompeting covenant, it is possible to amortize the value of the covenant over the life of the agreement. An astute seller may have problems in writing up the value of the depreciated assets and assigning a substantial value to the covenant not to compete. Any excess over the depreciated book value and the value of the covenant not to compete must be treated as ordinary income to seller.

One of the most important tax considerations of the buyer is to be sure as little value as possible is allocated to land, since it is nondepreciable.

---

[1]We are indebted to Mr. Woodrow Stewart, senior partner, Telford Law Firm, Gainesville, Georgia, for the guidance and information found in this chapter.

## Example 2

If the seller becomes a problem and refuses to sell under conditions of Example 1, then the purchaser needs to have his/her corporation purchase the stock of the seller at an agreed purchase price. The "target firm" (the purchased company) will then become a subsidiary. At the point of consummation of the transaction, the target subsidiary may be liquidated into the parent under section 334(b)(2) of the Internal Revenue Code. When this is done, the parent organization is able to spread the purchase price over the target's assets based upon their current market value. After this is done, and if the fair market value is greater than the current book value, the excess becomes current and ordinary income to the buyer to the extent of prior depreciation taken. Any amount in excess of the original cost is taxable at capital gains rate. Initially, this has a taxable effect on the buyer. However, the loss incurred from the additional taxes may be subsequently recaptured through the depreciation of depreciable assets (since the added amount above has an effect of raising the taxable basis). The result is a method of recapturing the "premium" portion of the purchase price.

*Special Note.* *Additional considerations.* The buyer should try to make sure that the buyer corporation's stock can be allocated to cover the value of the assets purchased. Any excess value will be treated as goodwill and will be considered nondepreciable. Consequently, insofar as tax benefits are concerned, they are irretrievably lost.

A buyer can look at such things as customer lists. If these lists have an ascertainable life, then they may be amortized in accordance with this life expectancy and can provide a tax benefit.

Assignments of patents, copyrights, and similar things may be amortized accordingly for tax benefits.

*Special note.* The past practice of buying a "loss corporation" in order to absorb profits of an existing corporation is virtually gone. Generally, the purchase of a loss corporation and the filing of a consolidated return will have the effect that the preacquisition losses of the target firm (acquired) can not be utilized on a carryforward basis in a consolidated return. Postacquisition losses can be, but of what good are they?

## Example 3

In a third example, the parent company acquires a controlling interest in the stock of target company (target company becomes a subsidiary of parent company).

*Alternative 1.* If the percent of old stock of the target company is reduced by more than 60 percent of stock owned prior to acquisition, the net operating loss carry-over of the target subsidiary is multiplied by 3.5 for any increased percentage points of more than 60 up to and including 80 percentage points. For any percentage points above 80, you use a multiplier of 1.5.

If you should want to use the net operating loss on a continuing basis, then you would purchase only 60 percent of the target company. In order to continue the use of net operating loss, it will be necessary for the previous ownership to retain at least 40 percent of the stock. Otherwise, the net operating loss will be reduced proportionately as indicated above.

*Alternative 2.* In the event that the parent company is experiencing high profits and the target company is doing all right profitwise, parent company can purchase the assets of target company and lease the assets back to target. The objective here is to purchase the assets at fair market value. Then, the write up of assets will provide depreciation to shelter part or all of the income generated by the lease payments. This alternative can, on occasion, provide a good return on this type of purchase investment, since this procedure will reduce current taxable income of the parent—especially good in the event that the buyer has excess income and earnings and is in need of tax benefits.

*Alternative 3.* In this case, the buyer is fairly heavily leveraged. An approach that might be used in this circumstance is to purchase the stock of the target company. The first step is to recapitalize the stock of the target and reclassify the stock. Usually, most of the common stock can be converted to preferred stock, with a view to dividends being paid to the preferred stockholder. This allows the purchaser to purchase the remaining common stock for little cash. In this case, the seller holds the preferred stock. This creates a preferred stock that can be converted to debt should the need arise. It is possible, under this arrangement to have an agreement with the preferred stockholders to redeem the stock over a period of years.

The advantage of this method to the purchaser is that it does not show as debt on the balance sheet. Therefore, the balance sheet gives a better picture to other interested parties. Besides giving a better financial statement appearance, this method enables the buyer to purchase the target company with very little cash.

# Estate Tax Planning

It is our intent to look at the various alternative considerations for estate tax planning in accordance with what is possible under the 1981 and 1982 Tax Acts. You should be aware, in estate planning, that the business aspects are entwined with the personal aspects of finance. In the circumstance of a closely held business, there always exists the potential for an estate tax problem.

## Primary Consideration

What can be done within an organization where there are younger family members?

The first need is to be able to control the older family member's estate tax problems. At a minimum, there may be a need to freeze the estate situation at its existing level. Otherwise, the estate tax liability will continue to grow. The procedures to follow will be determined by whether the business is a corporation or some other form.

*Alternative 1.* In this circumstance, we assume a partnership or the establishment of a partnership through which the estate of the older partner is frozen. By the establishment of a partnership agreement, the older partner will receive a fixed income in the nature of salaries and any other designated benefits desired. The younger partners (children, grandchildren, etc.) will pick up any residual income and growth in value. The transfer of partnership shares to the younger members could be dealt with under the 1981 Gift Tax Law. This law provides for a gift of $10,000 per donee per year. If the spouse of the donor joins in, then the amount becomes $20,000 per year. The latter is possible even if all of the assets are in the name of one person, if the other spouse also signs the gift tax return.

If the business is a service organization, it is likely that there will be little capital involved. Characteristically, service businesses are not as capital intensive as manufacturing or merchandising businesses.

In a capital-intensive business, each of the partners must have made a capital contribution to the business. By having a properly drawn partnership agreement, the principal donor may receive a level of income based on need. Then any residual income may flow to the other family partners. This arrangement, in fact, will *reduce* the *income tax liability* of the donor. Since the income will be spread among the younger family members who are in a lower tax bracket, it is possible in this situation for the family partnership to pay less income tax than the older family members did before. Often, more capital can be retained as operating capital for the firm. This results in more available capital to the business than would have been had if the assets were retained by the older owner. The estate tax benefits of the partnership arrangements are:

1. By the freeze at the point of creation of the family partnership arrangement, further growth in estate tax liability of the older owner is terminated, or
2. It is possible through the partnership–gift tax arrangement to eliminate estate tax liability.

In the event that the donor wishes to continue managing the business, a partnership agreement might designate the donor as the general manager. This is possible even though the gift of future growth has been made.

There are two different drafting options in a partnership agreement relating to the allocation:

1. Aggressive tax planning. This has to do with allocation between *risk* and *reward*—i.e., the degree of risk one is willing to assume based on the anticipated reward.
2. Conservative tax planning. When one desires less risk exposure, the decision is based on the risk-reward ratio.

This calls for assistance from an outside tax planning counsel.

***Alternative 2.*** Under this alternative we will consider the various aspects of estate tax planning under a corporate structure form.

The estate tax liability of the principal may provide a frozen status under the corporate form, just as in the case of the partnership. In the corporate situation, it is necessary to recapitalize the corporation. This is done by the issuance of preferred stock in exchange for common stock. In this arrangement, it is necessary for all the equity securities to be absorbed by the preferred stock. Any stock not covered should be dealt with through gifts.

A key to this arrangement is the evaluation of the stock and setting the preferred stock dividend. (Stock can be either voting or nonvoting). A redemption premium of the preferred stock may be utilized in order to help absorb the value of the common stock, and may be dealt with through gifts to the younger generation, ideally the stock which would have a value of zero or an amount equal to the gift tax exclusion. Dividends have to be considered cumulative or noncumulative. Noncumulative preferred does not require current or future payment of dividends. Cumulative dividends are not paid currently, but are deferred to a later date.

If the preferred stock is opted to be nonvoting, the older share-holder will probably want an agreement that authorizes the naming of a majority of the *board of directors*. (Our advising attorney prefers this method.) In the event there are minor family members, the stock may be held in trust for the minors. The parents of these minor children may serve as trustees for their block of stock. This arrangement will permit them (the parents) to make binding contracts.

The effect of this arrangement is that it freezes the stock at its value at the time of the stock conversion. This provides a special tax benefit for the donor.

### Estate Planning in Review

The important first step in estate planning is taking action to freeze the current status of the estate's assets. This is done in order that the estate tax problem will not be exacerbated. It is possible, through a gift program, to further reduce the estate tax liability problem.

The next step is to give some thought to the development of a properly planned estate plan. You may take advantage of the unified credit against the estate taxes by using the following schedule:

1. In 1983, the credit is an amount of tax equal to the amount of $275,000.
2. The credit equivalency grows as follows:
   1984—$325,000
   1985—$400,000
   1986—$500,000
   1987—$600,000 (it levels out here and remains at this level)

The point here is that each person has a credit and a properly designed estate plan will not permit the credit to be wasted at the death of the owner or spouse.

Under the 1981 Tax Act, it was made possible to have unlimited interspousal gifts and unlimited marital bequests at death. Prior to the 1981 Act, the law provided that the first $100,000 was free of tax; the second $100,000 was completely taxable; and after $200,000, one half was deductible and the other half was subject to estate tax. The plan then in vogue was to provide that one half the assets would be left to the surviving spouse to be sheltered by the marital deduction and allow the remaining one half to be subject to estate tax.

***Provisions of the New Law (1981).*** This law makes lifetime interspousal gifts and marital bequests by will unlimited. One spouse could leave by "will," in the proper manner, all of the estate and qualify for the marital deduction.

*Example.* This provision led some people to believe the solution to estate taxes is for one spouse to leave everything to surviving spouse as a means of beating the estate taxes (by way of "cross-wills"). However, for people with substantial estates, this simplistic method may be dangerous. In this case, the surviving spouse ends up with all assets; at the second death, all assets after the applicable credit are subject to estate tax. Since the estate tax has a progressive scale, the result is a tax that is higher than if both spouses had utilized their unified credit.

After 1987, at the death of a spouse with an estate of $1.2 million who has all the assets in his/her name and leaves all assets to the surviving spouse, there will be no estate taxes because of the marital deduction. But at the death of the surviving spouse, the estate tax will be $192,800. This is assuming a taxable estate of $600,000. The other $600,000 will be covered by the estate tax credit of $192,800.

*Example: Same $1.2 million, but different approach.* Generally, it is desirable for the spouse with greater assets to make gifts to the spouse with lesser assets in an amount equal to the estate tax credit. By making a gift to the spouse of $600,000, it makes no difference as to which spouse dies first. An amount equal to $600,000 in estate tax credit equivalency can be made available for the benefit of the surviving spouse for her lifetime or to her in such a manner that she may will her share to whomever she wishes. At the death of the surviving spouse, the estate can go to the children and grandchildren/heirs. The estate tax credit equivalency results in a $1.2 million estate with zero dollars estate tax. The estate tax credit should always be utilized. Each spouse should be sure their will makes use of the credit.

Prior to 1981, people sometimes had anxiety about leaving a spouse a substantial amount of property. This was based on the thought that if the surviving spouse were to remarry he/she could leave that estate to a new spouse with the net result being to cut off the children and grandchildren as beneficiaries of that portion of the estate. The 1981 Tax Act made it possible to leave the marital deduction to the surviving spouse for life and then directly to surviving heirs. This provided for a qualified terminable interest in the property for the second spouse. However, control of where the assets go after death of the surviving spouse can be retained by first spouse. Under this provision, the second spouse has no control over designating beneficiaries. The surviving spouse has the benefits from the qualified terminable interest property and can, when necessary, benefit from principal for comfort and support. Because of the 1981 Tax Act, it is now possible to provide for support of the

surviving spouse for life and to control who the ultimate beneficiaries will be.

## Buy-Sell Agreements

There are four things to keep in mind when formulating a buy-sell
agreement:

1. Life-time buy or sell option
2. Death-sale and purchase
3. Disability-sale and purchase
4. Minority shareholder

### Life-Time

This discussion generally applies to the corporate structure, but it
could apply to the partnership as well. This approach (life-time) is
recommended: If any partner wants out, then he/she should first
be required to sell to the corporation his/her stock. If the corporation does not want to purchase, then the remaining shareholders
should be given the second option, pro-rata. If any of these remaining shareholders disdain, then the other remaining shareholders
who do wish to purchase should be given the right to purchase the
stock pro-rata, which provides for keeping the ownership among
the remaining stockholders who wish to buy relatively the same
as among themselves.

The caveat is that you do not want the buy-sell agreement
structured so that the first option is to the shareholders and the
second option is to the corporation. The trap here is if the shareholders say "We will just pass on our option and let the corporation purchase the stock." Then, to the extent that the corporation
does purchase the stock, it can result in a dividend to the remaining shareholders equal to the purchase price. This is the worst of
all worlds, since the corporation has to purchase the stock with
*after-tax dollars* and the remaining shareholders get charged with
the dividend equal to the purchase price. A poorly drawn buy-sell
agreement, which has the options just outlined, will give you this
unfortunate result.

*Pricing the Option.* This discussion relates to the option to the
corporation, and the next relates to the option to the shareholder.
How do you price the option? Basically, two ways are usually used,
but there are many ways to do it.

*Formula.* The first method is on a formula basis; there are all
kinds of formulas. It might be based on the book value. In some

corporations this is as accurate a way as any. It could be done on a combination of book value and earnings. One that our counsel finds workable is a three-part formula. In this method, you take the current book value and let that be one third of your total purchase price. The second element is the average of the last four or five years of net earnings, after tax, multiplied by a multiplier of 7 to 10. Counsel finds that 7 or 8 works reasonably well by taking the average of the last five years of net earnings after tax, multiplied by eight; this becomes the second one third of the purchase price (it provides a history of earnings of the corporation). The third element is the trend. You take the immediately preceding year-end net earnings after tax, then multiply the net earnings by the same multiplier, (eight in this instance). This becomes the other one-third element. Then, you add up the book value (which is conservative), the average of the five years, (which is history), and the trend, (which is the last year multiplied), and divide these by three. The resultant sum is the formula purchase price. As indicated earlier, there are many different formulas that can be utilized. The main point here is that there are formula devices available so that, when some one wishes to sell, this is an option the corporation has.

*Annual certificate.* The annual certificate is another method that is available for use in a buy-sell agreement. The owners of the corporation get together at the year-end and decide what the stock in the corporation is worth, not knowing whether they will be a buyer or seller. So they have to think of it in terms of: "What would I want to take and what would I want to give?" Then they balance that off and, if they agree, plug it into the agreement as the new current value of the corporation. They sign a certificate which is attached to the buy-sell agreement. This then becomes the value of the stock until the next valuation. This arrangement makes it possible for someone to get out during the interim, if they so desire.

Counsel finds that many closely held corporations are lax about getting together and doing the certificate. Therefore, he usually provides a "fail-safe." For example, if for any reason shareholders have not agreed to a certificate within two years of the date of the last valuation, then the value usually becomes the higher of either the last valuation or the book value. For example, in an actual occurrence:

> Someone came to counsel on a buy-sell arrangement that had been in effect for 20 years. The stock had been valued 20 years ago at $10,000; in the event of one of the parties' death, the $10,000 would have been what the estate would have received. The stock was really worth $150,000. It was changed in the agreement, and within nine months the party died. Without the change, the estate would have been legally entitled to only $10,000.

The caveat is: if you use a certificate, how do you set up a fail-safe? In the event you do not attend to your business, there is a fall back. Insofar as life-time buy-outs, if one party wants out, you can have a binding obligation on the corporation to purchase. Counsel does not favor this option in a life-time situation. There should not be an obligation to purchase by the corporation while all owners are alive.

*Protecting minority stockholders.* However, you do need to address minority shareholders wanting to get out and not being able to get out because the corporation or the other shareholders do not see fit to exercise their option to purchase. One way this is sometimes done, if the corporation has the first option and declines and the shareholders have second option and they decline, is for the party wishing to sell to be able to go on the outside and sell his/her stock to anyone for any price. This appears to be an "ivory tower" theoretical solution that does not work in practice. In this situation you are dealing with unmarketable, nontraded, closely held stock. As a practical matter, there is little or no market for this kind of stock. So, in effect, the minority shareholder who wants to get out in effect, is locked in when the remaining shareholders do not want him/her to get out.

Counsel has devised a method to protect the minority stockholder. As an alternative to the previous discussion, the minority stockholder goes through the requirement of offering to the corporation and shareholders at an agreed price. When the options are not exercised, the party who wants out still has a choice. His choice is to offer to sell stock to the remaining shareholders or to buy the stock of the remaining shareholders, at whatever price and at whatever terms he/she may wish to place on it. This approach must be thought through very carefully because his offer is both an offer to buy or sell as will be seen. When the shareholder makes an offer to sell the stock at some price and some terms, the parties to whom that offer is made (the remaining shareholders) have two choices: They must either take that offer, or they must offer their stock to the minority stockholder on identical terms and conditions. If they reverse the offer, then the party who made the offer has to take it. So, it becomes "a fish or cut bait" solution. The party who makes the offer needs to think it through: "If I offer to sell and they decline, then it is going to come back to me and I will have to purchase." In this event, he/she has to be able to buy the stock of the other stockholders at the same price and terms.

If the minority stockholder makes the price unusually low, then the other stockholders will accept the offer. If, on the other hand, the minority stockholder makes the price of the stock unusually high, then the other stockholders will reverse it and put the offer back to the minority shareholder. In this case, the minority stockholder has to buy. This series of circumstances causes the minority stockholder to exercise caution and be sure that the price and terms of the offer are fair. This is an option that counsel likes to place in the buy-sell agreement as protection to the minority stockholder's interests. This offers a way to break the deadlock, a way to get in or get out.

The minority shareholder can put the offer on whatever price and terms he/she wishes, knowing that the offer becomes the price and terms. If the terms provide for a long-term deal, then the minority stockholder might be able to buy on a long-term basis, since he will own it all.

*Pricing Stock of Majority Stockholder versus Pricing Stock of Minority Stockholder.* Often, closely held corporations will have only two shareholders. The stock ownership may be 50%/50%, or if one of the shareholders has leverage, 51%/49%. In the event there are more than two stockholders, then you have a minority stockholder situation. In the case of 50/50 ownership, there is not too much concern. In the case, where there is a 51–49, there is a concern because the majority stock is worth more than the minority stock. In setting the value in this circumstance, you could use the certificate method. What happens when the majority stockholders is buying out the minority shareholder? In this instance, the majority stockholder is only buying appreciation rights and not buying control rights, so you can make an argument that the minority stock is worth less than it would be in the reverse situation. When the minority buys the majority, he/she is not only buying the earnings potential but is also buying control. This is worth something.

The way to address this is in your pricing. If you have a situation of pure minority-majority stockholders, then your formula should take into account the price of the majority stockholder's stock. For example, using the previously discussed 3-part formula (a straight-out way of objectively pricing the stock), you could do the minority the same way but discount the price of the stock at, say, 10 percent to 30 percent, which is not unusual. This should be addressed in the formula or in the certificate. By handling it in this manner, it becomes cut and dried and is not left to negotiations. Keep in mind that in a life-time buy-out, the corporation only has an option. In a life-time situation, it may not be wise for the corporation to be obligated to buy a minority stockholder's interest, since this situation might come at the worst time. Therefore, that is why the fail-safe buy or sell provision between shareholders is important.

## Death

*Resolving deceased ownership dilemma.* As a policy matter in a closely held corporation, it is generally wise to have a binding obligation on the corporation to purchase and on the estate of the deceased shareholder to sell. Only in rare and unusual circumstances is the widow/widower going to be a compatible, contributing, understanding shareholder. It is doubly important to the estate, because most closely held corporations do not have a dividend history and do not want to begin a dividend policy. For the estate of the deceased shareholder, who is not drawing a salary and is making no contribution to the business, there is in turn no return on investment. This is why the general policy of having the requirement that the corporation to purchase the stock from the estate is more desirable. In some states there exist some legal restraints on a corporation purchasing its own shares. Most corporation codes provide that a corporation can only purchase its stock out of the earned available surplus or the capital surplus available. Generally, in a death situation, there should be an obligation for the corporation to buy all the stock that it can legally buy before the remaining shareholders are required to purchase any shares of the deceased shareholder. If the buy-sell agreement places the primary obligation on the shareholders to purchase the shares with the subsequent decision to have the corporation purchase the shares, the payment by the corporation will likely result in a dividend to the *remaining* shareholders—a very bad result. In a situation where the corporation has insufficient earned surplus or capital surplus, you might consider increasing the capital surplus, by writing up the assets to market value rather than book value. If the market value exceeds the book value, then it creates a capital surplus.

Assume the corporation's assets are written up and the capital surplus is increased so that the corporation buys all the stock of the deceased shareholder it can legally buy, but there is still some outstanding stock. The agreement should usually provide that the remaining shareholders are obligated to purchase the remaining stock upon the same price and same terms as the corporation.

*Establishing Stock Value.* In establishing the value in a death situation, use the same approach as in life-time situations. Counsel usually uses the formula approach or the certificate method. The buy-sell option drops out on death because you do not want to place the estate in a buy-sell situation, since it would be bad policy for an estate to have to make an offer. The surviving stockholders could put it back to the estate to purchase, leaving the estate in a poor position to have to operate the corporation. For this reason, the buy-sell option should drop out on death. In summary the certificate method or the certificate method with a fail-safe is utilized by most practitioners as a procedure for valuing the stock.

The terms of purchase should be included in the agreement—for example, whether it is going to be cash or part cash, with the balance being paid in installments, and what interest rate the installments will carry and over what term. This should all be spelled out in the buy-sell agreement and should be spelled out in the life-time agreement. In the case of a life-time agreement, you may have longer terms than would be true in the case of death.

***Alternative Funding Options.*** Often, partially funding the death buy-out with life insurance is "good business," and certainly the owners should consider it. Given today's cost of term insurance, it is an economical way and will not impair the working capital of the corporation in the event of a premature death. Counsel usually references the insurance in the agreement, letting the corporation own the life insurance and be the beneficiary of the life insurance. The corporation will pay the premiums. At the time of death, the life insurance policy proceeds will be paid into the corporate coffers. The proceeds then fund part or all of the buy-out. Counsel thinks, from a policy standpoint, that the corporation should fund out of earnings that part of the purchase price which it can reasonably afford. This is based on the theory that life insurance can be used to cover that which you cannot afford to pay rather than that which you can afford to pay.

In the event there are two owners and one of them dies, there is a likelihood—because of the varying expertise—that the surviving owner would go out in the market and seek another shareholder. In this situation, the insurance should be structured outside the corporation as a cross purchaser (one stockholder owning and being the beneficiary of the life insurance on the other shareholder and the reverse). Then, in the event of death, the proceeds will be paid to the surviving shareholder, who is obligated under the buy-sell agreement to pay those proceeds to the estate; and the estate is obligated to sell the shares to the surviving shareholder. The money comes in to the surviving shareholder, from the insurance, income tax free. He/she purchases stock and gets a basis equal to the purchase price of the stock. Then when going into the market to find someone to replace the deceased shareholder, he/she can sell those shares to the new shareholder at the same price that was paid from the tax-free proceeds of the life insurance. The shareholder then receives the purchase price of those shares tax-free. The surviving shareholder ends up with tax-free proceeds. The estate of the deceased shareholder gets proceeds from the stock purchased with no income tax consequences, because of a "step-up" in the tax basis of the stock upon death. Although the value of the shares may be included in the estate of the deceased shareholder for estate tax purposes, it has no income tax consequences.

In those cases where you have two shareholders and there is a strong likelihood that the survivor will obtain a new shareholder, counsel perceives the above procedure as a good technique. Following this thought further, with this technique it is still possible to let the corporation pay for the life insurance. The premium on the life insurance will be under a *split-dollar agreement* between the corporation and the shareholders. The split-dollar agreement is no more than an interest-free loan from the corporation for the premiums. The corporation pays the premium and takes an assignment of the proceeds that equals, at death, the total amount of premiums that have been paid. A term rider is usually used on the policy so that the policy increases each year by the approximate same amount of the loan; at death, the face amount is still the same amount as it was at the time the policy was obtained, in so far as the beneficiary is concerned, after the corporation receives a return of the premium. For example:

> A corporation took out $200,000 on each stockholder, and had paid $50,000 in premiums on Shareholder A's life at time of his death. The face of the policy had increased to $250,000, the corporation received its $50,000 back, and the surviving shareholder got $200,000 which he used to buy the stock.

***Tax Status of Surviving Owner.*** There is some taxable consequence to the surviving shareholder by using the split-dollar agreement. The shareholder has to report as taxable income an amount equal to the lesser of the PS–58 cost* or the cost of the lowest-term product offered by the insurance company writing the insurance. The larger insurance companies, and some others, have recognized this marketing opportunity and have developed a very cheap term policy product. Because of this available low-cost term policy, the cost to the shareholder in terms of additional income is not consequential anymore.

This technique is very useful for one who wants to get a new shareholder. If there is no desire to get a new shareholder into the corporation, then the simplest approach is the redemption agreement where the corporation is the owner and beneficiary of the

---

*The main benefit received by the insured is the current insurance protection under the basic policy. The value of this benefit to the insured is calculated by use of the government's one-year term ("P.S. 58") premium rates.

policy. When there are more than two shareholders, then the cross-purchase agreement becomes cumbersome.

Presently, in the shareholder death circumstance, the procedural options discussed above seem to be the most appropriate way to satisfy the needs of the estate and surviving shareholder(s).

## Disability Considerations

According to counsel's experience, disability is the most overlooked part of the buy-sell agreement by practitioners and corporations themselves. In a closely held corporation, the permanent disability of one of the shareholders can be a traumatic thing, because the disabled shareholder usually will have inadequate personal disability insurance and can no longer work full-time or work at all at the company. Therefore, the family income is substantially affected. The remaining shareholders do not want to carry on all the work indefinitely. If they have to go into the marketplace and hire someone to take over for the disabled shareholder, and the company continues to show a profit this profit will inure to the benefit of the disabled shareholder and at his/her death the corporation still has to pay the agreed death provisions, this can cause a great deal of consternation and hard feelings.

*Short-Term Self-Insurance.* It is usually desirable to address this (disability) in the buy-sell agreement. Again, from a business standpoint, it is not bad policy to consider self-insuring the salary of a disabled shareholder for 90 days, or possibly 180 days because of the break on the premiums you get if you self-insure for the longer period. It is also desirable to go ahead and put in a disability plan for the shareholders. This may be funded by the corporation, which might pick up at, say, 180 days. This is all right but it still does not answer the question "What about a permanent disability?" which causes the problems alluded to above. Therefore, counsel thinks there should be in the buy-sell agreement a period in which, if disability continues to keep the disabled party from returning to full-time work, his/her stock will be automatically purchased by the corporation. The disabled shareholder has no alternative but to sell. This procedure gets the disabled shareholder out of the way.

*Disability Buy-out Insurance.* There is a relatively low premium product called "disability buy-out" insurance. Particularly for younger shareholders, it has a cost that is not very high. As an example of how it works, after a year of disability, the insurance company would then pay $200,000 or $300,000 to the corporation.

The corporation would utilize, or partially utilize, the money to buy out the stock of the disabled shareholder. Counsel has seen situations where, for as little as $350/year, you could pay the premium on a 30–40-year-old shareholder. This might pay as much as $200,000 or $300,000.

The long waiting period of this type plan is the thing that makes this so attractive, meaning that there is a combination of a six-month self-insured period and disability payments which would take up at the end of six months. At the end of 12 months' disability, the insurance company would fund or partially fund the buy-out of the stock. This should be explored at the original time of doing the buy-sell agreement. The idea in the insurance disability arrangement is to fund most of the purchase price of the stock, but some could be purchased out of earnings.

*Disability and Tax Liability.* Tax-wise it is not feasible to continue to pay the disabled shareholder a salary for two reasons. One is that it will be generally disallowed as a deduction to the corporation because he/she is not providing services for the salary. Second, it is a drain on the corporate coffers because the corporation is most likely having to hire a replacement; therefore, you would be paying two salaries for one job.

*Disability Clause Omission.* Counsel has found that the disability clause often is not considered in drawing up a buy-sell agreement. Statistically, the odds are approximately one in four that one of the shareholders will become disabled. The odds of a person age 30 becoming disabled at some time before dying are four times the odds that he/she will die prematurely.

## Minority Shareholders

If you want to protect minority stockholders and if you have shareholders who have varying financial positions, how do you proceed? It is easy to see how you could allow a situation to exist where a 25 percent stockholder might become a 5 percent stockholder. The directors might decide to issue more stock for cash. If the minority stockholder is not in a financial position to exercise his/her preemptive rights and buy stock in the same proportion as other stockholders, then stock dilution can become very real. This should be discussed and analyzed if you want to protect the minority stockholder(s) from such a result. It can be very easily done in the buy-sell agreement. In order to accomplish this provision, all that is necessary is simply providing that no additional stock will be issued to the shareholders in the absence of the unanimous consent of the shareholders. Therefore, the minority stockholder could object and keep additional stock from being issued to anyone who is presently a shareholder. It could be a two-edged sword; you might want that provision or you might not want that provision. In any event, it does provide considerable protection to the minority stockholder, who does not want his/her equity reduced because of an inferior financial position.

### Buy-Sell Agreements: Summary and Conclusion

The procedures discussed generally cover those areas that need to be covered in buy-sell agreements. The purpose of this section has been to make you the reader aware of your exposure and how you might plan to reduce or eliminate these possibilities as well as avoid or minimize the tax liabilities that might grow out of such situations.

*Buy-Sell Agreements—Management Continuity.* The most important thing that can be said about a buy-sell agreement is that it provides for continuity of management, a fair way to value the stock, and a fair way to treat the shareholders. From the shareholder's viewpoint, the most important thing that should be said about a buy-sell agreement is that the time to prepare the agreement is at the time the business is formed or at the time shareholders become shareholders and not later, after the corporation has become successful. The shareholders may have varying interests as to whether or not to prepare an agreement and how it should be prepared. Generally, people are very agreeable at the beginning and when money or the present position of the corporation is not the primary consideration. Generally speaking, if it is left until the problem occurs, then it is too late to satisfactorily deal with these problems. From a practical viewpoint, these buy-sell arrangements can not be emphasized too much. In other words, right after you form or buy a closely held corporation, the first order of business in addition to the election of officers and directors is the formulation of the buy-sell agreement.

*Buy-Sell Agreement—Tax Liability.* Another consideration that makes the buy-sell agreement extremely important, especially with businesses that are successful and where estate taxes are a consideration, is an arms-length, binding buy-sell agreement, on death, between unrelated shareholders, this kind of an agreement properly drawn, is binding on the Internal Revenue Service as to valuation. By that is meant that, if a shareholder dies with stock in a closely held corporation, and there is no binding buy-sell agreement as to value, the value may ultimately be what the IRS says that it is or what some court says that it is. It is "fair game," if the IRS says that the stock is worth more than any shareholder believes it is worth. Courts do not like valuation cases; they frown on them and usually will take an average somewhere between what the stockholder says that it is worth and what the IRS says that it is worth. This usually means more than the stockholder wishes. That is another reason to have a properly drawn buy-sell agreement. You eliminate those questions of valuation so far as estate taxes are concerned.

*Buy-Sell Agreement—Life Insurance.* In particular, if life insurance is owned by the corporation to help fund the buy-out situation and there is no binding "buy-sell agreement" as to valuation, you can have an increase in the value of the company by the infusion of the insurance proceeds themselves. A properly drawn buy-sell agreement will recognize the proceeds contributions as nothing more than the loss of a key man. The valuation of the corporation should be set forth in the buy-sell agreement even though there have been insurance proceeds infused. There should not be insurance owned by the corporation without a binding buy-sell agreement as to valuation in the event of death. Otherwise, you get that "double-barrel" treatment of increased valuation by the IRS as a result of the life insurance proceeds.

*Buy-Sell Agreement—Partnerships.* Most of the above statements will work in a properly drawn partnership agreement, using the same concepts in the partnership setting as in a corporate setting.

*The Gravity of Disability.* Going back to disability, counsel finds that people often do not think through the consequences of a serious disability to one of the owners. He has seen real-life situations where there was a buy-sell agreement, and the owner's contemplated disability and made very liberal payment provisions by the corporation to the disabled party without thinking the provisions through. Later, one of the owners had a heart attack, and the remaining shareholders had to do double duty. They continued to fund the salary fully for six months or longer, in time becoming very bitter about the situation. The disabled shareholder felt threatened; he needed the money, so he was not going to back off of the agreement. You should not be altruistic when looking at the buy-sell agreement because you have to anticipate the impact of a serious disability on the remaining shareholders. Do not commit yourself to pay more than what is reasonable and fair under the circumstances.

# Profit Sharing Plan

A growing business is in constant need of working capital and there are two ways to approach this. One way is to implement a profit-sharing plan. Such a plan may be drawn to allow the corporation to fund its tax deductible contributions by either paying cash to the plan's trust or by issuing the corporation's stock. Another way to generate capital is with an employer stock option trust, sometime called an ESOP or employee stock option plan (these terms are used interchangeably), which will be covered in the next section.

### Profit-Sharing Consequences

Taking the profit sharing plan first, the corporation is authorized to make contributions in the amount of 15 percent of the eligible payroll. One way to generate additional working capital is to take 15 percent of the eligible payroll and make a contribution of cash to the plan in trust. The trust immediately turns around and purchases stock in the corporation at the current appraised value—that is, it pays the corporation for that stock. There is no tax effect on the corporation by issuing this new stock for cash. So it has, in effect, the same money back in the corporation that it expended for the contribution. It gets an additional benefit, however, in that the contribution that it makes to the trust is a tax-deductible item. The net effect is that it reduces its income tax by the applicable rate on making the contribution. Therefore, it gets the full dollars or part of its dollars back into its bottom line for operating funds, etc. The key here is that the employees, when they retire, would have their stock purchased at the current fair market value. Some planning must be done, with either life insurance or term life insurance on the employees, with the trust being the beneficiary so that when an employee dies the trust receives a sum of money which can be utilized to pay the employee death benefits.

*Profit-Sharing and Retirement.* The corporation must understand that, upon the employee's retirement, it must provide funding. Another way to accomplish this is to purchase the stock for the first few years and then begin to fund it in later years, after the growth of the business has leveled out and there is less need of cash. The earnings on the cash contributed will accumulate tax-deferred and, therefore, provide a fund for cashing out the stock for people who retire. Employee turnover will help the corporation; in a turnover situation, before the employees are fully vested (which might be a 10-year vested schedule), they would forfeit their participation rights in the invested portion of their share. The forfeited part is then spread back over the remaining employees.

*Major Beneficiaries' Profit-Sharing.* The owners should realize that usually they are the highest paid employees; when contributions are made and stock is purchased, they are the beneficiaires of a usually significant and sometimes majority part of the stock. It should be understood that the trust is the owner of the shares and that they are usually nonvoting shares. Therefore, the minority shareholder does not enter into the picture as a threat because of trust arrangement.

*Profit-Sharing and Taxes.* A profit sharing plan is a good way to keep before-tax dollars in the corporation for growth purposes. Because the contribution to the plan is deductible from the before-taxes income each year, you can use part of the money to purchase stock and leave part of the money in the trust to be invested, to begin to accumulate a "sinking fund" to be used to redeem retired employees' retirement income. It is worth mentioning again that the owners, because of their high salaries and bonuses, may end up getting 60–80 percent (or even higher) of the plan's stock allocated to them, because the allocation of the stock in the plan is done on the basis of a single employee's salary as the numerator, determined by a fraction. The numerator is the employee's total salary (including bonus), and the denominator is the total payroll of all employees under the plan. For example, a $500,000 payroll with the two owners each receiving $100,000 means they would receive two-fifths (almost one half) of the stock.

## Employee Stock Option Plan (ESOP)

An ESOP works the same way as a profit sharing plan. There are two or three kinds. The payroll ESOP enables the corporation to get an extra 1 percent investment tax credit on its Section 38 property. The valuation of the corporation each year at the time the stock is purchased is an important factor, and the accountant should be called in to make a fair evaluation. This needs to be done every year, so that you buy the stock of the corporation at the current market value. As an additional incentive to the employees, the more they are efficient, "work hard," and are conscientious the more they help the shareholder's stock to increase in value. The increase accrues to the benefit of their retirement plan. Conversely, when the employees don't do a good job, their stock does not appreciate and may even depreciate; it hurts their employment plan. So they have all the incentive in the world (if they properly understand it) to make the corporation earn the maximum return in order to help their retirement plan.

An ESOP is basically the same concept as a profit-sharing plan, but in an ESOP you can only use stock, whereas in a profit-sharing plan you can use a combination or solely stock. In drawing up the profit-sharing plan, you must be careful that you provide it with the powers to acquire the employer's stock as an investment. The stock valuation requirement tends to be a little easier in a profit sharing plan than it is in an ESOP.

### Advantage of ESOP

The larger the corporation the more attractive becomes the ESOP, with the added value of the investment tax credit. Again, if you have a corporation that is growing and it needs all the working capital it can get, this should be explored as one possible way of accumulating after-tax working capital.

## Cooperatives

There are basically two kinds of co-ops. One is a tax-exempt co-op under Section 521, Internal Revenue Code, and there is a non-exempt co-op under Section 1381, Subchapter T of the Internal Revenue Code. There are two organizations to which it applies: any corporation that is exempt from tax under 521, and any corporation operating on a cooperative basis other than a 521 co-op. For all practical purposes, a 521 co-op is not usually advantageous. Therefore, you can let the corporation operate on a cooperative basis and get favored tax results. For example, under Georgia law,[2] if you organize your corporation under the Georgia Cooperative Association Law—the Cooperative Marketing Association provisions are such that you can not have any shareholder that owns more than 20 percent of the stock. Therefore, under the Georgia Cooperative Association laws, you must have at least five shareholders.

### Shareholder and Profits

Shareholdings have nothing to do with how profits are distributed. Profits are distributed based upon the volume of business done with the cooperative by its patrons. Assume that you have a marketing co-op and are selling your goods to the co-op. Or you might have a purchasing co-op which, for illustration purposes, is manufacturing feed, and you are buying your feed needs from the co-op. The profits of the co-op are distributable based upon a fraction: The numerator represents the pounds purchased by that particular patron, and the denominator is the total pounds purchased by

---

[2]Check the laws of your respective state for similar provisions.

all patrons. This fraction is then multiplied by the profits that may be attributed to these patrons' business. A marketing cooperative operates the same way as the purchasing cooperative, except that distribution of profit is based upon the pounds furnished to the co-op.

Again for illustration purposes, if you are selling turkeys, poultry, peaches, or any other agricultural commodities to the marketing cooperative, then you generally sell at cost. If you are buying feed, you buy feed at cost. The margin of profit of the cooperative, over cost, is returned to the patron as set forth above.

Let's take another example—a marketing cooperative. You sell your products (turkeys, peaches, apples, onions, etc.) to the marketing cooperative at what your actual cost of production is. You are paid for these products on a current basis, so that you maintain your operating capital. The cooperative then turns around and sells those same products (sometimes after processing or doing something to the products) on the market. Hopefully, the cooperative is selling the products on the market at a price that is higher than the costs. To the extent you are receiving a price higher than the costs, you are generating a profit at the cooperative level.

The cooperative, at the end of its year, looks at the total profits that it has made from patrons—i.e., those that have sold it products. Then the cooperative allocates to each patron those profits in accordance with the fractional formula discussed above, based on the pounds, tons, bushels, etc., of product that have been furnished by that patron (numerator/denominator − total units of all patrons × the profit of all patrons at year-end). The cooperative does not have to pay tax on the cooperative profits, which it distributes as "patronage dividends" to its patrons. The cooperative has nine months from its corporate year-end during which it must distribute these profits to the patrons. If the cooperative distributes those profits to the patrons during that nine-month period of time, it does not pay tax on these profits.

**Patron and Taxes.** The patron picks up, as taxable income, that portion of cooperative profits he receives as dividends. Basically, you have a one-tax situation. The payment to the patron is called a patronage dividend. *A dividend under normal corporate law is taxed to both the corporation that issues it and to the shareholder that receives it.* In a cooperative, there is no tax at the corporate level on a patronage dividend. As an illustration, let us see how that works to the advantage of the farmer, assuming this situation:

The farmer has a corporate year-end of August 31, and the cooperative has a year-end of December 31, 1983. The profits of the cooperative during taxable year 1983 are $1 million, and it holds them until September 1, 1984, and distributes them to the patrons. The patron's year-end is August 31, so he did not receive them until the first month of his corporate year ending August 31, 1985. He then utilizes those funds until August 31, 1985, and pays tax on December 15, 1985. Therefore, any profits that are in hand on December 31,1983, are not subject to federal tax until December 15, 1985.

You have a significant tax deferral that is perfectly legal under this arrangement.

## Tax Alternatives

*Alternative 1.* The cooperative can also buy from nonpatrons. Any business done with nonpatrons is nonexempt to the cooperative, and profits made are income on which the cooperative must pay tax. The cooperative may use these after-tax earnings as retained earnings. The cooperative must report these retained earnings just as any other corporation. Profits earned with patrons—patrons being cooperative members who are producers of agricultural products—are subject to a single tax. The cooperative could have a policy of paying all the profits out to everyone—treating everyone as patrons. Usually the owners of the cooperative don't do it this way. They simply elect to have the cooperative pay the tax on its nonshareholder's business. This is a decision that the board of directors can make. Gold Kist is an example of a cooperative that pays out all its patronage dividends, but usually not on a current basis.

*Tax Alternative 2.* How does the cooperative pay out the patronage dividends? It pays them out in cash, or it pays them out in revolving fund certificates. Revolving fund certificates are nothing more than a liability of the corporation to pay the money out at some point in the future. This will be determined by the board of directors from time to time. The cooperative corporation retains the money, but it does not pay tax on it because the patrons (by prior agreement) elect to pick up the funds as taxable income. In the event you have a cooperative that needs to make substantial capital improvements or that has substantial needs for working capital, this is a source that the cooperative has on which it has paid no tax. You recall that in the cooperative situation there is a single tax.

*Tax Alternative 3.* In the above situation, the patrons pay the tax on those cooperative earnings evidenced by revolving certificates. Another possibility is to distribute enough of the cash to the patrons to pay the tax on the revolving fund certificates. If, for example, the cooperative thought it should retain $1 million dollars in revolving certificates but the collective tax liability of the patrons is $300,000, it could pay out $300,000 in cash to the patrons and issue revolving fund certificates for $700,000. During the deferral period of the money, the funds can be utilized to purchase equipment, for investment, to pay interest, or for operating purposes.

*Cooperative Tax Advantage.* Not only is the cooperative subject to a single tax, but it provides the added feature of a deferral on the tax. As an example, if you have an integrated operation, where you have turkeys you could also have a feed mill. These would be in separate cooperatives. You would buy feed from the cooperatives at cost and utilize this feed to raise the turkeys. This keeps the costs down, and in this kind of cooperative, it breaks even. It would be possible to have an outside business that could sell feed to nonpatrons at market price. This segment of the business would generate profits on which the cooperative would pay tax. The cooperative could utilize the after-tax funds as retained earnings for its own capital improvements and working capital, thereby not requiring any working capital from its shareholders. In such a setup, you hopefully have conditions where you have outside sales sufficient to operate the mill and still sell to the patrons at cost. In this situation, the patrons have the best of all worlds. Since they are purchasing the feed at cost and are selling the finished product at cost to the marketing cooperative, they thereby get their funds back for operation and are able to defer their tax to a point in time "down the road."

Any time you have a farming/agricultural operation, even on a small basis, you should look at cooperatives. As a general rule, people tend to look at cooperatives as a conglomerate or a megacorporation. It works just as well for a group of 5 or more members of a regular corporation operating as a cooperative basis. You do not have to be a Gold Kist or a cooperative of the Midwest.

*Cooperative's Special Access to Financing.* Another advantage of the cooperative form of organization is that, as a cooperative, you qualify to borrow money from federal cooperative banks. These institutions are set up to make loans to farmers. A cooperative can finance its working-capital needs and other capital needs by borrowing from the appropriate cooperative bank. Usually these institutions have funds at very favorable interest rates. These rates are usually below the rates of commercial banks. There are some "stock purchase" requirements that are applicable when borrowing money from the cooperative banks. These requirements can be explored at the time the funds are sought.

# The Influence of Taxes on Operating Management's Decisions

## Taxes and Decision Quality

Tax decisions frequently affect operating decisions at all levels of business. For example, one attorney's policy is to meet with corporations that he represents, particularly closely held corporations, on a regular basis, twice a year—in the middle of the year to see how they are doing and to begin to make plans for the end of the year, and then in the last month of their fiscal year to make any last-minute adjustments. Invariably (even in sophisticated people, but particularly in unsophisticated business people who happen to be successful at business), the moment the company starts making money over and above the money that is needed for operations and to pay a salary, they will say "I don't want to pay any taxes. What do we do about mitigating taxes?" The job the business people cast counsel in is to try to show them how to reduce taxes. Many times the things that can be done to lessen taxes are not necessarily the best for the business. An "extreme" example of the latter situation:

## Example 1

> Counsel had a client who said, "I am making too much money, and the corporation is going to have to pay some taxes. Don't you think it would be a good idea to have the company buy a yacht?" Counsel responded, "What are we going to do with the yacht?" The client's response was, "I can entertain clients on it. I can use it for business promotion." Counsel then responded, "If it weren't for taxes, would you make that as a business decision?" Client: "No, not necessarily, but I've got to get my taxes down, and I can take investment tax credit and depreciation." Counsel: "That is absolutely the worst thing that you could possibly do. It is going to depreciate before you get if off the 'yard.' You are going to fight with the IRS, anyway, justifying the deductions. It doesn't matter what kind of log you keep. It will be a $60,000–100,000 investment, that will end up costing you a lot more than that, not only in terms of your poor investment; all you are going to do is to get a 1-to-1 write-off. Then you are going to sell it at a loss. You will have a loss that will reduce taxes all right, but you are going to hurt the business."

This is an extreme example of somebody who simply wanted to reduce taxes without giving any thought to *whether or not it was a good business decision.* The purchase of an airplane is another example, or someone who came in saying:

## Example 2

"Somebody talked to me about this cattle operation and says it's a good tax loss." Counsel's response was, "Oh yes, it is a good tax loss. I'll guarantee you that you will have a tax loss. You know you are going to lose money. If you want a tax loss, you can always give it to the church. It is 1 to 1, and you can get some tangible benefits rather than 'feathering some speculator's nest' by making an investment to reduce taxes. That is poor business."

## Example 3

In another example, counsel says:

People will come in and say, "I think I will buy X piece of equipment costing $350,000, because I have got to get my taxes down. This will give me a good investment tax credit and depreciation." I respond, "This sounds good, but what is it going to do for the business? What kind of internal rate of return do you think you will be able to get on that investment?" The client says, "I don't really need it yet but I have the money and I can reduce taxes on it." My answer is, "Unless you really need it in your business now, unless it will give you a return on your investment, don't do it. Don't make that decision based on taxes alone."

## Taxes and Operational Planning

Examples such as this go on and on. It seems simple to start with some sort of policy. Most people don't ever give themselves what is very important in a law firm or in a business, particularly a business—and that is a *one-year budget* and *five-year goals*. People need to push themselves to plan in terms of the future, and decide where they want the business to be five years from now. This should be updated every year—in other words, you keep pushing it five years down the road. You have a one-year plan and you have a five-year plan.

In the one-year plan, you will know what your history was at the end of the year; but in the five-year plan you update based on what you have learned. There is a certain psychology to doing this, because people do not seem to (or won't) realize that you can only have real growth in a company with after-tax profits. In other words, *you must have taxable income in order to end up with retained earnings.* You can put in a pension plan—a pension plan is a good way to have a fringe benefit—but it siphons off money that you need for growth. By so doing, you have kept your taxes down, but you have no way to get at the money when you need it for growth and development.

So, you should start with a five-year plan. You determine where you want to be five years from now. Then you calculate how much capital you are going to need to be at that level. Decide how much capital you will need to carry the inventory, to purchase equipment, and to carry the increased receivables. You look at that amount of money and you project backward on how much retained earnings (i.e., after-tax profits) you need each year in order to have that capital accumulated at the end of five years. Then it is a simple matter of budgeting. You try to see how much before-tax profits you can have.

Another syndrome related to this is tied with taxes:

> In a closely-held corporation, when the company starts making pretty good profits, the owners often say, "We have to get the corporate profits down. How about taking a $60,000 bonus?" A good counselor's response would be: "That is fine; do you need $60,000 additionally to live on?" Taxpayer's response: "No, I don't need the money; but if I leave it in the company and I want to get it out, then I have to pay tax on it again. "That's double tax."

## Taxes and Capital Accumulation

The taxpayer has missed the point. The point is that the stronger the company you build, the more security you have. If you take more money than you need out now in profits (as bonuses or increased salaries), there is a good chance that once you have taken it out you will spend it. You are going to spend it on items that are not going to give you any security. You will not be building the company. All you are going to end up with down the road is a company that's literally carrying you from hand to mouth. Why not leave the money in the company and build the capital? Because, to the extent you build the capital, it is comparable to the "goose and the golden egg." If you kill the goose, you get no eggs. The stronger the company is, the more security you have. If the company wants to undertake a major expansion as the result of a new opportunity, to go out and borrow the money at high interest rates or any interest rates is expensive. If you are able to finance it in-house, then you can make that expansion without having to justify it to the bank, without having to pay 15 percent interest (sometimes higher) or at least 1–2 percent over prime in order to get it. This is the advantage of blending your taxes and capital budget together—your five-year plan. (If you don't have more money after you have taken the tax-related action than you would have had without taking the action, you have taken the wrong action.)

## Corporate Tax Advantage

Most people do not realize that corporations have favored tax status, meaning that 46 percent is the maximum tax bracket for a corporation. Corporations presently enjoy a 5-step tax structure: 15% on the first $25,000 of taxable income; 18% on the taxable income over $25,000 but less than $50,000; 30% on the taxable income over $50,000 but less than $75,000; 40% on the taxable income over $75,000 but less than $100,000; and 46% on all taxable income over $100,000. Thus corporations are tax-favored. Use these favorable rates to accumulate wealth. No matter how much you make, even after state taxes,[3] you have 48 cents on the dollar that the government does not get. No one is in the 100 percent bracket; so when you say, "I am giving it all to the government," that is not true. People tend to get locked into a "tax mentality"—all they look at is the amount of the check that they write to Uncle Sam. They don't want to look at the amount of money that they keep. A well-informed tax counselor would come back and say that once you get your salary at a comfortable level, then you shouldn't take exorbitant bonuses unless you have a current need for cash. Leave the money in the company and use it to grow. Most people want a company to grow; however, business people should realize that it takes capital in order to grow. You need capital in terms of computers, salesmen's commission's, trucks, etc., and sometimes in terms of executives and higher-paid professionals. These are needs even in a service organization, even in a law firm. As the country moves away from an industrial society into one that is going to be a service oriented society, capital needs will continue.

## Exporting and Taxes

If your business is engaged in exporting, it would be desirable to utilize the domestic international sales corporation (DISC). In this situation, you defer your tax simply by using a corporate structure that is a subsidiary. You have an agreement between the subsidiary and the parent, but even it is designed to accumulate capital to increase sales. The concept here is solid—you increase the amount of capital as your sales and receivables increase. This results in your inventory needs going up, which means your receivables needs will go up, and you are, therefore, accumulating capital for that. In effect, this is a deferral for tax purposes. This concept is valid even though you are not in the exporting business.

---

[3]In some states, state corporate taxes may be higher than 6 percent.

Again, if you will make yourself do a five-year analysis—figure out where you want to be in terms of company profits five years from now—then ask yourself: How are we going to have that? What is going to be required in the way of capital in order to attain that kind of income? How much is it going to take in capital in order to have the needed sales?

> One business person has a five-year plan that details how he wants to have his company have an extra $3–6 million in sales five years from now. As a result, he begins to focus on what it is going to take in the way of capital. Then he must realize that in order to have capital he has to have taxable profits. There is no other way, short of fraud, that he can have capital without having taxable profits.

### Building a Capital Base

If you have invested your assets in some form of tax shelter, it may be in an unrelated field (a leasing program, a cattle operation, etc.). Usually, these are highly speculative and mostly all that you will save is your tax savings. If it is not a good investment on its "own legs," then it is not a good tax shelter. In these circumstances, all you are doing is literally sheltering taxes. The money you keep is the money you make on the saved taxes. In many cases you are a lot better off to go ahead and pay the taxes. You should use the retained earnings to build your capital base because corporations, until they get to the point where they need the capital, can take capital (surplus money) and invest in such things as a good preferred stock.

For example, if you were to invest in Southern Company preferred stock, paying 11 percent, then 85 percent of that dividend is not taxable to the corporation. You only pay tax on 15 percent. If you pay tax at 46 percent of 15 percent, this is 6.9 percent tax you are going to receive on that money. As long as you have a business need that is documented in your corporate minute book (this is important), a business need for which you are accumulating the capital for, then the IRS cannot attack you for unreasonable accumulation of income. A business corporation can have a quarter of a million dollars as surplus capital without having any excuses for it. For everything over a quarter of a million dollars there must be a good business reason. However, if you have a valid business reason, and document it, you can accumulate any amount of money.

### Positive Tax Management

Again, while you are waiting for a capital investment opportunity or for the time to make your expansion by building an addition to your building or buying some more equipment, you can have the money working for you by a tax-advantage method. In this way, you are only paying a small amount of tax on the accumulated money that is truly surplus money.

### Negative Effects of Poor Tax Management

Most people, however, will in effect drain the corporation of its current funds in order to reduce the corporation's taxes. Then, when they reach expansion time, they don't have the money; and the corporation certainly does not have the money because it has spent it in the form of bonuses and salaries. The corporation must then go to the bank and borrow the money. This is usually the "tight loan" agreement (the loan agreement covenants) that restricts the operation of the corporation, and many times it restricts you to the point that it actually hinders the business. In effect, the bank ends up managing the company instead of the chief operating officers.

The purpose of this discussion is not to talk about ways to mitigate the corporation's taxes, but it should be understood that those opportunities will come. You will get the investment tax credit, plus the depreciation, at the time you are ready to make a capital expansion and spend the money. In effect, you then recoup some of those taxes that you previously paid.

### Business Taxes in Perspective

It is often very difficult to get the average business person to see that there is no evil in paying taxes at the corporate level. This is frequently the tax lawyer's most difficult task. He/she can help them to reduce their taxes, but many times it is not in the corporation's best interest or their personal best interest. Their personal interest is tied to the strength of the corporation.

If the company has accumulated a large sum of retained earnings, it is assumed to be successful and another company may want to buy it. The options open to Company X are to sell the assets or to sell the company. If Company X sells the assets, the company can retain all the cash and get *capital gains* on it. The maximum tax rate on the capital gains is 20 percent. If these funds are invested in preferred stock or tax-free securities, then they (the Corporation X principals) will have recouped just on the investments. They will have recouped a good deal of what they have already spent as taxes, because 46 percent of 15 percent is a good shelter. This is accomplished with safe investments, and again you are accumulating it. It is important that you do document what your expansion plans are. Plans over a period of time, if they are not carried out, become a "red flag" to the IRS. Plans need to be legitimate.

## Personal Holding Companies

Most people seem to avoid a personal holding company as if it were "the plague." It appears that there are some tax advantages from the personal holding company. You can have a holding company that owns a number of separate companies, or you can have a one-company holding company. In these circumstances, you are passing the dividends upstream, out of the after-tax profits of the subsidiary up to the parent company which is nothing but a holding company. These funds can be passed up without any tax consequences to the holding company. A holding company receives these funds and invests them, for example, the holding company invests in tax-free bonds, the income from these bonds is tax free, an investment vehicle that isn't subject to income tax. Another application of a holding company is that it can be used in a joint venture. Venture capital is something that is always available. Then, if you have money you can make investments as a joint venture with someone who has some expertise, integrity, and moxie. There is a joint venture capital basis, and a normal piece of that will enable the accumulation of capital, in addition to the company you are operating. If you truly do have surplus money, then the idea is to devise a system whereby you can use those monies. As an example, for a string of 22 finance companies owned by a holding company, there is a decided advantage here. The funds may be passed up to the holding company, which in turn may lend them back to the subsidiary companies at the going rate. Instead of having to obtain those funds from an outside source, a double benefit is gained by using the holding company funds.

The holding company is a way of building corporate fences. If the operating company gets hit by a major lawsuit, a truly major lawsuit above and beyond the products liability coverage, your *holding company* is protected.

## Sound Business and Unsound Business

When a business is run on the basis of minimizing the tax liability, the business is not going to be run as well as if the same people were running that business on the basis of "How can we make the greatest profit?" They have less money and the company will be a lot weaker; consequently, they are not in a position to take advantage of opportunities. An opportunity that cannot be taken advantage of because of inadequate capital is worse than an opportunity that never comes to your attention. Opportunities come if business people have the resources to do something about them. A business that has capital on hand is usually able to find a *good productive use for those funds* by: expanding their own business by taking on a new line; buying another company and merging it with their company; or by joining a joint venture capital of an unrelated business. The opportunities are unlimited. If an opportunity comes up and the company is not able to take advantage of it, that lost opportunity may jeopardize the business.

## The Fictional Concept of Taxes

The average taxpayer, whether personal or business, has a fictionalized concept of the tax law and tax rates. Frequently taxpayers say, "We have got to do something, we are paying everything we make to the government." No one pays everything they make to the government, not in the United States. When a taxpayer says that, it is a fiction. They are looking at the size of the tax bill rather than the size of the after-tax profits retained.

## Minimizing Taxes

There are always opportunities to minimize taxes within organizations. What is being discussed in this section does not mean that you should not try to minimize taxes. Such opportunities always exist. You should have a good independent accounting firm or perhaps a good tax lawyer to help you with your tax planning so that, within your organization, you will make sound plans for paying the least amount of tax that you legally have to pay. If you, in order to reduce taxes, make a business decision that you would not have made were it not for reducing taxes, you can be sure that it is a bad business decision. The solid premise ought to be that you are going to make a profit as large as you can make. Within a corporate framework, you will minimize your taxes by every legal means available, without making any decisions that would not be made were it not for taxes.

Why do people make bad tax decisions? What really happens in a small firm is that many bad decisions are made toward the end of the year. For example, a firm is making a profit, but as they come to the last quarter they suddenly realize that they have made a lot of money and it has gone back into the business in the form of inventory, work-in-process, accounts receivable, and possibly some capital expansion (new equipment). There is no money to pay the taxes. Then, they make a decision which will artificially lower their taxes in order not to have to come up with that money. That decision will end up costing the business money.

### Resolving This Dilemma

Our earlier, major premise is that a sound business, at the end of each month, prepares an operating statement, accrues the taxes, and sets aside on an annualized basis the tax on that month's income. This should be placed in a reserve account in the bank to draw interest. The remaining cash should only go back into the business. Thus, when the end of the year comes, you will have enough money to pay the taxes and all the remainder of the money has gone back into the company. You do not have split-second decisions made for the sole purpose of reducing taxes and not with the intent of what is best for the business.

There are times when the problem will compound. The business person will prematurely make a decision on spending some money for a piece of capital equipment to reduce the taxes. That decision will end up being a good business decision, which will in turn generate more profits the next year. Then they will encounter a bigger tax problem the next year.

The simple thing to do is accrue those taxes, but many small firms do not. A lot of the smaller firms do not have monthly financial statements, much less accrue taxes. They do not have the money on hand. They end up making a bad business decision, in order to reduce taxes. The problem could have been avoided if the firm had simply accrued the taxes and set them aside and taken the rest of the money and invested it back in the business. What they do is invest all the money back in the business. They do that each month and they come to the end of the year without having the funds to pay the taxes. This reflects the lack of cash management. This one methodology, if applied, would prevent a lot of bad decisions being made (crisis decisions).

### The Profit Status of Many Businesses

We have observed that among many smaller independent business people, their books are their checkbooks. If they have money in the bank, they think they are making money. On the other hand, if they don't have money in the bank, then they think they aren't making money. Yet, there are a number of good business people who will say, "If we made $300,000, where the _____ is it?" They can be shown by just flipping over to the part of the financial statement that talks about uses and application of working capital. It is at this point that the business person wants to change the whole operation. They want to reduce their taxes, but the crisis would have been avoided if they had just *accrued* and *reserved*. Then they would not be faced with this crisis.

## In Conclusion

The material in this section has been prepared for those who are reluctant to seek the counsel of a competent, independent accountant or a competent tax lawyer. While the small or independent business person needs to seek expert tax counsel a great number will not. It is for these persons that this material has been prepared. By reading this information, you will become aware of the actions you need to take, including getting the advice of expert counsel, in the interest of better management of your assets.

It should always be the objective of a firm's management to achieve the *optimum profit results* and let taxes take care of themselves. This statement does not mean that the firm should not rely on the advice of the tax expert; but let profit not taxes be the dominant consideration.

# Chapter Eighteen

## Asset Preservation: Bankruptcy and Creditor Considerations

### Introduction

As an independent business person, you are concerned with the options for protecting your firm's assets from actions you or others may take that will impact on the value and quality of the assets. In the development of the material for this chapter, the intent has been to create an awareness of the risks and the defensive measures that will affect you as both a creditor and a debtor. These issues will be developed, in an appropriate order, as we perceive them.

As much as it may be desirable, it is not always feasible, reasonable, or possible for the firm to function in a prosperous and secure manner. There are times when the actions of others or your own action(s) may produce a financial crisis. Then the key questions become: How can I defend myself from my creditors? How can I minimize my losses? More importantly, how can I save my business?

Assuming you have stalled paying your creditors as long as they are willing to tolerate your delinquency, there are two methods of saving the business available to you. These are a "Composition of creditors" or one of the three chapters of the 1978 Bankruptcy Act (7, 11, and 13).

### Composition of Creditors

In viewing your options, the better choice seems to be the composition of creditors. This should be the least expensive and most effective way of dealing with a financial crisis. A composition of creditors is a contractual arrangement between the business firm and its creditors. This should grow out of an assemblage of the principals or their agents. The purpose of this assemblage is to formulate an agreement which will enable the business firm to continue its operation and to provide, over a reasonable time period, for satisfying the claims of the creditors. In brief, the contract contains a series of protective covenants protecting the rights of all principals. This agreement is supervised by a trustee whose responsibility is to assure compliance with the covenant stipulations.

The legal and accounting expense of this arrangement is minimal as compared to those incurred in a bankruptcy situation.

## Bankruptcy

Under the 1978 Bankruptcy Act, there are 3 chapter designations for bankruptcy action: Chapter 7, Chapter 11, and Chapter 13. The jurisdiction of the Act is under a legal cloud, based on action of the U.S. Supreme Court in June 1982. The court, at that time, called upon the Congress to rewrite the 1978 law by December 1982. In early 1983, Congress was still in the process of responding to the June 1982 decree.

## Who May File

### Chapter 7

Individual, partnership, and/or corporation.

### Chapter 13

An individual with regular income, secured debts not in excess of $350,000, and unsecured debts not in excess of $100,000.

### Chapter 11

Any entity other than stock broker, commodity broker, bank, domestic insurance company, or credit union.

### Chapter 7 Bankruptcy

Under a Chapter 7, the provision is for the voluntary liquidation of the debtor's assets can also be involuntary. Then these benefits are utilized toward the satisfaction of creditor claims. The debtor can reassume some debts with the approval of the court. This method is considered to be the least desirable of the three bankruptcy procedures.

## Chapter 11 Bankruptcy

Under a Chapter 11 proceeding, the intent is to enable the management of the firm to "buy time"—that is, the firm is protected by the court from its creditors by preventing the creditors from taking legal action to collect their claims through a foreclosure/sale, so long as the secured creditors are adequately protected. This procedure applies to those circumstances where the firm may be anticipated, through reorganization and a moratorium period on paying its obligations, to be able to correct its cash-flow deficiencies and in time be able to satisfy the claims of its creditors. Under these conditions, a Chapter 11 seems to be the appropriate process. However, it should be understood that this action falls under the control of the bankruptcy judge in whose jurisdiction the case rests. All major actions and contractual arrangements must be approved by this judicial officer and the creditors committee. Otherwise, these claims and other contractual actions lack legal validity. It is an expensive process, since various principals' interests are represented by counsel, whose fees are paid from the asset corpus of the Chapter 11 firm. However, prior to payment, all such payments must have the approval of the court. In addition, the Chapter 11 circumstance tends to require the frequent services of a reputable CPA firm, preferably one of the "Big Eight" group.

One of the authors is familiar with a Chapter 11 case that had its inception in May 1980. The assets were sold by the court for $791,000 in August 1981. The initial claims against the firm were $590,000. In early 1983, the case remains in the hands of the court. In the interim, a significant portion of the corpus has been consumed by legal and accounting fees.

Another example of a Chapter 11 case is the well-publicized "Manville case" relating to its asbestos liability dilemma. Re Chapter 11 cases, "Where to Look for Further Information" at the end of this chapter.

## Chapter 13 Bankruptcy

Under the 1978 law, this device has been most frequently utilized in cases of personal bankruptcy. There are two types of Chapter 13 plans—*extension* or *composition plans.*

Under the provisions of Chapter 13, the individual debtor is given certain asset and income exemptions. Upon presentation of a liability, asset, and income statement, a "plan of resolution" is developed with the approval of the court. It has not been uncommon for the plan to provide only token payments to unsecured creditors, usually covering a three-year period. Under the Chapter 13 arrangement, the debtor is able to retain a significant portion of residual assets including a house, furnishings, and (in some instances) one or more automobiles.

Obviously, a Chapter 13 situation works to the detriment of the creditor. Because of this circumstance, it then becomes of paramount importance for creditors to formulate advanced plans, with the assistance of attorneys, in order to minimize losses from the debtor.

## Summary

It has been the purpose of this chapter to familiarize you with your status both as a debtor and as a creditor.

In the presentation of the composition of creditors and bankruptcy material, it has not been our intention to provide you with complete and comprehensive answers. Rather, we have tried to make you aware of the defenses and risks to your assets under these circumstances. We counsel you to seek the advice of a competent attorney in dealing with these matters.

## Where to Look for Further Information

For more detailed information, relating to events surrounding the use of Chapter 11 bankruptcy, we refer you to these articles:

"Bankruptcy Laws: Stretched Too Far?" *Business Week*, May 9, 1983, p. 33.

"A Retailer's Chapter 11 Has Creditors Enraged." *Business Week*, May 9, 1983, p. 71.

# *Chapter Nineteen*

# Providing for Management Succession

There are two potential problems involved in owning and/or managing an independent business. First, there are the problems associated with failure. The information presented in the preceding chapters is based upon the assumption that your business has been successful, and you have not failed. Therefore, the second problem—that the business may have grown too rapidly—is important. We hope that your organization followed a normal path of growth and development and that everything is in order and you have overcome both these problems.

## Need for Management Succession

If neither of the above problems has occurred, you may be facing a third possibility, the need to provide for management succession for your ongoing business.

### An Overlooked Problem

In most independent firms, the development of managerial personnel and the provision for management succession are greatly neglected, often until it is too late to do anything about them. Therefore, now that your firm is operating successfully, you should answer these questions: Who will fill my shoes so that I can retire when I choose? Is there someone to operate the firm so I can take vacations or go to training programs or conventions? If my business is a proprietorship, do I want my spouse or child(ren) to manage it when I leave? If my company is a partnership and I leave it, do I want my spouse or children to be a partner? How will my death or incapacity affect my firm?

> The premature death of the owner of a family business presented the wife and other family members with a crisis concerning its future management. The eldest son, with a technical degree from one of the nation's leading colleges, was settled into a professional position with a promising future. After much soul-searching, he yielded to family loyalty and resigned his position to return home to be the business's general manager.

### What Is the Real Problem?

Your children, grandchildren, and other relatives may not have the capabilities—or the interest—to manage the firm. You need to be exceedingly competent to be either a judge of their managerial talent or a teacher to provide management training. The *real* problem, according to one management consultant, is that the model isn't today's business corporation. "It's the Kingdom. The Old Man is the king, and the kids are the princes and princesses."[1] The "old man" usually has trouble accepting the kids into *his* business, in which he started and devoted his whole life.

## Some Problems in Managing a Family-Owned Business

> When close relatives work together in a business, emotions often interfere with business decisions. Conflicts sometimes arise because relatives look at the business from different viewpoints. For example, relatives who are furnishing the capital or are the "money people" may consider only income when judging capital expenditures, growth, and other major matters. Relatives engaged in the daily operations judge money matters from the viewpoint of securing the production, sales, and personnel necessary to make the firm successful. These two viewpoints may conflict.

### Individuals' Interests Conflict with Firm's Objectives

Many times in a family business, the individuals' interests take precedence over centralized objectives and a supporting organizational structure. Such was the case of the Chapman family.

---

[1]Sanford L. Jacobs, "It's Often Hard in Family Firms to Let the Children Take Over," *The Wall Street Journal*, March 14, 1983, p. 33. We strongly urge you to read this interesting and informative article!

The Chapman House grew like Topsy into a profitable chain of restaurants, motels, and textile industries. In time, the second generation took over more and more from the matriarch, and the third generation began its entry into the business. It soon became evident that there were too many chiefs, with a resulting proliferation of activities and increasing internal conflicts and decreasing profitability.

The passing of the matriarch was followed by 90 days of internal strife. At the end of this period, a third-generation family member, with an MBA from State University and outside employment experience in a major industrial corporation, was able to hammer out some centralized objectives. This settlement was followed by the development of an appropriate organizational structure to reach the objectives. Fortunately, in this case, the family members recognized that their individual economic advantage was in keeping the business intact and expanding only in those areas offering the best return on investment.

### Difficulty of Making *Rational* Decisions

The firm's top manager should recognize the extent of the emotions involved and make objective decisions. It is often hard for the manager and other relatives to make rational decisions about each other's skills and abilities. Also, quarrels and ill feelings of relatives may spread to nonfamily employees, or family quarrels may carry over into the firm's operations and interfere with its effectiveness. The manager should not permit the business to become divided into factions. It is necessary to convince nonfamily employees that their interests are best served by a profitable company rather than by allegiance to any particular family member. Another complication that often occurs is that nonfamily employees tend to base their decisions on the family's tensions. They know how their bosses react, and they react accordingly.

### Incompetence of Family Members—or Worse

Some family-owned companies are handicapped with high turnover among their most capable nonfamily employees. Relatives are sometimes to blame, for they may resent outside talent and make things unpleasant for nonfamily managers. An incompetent family member may occupy one job after another without being successful in any one of them. But this person still has a job, a title, and a salary. Relatives may indulge in excessive family talk during working hours, hampering their performance as well as the performance of others. A relative can demoralize an organization by loafing, avoiding unpleasant tasks, taking special privileges, or making snide remarks about the manager and other relatives. One may even go so far as to spy on other employees.

> In a retail clothing store, the aunt of the owner-president is notorious for making life miserable for other workers, especially females. She sneaks into the ladies' room and reports anyone found smoking. The employees always look behind clothing racks to see whether she is listening before they say anything personal or derogatory about the family. They refer to her as "the Gestapo." Needless to say, morale is constantly low. Turnover is far greater than that for comparable stores.

Another kind of problem is that family members in control may require clearance of all routine matters.

One of several alternative steps can be taken to correct the above situations, but each has its drawbacks. A troublesome relative may be discharged (with difficulty), assisted in starting another business in a noncompeting line, exiled to a branch office, or assisted in obtaining a job elsewhere. A useless manager may be shifted to some newly created, menial position with title and salary but no actual work to perform. The job may be designed for minimum contact with other employees and require no important decisions.

The manager should set the example and insist that other relatives refrain from family talk while on the job. If the company can afford it, one way to obtain objective control in a family-owned business is to hire an outside professional manager to handle day-to-day operations. To retain nonfamily employees, avenues for promotion and other reward systems must be kept open.

## Lack of Definite Authority

Responsibilities of family members should be specified, and the extent of the authority, duties, and activities of each should be clearly stated. A manager's authority to suspend or discharge flagrant violators of company rules should also be specified. Control is weakened if the manager must make special allowances for family employees. Definite lines of authority and responsibility are an absolute necessity.

> In 1950, when Joseph Rothberg founded Manhattan Distributing Co., it had a staff of 10, one line of product, and grossed $300,000. After 32 years of struggling, pushing, prodding, and nurturing, it had 90 employees, 40 lines, and grossed nearly $30 million. It was his "alter ego," and he managed it by himself until 1974, when he either had to sell out or bring in someone to help him. He invited his son-in-law, Nolan Crane, to join the firm.

With little discussion—especially of authority-responsibility relationships—they started working together and spent six years feuding with each other. Mr. Rothberg, a self-made man dedicated to the value of sacrifice and hard work, had difficulty relinquishing authority to Mr. Crane, a product of a more leisure-oriented generation, who-had worked 10 years for a large corporation. The younger man, who was ambitious and eager to succeed in the family business, sometimes appeared to the older man to be assertive, brash, and impatient. Both became frustrated, and Mr. Rothberg retreated into isolation and made decisions in a vacuum. Mr. Crane was never quite confident about his role and lacked authority to make the decisions that were required to save the firm.

A crisis was precipitated when an order placed by Crane was canceled without any discussion from Mr. Rothberg, and the son-in-law stormed in and resigned. This was the turning point in their relationship, as it was the first time they had shown their true feelings. They began to communicate and show respect for each other. With the help of Margaret, the daughter-wife who had been caught in the crossfire, they worked out some 16 simple, practical rules that should be followed when anyone brings a family member into an ongoing business.[2]

Often the owner-manager may believe an expenditure should be made in order to improve efficiency; yet, other family members may oppose it because they consider it to be money out of their pockets. The manager may base arguments for the expenditure on information that nonfamily employees have derived, or show the relatives that the investment can be recovered in a few years. Outside business advisers—including bankers, accountants, attorneys, or consultants—may assist the manager in convincing the relatives of the merits of the expenditure.

Some relatives in a family-owned business develop a desire to maintain the *status quo* as they grow older. They can block, or at least hamper, company progress. These relatives may be given an opportunity to convert their common stock to preferred stock or to sell some of their stock to younger relatives. Perhaps they can be "gradually retired" through salary reductions over several years and induced to relinquish some of their interest in the firm.

### Sharing the Profits

Provisions for paying family members and dividing the profits equitably among them can also be difficult. If the business is a corporation, stock dividends may be appropriate.

---

[2]See Margaret Crane, "How to Keep Families from Feuding," *INC*, February 1982, pp. 73-79, for a list and discussion of these rules.

The salaries of family members should be competitive with those paid others of comparable rank and ability in the same area. Fringe benefits—such as deferred profit-sharing plans, pension plans, insurance programs, and stock purchase programs—can be useful in dividing profits equitably.

### Some Sources of Help

If you are the manager of a family-owned business, you are not alone. Other individuals managing family companies in the same community may be a source of information and assistance. Exchange ideas with them and learn how they have solved problems similar to yours. Also, if you manage a small corporation, the presence of outsiders on the board of directors can be beneficial. Another source of help for children trying to enter family businesses is the National Family Business Council (NFBC) with chapters around the country.[3]

## Some Difficult Problems with Managers

You may have problems with your managers, whether they are members of the family or not. You should be familiar with three staffing problems that are particularly difficult in small firms: (1) the manager who thinks only in terms of the past, (2) the one who makes work, and (3) the one guilty of work duplication.

### What to Do with Incompetent Managers

The first of these managers retains the old ways and refuses to learn and adopt new methods of management regardless of how effective they may seem or how badly they are needed. Either dismissal or transfer to another assignment is appropriate in this case.

The make-work manager may have been hired to perform a specific job—such as doing a market survey—but the need for those services no longer exists. Dismissal or transfer to a more productive position may be appropriate.

The problem of work duplication may exist because two managers are both supervising the same project. Their duties should be reappraised.

If you are faced with similar staffing problems, start with one or two changes at a time and see how they work out. You should

---

[3]For more information, contact the NFBC, 1000 Vermont Avenue N.W., Washington, D.C. 20005.

also try to anticipate and make changes before they become a critical necessity.

## Replacing Key Executives

Another type of staffing problem occurs when key executives leave. Some dislocation inevitably occurs, but you usually have some latitude in the kind of replacement you seek. Consider reorganizing your management, redistributing the present assignments and using present managers more effectively. The job specifications for a new manager could be written less narrowly, and the range of choices broadened. Managers should participate in this planning because they will feel that they have contributed to the decision, and will accept the newcomer more readily.

Often managers prefer that an individual *from within the firm* replace a key manager who has left. This attitude usually appears not only in the manager who expects to be promoted, but also in other employees. If you decide upon an outsider, you should discuss the reasons with the person(s) who expected the promotion and with other managers prior to filling the vacancy.

If you recruit someone *from the outside,* have your people who will be working with the new manager meet and talk with candidates. Observe their reactions and ask for their evaluations of each prospect. Seek answers to these important questions: Will the prospect fit into the community? Will the family be able to make the adjustment? Give the prospective manager ample opportunity to consider the situation carefully before deciding.

You can *appraise a prospective manager's ability* by considering several kinds of information: records of past performance, personal statements, and evaluations by others. Perhaps a prospective sales manager provides data that show a 60 percent increase in sales volume over the last five years while the sales force rose only 20 percent. A candidate's personal statements may reflect an interest in high-quality, custom-built products with low volume and high margin. You should determine whether there are inconsistencies in the candidate's statements. If you have doubts, ask more questions. Do not automatically reject the prospect because of a poor reference. The evaluation may have resulted from a personality conflict, the circumstances of resignation, or some other situation that does not affect the prospect's suitability for your company.

In *determining compensation,* review the remuneration of your present managers to see whether it is adequate and equitable, whether it is properly related to their contributions to the firm, and whether it is comparable to that of the new manager. Have a five-year compensation plan in mind for a new manager. Keep in mind that, if your offer is too high now, you may limit your ability to increase rewards for improved performance in the future. However, do not drive too hard a bargain. To help make the new manager's interests coincide with yours, consider offering a share of ownership in your firm.

When you hire a manager, you should discuss with him or her *how the relationship can be terminated.* There should be some penalty for termination, but it should not be so great that you keep an unsatisfactory manager rather than pay the penalty. Avoid giving the manager a bonus for taking a better job elsewhere. Do not conceal any unpleasant conditions that must be confronted soon after the new manager reports for work.

Some turnover in your middle management group can be beneficial if it does not happen too often. If you have a young manager with ability and ambition, be frank about the opportunities you can offer. If such a person should desire to move, offer help in finding a better position. This assistance is preferable to the manager's job-hunting without your knowledge.

> An owner-manager was reading the *New Orleans Times-Picayune* want ads. Suddenly he exclaimed, "That's my telephone number!" When asked what he meant, he indicated a "Position Wanted" ad that gave one of his office phones for prospective employers to call. Needless to say, he was very upset with the young man who had placed the ad.

Replacing a manager can sometimes be helpful to the firm. For example, suppose a production manager who has excelled in plant layout, tooling, and production methods leaves you. In replacing this person, you might seek a manager with a different mix of skills—perhaps including labor relations, employee productivity, and quality of supervision.

## Preparing for Your Successor

What preparations should you make when you are planning to retire, acquire another business, or otherwise turn the business over to someone else? Too often a small company suffers under these circumstances. Sales may decrease, or production may lag. These difficulties can be prevented by preparations that enable the new manager to pick up where you leave off. The key is to make available to your successor the specialized knowledge that you have accumulated over the years. But be prepared for that knowledge *not* to be used, or at least to be modified.

## Providing Adequate Information

You should create a reference source for a new manager by making an inventory of the various kinds of information used to manage and operate the business. The inventory should consist of three kinds of information:

1. Facts about the general management of the company.
2. Data concerning the firm's finances.
3. Information about operating and technical aspects.

Examples of these inventories are included in the appendix at the end of this chapter. This type of inventory should also help you evaluate your firm at any time, even if you're not leaving it.

You should set down some information about goals and objectives you hope to see the company reach, both before you leave and afterwards. An illustration of this type of objective might be the accumulation of funds to replace an old plant. This plan should be supplemented with profit-and-loss and cash-flow projections.

## Starting Early

Even though your top assistant should have essentially the same capabilities as you, try to find someone who complements your abilities. Two dynamic and aggressive individuals often clash. Ideally, "The capable assistant is usually one whose strengths match your weaknesses, rather than one whose strong points match yours."[4]

To facilitate a smooth transition, bring in the new manager as early as possible. The length of the transition period varies according to your plans, the type of business, the new manager's experience and knowledge, whether the person is a relative or a hired outsider, and the size of the firm. The period may vary from three to five years.

## The Moment of Truth

Mr. Leon Danco, president of the Center for Family Business in Cleveland, advises owners who refuse to face the problem of preparing for their successors: "You must perpetuate or liquidate."[5] Ultimately, the moment arrives when you must turn over to someone else the business you have created with your own ambition, initiative, and character. *If you have built well, it will survive as testimony of your creativity!*

---

[4]Med Serif, "Pointers for Developing Your Top Assistant." *Small Marketers is Aids No. 101* (Washington, D.C.: Small Business Administration, 1972).

[5]Jacobs, "It's Often Hard in Family Firms."

A sales representative in the rubber industry and an experienced and technologically competent production manager in his early 60s formed a business to produce a component used in the shoe industry. The production manager owned two thirds of the firm and the sales representative one third.

The sales representative was weak in his management abilities, so that the real management burdens rested on the production manager, who in fact was the general manager.

After four years of operations, the general manager was in his late 60s, and the business was still short of the profit objectives. The general manager had planned to retire at 70, but now he began to wonder how he could. It seemed that not only was his time needed in the plant, but more and more of it was spent in the field; and when he was away from the plant, its efficiency suffered. The nagging question was (as is so often the case in similar circumstances): What can I do when there is no one to whom I can delegate some of my activities?

## A Management Audit

You have now come to the point where you are asking yourself, "How well am I actually doing?" To determine your individual situation, you can use the questionnaire "General Management Audit," found in Exhibit 19–1 at the end of this chapter. This material has been field tested and has proved useful in aiding owners and managers of ongoing independent businesses to take an objective look at their managerial status and the managerial status of their business.

## Summary

Because of the time, effort, and money you have expended to make your small business a success, it is important that you do everything possible to provide for effective management succession. In order to do this, you must make adequate provisions for the selection, development, and motivation of competent professional managers to succeed you and assure your firm's continuation. Some ideas to make this possible have been presented in this chapter.

Relatives in family businesses can cause many problems that test a manager's ability. Establishing and communicating lines of authority can help to resolve conflicts, particularly those involving nonfamily employees. Loss of key executives should be avoided when possible.

Use of the forms in the exhibits that follow can aid in analyzing your company and your position in it.

# Appendix: Inventory of Information Used to Manage and Operate a Company[1]

## Inventory of Facts about General Administration

*Company history:*
Date organized, key founders, and major events.
Clippings of stories from newspapers and trade journals concerning your company.
Brochures concerning new products, processes, sales personnel, etc.

*Company organization:*
Organization chart.
Job specifications.
Description of key employees, including your evaluation of their potential.
Report of studies of your company made by employees or an outside consultant.

*Policies:*
Information on credit and selling terms, vacations, retirement plans, employee loans and advances, etc.

*Legal matters:*
Patents, licenses, and royalty agreements.
Information on where each formal document is filed.
Employment and labor agreements.
Leases.
Contracts with suppliers and customers.
Outcome of past lawsuits and pending suits.

*Outside services:*
List and brief description of outside professional people who work with your company, including bankers, accountants, insurance agents, advertising agencies, consultants.

## Inventory of Financial Data

Profit-and-loss statements for past 10 years.
Copy of most recent balance sheet.
Copy of most recent budget.
Brief description of company's working-capital turnover trends, return-on-investment trends, operating ratios, etc.

---

[1]Source: Frederick F. Halstead, "Preparing for New Management," *Management Aids for Small Manufacturers No. 183* (Washington, D.C., Small Business Administration, 1972).

## Appendix *(concluded)*

List of current bank accounts, including average balances and name of bank employee who handles accounts.

List of prior banking connections, indicating the line of credit and bank officers who arranged it.

List of paid tax bills.

List of insurance policies, including a description of coverages and premiums and name of agent.

Copies of your financial and control reports, with notation about frequency of preparation and distribution.

Copies of procedures or procedure manuals.

### Inventory of Operating and Technical Information

*Marketing:*

List of company's products or services, and notes concerning customer acceptance, profitability, and future potential.

List of geographical areas in which each product is sold, types of customers, and the largest customers.

List of distribution channels.

Brief outline of advertising program, including how it is coordinated with other sales efforts.

Brief descriptions of sales training programs.

Brief description of how prices are set for current and new products.

Brief description of competitors, including a list of their products, location and size of their plants, share of the market, pricing policies, and channels of distribution.

*Production:*

List of major pieces of equipment. Brief appraisal of efficiency of the plant and equipment.

List of product and manufacturing specifications and process procedures.

List of studies made to improve layout and quality control, to replace existing equipment, etc.

Brief description of how production is scheduled and controlled (orders on hand or for stock).

Brief description of standards used for measuring performance and methods for eliminating waste.

*Purchasing:*

Lists concerning: (1) major materials purchased, (2) names of suppliers, (3) present contracts with suppliers, and (4) procedures for buying, including kind of approval needed for various types of purchases.

Inventory of knowledge in special areas: research and development, engineering, quality control, etc.

# Where to look for Further Information

Corley, R. N., and Black, R. L. *The Legal Environment of Business.* 5th ed. New York: McGraw-Hill, 1979.

Donnelly, J. H.; Gibson, J. L.; and Ivancevich, J. M. *Fundamentals of Management.* 3d ed. Plano, Tex.: Business Publications, 1978.

Gross, Harry. *Franchise Investigation and Contract.* Rev. ed. New York: Pilot Books, 1979.

Halstead, E. Frederick. "Preparing for New Management." *Management Aids for Small Manufacturers No. 183.* Washington, D.C.: Small Business Administration, 1972.

Levinsen, Robert E. "Problems in Managing a Family-Owned Business." *Management Aids for Small Manufacturers No. 208.* Washington, D.C.: Small Business Administration, 1970.

Megginson, Leon C.; Mosley, Donald C.; and Pietri, Paul, Jr. *Management Concepts and Applications.* New York: Harper & Row, 1983, chap. 4.

Robinsen, Joseph A. "How to Find a Likely Successor." *Management Aids for Small Manufacturers No. 198.* Washington, D.C.: Small Business Administration, 1968.

Samuelson, P. *Economics*, 11th ed. New York: McGraw-Hill, 1980.

Weston, J. F., and Brigham-Holt, E. F. *Essentials of Management Finance.* 4th ed. New York: Holt, Rinehart & Winston, 1977.

# Exhibits

You should now have successfully completed reading and studying the material in Part 5. We hope it has been of help to you in owning or managing your ongoing independent business. You may wish to complete the following form as a self-audit of the general management of your organization.

As with the other exhibits, you should answer the questions as completely, objectively, and honestly as possible. When you have completed this, you may want to go over it again, objectively evaluating how you are doing. An alternative is to submit this to someone you trust—a consultant, banker, or friend—and have him or her evaluate how you are doing.

Good luck to you!

**Exhibit 19–1**
**General Management Audit**

1. Organization
   a. Do you have a board of directors?
      Yes _____ No _____
   b. Who constitute your board? _____
      _____
      _____

   c. How often do you meet? Monthly _____
                             Quarterly _____
                             Semiannually _____
                             Yearly _____
   d. Are these meetings of any actual benefit?
      Yes _____ No _____
   e. Does any action result from suggestions made in board meetings? Yes _____ No _____

2. President—function and status
   a. How old are you? _____
   b. What is the state of your health? Excellent _____
                                        Good _____
                                        Fair _____
                                        Poor _____

   c. Do you have any specific health problems? _____
      _____
      _____

   d. What do you do in running your company? _____
      _____
      _____

   e. Who looks after things when you are away? _____
      _____

   f. Are you satisfied with what goes on in your absence?
      Yes _____ No _____

*Exhibit 19–1 (continued)*

g.  If, for some reason beyond your control, you were not able to be there to run the business, what would happen?

_____

_____

_____

_____

h.  Could your business continue if you were killed in an automobile accident? Yes _____ No _____

i.  Are you training someone to assume your managerial responsibilities? Yes _____ No _____

j.  How long have you been training this person? _____

k.  Why did you select him or her? _____

_____

_____

_____

l.  How much consideration have you given to detailing the activities that take place in your company?

_____

_____

_____

_____

m.  Have you assigned specific people to be responsible for specific activities? Yes _____ No _____

n.  Are you happy with everybody's performance in his or her assigned role? Yes _____ No _____
Who? 1 _____ 2 _____ 3 _____ 4 _____ 5 _____

_____

_____

Why? _____

_____

_____

_____

o.  Do you ever go through your organization and evaluate the performance effectiveness of those people assigned to some type of managerial responsibility? Yes _____ No _____

p.  Do you expect these people to do the same thing as the people they supervise? Yes _____ No _____

q.  Construct an organization chart of your business. First do it by functional activity without the people; then add the people.

3. Management information
Provide information that reveals what actually has occurred in a specific time frame. This information should be utilized to deter-

*Exhibit 19–1 (continued)*

mine accurate costs, to plan more effectively for profits, and to determine asset-and-liability status.

4.  Paper-flow analysis
    (Sales orders → Who → What happens → Where?)
    *a.*  What happens when an order is received? _____
    _____
    _____

    Is a credit check obtained? Yes _____ No _____
    *b.*  How is it recorded? _____
    _____
    _____

    *c.*  If it is recorded on a sales order, what is the sequence of events that follows? Who handles it (step by step through production and shipment)? At the end, who takes final action and files orders?
    _____
    _____
    _____
    _____
    _____

    *d.*  How do you maintain a file of orders? _____
    _____
    _____
    _____

    *e.*  Who is responsible to see that orders are filled and shipped?
    _____
    _____

    *f.*  Are the sales orders dated and numbered?
    Yes _____ No _____
    *g.*  Are purchase orders issued on prenumbered forms?
    Yes _____ No _____
    *h.*  How are purchase orders initiated? _____
    _____

    *i.*  Trace the paper flow of purchase orders.
    _____
    _____

*Exhibit 19–1 (continued)*

j. What system of record keeping exists for purchases? Do you check invoices against purchase orders?
Yes _____ No _____

k. Do you have receiving reports? Yes _____ No _____ Who gets them?

_____

l. Are they matched against purchase orders and incoming invoices? Yes _____ No _____

m. Do you invoice your orders on prenumbered invoice forms?
Yes _____ No _____

n. How many copies of invoices are made? _____
Who receives them? _____

_____

o. When are invoices issued? _____

p. In sending invoice to customer do you send copies of all appropriate documents, B/L, other related information?
Yes _____ No _____

q. What procedures control sales invoices? Are they transferred to Accounts Receivable, Accounts Receivable Aged, etc?

_____
_____
_____
_____
_____

r. Is it possible that a salesperson or other person might make up an invoice, collect for it, and not turn in such receipts?
Yes _____ No _____

s. Do you keep a record of adjustments? Yes _____ No _____

t. Who is authorized to make adjustments?

_____

Do you permit salespeople to make adjustments?
Yes _____ No _____ (There is danger of collusion between salesperson and customer in making adjustment.)

u. Do you get sales reports on calls activity, information obtained, indication of expected activity or lack of it?
Yes _____ No _____

v. Do you develop a monthly sales expense, by salesperson?
Yes _____ No _____

*Exhibit 19–1 (concluded)*

 *w.* Do you develop a production order? Yes _____ No _____
   For what time period:

    Daily _____    Semiannually _____
    Weekly _____    Quarterly _____
    Monthly _____    Yearly _____
    Every six weeks _____

 *x.* List audience paper flow distribution by time through operating period. _____

   _____

   _____

   _____

   _____

   _____

5. Profit Analysis
 *a.* Cost breakdown:
   (1) Overhead _____
   (2) Operating
    (*a*) People _____
    (*b*) Material/goods _____
 *b.* How do you *price* your product? _____

   _____

   _____

   _____

   _____

 *c.* Collection cycle? _____

 *d.* How do you plan for profit? Bottom line? Pricing formula?
   Explain: _____

   _____

   _____

6. Marketing
 What plans and what activities are taking place in your organization to assure a future market?
 *a.* Are you replacing retiring dealers with younger people?
   Yes _____ No _____
 *b.* Are you promoting the development of new customers to assure a continuing market? Yes _____ No _____
 *c.* How are you approaching the market to accommodate the changing age distribution in the population? Are you developing products with special appeal to the younger generation? Yes _____ No _____
 *d.* Other: _____

   _____

## Exhibit 19–2
## Should You Go Out of Business?

The purpose of this questionnaire is to guide you through the painful analysis of whether to liquidate your business or to continue its operation. Unfortunately, many people postpone accepting the economic realities that confront them and their business and stay too long. The result may be a complete economic loss when an earlier liquidation/disposal would have enabled the salvaging of some resources.

1. List your net sales for the past five years on a yearly basis:
   a. Year 1:                    $_____
   b. Year 2:                    $_____
   c. Year 3:                    $_____
   d. Year 4:                    $_____
   e. Year 5:                    $_____

2. List your net profit for each of those five years:
   a. Year 1:                    $_____
   b. Year 2:                    $_____
   c. Year 3:                    $_____
   d. Year 4:                    $_____
   e. Year 5:                    $_____

3. List the dollar amounts of money/goods/services/benefits you have taken out of the business for each of the five years:
   a. Year 1:                    $_____
   b. Year 2:                    $_____
   c. Year 3:                    $_____
   d. Year 4:                    $_____
   e. Year 5:                    $_____

4. List your balance sheet position, at year-end, for the items listed below for the past five years:

| Item | Year 1 | Year 2 | Year 3 | Year 4 | Year 5 |
|------|--------|--------|--------|--------|--------|
| Cash | | | | | |
| Inventory | | | | | |
| Buildings | | | | | |
| Land | | | | | |
| Equipment | | | | | |
| Accounts Receivable | | | | | |
| Current Assets | | | | | |
| Bad debts | | | | | |
| Accounts payable | | | | | |
| Notes payable | | | | | |
| Current liabilities | | | | | |
| Net worth | | | | | |

5. List the information requested below on a current basis:

| | Cost | Book Value | Replacement Cost |
|------|------|------------|------------------|
| Building | | | |
| Equipment | | | |

## Exhibit 19–2 (concluded)

6. How much new investment does your business need at this time? $_____

7. If you were to make this investment, how long would it be before the results were operational? _____

8. What return may you reasonably expect from this investment? _____%

9. How long will it take you to amortize this new investment? _____

10. What other investment alternatives are available to you?

_____

_____

_____

_____

_____

What rate of return?_____

11. If you were to invest this money in your business, what assurance do you have that it would produce satisfactory results?

_____

_____

_____

_____

_____

12. Are you experiencing:
    a. Labor turnover problems? ☐ Yes ☐ No
    b. Work absenteeism? ☐ Yes ☐ No
    c. Difficulty in obtaining suitable personnel to work in your business? ☐ Yes ☐ No

13. Are you having difficulty in maintaining adequate sources of supply? ☐ Yes ☐ No

14. Do the pricing policies of your suppliers enable you to compete favorably with your competitors? ☐ Yes ☐ No

15. Are you finding it difficult to compete? ☐ Yes ☐ No
    Why?_____

_____

_____

_____

16. How many competitors do you have at this time?

_____

17. What change has taken place in the number of your competitors in the last five years:
    a. Number gained? _____
    b. Number lost? _____
    What are the reasons for the differences?

_____

_____

_____

_____

_____

18. List the problems that confront you at this time in your business:
    a. _____
    b. _____
    c. _____
    d. _____
    e. _____
    f. _____
    g. _____
    h. _____
    i. _____
    j. _____
    k. _____
    l. _____
    m. _____
    n. _____
    o. _____
    p. _____

19. Do you believe it reasonable to assume that you can resolve these problems? ☐ Yes ☐ No

20. Start at the beginning of this questionnaire, and read it carefully and thoughtfully. At the conclusion of this analysis, do you honestly believe that you should continue your business? ☐ Yes ☐ No

## Exhibit 19–3
## Providing for Management Succession

The purpose of this questionnaire is to enable you to determine whether you are providing for management succession in your company most economically and effectively.

**Managing a family-owned business**

1. If you are managing a family-owned business, do you find that emotions often interfere with business decisions? □Yes □No

2. Do relatives who are furnishing the capital consider only income when judging capital expenditures, growth, and other major matters? □Yes □No

3. Are you and your relatives able to make rational business decisions about one another's skills and abilities? □Yes □No

4. Do quarrels and ill feelings of relatives spread to nonfamily employees? □Yes □No

5. Do nonfamily employees tend to base their decisions on the family's tensions? □Yes □No

6. Is your company handicapped with high turnover among your most capable nonfamily employees? □Yes □No

7. Does your company have a family member who has occupied one job after another without being successful in any of them? □Yes □No

8. Are ceilings imposed by your relatives on the amount of money that you can spend without permission so low that you are unable to capitalize on productive situations? □Yes □No

9. Does excessive family talk during working hours hamper your relatives' performance and that of others? □Yes □No

10. Have you specified the responsibilities of family members and the extent of their authority, duties, and activities? □Yes □No

11. Do you have the authority to suspend or discharge flagrant violators of company rules even if they are family members? □Yes □No

12. Do your older relatives want to maintain the status quo? □Yes □No

13. Are the salaries of family members competitive with those paid others of comparable rank and ability in your area? □Yes □No

14. Do you exchange ideas with other individuals managing local family-owned companies and learn how they solve problems similar to yours? □Yes □No

**Difficult problems with managers**

15. Do you have managers who retain the old ways and refuse to learn and adopt new methods? □Yes □No

16. Have you found either dismissal or transfer to another assignment appropriate in handling these managers "of the past"? □Yes □No

17. Do you have "make-work managers" who were hired to perform specific jobs which no longer exist? □Yes □No

18. Does work duplication exist in your company? □Yes □No

19. When one of your key executives leaves, do you:
    a. Reorganize your management? □Yes □No
    b. Redistribute the present assignments? □Yes □No
    c. Use present managers more effectively? □Yes □No

20. If you decide upon an outsider as a replacement manager, do you discuss the reasons with the manager who expected the promotion and with other managers prior to filling the vacancy? □Yes □No

21. Do you observe your people's reactions to prospective managers and ask them for their evaluations? □Yes □No

22. Do you appraise a prospective manager's ability by considering this information:
    a. Records of past performance? □Yes □No
    b. Personal statements? □Yes □No
    c. Evaluations by others? □Yes □No

23. In determining compensation, do you:
    a. Review the remuneration of your present managers to see whether it is:
       (1) Adequate and equitable? □Yes □No
       (2) Properly related to their contributions to the firm? □Yes □No
       (3) Comparable to that of the new manager? □Yes □No
    b. Have a five-year compensation plan in effect for a new manager? □Yes □No

24. When you hire a manager, do you discuss with him or her how the relationship may be terminated? □Yes □No

25. If you have a young manager with ability and ambition, are you frank about the opportunities that you can offer? □Yes □No

**Preparing for your successor**

26. Are you making available to your successor the specialized knowledge you have accumulated over the years? □Yes □No

27. Have you created a reference source for a new manager by making an inventory of this information:
    a. Facts about the general administration of your company? □Yes □No
    b. Data concerning your firm's finances? □Yes □No
    c. Information about the operating and technical aspects of your firm? □Yes □No

28. Do you plan to set down objectives that you hope to see your company reach both before you leave and afterward? □Yes □No

29. If your top assistant has the same capabilities as you have, have you also tried to find someone who complements your abilities? □Yes □No

30. To facilitate a smooth transition, do you plan to bring in the new manager as early as possible? □Yes □No

31. Do you intend to have the transition period last from three to five years? □Yes □No

# Part 6
# Planning and Organizing a New Business

In Part 1, you were introduced to the independent business and its owner. Part 2 introduced you to producing your product or service. Part 3 prepared you for marketing your product or service. Part 4 gave you guideline information for profit planning and control. Part 5 gave you some focus on some of the special considerations in managing an independent business.

The chapters in this part provide some insights into: determining the nature of the economic environment for your business; considering the option of a franchise; your entering an existing business; establishing a new business; viewing your alternatives for planning the legal and financial structure of your business; and, finally, planning the administrative structure for your business. Figure 1 is a graphic presentation of some of the activities involved in starting up a firm. It illustrates the sequence of activities needed, from the original idea for a business to the final objective profit.

"Management is getting things done through people," said Lawrence Appley, former president of the American Management Association. We agree with his conclusion, but there is more to managing an independent enterprise than that. As Figure 2 shows, you must also make decisions and allocate scarce financial, physi-

**Figure 1**
**Concept of Entering Business**

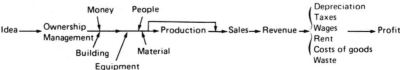

cal, and human resources so that the business will achieve its objectives.

The seven functions shown in the center of Figure 2 must be performed by any person running a business, whether the owner of the business or a professional manager running someone else's business. While all the functions are discussed in the text, individual chapters are not organized around them.

***Figure 2***
**Definition and Functions of Management**

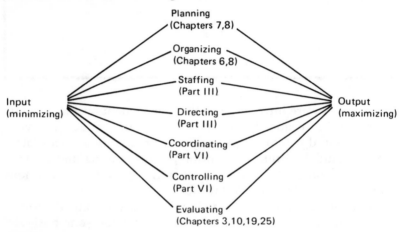

Management is:
1. Doing through others,
2. Decision making, and
3. Allocating scarce resources, so that
4. Objectives are reached.

Because a new business needs to be managed effectively by someone, you must now answer a most significant question: "Should I be the owner of the firm and hire someone else to manage it for me, or should I both own and manage it myself?" If you choose to be the manager yourself, be prepared to become a generalist manager. The generalist-type manager has the conceptual skills necessary to analyze the total situation, detect problems, determine causes, and bring about effective solutions.

Finally, do not necessarily imitate practices and methods used in larger firms, because they could produce operating procedural inefficiencies in your company. Procedures and methods should utilize personal strengths and offset personal deficiencies.

# Chapter Twenty

## Studying the Economic Environment for the Business

It is now time to give careful consideration to the type of business that satisfies your personal goals and objectives, to study its economic environment, and to decide whether to buy an existing firm or to start a new one of your own. These decisions will largely determine whether you will be successful and satisfied during your business career.

The process of choosing the type of business to enter will be influenced by your personal value system, education, training, financial ability, and family situation. Since owning an independent business is such a very personal matter, you should consider as broad a range of options as is feasible. In conducting this survey and analysis of possible business opportunities, however, do not become so involved in details that you lose sight of your overall objective. Instead, your mission should be to find that business which helps achieve your objective while still satisfying your other personal needs.

The volume of government regulation and its accompanying paperwork have had a great impact on the owners of smaller businesses, who have the sole responsibility for compliance. In contrast, the larger firm often has staff specialists whose responsibility is to assure compliance with government regulations. The regulatory environment is not uniform in its impact on various kinds of business. Therefore, for the specific choice of a business, you will want to explore its position in the regulatory environment.

As the economic environment will play a vital role in the success or failure of your firm, you should study it very carefully. All too frequently, it becomes obvious from later events that little effort was made to determine whether the economic environment was friendly or hostile to the new owner-manager. Also, people often commit funds to a business without adequate preliminary investigation concerning the venture's feasibility.

> Such was the case of the young college graduate. Though she had been involved with several aspects of eating establishments, she had not actually owned or managed one. Seeing a vacant building, she saw the opportunity to open a fancy restaurant. A contract was signed for the purchase of the property, and funds were spent for preliminary plans and other related activities.
>
> Then the problems began to appear! The cost of renovation ran many times her original mental estimates; there existed an old restrictive covenant in the deed that prevented a new owner from having complete freedom in using the property as desired.
>
> In the end, the project had to be terminated, and the investment of several thousand dollars produced nothing but another example of the need for a feasibility study.

Our intent in this chapter is to outline a procedure to use in studying the economic environment for your business. The material should also help you determine whether your idea for a business is economically feasible and aid you in deciding whether to buy an existing firm or to start one of your own.

## Selecting the Type of Business to Enter

Probably the best point of departure to use in selecting the type of business to enter is to review the introspective personal analysis made in Chapter 1. The purpose of this reevaluation is to eliminate those options that are not compatible with your personal likes and dislikes. You would probably be miserable if you chose an activity found to be inconsistent with your abilities and personality.

### Reviewing Your Abilities

The main purpose of the personal analysis should be to identify what physical, mental, emotional, and spiritual abilities you have, including:

1. Your intellectual abilities.
2. Your education, training, and experience, which determine the expertise you have for certain types of business. As a rule of thumb, you should have a minimum of three years' experience—preferably some of it managerial—in the particular line

in which your proposed company will be engaged. Through this experience, valuable information about the management, operations, and statistics of the company should have been obtained.

3. Your philosophies and ethical value system, which will keep you from being satisfied in many kinds of business.
4. Your attitudes and feelings, which will limit your success to only a small variety of activities.
5. Your physical health and stamina.
6. Your personal goals, which should probably include the level of income desired from your business.

A significant question that you should answer is, How much profit do I expect tò receive from this business as remuneration for my time and investment in it? Profit potential at least for the first year, preferably for the first two years, should be determined. Other considerations are your spouse's likes and dislikes, whether you want to be near your relatives and/or friends, and what it would take to make you a satisfied—and therefore a successful—person.

This analysis is the first culling procedure; it should drastically reduce the number and variety of choices available to you.

If you would feel more comfortable by taking attitude, interest, and aptitude tests to assist you in making your decision, such tests are available through your university, college, junior college, or vocational-technical school. In addition, a professional psychologist might assist you.

## Eliminating Undesirable Businesses

The next rejection process is to eliminate the businesses that will not provide the challenges, opportunities, and rewards—financial and otherwise—that you are seeking. Be rather ruthless in asking, What's in it for me? as well as inquiring, What can I do to be of help to others? Ask questions similar to the following about each business you consider.

1. How much capital is required to enter and compete successfully in this business?
2. How long will it take me to recoup my investment?
3. How long will it take me to reach an acceptable level of income?
4. How will I live until that time?
5. What is the degree of risk involved? Am I willing to take that risk?
6. Can I "hack" it on my own? Or will I need the help of my family? Others?
7. How much work is involved in getting the business going? In running it? Am I willing to put out that much effort?

8. Do I want to acquire a franchise from an established company, or do I want to start from scratch and go it on my own?
9. What is the potential of this type of business? What are my chances of achieving that potential?
10. Are sufficient data available for me to reach meaningful decisions? If so, what are the sources of information?

A psychology professor involved with research in learning theory believed he had discovered a phenomenon centered upon the "right" space between the lines and the "right" height of the letters that would simplify and assure the early development of writing and learning skills of children in their early school years. He believed that a series of products such as lined writing paper, with alphabetical letters of the "right" height, incorporated into toys and games, and alphabet cereal could be produced around these ideas.

His initial idea was to work through existing businesses. After some disappointments in trying to interest companies producing writing papers, he turned to one of SBA's counselors for assistance.

The counselor was impressed with the strong commitment by the professor but was not convinced that the concept had a "proprietary value," since some years earlier he had seen some writing paper with letter examples that seemed almost identical. In an effort to confirm or disprove the value of these ideas, the counselor contacted several authorities, who confirmed the lack of proprietary value.

The professor's commitment would not permit him to accept these judgments. He resigned his university position in order to devote full time to the project in spite of the facts that he had a wife and two children and had no other means of economic support.

Upon further questioning, the professor admitted that he had not written for publication any of his research findings, so the counselor suggested—to the chagrin of the professor—that possibly his best approach was to return to an academic post and devote his full energies to gaining professional recognition for his research findings. The last knowledge the counselor had of the professor was his continued dogged determination to establish his own production company—without success.

## Using a Checklist

You might want to prepare a checklist in order to be more methodical and objective in this evaluation. Figure 20–1 shows a list used by a consultant who helps people decide what business to enter. This list may be modified to meet your unique needs.

Where can you find the information needed to make this type of analysis? The first place to look is in the technical section or the government-documents section of your nearest library. The librarians in either of these sections can assist you in finding industry

**Figure 20–1**
**Business Selection Survey Checklist**

| Capital required | Degree of risk involved | Amount of work involved | Independent ownership or franchise | Potential of the business | Source of data |
|---|---|---|---|---|---|
| | | | | | |

data. Study carefully the U.S. census data on population, business, housing, possibly even agriculture. The Small Business Administration, in Washington or a regional office, can be of great help to you. Also, the following may be helpful:

1. The research division of the local chamber of commerce.
2. The trade association for the industries you are interested in.
3. Local business leaders.
4. Bankers and other financial experts.
5. Your congressional representative.
6. Your local small business development center.

## Classifying the Types of Business

While there are several ways of classifying the types of business available, we chose to group them as: (1) retailing, (2) service, (3) wholesaling, (4) research and development, (5) consulting, and (6) manufacturing. A more detailed classification is provided in Figure 20–2, showing the options in each group.

## Choosing the Business to Enter

The point has now been reached where you need to have an exercise in brainstorming. Get a group of friends together and ask them what kinds of products or services they need. Then ask them if those needs are being met adequately. If not, what would be necessary for their needs to be satisfied? Try to get them to identify not only existing types of business, but also as many new kinds of business as possible. You should then consider the kinds of products and services that are not now available, but that are needed and could—if available—find a market.

You might also assemble a diversified group of local independent business managers to brainstorm with you on business op-

**Figure 20–2**
**Some Business Options, Classified into Related Groups**

1. Retailing.
   a. Food.
      1. Grocery.
      2. Fast-prepared.
      3. Convenience.
      4. Restaurant.
      5. Lounge.
      6. Specialty shops.
   b. Appliance.
   c. Hardware and building
      material.
   d. Specialty.
   e. Clothing.
2. Service.
   a. Service station.
   b. Auto repair.
   c. Appliance repair.
   d. Building repair and
      renovation.
   e. Janitorial.
   f. Plumber.
   g. Electrician.
   h. Floor covering.
   i. F.B.O. (fixed-base operation
      aircraft).
   j. Travel agency.
3. Wholesaling.
   a. Jobber.
   b. Broker.
   c. Distributor.
   d. Manufacturing agent.
4. Research and development.
   a. Materials.
   b. Products.
   c. Software information
      systems.
   d. Specialized machinery.
   e. Manufacturing systems.
5. Consulting.
   a. Management.
   b. Management information
      systems.
   c. Financial.
   d. Investment.
   e. Marketing.
   f. Risk management.
   g. Land use and development.
   h. Engineering.
   i. Economic.
   j. Government.
   k. Various additional highly
      specialized areas.
6. Manufacturing.
   a. Metals.
      1. Sheet metal.
      2. Machine shop.
         (a) General.
         (b) Special equipment.
      3. Foundry.
      4. Mini-steel mill.
   b. Plastics.
      1. Extrusion.
      2. Applicatory.
      3. Formulatory.
   c. Food processing.
      1. Meat.
      2. Vegetables.
      3. Bakery.
      4. Specialty items.

portunities. Another possible source of participants for this exercise might be members of the local ACE (Active Corps of Executives) or SCORE (Service Corps of Retired Executives) chapters.

An example of a business that originated from ideas of local business managers was a sheet metal shop that was established to supply the sheet metal requirements of a machine shop.

When obtaining advice from outsiders, always remember that it is your resources that are at stake when the commitment is made. Thus the ultimate decision must be yours.

After such exercises in freewheeling thinking, the next step is actually to select that business which seems best for you. Your earlier checklist now comes in handy in making the choice. In fact, you may want to make more than one choice and leave yourself some options. Remember to consider your personal attributes and objectives in order to best utilize your capabilities, yet an effort should be made to maintain an attitude of objectivity and let your mind—not your emotions—govern your decisions.

Once the choice has been made, it is necessary to conduct an economic feasibility study to determine, as best you can, its economic possibilities. As one former student put it, "The time spent in doing these various exercises pays off in the end. It actually helps achieve your purpose in less time by guiding you to do those things you need to do." He has evidenced this by starting three businesses in distinctly different but related fields and achieving success in sales and profits in the first year of operation of each of them.

## Studying the Economic Environment

A study of the environment may be carried out either rationally and objectively or with little thought. As shown in Figure 20–3 you may either use the analytical and rational approach of a computer or play the odds and rely on chance, as in playing a slot machine. The game of business requires the best objective, rational, and reasoned effort if you are to succeed.

### Studying the Economic Environment for the Business

Begin your study by analyzing the characteristics of the economic environment related to the particular kind of business in which

**Figure 20–3**
**Which Method to Use in Making Your Decisions**

you are interested. An overview of the economic status of the industry of which your potential business will be a part may be provided by obtaining answers to these questions:

1. How many firms are there in this type of industry?
2. Do they vary in size, or do they seem to be uniform in size and general characteristics?
3. What is the geographic distribution of the firms in the industry? Are they concentrated in one area, or are they widely distributed? (Rising transportation costs have increased the importance of this factor.)
4. What is the relationship between smaller firms of this type and larger firms and other industries? There may be adverse features associated with this relationship. As an example, carpet plants solely dependent on the auto industry for customers are subject to the fluctuations of auto sales.
5. Does the firm serve only the domestic market? Or are there opportunities to serve foreign markets as well?
6. What are federal, state, and local government agencies' attitudes toward this type of business?
7. What is society's attitude toward this type of business?

After deciding the overall economic environment in the industry, study the business climate for your enterprise in the area in which you would like to operate. One approach that is frequently used in analyzing an area is to evaluate the objective and subjective factors that influence the region's business climate. Additional data that pertain to your particular type of business may also be obtained.

### Studying the Market for Your Business

Next, determine what is happening in the marketplace and the possible future your business will have in that market. The size, nature, and other characteristics of the market, as well as your firm's future possibilities, may be derived from answers to questions such as these:

1. What is the relationship of population to the proposed business?
   a. Identify the age distribution among the population. Is a specific age group of special importance to this business?
   b. Identify the population by sex, race, education, fertility rate, occupation, and other characteristics that affect the demand for goods and services.
   c. Define the size of the population and trends in size, age, sex, racial, educational, and occupational distributions. A declining population, or a declining population segment, in a specific geographic area may indicate an unsuccessful fu-

ture for some businesses. A changing birthrate can affect many industries oriented toward the baby, teenager, and youth markets.

2.  What are the size and distribution of income within the population?
3.  Is the sales volume for this kind of business growing, stable, or declining?
4.  What are the number and size of competitors?
5.  What is the success rate of competing businesses?
6.  What are the technical aspects (state of the art)?
7.  What are the sources of supply?
8.  What are the capital requirements?
9.  What is the rate of return on investments?

***Estimate Size of the Market.*** The above answers can help you estimate the size of your market. Additional data may be obtained from trade associations, chambers of commerce, and various federal, state, and local government agencies. Examples of specific sources are the U.S. Department of Commerce (through its Office of Business Economics) and the U.S. Bureau of the Census. The divisions of research of colleges and universities also may be of assistance.

Statistical information gathered and tabulated by the Bureau of the Census may be particularly useful in evaluating the following variables, which determine the size and composition of your market:

1.  Population characteristics.
2.  Employment patterns.
3.  Personal income.
4.  Business sales and income.

***Estimate the Competition.*** In studying the market area, you should ascertain the number of similar businesses that have been liquidated or merged with a competitor. When the number is high, it is usually a sign of economic weakness.

Analyze competitors' activities to determine how effectively a new company can compete. Is the market large enough for another firm? What features—such as lower price, better product, or more promotion—will attract business? What features can be developed for a new firm?

Determine the kinds of technology being applied by other firms in your industry. For example: Are other machine shops using hand equipment? Or are they using the latest equipment, including numerically controlled devices? The state of technology is significant in determining operating costs.

*Estimate Your Share of the Market.* Now you should be able to arrive at a "ball park" figure for your total sales volume and your share of the market. In arriving at this kind of estimate, select reasonable and conservative figures. You —as the planner of a new business—should first determine the geographic boundaries of the market area and then, from your knowledge of the potential customers in the various communities located in this area, make an estimate of products that might be purchased. It is better to plan for a relatively low level of sales in order to budget more effectively the business's operation.

## Set Up a Plan

If you call on your own resources and those of other people who are specialists in your area, you should be able to develop a detailed plan for your business. This plan would include land, building, equipment, inventory, working capital, and personnel. You should then be able to determine the capital requirements for each of these productive factors, as well as the total of your capital requirements. Some additional capital should be provided for contingencies. How much inventory you need is determined by the number and location of suppliers.

*Estimate Your Capital Requirements.* Information concerning your capital requirements may be obtained from potential competitors. You may even find that owners of existing businesses will cooperate with you by supplying various types of useful information, so long as you approach them in a manner to merit confidence. Some owners play the old game "I've got a secret," but our experience indicates that these people are in the minority. Other sources of information may include suppliers, wholesalers, and manufacturers.

> A consultant was searching for comprehensive information relating to the opening of a retail fabric shop. He called a major textile manufacturer, who indicated that this information was readily available from McCall Patterns and Simplicity Patterns. Each of the pattern makers maintained comprehensive market research programs and made such information readily available.

*Estimate Your Return on Investment.* By using the capital requirements and developing an estimate of expected profits after taxes, you should be able to estimate the rate of return on your investment and on each dollar of sales. You will probably want to set a return-on-investment objective that, when added to your estimated value of your own services, should compare favorably with the average profit potential for your type of business.

By using the rate-of-return figure you decide upon, and given a knowledge of the market in which you plan to operate, you can compute what sales will be needed to provide a satisfactory return.

> For example, suppose you invest $25,000 in a business and your objective is to receive a 12 percent return on your investment. You could earn $12,000 a year working for someone else. You should then expect to receive an annual income from the business of at least $15,000, which is the equivalent of $12,000 salary plus $3,000 return on investment.
>
> You further estimate your market to consist of 5,000 companies spending an average of $1,000 per year for the items you will sell. This represents a total market potential of $5 million. The typical profit-to-sales ratio for that industry is about 6 percent. By dividing your hoped-for earnings of $15,000 by the profit margin of 6 percent, you find that you must have sales of $250,000 in order to achieve your profit objective. This means you would need at least a 5 percent share of the market for your products.

### Use SBA Resources

In addition to the data sources previously listed, the Small Business Administration has developed a variety of information resources that may be obtained from the nearest SBA office, one of the Government Printing Office retail outlets, or the Superintendent of Documents, Washington, D.C.

After completing all these mental exercises, you should know whether the rate of return for the business you have chosen is acceptable, based on current economic information. Since you want to achieve the highest possible rate of return, make fresh comparisons with alternative investment opportunities. Then decide whether this business is the opportunity sought. If it is, then the decision is Go!

## Deciding Whether to Start a New Business or Buy an Existing One

You have now decided that you are the entrepreneurial type and that you want to own a business. You have also determined what type of business you want to enter and have found it to be economically feasible. The next step is to choose from the alternatives of entering an established business or conceiving, planning, organizing, and operating a new business of your own. In this respect, you are like the traveler on the road in Figure 20–4, who must make a decision. Select the alternative that seems to afford the best opportunity of accomplishing your goals. However, just as the traveler, you may find yourself in the dilemma of not knowing which direction to take. After viewing the options, you must make a decision— a decision that you hope will carry you to success.

The following material should help you make this decision most effectively. Specifically, it presents the reasons for and against entering an existing firm and starting a new one from scratch.

**Figure 20–4**
**Which Road to Take**

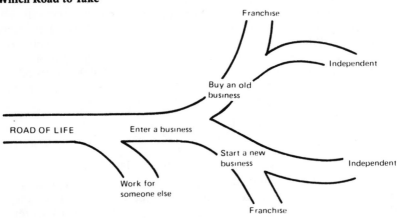

There are several sources from which you can obtain information on available business opportunities. Included are *The Wall Street Journal,* a list of bankruptcy sales in your local paper, your banker, and chambers of commerce.

One word of caution is important at this point. The past success or failure of such businesses is not alone enough to justify a decision on whether or not to buy a given business. Instead, you must make a thorough analysis of the present condition of the business and an appraisal of what it might do in the future.

## Entering an Established Business

Before you are able to make the analysis you desire, first locate the business or businesses available for purchase. In your search, you will find that some firms are not available at any price, others will become available but at a high price, and still others are actively seeking a buyer.

Buying a business can mean different things to different people. It may mean acquiring the total ownership of an entire business. It may mean acquiring only the assets of a firm, or its name, or only certain parts of the business. Keep this uncertainty in mind as you study the following material.

### Some Considerations in Acquiring an Ongoing Firm.

One important factor is always the price asked for the firm. Sometimes a successful ongoing business may be acquired at a bargain price. For some reason, it can be bought at a fraction of either the dollar cost or its replacement value.

> For example, a small stone company was owned by a few stockholders who wanted to sell out in a hurry for personal reasons. The company had more assets, including accounts receivable and cash on hand in the bank, than the purchase price the owners were asking. Some outsiders purchased all the outstanding shares. They were able to take the cash on hand and that received from the receivables to reimburse themselves for all the shares they had bought.

You should be ready to grab similar opportunities.

A retailer may be willing to sell a business for the current price of its inventory. However, you should be cautious. The value of its accounts receivable should be checked and caution exercised in including this in the purchase price. The extent of liability needs verification. Be sure to have your own CPA audit the records and verify the inventory and its value.

> A grocer who wanted to sell her store reduced her retail prices in order to attract a large number of customers. It mattered little to her that many items were reduced to cost or less. A "sucker," who saw the large number of customers, took the bait and bought the store. About three weeks after assuming ownership and management, he had to replenish his stock. He had to raise his prices, but then his business dropped off, and he was very unhappy over his situation.

Another element of consideration is your managerial ability. Some people have a talent for acquiring businesses that are in economic difficulty or are not achieving the results possible. These persons are able to come into a business and initiate changes that turn the business around. Once the business prospers, the new owner looks for another buyer to purchase the successful business. The seller then seeks another similar opportunity.

### Reasons for Acquiring an Established Business.

While it is difficult to discuss this subject intelligently without knowing the specific details of each situation, at least some generalizations can be made. Some advantages of acquiring an established business are:

1. The facilities—building, equipment, inventory, and personnel—are already functioning.
2. A product or service is already being produced and distributed.
3. A market has been established and exists.
4. Revenue and profits are being generated.
5. The location may be very desirable.
6. Financial relationships have been established with banks and trade creditors.

An experienced businessman recently sold one of his businesses. He searched for an existing business in which he might become involved. His interests were managerial challenge, economic growth, and profit. After viewing several possibilities, he acquired a small company that manufactured a top-quality airport service vehicle. The company needed additional capital and more effective management. The new owner was able to bring these two ingredients.

***Reasons against Acquiring an Established Business.*** Buying an ongoing business may also have these disadvantages:

1. The physical facilities (building and equipment) and product line may be old and obsolete.
2. The personnel may be stagnant and have a poor production record.
3. Union-management relations may be poor.
4. The inventory may contain an excessive amount of "dead stock."
5. Too high a percentage of the assets may be in poor-quality accounts receivable.
6. The location may be bad.
7. The financial condition and relations with financial institutions may be deteriorating.

A group of investors was considering buying a firm in the extractive industry. A very favorable market existed for products from that type of business. However, on examination, they found that the raw material available was of such poor quality that the market would not accept the firm's product. The group decided not to invest.

### Starting a New Business of Your Own

In considering the possibilities of establishing a new business, you should recognize that you have more freedom of choice in defining the nature of the business than if you purchased an existing firm. Remember that there are both pluses and minuses in choosing this alternative. You should view a particular business in terms of whether it will enable you to achieve your personal objectives.

Also, how do the advantages and disadvantages of this option compare with those of entering an ongoing business? Is there—on this basis—a reasonable opportunity for success?

As previously stated, some people have as their goal in life the initiation of new businesses. They find a pleasure in establishing new ventures, getting them operating at a profit, and then finding a buyer for them. Then they start the process over again. Other people enjoy the challenge and sense of accomplishment that come from creating something new. They feel that they have been useful, and will probably keep the business and run it themselves. Yet, they may later start and operate other firms.

> The Chapman family business originated by accident. In the early days of the automobile, two nationally prominent industrialists were touring the hinterlands by auto. During one day's travels, they found themselves many miles from a restaurant or hotel. They had their driver take them to a farmhouse that stood some distance from the main road. When greeted by the lady of the house, they inquired if she might prepare a meal for them, for which they would gladly pay. A short time later she fed them the meal that had an "outstanding quality of palatability."
>
> The word spread, and others came with a similar request in an ever increasing frequency. In time, the farmhouse became a familiar, friendly place for the wayworn traveler, known far and wide as Chapman House.
>
> The years passed; the children grew into adulthood, married, and had children of their own. In the meantime, Chapman House's activities continued to expand to include a motel—as well as an enlarged restaurant—where textile and food products prepared by the local citizens were sold.

**Reasons for Establishing a New Business.** Some of the reasons for starting a new business of your own instead of buying one may include the opportunities to:

1. Define the nature of your business.
2. Create the type of physical facilities you prefer.
3. Take advantage of the latest technology in selecting equipment, materials, and tools.
4. Utilize the most recent processes and procedures.
5. Obtain fresh inventory.
6. Have a free hand in selecting, training, developing, and motivating personnel.
7. Design your own management information system.
8. Select your competitive environment—within limits.

A young entrepreneur wanted to enter the food, beverage, and lodging business. He could purchase one or more of a number of existing facilities. Each had a community image. His other option was to restore a historic building, which had earlier served as a hotel, into a superior-quality facility.

***Reasons against Establishing a New Business.*** Some of the disadvantages of starting a new business "from scratch" are:

1. Problems of selecting the right business.
2. Unproven performance records in sales, reliability, service, and profits.
3. Problems associated with assembling the resources—including location, building, equipment, material, and people.
4. Necessity of selecting and training a new work force.
5. Lack of an established product line.
6. Production problems associated with the start-up of a new business.
7. Lack of an established a market and channels of distribution.
8. Problems in establishing a basic accounting system and controls.
9. Difficulty in working out the "bugs" that develop in the initial operation.

A new restaurant, catering to a high-class clientele, was established with the support of influential people. In spite of heavy advertising, the business failed. A small-business specialist attributed the failure to its location in a not-very-accessible neighborhood.

The questionnaires in Exhibits 20–1 and 20–2 should help you in deciding whether to start a new business or enter an existing one.

## Summary

This chapter has presented the essential steps in choosing the type of business to enter. You need to review your abilities; eliminate businesses that do not meet your abilities, desires, or economic potential; and consult and brainstorm with others. The economic environment for a business requires analysis. The many economic factors that affect business relate to the market, competition, capital requirements, and return on investment.

Also, a decision must be made on whether to buy an existing business or to start a new one. The advantages and disadvantages of each were listed. The next two chapters examine the processes used to analyze the alternatives.

## Appendix: Deciding Whether to Start a New Business or Buy an Existing One

Should I start a new business or buy an existing one? At this point in your career, this should be a very important question for you. The material in these forms should aid you in making this choice.

You might want to reproduce these pages and do the same thing for several businesses you have in mind. We recommend that you answer the questions concerning any business you have in mind as conscientiously as you can.

If, after answering the material in Exhibit 20–1, you decide to enter an established business rather than to establish one of your own, then you should proceed to the material in Exhibit 20–2. You should complete this form for each specific business you are considering entering.

## Exhibits

*Exhibit 20–1*

Before deciding whether you will establish a new business or purchase an established business, you need to give consideration to the positive and negative features of each. More important, you should rate each point a plus or minus as you perceive the significance of the point and its value to you.

1.  Define the nature of the business:

    _____

    _____

    _____

2.  Favorable points for establishing a new business: Plus (+) or Minus (−):
    a.  Opportunity to create the type of physical facilities I prefer.                                                    _____
    b.  Ability to take advantage of the latest technology in selecting equipment, materials, and tools.                    _____
    c.  Opportunity to utilize the most recent processes and procedures.                                                    _____
    d.  Opportunity to obtain a fresh inventory.                       _____
    e.  Opportunity to have a free hand in selecting, training, developing, and motivating personnel.                       _____
    f.  Opportunity to design my own management information system.                                                         _____
    g.  Opportunity to select my competitive environment within limits.                                                    _____

3.  Favorable points for selecting an established business (plus [+] or minus [−]):
    a.  Avoiding the difficulty of a business with an unproved performance record in sales, reliability, service, and profits.                                                         _____
    b.  Avoiding the problems associated with assembling the composite resources—including location, building, equipment, material, and people.                                         _____
    c.  Avoiding the necessity of selecting and training a new work force.                                                   _____
    d.  Avoiding the lack of an established product line.             _____
    e.  Avoiding production problems associated with the start-up of a new business.                                         _____
    f.  Avoiding the lack of an established market channel for distribution.                                                 _____
    g.  Avoiding the problems in establishing a basic accounting and control system.                                        _____

*Exhibit 20–1 (concluded)*

    *h.*   Avoiding the difficulty in working out the "bugs" that develop in the initial operation.      _____

4.   Checking back over the points covered in 2 and 3 above, I conclude:

    *a.*   I want to establish a new business.     (   )

    *b.*   I prefer to enter an established business.     (   )

5.   If your answer in 4 is *b*, then proceed with Part B, which follows.

*Exhibit 20–2*

Considerations for selecting an established business, your responses, those of the present owner, and the facts concerning the status of the business should guide you to a comfortable decision as to whether this business is for you.

1.   Why is the business available for purchase? _____

    _____

    _____

    _____

2.   What are the intentions of the present owner? _____

    _____

    _____

    *a.*   Does the present owner plan another business to compete with you? Yes _____ No _____

    *b.*   Is the present owner in good health? Yes _____ No _____

    *c.*   Does the present owner wish to retire?
Yes _____ No _____

    *d.*   Does the present owner wish to continue to be associated with the business? Yes _____ No _____

3.   Is the market for the firm's product/service declining?
Yes _____ No _____

    *a.*   Changing neighborhood? Yes _____ No _____

    *b.*   Declining population? Yes _____ No _____

    *c.*   Technological change? Yes _____ No_____

4.   Are physical facilities suitable? Yes _____ No _____

    *a.*   Worn-out or outdated? Yes _____ No _____

    *b.*   Proper size for demand? Yes _____ No _____

    *c.*   Laid out properly? Yes _____ No _____

5.   Is the business operating efficiently? Yes _____ No _____

    *a.*   How effective are the personnel?

        (1)   What is the rate of labor turnover? _____%

        (2)   What is the rate of absenteeism? _____%

*Exhibit 20–2 (continued)*

   (3) Is the business unionized?  Yes _____ No _____

   (4) Is productivity high?  Yes _____ No _____

  *b.* What is the amount of waste?

   (1) Material _____% $_____ per day

   (2) Machine time _____% $_____ per day

   (3) Personnel time _____% $_____ per day

  *c.* Is the quality of product / service good?

   Yes _____ No _____

   (1) What portion of product is wasted? _____%

   (2) How many complaints about service are received? _____ / year

   (3) Are deliveries on time?  Yes _____ No _____

  *d.* Is inventory satisfactory?  Yes _____ No _____

   (1) Does the inventory contain mostly "dead stock"?

   Yes _____ No _____

   (2) Is its level appropriate for the firm?

   Yes _____ No _____

6. What is the financial condition of the firm?

 Good _____ Fair _____ Poor _____

7. Analysis of accounting information:

  *a.* Have you had a reputable CPA appraise the firm's assets and liabilities?  Yes _____ No _____

  *b.* Validity of financial statements:

   Accurate _____ Overstated _____ Understated _____

   Warning: Check to see: Relationship of book value of fixed assets to replacement costs; percentage of total accounts receivable over 90 days (_____%); records kept of age of accounts receivable? (Yes _____ No _____); dollar amount of bad debts charged off last 6 months ($_____), 12 months ($_____), 36 months ($_____).

  *c.* Cash position:

   (1) Cash on hand: $_____

   (2) Cash in bank: $_____

  *d.* Is cash flow adequate to meet obligations?

   Yes _____ No _____

  *e.* Current ratio: _____

   (current assets/current liabilities)

  *f.* Quick ratio: _____

   (current assets − Inventories)/(current liabilities)

  *g.* Debt-to-equity ratio:

   (Debt [current liabilities, notes, bonds] ÷ owner's funds [common stock, preferred stock, capital surplus, and retained earnings]) _____

*Exhibit 20–2 (concluded)*

    *h.* Ratio of net income to sales:
(net income/net sales) _____

    *i.* Net income to investment ratio:
(net income/investment) _____

    *j.* Amount of debt:
        (1) Notes: \$_____
        (2) Bonds: \$_____

    *k.* Terms of Debt: _____

    *l.* Adequacy of cost data:
Can you accurately determine the cost of the product or service? Yes _____ No _____

    *m.* Are there available data to enable you accurately to break down the price of a product or service into costs and profit? Yes _____ No _____

    *n.* Is the business solvent? Yes _____ No _____

8. How much investment is needed? \$_____

9. What is the estimated return on your investment? _____%

10. What is your decision? _____
_____
_____

# Chapter Twenty-One

## Operating a Franchise

Franchising has effectively existed for many generations. Through time, its structure, organization, characteristics, operations, and total being have envolved in response to a changing environment. Many new activities have begun to be franchised.

Our concern is to deal with the subject as it has most recently evolved and exists in the early 1980s. There continue to be many franchising opportunities, as seen in the daily paper (see examples in the want ads business opportunity section, block ads in the business section, and so forth) and various business publications, including the magazine *Franchising*. Yet, the fact that franchising opportunities exist does not mean that the probability for success in each situation is good, for the spectrum ranges from the gyp to almost-guaranteed economic success. Be cautious in dealing with franchisors who promise a guaranteed return on your investment. Often, contracts with these elusive or vanishing organizations have proved worthless.

We want you to be aware of what it means to be a franchisee and how best to proceed in selecting the franchise that is right for you. Perhaps, after giving analytical consideration to the matter, you may conclude franchising is not for you.

### Importance of Franchising

Franchising has been one of the most rapidly expanding areas of business activity in recent years. The large percentage of new busi-

**Figure 21–1**

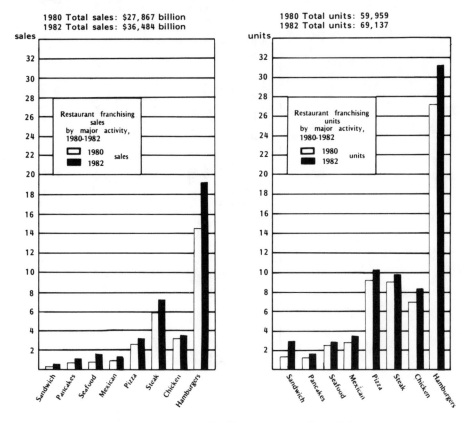

1980 Total sales: $27,867 billion
1982 Total sales: $36,484 billion

1980 Total units: 59,959
1982 Total units: 69,137

Restaurant franchising sales by major activity, 1980-1982
☐ 1980 sales
■ 1982

Restaurant franchising units by major activity, 1980-1982
☐ 1980 units
■ 1982

Source: "Franchising in the Economy." Table 58, January 1982, p. 67.

nesses that fall in this category explains its prominent treatment in this part of the book. While service stations are considered a form of franchising, government documents separate service station franchises from other types. We include a discussion of them in this chapter, however, from a practical point of view.

Franchise activities are growing, as can be seen by Figure 21–1. The total number of franchise establishments grew 5.24 percent from 1980 to 1982. It is estimated that franchising accounts for about $437 billion in annual sales.

Table 21–1 shows the average sales per establishment from 1980 to 1982. Of particular interest is the volume of sales by the kinds of franchise business. Also of interest is the fact that usually the average sales in establishments owned by a franchisee are greater than in those owned by the company.

**Table 21-1**
**Franchising in the Economy: 1982***

| Kinds of Franchised Businesses | Establishments (number) | | | Sales ($000) | | |
|---|---|---|---|---|---|---|
| | Total | Company-Owned | Franchisee-Owned | Total | Company-Owned | Franchisee-Owned |
| Automobiles and truck dealers[1] | 28,320 | 150 | 28,170 | $194,295,000 | $1,046,000 | $193,249,000 |
| Automotive products and services[2] | 43,151 | 4,351 | 38,800 | 8,289,963 | 2,599,526 | 5,690,437 |
| Business aids and services | 50,193 | 6,780 | 43,413 | 9,081,280 | 1,600,846 | 7,480,434 |
| Accounting, credit, collection agencies and general business systems | 2,743 | 49 | 2,694 | 154,482 | 12,875 | 141,607 |
| Employment services | 5,395 | 1,499 | 3,896 | 2,186,732 | 935,520 | 1,251,212 |
| Printing and copying services | 4,171 | 146 | 4,025 | 545,398 | 22,764 | 522,634 |
| Tax preparation services | 9,644 | 4,518 | 5,126 | 371,191 | 202,691 | 168,500 |
| Real estate[4] | 21,116 | 224 | 20,892 | 4,475,469 | 148,985 | 4,326,658 |
| Miscellaneous business services | 7,124 | 344 | 6,780 | 1,348,008 | 278,011 | 1,069,997 |
| Construction, home improvements, maintenance, and cleaning services | 16,422 | 643 | 15,779 | 1,958,850 | 272,450 | 1,686,400 |
| Convenience stores | 17,312 | 10,076 | 7,236 | 9,052,060 | 5,557,297 | 3,494,763 |

| | | | | | |
|---|---|---|---|---|---|
| Educational products and services | 4,128 | 666 | 3,462 | 450,395 | 94,150 | 356,245 |
| Restaurants (all types) | 69,137 | 20,056 | 49,081 | 36,483,817 | 11,710,723 | 24,773,094 |
| Gasoline service stations | 147,000 | 26,460 | 120,540 | 117,762,000 | 21,197,000 | 96,565,000 |
| Hotels, motels and campgrounds | 6,904 | 1,008 | 5,896 | 11,819,636 | 3,124,863 | 8,694,773 |
| Laundry and drycleaning services | 3,346 | 61 | 3,285 | 304,574 | 31,200 | 273,374 |
| Recreation, entertainment, and travel | 5,293 | 105 | 5,188 | 829,964 | 35,361 | 794,603 |
| Rental services (auto-truck) | 7,989 | 2,161 | 5,828 | 3,728,810 | 1,564,735 | 2,164,075 |
| Rental services (equipment) | 2,797 | 277 | 2,520 | 447,827 | 115,582 | 332,245 |
| Retailing (nonfood) | 39,306 | 13,368 | 25,938 | 12,886,981 | 5,671,791 | 7,215,190 |
| Retailing (food other than convenience stores) | 17,362 | 1,200 | 16,162 | 9,213,324 | 2,413,105 | 6,800,219 |
| Soft drink bottlers [1,3] | 1,700 | 75 | 1,625 | 20,089,000 | 1,406,000 | 18,683,000 |
| Miscellaneous | 5,234 | 337 | 4,897 | 746,070 | 123,990 | 622,080 |
| Total—All Franchising | 465,594 | 87,774 | 377,820 | $437,439,551 | $58,564,619 | $378,874,932 |

1982 data estimated by respondents.

[1] Estimated by BIE, based on the Bureau of the Census and trade association data.

[2] Includes some establishments with significant sales of nonautomotive products such as household appliances and garden supplies.

[3] Includes soft drinks, fruit drinks, and ades; syrups, flavoring agents, and bases. Data do not include figures for independent private label and contract-filler bottling companies which accounted for 22 percent in 1980, 22 percent in 1981, and 22 percent in 1982 of the value of shipments of the total industry.

[4] Gross commissions.

## What Can a Franchise Do for Me?

In our survey of the field, we have generally concluded that a franchise can take your money or it can make you financially in-dependent—depending upon which franchise you choose. At this point, your focus should be "What can a franchise do for me that I cannot do for myself?" In some instances, the answer may be noth-ing; while in other circumstances, a franchise can lead to success. Some of the more successful franchisors provide:

1. A training program that will equip you to manage your unit. (The more successful ones have their own special training schools—for example, McDonald's Hamburger University and Holiday Inn's Holiday Inn University.)
2. A standardized accounting and cost-control system. These rec-ords are audited periodically by the franchisor's staff. In many instances, standard monthly operating statements are re-quired. The franchisor develops a set of standard performance figures based on composite figures of reporting franchisees, and returns a comparative analysis to the franchisee as a man-agerial aid.
3. Financial assistance, in some instances, when minimum eq-uity requirements are met by the potential franchisee. This financing covers land, building, equipment, inventory, and working capital.
4. Site selection and a turnkey facility. This includes the pur-chase of the site and the construction of a standardized struc-ture of a design identified with the franchise.
5. Counsel and specifications for erecting and equipping the facility.
6. A local, regional, or national image.
7. Well-planned and implemented national or regional advertis-ing programs, establishing and maintaining a uniform image.
8. A set of customer service standards. These are established by the franchisor and professional staff, who make regular in-spection visits to assure compliance by the franchisee.
9. Continuing management assistance, training, and guidance.
10. A sensitivity and responsiveness to changing market opportunities.
11. Possible buyer advantage of a larger corporation. (It is impor-tant to check on a comparative basis.)
12. An operations system that has proven successful.

An example of franchisors' responsiveness to market opportunities is described in an article in the April 26, 1976, issue of *The Wall Street Journal* about the success fast-food franchisors are achieving by moving into the small-town market. In many instances they have developed a smaller-size unit to accommodate this market.

## Classification of Franchises

Recognizing that there are many categories of franchises, we have selected seven whose records make them worthy of your consideration. These are: fast foods, motels, retail hardware stores, automotive businesses, service stations, convenience markets, and real estate. We do not intend to imply that all franchises in these categories are of a quality worthy of your selection. Nor do we imply that they are the only ones worthy of your consideration. Some current active areas of franchising are shown in Table 21–2.

*Table 21–2*
**Some Types of Currently Popular Franchises**

| Type of Business | Approximate Number of Franchises |
|---|---|
| Automotive products services | 100 |
| Auto/trailer rentals | 14 |
| Beauty salons and supplies | 12 |
| Business aids/services | 95 |
| Campgrounds | 4 |
| Clothing/shoes | 19 |
| Construction/remodeling materials/services | 31 |
| Cosmetics/toiletries | 5 |
| Educational products/services | 19 |
| Employment services | 48 |
| Equipment/rentals | 8 |
| Food—donuts | 9 |
| Food—grocery/specialty stores | 36 |
| Food—ice cream/yogurt/candy/popcorn/beverages | 31 |
| Foods—pancake/waffle/pretzel | 8 |
| Foods—restaurants/drive-ins/carry-outs | 205 |
| General merchandising stores | 5 |
| Health aids/services | 23 |
| Hearing aids | 1 |
| Home furnishings/furniture—retail/repair service | 35 |
| Laundries, dry cleaning—service | 7 |
| Lawn and garden supplies/services | 6 |
| Maintenance/cleaning/sanitation—services/supplies | 23 |
| Motels, hotels | 19 |
| Paint and decorating supplies | 1 |
| Pet shops | 4 |
| Printing | 13 |
| Real estate | 30 |
| Recreation/entertainment/travel service/supplies | 21 |
| Retailing, miscellaneous | 63 |
| Security systems | 4 |
| Soft drink/water bottling | 6 |
| Swimming pools | 5 |
| Tools/hardware | 10 |
| Vending | 3 |
| Water conditioning | 7 |
| Miscellaneous wholesale and service businesses | 23 |
| Drug stores | 2 |

## Fast Foods

The success of fast-food franchises is related to many factors. Some of these are the demographic environment evidenced by the high percentage of young adults in the population; the large number of singles, both male and female; the increasing percentages of working housewives; and the lack of available domestic help. Other factors that seem to have had a positive influence on the course of events are products appealing to the palate of a significant segment of the market, fast service, a sanitary environment, and a structure that is easily recognizable.

Wendy's International, Inc., is one of the fastest growing fast-food franchises, primarily because it appeals almost exclusively to young adults, who make up the fastest-growing segment of our population. It specializes in made-to-order, quality hamburgers served in a place with stylish and comfortable decor.

McDonald's Corporation continues to expand its share of the market by catering to new clientele—such as the patrons of Water Tower Place in Chicago, a complex of expensive condominiums and elite shops. The wealthy customers enjoyed the food so much that McDonald's had to double the size of its restaurant in nine months.[1] It has also expanded its line to include new products such as its Egg McMuffin breakfasts and McChicken sandwiches. Plans for the future include the addition of 450 to 525 new units per year and remodeling older units by localizing the decor to attract more customers. Currently 25 percent of the franchises are company owned. For information on the franchise arrangement, see Figure 21–2.

The year 1980 marked a turnaround for Denny's, Inc., the coffee shop and doughnut house chain. This was achieved by reducing the annual expansion rate from 103 coffee shops to 40, closing 150 unproductive Winchell Donut houses, and writing off $10 million created by these actions. By the September quarter, revenues were up 22 percent and net income was up 16 percent over the previous-year.

Denny's managerial philosophy continues along its previously defined basis:

1. Maintain multiple levels of management to ensure quality and consistency of product.
2. Maintain intensive training and apprenticeships for restaurant managers.
3. Improve incentive programs to encourage entrepreneurship.
4. Broaden menu to raise customer tabs.

This may be contrasted with Sambo's, whose revenue and in-

---

[1]"The Fast-Food Stars: Three Strategies for Fast Growth," *Business Week*, July 11, 1977, pp. 56ff.

*Figure 21–2*
**Franchise Program: McDonald's Corporation\***

*Franchisee Requirements:*
1. Flexible with respect to relocation.
2. Devote 100 percent business time and efforts to their McDonald's restaurant operation.
3. Minimum of 50 percent liquid capital (excluding much of equity in personal residence, personal property, cars, etc.) available for business. Balance of financing conventional source (bank) based on personal financial statement. (McDonald neither finances or guarantees the loans of franchisees.)
4. Responsible for equipping facility with all necessary and approved items of kitchen equipment, sealing and decor, signs and landscaping. All preopening expenses, such as inventory, uniforms, and crew training, are responsibility of franchisee.

*License Cost of Franchise and Requirements:*

| | |
|---|---|
| 1. Initial fee | $ 12,500 |
| 2. Security deposit (refundable) made payable to McDonald's Corporation | $ 15,000 |
| 3. Total cost of franchise (dependent on size of restaurant | $275,000–340,000 |

4. Term of franchise normally 20 years
5. Franchise documents, including license and lease, require personal signature.
6. Ongoing fees 11.5 percent of gross sales during term of franchise

*Franchisor provides:*
1. Necessary operational training assistance.
2. Operation monitoring.
3. Composite feedback with suggestions to franchise based on monthly accounting reports required by franchisor.

\*This information came from an earlier telephone interview and current McDonald's Franchise *Preliminary Information.*

come trends are the reverse—but whose managerial and personnel philosophies are shifting.[2] (After this article Sambo's found it necessary to take a Chapter 11.)

Some of the personal attributes that franchisors look for are a record of stability; a pleasant and personable attitude; an organizational outlook (that is, the attitude of a person who can accept operating within the organizational framework, not the innovative, entrepreneurial type who adapts things to personal wishes); a track record of reasonable success; two years or more of college; and sufficient personal financial resources to satisfy the franchisor's minimum capital requirements. Generally, franchisors are very public relations oriented. Their paramount interest is to maintain the company image of quality service and product which contributes to the financial success of both the franchisors and the franchisees. Figure 21–1 shows the distribution of restaurant and franchising sales by menu type, and franchising units' share by menu type.

[2]For more detailed information, see *Business Week*, December 15, 1980, pp. 98–105.

## Motels

During the past three decades, the motel industry has had phenomenal growth. We have seen it grow from "mom and pop" units with an often questionable image to an industry dominated by large corporate complexes. These corporations have company-owned units and also a franchise division operating units under the company trade name with cooperative participation by unit owners. (See Table 21–3 for the costs of selected-size franchises of one chain.)

**Table 21–3**
**Best Western Membership Fees**

| Units | Entrance Fee | Annual Travel Guide Dues | Annual Membership Fee | Reservation Fee | Total Annual Recurring Costs |
|---|---|---|---|---|---|
| 20 | $ 6,208 | $ 831 | $ 4,088 | $ 730 | $ 5,694 |
| 40 | 6,968 | 1,391 | 7,957 | 1,460 | 10,808 |
| 60 | 7,728 | 1,771 | 11,534 | 2,190 | 15,495 |
| 80 | 8,488 | 1,971 | 14,892 | 2,920 | 19,783 |
| 100 | 9,248 | 2,171 | 18,250 | 3,650 | 24,071 |
| 120 | 10,008 | 2,371 | 21,536 | 4,380 | 28,287 |
| 125 | 10,236 | 2,431 | 22,521 | 4,563 | 29,341 |
| 140 | 10,768 | 2,571 | 24,820 | 5,110 | 32,501 |
| 150 | 11,148 | 2,671 | 26,463 | 5,475 | 34,609 |
| 160 | 11,528 | 2,771 | 28,069 | 5,840 | 36,680 |
| 175 | 12,098 | 2,921 | 30,478 | 6,388 | 39,787 |
| 180 | 12,288 | 2,971 | 31,281 | 6,570 | 40,822 |
| 200 | 13,048 | 3,171 | 34,493 | 7,300 | 44,964 |

Source: Best Western 1982 fee schedule.

A pioneer in the motel image change has been Holiday Inn.[3] It set standards of consistency and uniformity of accommodations, service, and rates. Its success through providing a uniform image, complemented by its free Holidex reservation system, became a model for a new segment of the hostelry industry.[4]

The advent of the interstate highway system and the affluence and mobility of the American public created a market with great potential. Almost every interstate highway interchange became a potential motel site. Success seemed assured. Perhaps, in part, the earlier successes may have been responsible for what became an industry with excess capacity. No one heeded the few who foresaw the energy crisis and its ultimate effect on gasoline prices and American lifestyles. Nevertheless, the crisis came, along with a

[3]For information, see the 1983 Holiday Inn Franchise Prospectus.
[4]The credit card arrangement with Gulf Oil Corporation, as well as the use of other national credit cards, further contributed to their success.

changing mood and customer interest in the amenities a motel should provide. Many of the existing properties are now as obsolete as the mom-and-pop motels became with the coming of the national motels. The architecture, location, amenities offered, market, and/or finances of these properties do not make them suitable for modification. Instead, many are scheduled to be phased out by the franchisor—so beware!

*Old-Motel Opportunities.* In considering the acquisition of an existing franchise motel property, whether new or old, you should make a careful determination of its status. In determining the old motel's status, you should study the current and projected traffic patterns and densities. Also, you need to identify the travelers and the types of accommodation they use. (State tourist bureaus or departments of transportation often can provide this information.) Look at the occupancy rates for at least the past three years to see trends and relationships to the breakeven rate. Identify all the cost factors to see whether the current rate structure covers all the costs plus an adequate profit.

A visual inspection of the facilities determines the condition of the structure, both external and internal. Be particularly careful in checking to see that conference rooms and facilities have adequate lighting, cooling, heating, and sound equipment, and superior acoustical properties. The lobby and office space—and equipment and furnishings—should also be inspected. In looking at the exterior, check the ramps, passageways, elevators, roof and gutters, stairways, swimming pool and deck area, grounds and shrubbery, and the drainage, parking, and fire protection systems.

*New-Motel Opportunities.* Although the motel industry may be overbuilt and some properties are obsolete and should be phased out, new properties are still being developed. From a review of the present status and the future of the franchise motel business with some of the recognized people in the business, certain facts seem to stand out; they should be given careful attention if motels are a field of interest. You should give consideration to the following:

1. The number of units operated by the more reputable motel organizations will tend to remain constant.
2. New units will generally be in the 300–500 room size.
3. Most new units will be constructed in metropolitan locations selected to serve a segment of the convention market.
4. Some major motel companies are expected to increase the percentage of units owned and operated by the company.
5. An opportunity continues to exist for new franchisees to develop new properties that will be good revenue producers, but greater care is demanded in site selection than in the past.

## Retail Hardware Stores

In recent years there has been an increasing interest in cooperative franchising among retail hardware stores. This is an arrangement tying the retail unit to a hardware wholesaler corresponding in name to the franchise name. If you are interested in this type of franchise, you should contact the wholesaler for details. Examples are Ace, ARMA, Servistar, (trade name is the property of American Hardware, Butler, Pennsylvania), and True Value.

## Automotive Businesses

Automotive franchises have been around for some time. The franchises have historically been retail outlets for parts and accessories. Some of the units have been affiliated with nationally known tire manufacturers. Others have been related to national automotive parts manufacturers. A comparatively recent entry into the automotive franchise field is the specialty service shop. Some examples are those specializing in transmission repairs and parts; those specializing in muffler and shock absorber repairs and parts; the speed shops providing technical assistance, modification, and specialized parts; and diagnostic centers with their gradations of sophisticated electronic, computerized equipment.

In recent years, there has been a significant growth in the wholesale-retail franchise auto parts outlets. Also, the number of automotive tune-up franchises has been growing as gasoline stations shift from full service to self-service. Many of these franchises use former service stations.

The qualifications that automotive franchisors seek in their franchisees are significantly different from those desired by other franchisors. Automotive franchisors tend to look for the male chauvinist. They prefer that the franchisee's wife and family not be associated with the business. A high school education seems adequate except for diagnostic centers, where technical training should be required. It seems that friendliness is not considered an essential attribute. Since the greatest concern of the franchisor seems to be the ability of the franchisee to pay bills and carry a sufficient inventory, adequate personal finances and financial stability are considered very important.

In general, the capital requirements of the autmotive franchise are less than for some fast-food or motel franchises. Most of the automotive franchises give little help in terms of management assistance, site location, financial assistance, and training. Yet there may be advantages in the system, product line, and national advertising. Each situation should be carefully considered on its own merits.

## Service Stations

From 1972 to 1979, the number of service stations in the United States declined from about 226,000 to 171,000, or about 24 percent.[5] Some observers of the oil industry have predicted that the number might even dip to 125,000 by 1985. Even though it does not appear that this prediction will materialize, it is evident that the number of entrepreneurial opportunities for service station management and operations is decreasing.

During the same period, the average sales per station rose about 186 percent, to about $368,000 per year. However, the net profits of stations were unattractive during the 1970s.

Significant factors affecting the character of opportunities in this area are:

1. In operating:
   a. A higher percentage of stations are self-service, company owned, or combined with stores.
   b. Employee jobs and demands have changed.
2. In financing:
   a. An increase in required investment.
   b. More open accounts and possible credit card usage charges.
   c. High rate of money exchange.
   d. More pilferage.
3. In marketing:
   a. Increasing negative reactions to higher gasoline prices.
   b. Changing traffic patterns.
4. In governing:
   a. Unstable relations with oil companies.
   b. Changing regulations of the Federal Energy Administration, Environmental Protection Agency, and agencies of the states.

The net effect of all these factors is that future independent dealers must be better qualified because the companies have become more selective, fewer stations are available, and broader technical knowledge and skills are required. Many major petroleum companies provide training schools and in-house advisory services to their dealers.

## Convenience Markets

While the term *convenience market* is usually associated with food outlets, it may in fact cover a variety of specialty shops. The latter

---

[5]The material for this part was developed with the assistance of M. M. Hargrove, *National Petroleum News,* and from an interview with a major oil company marketing executive.

perform a service by assembling merchandise or materials into a single location, making selection and purchase convenient. Some examples of these types of franchises are 7–Eleven food markets, Craft Shack, and Radio Shack.

### Real Estate

Franchising is being used more frequently in an increasing variety of business activities, including real estate. Franchising is not new to the real estate field. In the past, however, most of the real estate franchises were related to farm real estate. Now, activity is primarily concerned with urban real estate organizations—for example, Electronic Realty Association, Inc., and Century 21.

A major selling point in marketing real estate franchises is the benefit of national referrals. Advantages once restricted to large firms are now available to smaller firms through the franchise system. Basically, the franchise makes the smaller firm more competitive with the larger organization. One national real estate authority believes that in 10 years a significant majority of the smaller real estate firms will be affiliated with a franchise organization.

Fees are split with the referral firm, but in today's mobile society, the selling firm hopes to offset such fees through referrals back to the referring firm. The newness and rapid expansion of real estate franchises indicate that a period of experience is needed before the stability achieved by franchisors and franchisees in other fields will be achieved in real estate. In considering a real estate franchise, you should apply some of the criteria mentioned earlier for fast foods and motels and keep up with the changes occurring in this dynamic field.

## What Franchise to Choose

The purpose of the material that follows is to aid you in selecting the right franchise—the one that will help achieve your objectives without jeopardizing your resources.

### Some Risks in Franchising

Many franchise situations are loaded with pitfalls. Some of these dangers were pointed out in a Small Business Administration press release of a study done for the U.S. Senate Select Committee on Small Business.[6] Such franchises left hundreds of disgruntled, disappointed, disillusioned people strewn in the aftermath of their

---

[6]See Urban B. Ozanne and Shelby D. Hunt, *The Economic Effects of Franchising* (Washington, D.C.: Small Business Administration, 1971), especially pp. 1–2.

onslaught. Unfortunately, many of these persons had naively placed their life savings in ventures that were doomed to failure from the start. There was a broad array of these activities, from gum-vending machines, candy machines, and stamp machines to fast food (fried chicken, specialty food items, soft custard, and hamburgers), motels, coin-operated laundries, and ice cream parlors.

> A man put up $2,000, on a guaranteed investment, for gum and candy machines. The franchisors promised to find good locations for the machines. However, these failed to materialize because all desirable locations were already being used. As a result, the man lost his $2,000. In the meantime, the franchisor disappeared and the guarantee on the investment was of no value.

> A well-known radio-TV entertainment personality became involved with a fried chicken franchise operation. The fine print on the front page of the prospectus revealed more padding of assets than real value. From the outset, the franchisor did a poor job in assisting the franchisees. Consequently, the franchisees went down.

> A flurry of activity in mobile home sales and mobile home park franchises led many people to invest in the stock of the companies and buy their franchises. Many "fast buck" operators rode to the pinnacle of paper success, but most investors lost substantial sums when the house of paper came crashing down.

> Camping park franchises appeared vacant or sparsely populated during the 1973–74 energy crisis.

Federal Trade Commission regulations make it mandatory for a franchisor to file disclosure papers which provide facts about itself in 20 different areas. The disclosures help to avoid misrepresentation by the franchisor and to record a franchisor's commitments. In addition, 15 states require potential franchisors to register with the state before selling franchises there. The government agencies check the facts in these reports. If any information looks questionable, more information is requested. A potential franchisee should review these records to become informed and to reduce the risks in purchasing a franchise.

## Some Pertinent Questions to Ask

In viewing a franchise possibility, you should investigate the objectives of the franchisor. Here is a simple list of questions you might want to answer before "putting your money on the barrel head."

1. What is in it for me?
   a. Return on investment.
   b. Salary I can reasonably expect.
2. Is the franchisor just unloading a "white elephant" on me? An

example was a franchisor who tried to sell home swimming pools by requiring the franchisee to purchase a display model at a price comparable to standard retail price.

3. What services does the franchisor provide the franchisee? Are the services priced at a discount or priced too high for the benefits they offer?
4. What is the attitude of the existing franchisees? Are they seeking to unload, or are they happy with the results they are achieving?
5. What is the attitude of your banker, CPA, Better Business Bureau, chamber of commerce, and community toward the franchisor and existing franchisees?
6. Is there a clause in the franchise contract that permits the franchisor, at will, to purchase the franchise on terms favoring the franchisor?

## Some Conclusions Concerning Franchising

Even in the best franchise situations, the franchisor tends to hold an advantage. Usually, this relates to operating standards, supply and material purchasing agreements, and agreements relating to the repurchase of the franchise. However, franchise operations may offer you an opportunity to derive a satisfactory income on your investment and efforts.

A large number of court cases relating to franchise activities are now being adjudicated. Among the issues involved are territorial rights held by the franchisor and by the franchisee, and the right of the franchisor to require the franchisee to purchase supplies and inventory from the franchisor. Decisions seem to indicate that the franchisee may gain some advantages—and lose some—from these legal actions.

The growth of some types of franchises has had a negative effect on established businesses, and some are fighting back. For example, fast-food sales have hurt supermarket sales; as a result, frozen-food processors are producing easily prepared quality menu items, and supermarkets are establishing delis and bakeries.

Two significant changes are underway, at least in the fast-food franchising area, that may affect your decision to go into this type of operation. First, many of the companies are buying back the franchises from individuals and operating them themselves. Companies find that they can make more money this way, particularly in the more profitable areas. A second trend is to grant a group of franchises to existing franchisees who have a proven record of profitable operations.

# Summary

This chapter has given you an overview of some of the advantages and disadvantages of operating a franchise, as well as some of the considerations in choosing the type of franchise you would like to operate. On balance, the future of franchising seems to be quite favorable, in spite of some slight evidence of a trend away from the practice.

The material in this chapter has placed the greatest emphasis on fast-food and motel franchises because of the significant growth in fast foods, which continues, and the growth and size of the motel industry. In both of these categories, there are franchises that are sound and solid opportunities for their types of business. The characteristics of these operations seem worthy to serve as models for evaluating other franchise organizations and the opportunity they pose.

# Where to Look for Further Information

Department of Commerce, Domestic and International Business Administration, *Franchise Opportunities Handbook*, April 1977.

# Chapter Twenty-Two

## How to Enter an Existing Business

After making the choice to enter an independent business, determining that your business idea is valid and economically feasible, and deciding to enter an existing firm, you are now ready to take that important step. The material in this chapter presents a plan of action to help you achieve that goal.

By this time, you should be aware of the many problems and challenges awaiting individuals moving into an independent business ownership and management. Problems in an established business may be well concealed. It is the intent of this chapter to aid you in seeing an established business in true perspective—its strengths as well as its weaknesses.

While there is some similarity between establishing a new business—which is discussed in the next chapter—and entering an ongoing enterprise, there are several significant differences. These are covered in this chapter. The procedures and analyses that follow are intended to provide you with an overview of how to evaluate an existing firm and to aid you in determining (1) whether or not to purchase a given business, and (2) if you do buy it, what you should do to implement your plans and begin operations.

### To Buy or Not to Buy?

In considering options in selecting an established business, it is likely that you will narrow them down to a single choice. At that point, you should check the business out before making the final decision. The procedure might be compared to the steps involved in moving an aircraft from the boarding gate of the terminal to the taxiway, to the runway, and into the air. Certain items must be checked off at each step of the way, with the pilot having the right to abort the flight—up to the point of commitment to taking the aircraft into the air. So it is with the purchase of an established business: up to a certain point, you may cancel out; but from that time on, you are committed to take over the business. Figure 22–1 is intended to illustrate this comparison.

**Figure 22–1**
**To Go or Not to Go**

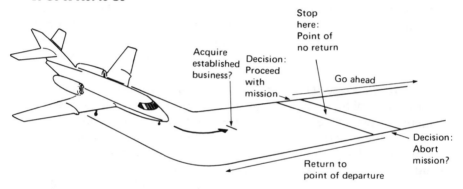

## Why Is the Business Available? (1)[1]

You should determine why the firm is available for purchase, as this in itself can be a "red flag" warning that something may be wrong. You need to determine if something is the matter and, if so, what and why and what can be done about it.

The answer to the question Why is this business available for purchase? should help you establish the validity of the owner's stated purpose for selling the business. Maybe it is in accordance with the old cliché "Anything I have is for sale, at a price—that is, for the right price." Some reasons provide a positive opportunity, while others may be negative. The following analysis should help you determine the potential opportunity to be found in a firm.

Does the present owner have too many irons in the fire? Sometimes too many businesses are run by one individual who is unable to allocate sufficient time to manage all of them successfully.

---

[1]The numbers shown in parentheses after headings refer to sections of Exhibit 20–2 in the appendix at the end of chapter 20.

Bob Bleckley had dropped out of college in his senior year for financial reasons. After working several years for a building supply firm, he went to work for a partnership engaged in diversified construction of commercial buildings. He was made manager of the metal door division. The partners were so busy with their other activities that they gave him little assistance or interest. Bob was running the division.

Bob offered to buy the division from the partners, and they accepted. He is now the owner-manager of that firm and two other small activities.

## What Are the Present Owner's Intentions? (2)

If you purchase a company, the present owner will be free to do what he or she desires, unless restricted by a contract. What has been said and what is done may not be the same. As a precaution, make a thorough check of the owner's intentions.

### Will the Present Owner Remain in Competition?    Sometimes, for reasons of location or because of the age of the facility or equipment, an owner decides to dispose of the firm, open another one, and compete with the purchaser of the old firm. For protection, you should have an attorney draw up an agreement that the present owner will not reenter a similar business in the same community or market area for a reasonable period of time. These agreements are sometimes difficult to enforce, but most business people do live up to their agreements.

The owner of a pest control franchise needed to change locations for family reasons. The new location was within the franchise area, so the purchasers required him to sign an agreement that he would not reenter the business for five years.

In the meantime, he opened a restaurant and related business and became quite successful. At the end of the five years, he opened an independent pest control business in his new location.

### Is the Present Owner in Good Health?    If the owner is in poor health, you should determine that it is physical and not economic.

Bob Howard was interested in owning his own business. One Sunday, he was reviewing the want ads in the newspaper when he spotted an item of interest:

FOR REASONS OF HEALTH, OWNER WILLING TO SACRIFICE SUCCESSFUL, PROFITABLE SANDWICH SHOP. PRICED FOR IMMEDIATE SALE.

Bob dashed over to Easy Sandwich Shop. The place was full and business great. (All the owner's friends just needed a sandwich that day.) After some delay, Bob was able to engage the owner in serious negotiation. After some haggling, the principals shook hands, and Bob wrote a check from his savings for $10,000.

A month later, Bob was chagrined to learn that the business was ready to fold when he took the bait. The former owner's friends were gone, and business was terrible. The $10,000 received by the former owner had worked a fast cure for his ill health.

***Does the Present Owner Desire to Retire?***    The owner may have reached retirement age, which is a valid reason for offering a business for sale. Because of taxes, the owner may want to be paid for the business over a number of years. In addition, he or she may want to contract for a specified number of years to serve as a consultant or to fill some managerial role.

A word of caution is appropriate. Sometimes the continued association of a former owner can be detrimental to the new owner. By continued association with the firm, the former owner may cause the new owner to be unsuccessful and thereby regain ownership of the business.

At the least, the presence of the old owner restricts the freedom of action of the new owner and can otherwise inhibit his or her actions.

Barbara Jones, an experienced insurance agent, became the controlling partner in an insurance firm which also owned a savings and loan association. The previous owner, 75 years old, remained as chairman of the board of the savings and loan association and active partner in the insurance company.

The next 10 years were miserable for Barbara, for she was treated as a junior clerk by the minority partner. She finally sold her interest to someone else.

## Is the Market for the Firm's Product Declining? (3)

The demand for a business's product may be declining for one or more of the following reasons:

1. Changing neighborhood. There may be a change in the residents' economic status; there may be a change from one ethnic group to another, from one age group to another, or in the lifestyle of the inhabitants.
2. Declining population. The movement of population in both urban and agrarian areas has had a devastating economic effect on some firms. New roads, residential areas, and shopping malls have influenced this movement.
3. Technological change. The advent and installation of new technology may immediately cause a firm to become obsolete.

The owners of a company in Florida processing large cans of grapefruit juice decided to build a new, more efficient plant. As soon as it was completed, they found themselves competing with a new plant producing fresh-frozen juice concentrates.

**Preparing an Economic Feasibility Study.** An economic feasibility study for an ongoing business is similar in nature to the economic feasibility study for a new enterprise, which is presented in the appendix to Chapter 20. To avoid being trapped by economic conditions that may result in either economic disaster or stagnation, you should determine the business's feasibility. The data for the study could be gathered and analyzed under the following classifications:

1.  Population trends of the market. The area may be experiencing an increase or decrease in population. The population may be stable, or one ethnic, economic, or age group may be moving out and another moving in.
2.  Age distribution of the population. If the demand for a firm's product or service has been from a particular age group, the size and trend of that group should be identified.
3.  Income levels and distribution of the population. Sales are affected by both purchasing power and its distribution within the population. You should study the relationship between the income distribution among specific age groups and the demand for goods and services.
4.  Market size. From the *Journal of Marketing, Sales Management,* census reports, local chamber of commerce data, area planning and development commissions, local newspapers' market data, and other sources, you can obtain information to help define the size of the firm's market.
5.  Share of market. By estimating the size of the market and by defining the amount of competition and its quality, you can search for areas upon which you can capitalize.
6.  Impact of expected changes. Changes in the legal, physical, social, cultural, economic, and religious environments can affect your chances of success. Some of these are as follows:
    a.  Zoning changes may have some influence if the business is retail in nature. Over 30 families deposited $5,000 each for new homes to be constructed. None were finished. According to town officials and engineers, the builder was incompetent and was unable or unwilling to comply with the building code regulations.
    b.  Construction of traffic arteries or changes and relocations may cut businesses off from their customers. Jo Anne's Dress Shop was located in a small shopping center on a highway leading into and out of Capital City. The street was closed

for about 18 months for widening and relocation. Jo Anne's clientele, composed primarily of middle-income house-wives, shifted usual traffic patterns. By the time the street reopened, Jo Anne's business had declined to the point that she went bankrupt.

c.  The emphasis being placed on the environment and ecology has resulted in constraints on some businesses. You should be careful that a confrontation with the environmentalists does not occur. Changes in laws regulating pollution con-trols have also increased the costs of doing business.

d.  Changes in tax laws and other government regulations af-fect the volume of paperwork and the time necessary to prepare the required reports.

e.  Labor laws have a direct effect on the cost of doing business. An example is the federal Occupational Safety and Health Act (OSHA), which establishes specific safety standards. (See Chapter 5 for details.)

f.  Technological changes may affect you. For example, inno-vations in the local newspaper equipment field, such as new and cheaper offset systems and computers aiding in the composition of the paper, have caused many publishers to abandon their existing equipment.

## Are Physical Facilities Suitable? (4)

A firm's ability to sell its product or service is based on its ability to produce and serve, as well as on its market potential. Physical facilities such as buildings, machines, display racks, and carpeting should be checked for ability to perform the services desired.

*Are the Physical Facilities Worn Out?*  If the plant, equipment, tools, and furniture are worn out, it is likely that the business's maintenance costs will be excessive. It is also likely that the firm can no longer effectively compete in the marketplace.

> A druggist and his wife had been running their drugstore for 40 years—largely without making changes and improvements in their physical plant. After the death of his wife, the druggist (who was approaching 70) decided to sell the business. He was unable to find a buyer, for the equipment was so antiquated and in such poor condition that it was useless to others. He finally sold only his stock and prescription file to another pharmacist.

Occasionally, old equipment that is well maintained, but that has been fully depreciated, offers a cost advantage over newer, more modern equipment. It is possible that the continued use of older equipment may produce a greater profit, but it may not.

Sometimes it is necessary to purchase new equipment on an installment basis. The effect of such a step on the cash flow should be carefully analyzed.

*Are Facilities Planned Properly?*  Facilities should be of sufficient size and design to meet current and projected requirements. Also, optimum results can be attained only if the plant is effectively laid out. An important item to consider is whether the equipment is spaced and laid out in a sequence of productive steps, so that only a nominal amount of work-in-process inventory is needed. The greater the number of operations that require doubling back and crossing over, the greater will be the requirements for this type of inventory.

The manner in which a plant is laid out also has a direct relationship to labor requirements and therefore to labor costs.

> A veneer mill and plywood plant was designed and laid out to take advantage of cheap labor. There were a minimum of conveyors and a maximum amount of handling by the workers. The net result was excessive cost and negative profit.

A retail store should be laid out to promote the proper flow of customers, a good display of merchandise, and an inviting environment.

### Is the Business Operating Efficiently? (5)

In acquiring an ongoing business, you will probably keep most of the operating employees and key management personnel. Therefore, it is desirable to look for performance and behavioral characteristics that may serve as a basis for appraising how effectively each employee performs.

*How Effective Are the Personnel?*  Employee attitudes and skills are important to the productivity of a firm. Attitudes can be judged by measuring employee turnover and absenteeism, by the firm's record of resolving employee-management conflicts, and by the tenure of employees. Records of the extent of training and experience of employees provide a basis for rating skills.

Your attitude toward unions should be considered; it is difficult to change the state of unionization or nonunionization.

*What Is the Amount of Waste?*  The amount of waste serves as an important key to profit or loss. By being particularly observant of operations, you can determine the amount of material and supplies being needlessly wasted in operations.

A carpet mill was observed to be looping out to the edge of the jute or polypropylene backing. Yet, from one to three inches was sliced off each side after the carpet was finished. It was estimated that the mill was unnecessarily using about $10,000 worth of fiber per day by not stopping the looping process approximately an inch from the edge of the backing.

Machine time and employee time that are not being utilized are important wastes. Investment in equipment is usually costly, and this cost must be offset by keeping the equipment operating as much as possible. As wage rates increase, employee idle time becomes more expensive. On the other hand, keeping salespeople so busy that customers must wait means lost sales. Customers may leave a store before making purchases and may not return.

**What Is the Quality of the Product or Service?** The quality of products, or the quality of service produced by the employees, should be graded. The firm can be judged by measuring the percentage of good product or service turned out and the percentage of sales returned. Also, the number and character of complaints about the firm's service is a measure of quality. The keeping of records of these quality measurements, with actions taken to cure the problem, indicates management's interest in providing quality service.

**Is Inventory Satsifactory?** The ratios of inventory to sales tend to be about the same for independent businesses in the same industry. However, some items may be obsolete, some are sold infrequently, and some move out of inventory quickly. A careful examination of the types and number of items reveals the quality of the inventory.

The owner of a hardware store decided to sell it in 1970. The prospective buyer found 200 horse collars among the antiquated stock.

## What Is the Financial Condition of the Firm? (6)

An audit by a reputable accountant or accounting firm is a check on the reliability of the accounting information. This should include both a physical inventory to determine the accuracy of the recorded information and a quantitative analysis of the economic value of the assets and liabilities.

*Validity of Financial Statements.* (7) You should verify the validity of the financial statement items. Each item listed on the financial statements should be verified by physically counting the listed items to determine whether they agree with the amount shown. Also, you need to find out whether the items are of the stated value.

You should check on the age of the accounts receivable. Some businesses continue to carry accounts receivable that should be charged off as bad debts, resulting in an overstatement of the firm's profit, income tax liability, and value. A tabular summary classifying them by age (such as 30, 60, 90, 120, 180 or more days), would give some perspective of the effectiveness of the existing management's credit policies and practice. The age of accounts payable should also be determined.

The reason for analyzing the firm's accounting data is to determine its economic health. In performing your analysis, there are numerous items you should check. The most important of these are now presented in general terms.

*Cash position.* Is the firm's cash position high or low, considering the industry, location, and so forth? Due to taxes, a firm may accumulate a strong cash position. The owner may prefer to sell the firm and take advantage of the capital gains benefit over ordinary income. Other reasons for having a strong cash position are to take care of poor funds management or to provide for flexibility to take advantage of any profitable opportunity that presents itself.

*Cash-flow analysis.* It is important to consider the monthly cycle of cash revenue and cash payout. Examine the firm's cash inflow and outgo for the past year. Develop an estimated cash budget for the coming year. This budget shows whether the cash flow is adequate to meet obligations.

*Analysis of ratios.* Many financial ratios can be used in estimating the economic health of a firm. While these are usually used in managing a going concern (as shown in Chapter 12), they can also help you make a purchase decision.

Current ratio is defined as current assets divided by current liabilities and is a measure of short-term solvency. Current assets normally include cash, marketable securities, accounts receivable, and inventories. Current liabilities are composed of accounts payable, short-term notes payable, income taxes payable, and accrued expenses. In general, the current ratio should be about 2 to 1.

Quick ratio is obtained by dividing current liabilities into current assets minus inventories. You can use this ratio to estimate the ability of a firm to pay off its short-term obligations without having to sell its inventories. Inventories tend to lose value faster than other assets when sold in a hurry. In general, the quick ratio should be about 1 to 1.

Debt-to-equity ratio, obtained by dividing debt by equity, shows the firm's obligations to creditors, relative to the owner's funds. Debt includes current liabilities and bonds; owner's funds include common stock, preferred stock, capital surplus, and retained earnings.

Ratio of net income to sales is calculated by dividing net income by net sales. You may use net income before taxes or after taxes. General guidelines include competitor and industry ratios.

Net income-to-investment ratio is found by dividing net income (before or after taxes) by total assets. A convenient guideline is to compare this value with returns on alternative investments.

*Determination of debt.* You need to check both the amount of debt and the terms of debt. The amount of debt is important, for it shows your financial obligations. You are primarily concerned with short-term notes (less than one year), term notes (one to five years), and long-term debt (anything in excess of five years).

Concerning terms of debt, you should learn the rate of interest, the firm's ability to repay the debt in its entirety without penalty, whether a minimum deposit balance is required by the lender, and whether an acceleration clause would operate in the event of default in payment of interest and principal.

*Adequacy of cost data.* You should determine whether cost data are adequate and accurate. The accounting system used, even when supervised by a CPA or by one of the national accounting firms, often fails to reveal the actual costs of individual activities. Thus, it is impossible to determine the price for each product or service in order to satisfy a predetermined profit criterion. Nor is it possible to explain undesirable variances.

*Analysis of pricing formula.* You should analyze the pricing formula used by the firm. Be sure that the price for individual products or services includes all elements of costs and a provision for an adequate profit.

*Is the business solvent?* The business should be solvent. Unfortunately, there have been instances when people have discovered all too late that the firm they purchased has less assets than liabilities.

A building contractor sold 150 homes for down payments totaling over $500,000. Because of abysmally inadequate financing, he was unable to complete the houses. The firm was sold, but the new owners had either to return the money or to give title to their property to the purchasers.

The above incident indicates the need for making as complete a check as is reasonable. Many more questions need to be answered if there is any indication of insolvency.

*How Much Investment Is Needed? (8)* Your investment includes the purchase price for the existing firm plus additional capital for start-up purposes less loans you may obtain.

*What Is the Estimated Return on Investment? (9)* This return should be based on the analysis of answers to the questions listed in the designated form, any other analysis, and your best projection of the future. It should be realistic. Reading previous chapters should aid you in developing a good estimate.

### What Is Your Decision? (10)

The results of the previous analyses may be so disappointing that you will reject the purchase. However, even if this alternative looks very good, you cannot answer the question until you have explored other alternatives. Buying another existing and available business or starting a new business must be assessed. (The latter alternative is discussed in Chapter 23.) Finally, you may want to obtain the opinion of an appraiser specializing in this type of business.

## Implementing Plans

If you have decided to buy the business, you are ready to activate "operation acquisition." Figure 22–2 indicates the sequence of steps that you will probably follow in moving from the decision to purchase the old business to the point of taking over and running the business's operation. The rooms may be considered as the places where the important designated activities take place. The sequence of rooms is intended to impress upon you the importance of following the appropriate sequence of activities.

### Financing the Business

You are now ready to develop a plan for financing the business. As indicated earlier, financing an existing business will depend to a significant extent on the terms asked by the seller. A protective measure is to use escrows, whereby part of the purchase price is put in safekeeping until all aspects of the sale have been completed.

### Considering Changes in Method of Operations

As a result of operational analysis suggested earlier in this chapter, you should have developed some ideas concerning the changes you would like to make in the business's existing method of operations.

**Figure 22–2**
**Points of Decisions**

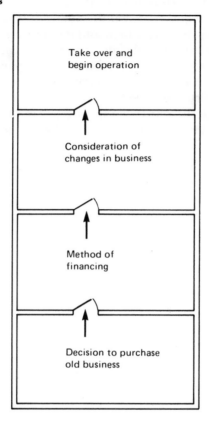

### Developing a Formal Plan

You should now prepare a formal plan of change to be integrated with a formal plan of action. You may wish to combine the two plans into a manual of operating procedures.

### Taking Over the Business

It is now time to start operations. If you have followed the procedures outlined above, the probabilities of your succeeding in your new business will be greatly increased. Yet, you should be prepared for unforeseen contingencies and be ready to react promptly to any difficulties that may arise.

## Summary

Well, you are now committed to being an independent business manager. You have: (1) found a business you like; (2) determined the reasons that the present owner wished to sell; (3) analyzed the market, competition, physical facilities, personnel, and operations; (4) validated and analyzed the financial information; (5) determined the required investment and the return expected from it. You may or may not have decided to buy, depending on evaluations of other alternatives. If you did decide to purchase the existing firm, you develop plans for financing, for making changes, and for acquiring and running the firm.

After you take the reins, you must manage the firm. How you can successfully do that is discussed in other sections of this book.

# Chapter Twenty Three

## How to Establish a New Business

You should by now have developed a basic concept of the nature of independent business and how you expect to relate personally to a specific type of independent business. You should also have decided whether you would like to become a franchise to take over an existing firm, or to plan a new venture. It is the purpose of this chapter to show you how to plan successfully a new independent business. The material should enable you to move in an orderly fashion from the idea stage to making the new business a reality. In addition, should the need exist, the formal plan may serve to interest others in investing in the new venture.

As far as you—the potential new entrepreneur—are concerned, the outlined procedure should aid in avoiding costly blunders. It should conserve time and result in a more polished final product. Insofar as potential investors are concerned, the formal proposal should demonstrate that your idea has been well studied and appropriately structured. Often, the potential new independent business owner approaches investors with little more than a dream. The response is likely to be negative. This material should help you avoid these—and other—pitfalls.

In general, the business process involves putting financial, physical, and human resources into an organization in the form of inputs. These are converted through some form of operations or production into goods or services. These, in turn, are distributed

to other processors, assemblers, wholesalers, retailers, or the final
consumer as outputs. Figure 23–1 presents a generalized chart of
such a process. You can establish a company to perform any one
or more of the segments of this total process.

**Figure 23–1**
**The Business Process**

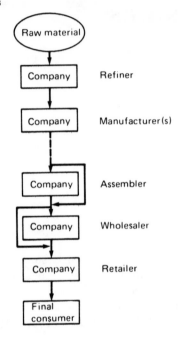

The specific steps needed to start this process include at least
the following:

1. Developing a timetable.
2. Establishing business objectives.
3. Setting up organizational structure.
4. Determining personnel requirements.
5. Determining physical facility needs.
6. Planning your approach to the market.
7. Preparing a budget.
8. Locating sources of funds.
9. Implementing the plans.

## Developing a Timetable

You should establish a timetable for developing the business in an
ordered, coordinated fashion. Data should be developed relating

to performing each step in starting the business. Next, a time frame for accomplishing each of the steps should be determined. Many of these steps can be, and often are, performed simultaneously.

## Establishing Business Objectives

In order for your enterprise to have purpose and direction, you should establish the objectives you hope to achieve for yourself and your firm. These should be compatible with the objectives discussed in Chapter 2. Examples of some possible categories of objectives are:

1. Size:
   a. Physical.
   b. Financial.
2. Type of products:
   a. Number.
   b. Kind of product lines.
3. Number of employees.
4. Sales.
5. Profits.

For each of these categories, you will want to define the objectives you hope to have achieved after 1 year, after 5 years, and after 10 years.

## Setting Up the Organizational Structure

As previously stated, you must develop a unified organizational structure, taking into consideration the legal, financial, and administrative aspects of the business. Keeping in mind the basic premise that "my business is very personal," it is important to select those forms that are in your best interest. Also, you should organize for the long run and not just for the short run. The outline that follows is intended to show the options available at each juncture and to assist you in making the best choice.

1. Legal alternatives. Choose one of the following that seems most appropriate to your needs, objectives, qualifications, and philosophies.
   a. Proprietorship.
   b. Partnership.
   c. Corporation.
   d. Holding company.
   e. Co-ops.
2. Capital structure. Determine the extent to use equity and debt based on:
   a. Amount of personal funds you wish to commit to the business.

   b.  Amount of personal funds other principals wish to commit.
   c.  Availability of equity and borrowed capital and at what costs—interest and concessions.
   d.  Degree of risk you are willing to assume.
3. Administrative structure. Develop a formal plan of organization based upon these factors:
   a.  The main mission or purpose of the business.
   b.  Your primary personal and business objectives.
   c.  The plans, programs, policies, and practices that will achieve those objectives.
   d.  The authority and responsibility relationships that will accomplish the mission or purpose of the firm.

An element often overlooked by the independent business manager is the importance of having access to a board of directors (or advisers, if the firm is not a corporation) to evaluate the firm's operation and to make recommendations relating to future activities. You must be willing to be responsive to its guidance. You should expect to pay these people reasonable honoraria for each meeting, plus expenses. The board is usually composed of at least three people from outside the business and an equal number from within.

In selecting outside members, you should try to obtain a balance of expertise and experience, such as: (1) a business manager with a record of success in business, preferably in a related but different field; (2) another business manager with a different background, but equally successful; and (3) if available, an academic person with a general management background that encompasses the operations of independent businesses.

## Determining Personnel Requirements

The next organizational step is to determine the duties and responsibilities (job descriptions and specifications) needed to perform the activities of the business. Then the process of estimating personnel requirements can be undertaken.

One problem area seems to be more prevalent in smaller firms than in larger organizations. Frequently the business is closely related to the family unit, and this relationship may contribute to morale problems if outsiders are brought in. The independent business owner-manager should be aware of these potential problems and take deliberate steps to prevent them.

## Determining Physical Facilities Needed

Two important decisions must now be made: (1) what location to choose and (2) whether to buy (build) or lease your physical facilities.

## Location

The type of business you are going to operate (retail, service, or manufacturing) also influences your location decisions. This factor is important: it relates to access to customers, suppliers, work force, utilities, and transportation, as well as compliance with zoning regulations. The mission of the business serves as a basic consideration in seeking the right location.

Each type of firm has its own set of factors to consider and gives priority to those that most affect the firm. Retailer location is primarily based on a marketing analysis. A manufacturing plant is concerned with costs and availability of a series of items such as labor, utilities, and transportation. Service organizations use different combinations of marketing-cost factors in selecting their locations. Let us look at retailing, manufacturing, and then general factors in location analysis.

*Retailing.* A retailer first finds an area where the potential market exists for the sale of its goods; this is called a trading area. Within this area, the retailer must locate a site where it is easy, attractive, and profitable for customers to shop, so that customers think of going to that site first when considering buying. The location can be in the central business district, a shopping center, a neighborhood, or another location. The site cost must be within the means of the firm.

> Kitty had operated her medium-priced ladieswear shop for a number of years in the same location. It was in a small shopping center across the street from one of the community's traditional shopping centers. A representative of the shopping mall tried to persuade Kitty that it would be good business for her to move to the mall.
>
> After inquiring about the rental terms, Kitty was somewhat awestruck. The basic rent would be $14.50 per square foot, and then there would be an additional charge of 5 percent of the gross sales. Later, Kitty was relating her experience and thoughts concerning the mall situation. "Do you know that just the basic rent would have cost me $800 a month? Then, I would have to add on that 5 percent. Can you imagine what I would have to charge for my clothes if I were going to make a profit? I think I'd better stay put."

Cost of a location in a shopping mall may be high, but may be balanced by high traffic. Many statistics have been collected and are available to aid in location analysis.

*Manufacturing.* Manufacturing firms want to locate plants near customers and vendors for ease of transporting goods and material. Comparatively, manufacturing plants employ more people, use more energy and other utilities, and emphasize cost reduction more than retailers do. Thus, labor rates and availability, union activity, cost and availability of utilities, tax rates, and zoning restrictions assume a greater influence in location analysis.

*General Factors.* The following factors are important in location analysis, particularly for manufacturing:

*Access to work force.* Essential for success is the availability of people with the personal attributes and skills the business requires. You should consider the possibility of blending part-time with full-time employees in order to provide more flexibility and a more economic operation. Another consideration is the distances and types of residential areas from which you will draw employees. If you can locate your business where employees can walk to work and possibly even go home for lunch, you may have an advantage in pay negotiations, worker loyalty and interest, and better job attendance.

*Availability of utilities.* Access to needed utilities (such as electric power, gas, water, sewerage, and steam) is also very important. Two other factors to consider are flexibility in operation and economics (not only the initial installation costs, but also operating costs). Energy is of increasing importance in location decisions because of its spiraling costs and variations of as much as 50 percent in its rates.

*Availability of vendors.* Are there a sufficient number of vendors to supply the needs of the business? In the selection of vendors, you should determine the types of supportive service each seller can provide. The kinds of support that may be derived are: (1) assistance in designing a product or products, (2) aid in the selection of machinery and plant, (3) technical assistance in solving problems, and (4) assistance with pricing and formulating trade credit practices.

*Access to transportation.* Can the most economical form of transportation for both your inbound and outbound shipments be made? Are there railroad spurs to the location? Truck lines? Buses? Does the site allow for enough parking?

*Taxes and government regulations.* The location of a firm is influenced by rates and types of taxes, licenses, zoning, waste disposal, and other restrictions, and by government attitude toward business. In particular, these factors must be assessed at the local and state levels. The value of the services available, such as recreation and education, should be balanced against the costs.

The best location is one which satisfies your requirements and provides optimum benefits. For example, if you are going into the retail business and are considering a specific piece of vacant property, it is desirable to determine the reason behind the vacancy.

### Buy or Lease

The question of whether to buy or lease the physical plant is important; the supply of capital may be the determining factor. The rate and amount of return you can receive on capital invested in other ways is another consideration. The nature of space requirements and the availability of the structure are also significant. You should not overlook the role of depreciation and its effect on cash flow. Also, do your building requirements indicate the need for a specialized or a general-purpose structure? You should be cautious in committing yourself to a special-purpose structure because of the long-range problems of disposing of it if you decide to move or go out of business.

## Planning Your Approach to the Market

Three marketing factors should be considered before opening your business to the public: (1) building an image, (2) channels of distribution to use, and (3) pricing. While these factors are discussed in greater detail in Part 3, facts you should know before starting your business are provided here.

Some years ago, a man living in New England conceived an idea for a new kind of dustpan that could be made of rubber in a variety of colors. Lacking the production resources, he had a dozen samples of this new product custom-made.

Armed with his dozen multicolored dustpans, he went to Boston to hawk his wares to Filene's and Jordan-March, neither of whom seemed interested in them. He was sure that housewives would buy his product, since it could be made to fit any floor irregularities and would not mar the floor. As he was returning home irritated by the rejection of his product, these things weighed on his mind.

What could he do to prove his idea was good? While he was passing through Pawtucket, Rhode Island, the idea hit him. "Why not market-test it by calling on housewives?" Pulling into a residential street, he parked his car and set out to ring doorbells. Forty-five minutes later, he returned to his car with only 2 of the 12 left.

Convinced that his idea was good, he developed a company to market the product. In time, the company grew, its product line ever expanding.

## Building an Image

The image of a firm determines a potential customer's acceptance or rejection of it as a desirable place to purchase goods or services. The public's perceptions come from a company's actions and from statements of reliability, integrity, price, and quality. A new firm must develop an image that will attract customers.

A number of factors should be considered in building an image for a firm. What segment of the market offers the best potential opportunity? What advertising media will best reach this market?

> A radio station operated on both AM and FM frequencies. After a substantial time period, its sales manager evaluated the results of its efforts to sell advertising and discovered that its advertising customers obtained 45 percent or more of their business volume from the black community. The members of this community, however, made up a meager portion of the station's FM listening audience. The FM had never attracted the desired volume of advertising revenue. A shift to black disc jockeys and a program format attuned to this community produced a substantial increase in advertising revenues.

Too much money may be spent on the exterior of the building, decor, billboards, or an ineffective advertising program. Expenditures in these areas may attract customers, but they can result in a reduction in the quality of service and merchandise. It would be better to reverse the pattern by giving excellent service and providing, good-quality merchandise, for these are remembered longest and provide the desired customer appeal and following.

> A hotel coffee shop was located in a small town on a major tourist route. The building of an interstate highway on the periphery of the town did not cause a loss of customers. People said, "I have been coming here for 25 years and I enjoy the service and food." Others said, "I have driven an extra 150 miles to get here."

## Channels of Distribution

The nature of your business and the economic characteristics of the industry will partially determine channels of distribution. There are various classes of business, and each has a number of options for marketing its products. Some alternatives you have are:

1. Industrial products:
   a. Direct sales to customers.
   b. Manufacturers' agents.
   c. Distributors (wholesalers-warehouses).
2. Consumer products:
   a. Direct sales

        **(1)** Door to door.
        **(2)** Independent retail outlets.
   **b.** Wholesalers.
   **c.** Chain retail outlets.
   **d.** Your own retail outlets.
        **(1)** Direct ownership.
        **(2)** Franchise.
 **3.** Service (direct to consumer).

### Pricing Policies

Whatever the business, pricing is important. In pricing your goods or service, you should consider all the relevant factors, including costs of production and distribution as well as possible market acceptance, then add an additional percentage to provide a planned profit.

Certain rules of thumb are available for use in determining prices in most businesses. In the restaurant industry, total food costs generally have not exceeded 33 percent of the sales price. More recently, a price based on food costing from 25 to 44 percent is believed to be more realistic.

> A restaurant owner in a college town was not sensitive to the relationship between food cost and price. He was in financial difficulty and sought the aid of the Small Business Administration. A SCORE volunteer was assigned as consultant. His first question was, "What is the most popular item on your menu?" The restaurant owner replied, "Our $2.25 steak." The consultant asked for a scale and a raw steak. He showed the businessman that the raw steak cost $1.85. Obviously, the reason for the steak dinner's popularity was the markup of less than 22 percent for the meat. It was also the reason why the business was in financial difficulties.

In formulating pricing policy, consider the competition's prices but also consider how much impact price has on business volume. Is the quality of the product or service more important to the consumer than price is? What factors are most important in price determination?

## Preparing Budgets

It is now time to pull together all the revenue and cost items for which you have planned. This process is called budgeting.

Budgets should be considered as instruments of both planning and control. They help you plan how to allocate your firm's resources. The main objective is to maximize your revenue, minimize cost, and increase profit. Profit should be included in the total budget. Specific profit figures depend upon many factors, including the type of industry, location, and efficiency.

Concerning management information, you need to ask these two questions:

1. What decisions do I need to make?
2. What information do I need in order to make those decisions?

Answers to these questions should serve as guidelines in preparing your budgets. Some of the items to consider are: expenses, including the cost of the money you will use (remember that money has a cost, whether it is owned or borrowed.), depreciation, obsolescence, utilities, maintenance, supplies, personnel, fringe benefits, insurance, material handling, waste, transportation cost, and start-up cost; revenues, including sales of your product or service, sale of property, and interest on money invested; and the resulting profit—or loss. Records are needed to aid in developing budgets and cost information and to aid in controlling. This is a good time to plan your basic accounting system and records.

### Types of Budgets

The most important budgets for a small firm are:

1. An operating budget.
2. A capital budget.
3. A cash-flow budget.

*Operating Budget.* In preparing the operating budget, try to anticipate the costs of obtaining and selling your products, and the income received from them. This budget serves as a basis for comparing budgeted activities with actual performance and for determining the cause of variances from your plans.

*Capital Budget.* The capital budget reflects plans for obtaining, replacing, and expanding your physical facilities. It assists you in beginning operations and being able to have the needed buildings, tools, equipment, and other facilities.

*Cash-Flow Budget.* The cash-flow budget is a statement of how much cash will be needed to pay what expenses at what time, as well as indicating the sources of cash. The lack of ready cash resources is the primary reason that firms get into an illiquid position, causing a forced liquidation. By using the cash-flow budget, such a situation may be avoided.

## Anticipating Difficulties

At the danger of being alarmists, we should point out that you should look realistically at the possibility of failure and begin to guard against it. In preparing the budget for a new business, you must understand and accept the equity risk and the investment required. Look at the costs involved in acquiring assets, using them, and then having to liquidate the business if it fails. Table 23–1 should help you understand some of these risks.

**Table 23–1**
**The Value of Assets in a Going Concern and in Case of Liquidation**

| Items | Going Concern Value | Failing Business Liquidation Value |
|---|---|---|
| Start-up costs | 0 | 0 |
| Cash drain until breakeven level of operation is attained | 0 | 0 |
| | | Cash 100% |
| Basic working capital investment for a mature level of business (includes cash position adequate to take care of _____ weeks of payroll and operating expenses) | Good value | Accounts receivable depends on quality of debtors or depends on inventory market value (less handling costs) |
| Equity in plant, product, and equipment | Some value | Some value |
| Goodwill and other intangible assets | No value | No value |

## Locating Sources of Funds

After having budgeted the amount of funds needed for capital expenditures and for beginning operations, locate the sources from which you can obtain those funds.

Your ability to raise funds is one of the significant determinants of the size and type of business you can enter. Methods of financing change, and there is no one best method. While some methods have advantages over others, the attitudes and desires of the investors or lenders determine the sources of financing available at a given time. The following discussion should help you find the needed money to begin operations.

### Your Own Funds

Some people believe in using only their personal funds and not borrowing in any business venture. Other people believe that they should use as little of their personal funds as possible, instead obtaining as much leverage as possible by using the funds of others. Assuming that you must, or wish to, use funds of others, several sources of outside funds are available.

### Funds of Other Individuals

You may find other individuals with excess funds who are interested in investing in a venture opportunity. Such a person might be found among friends or through an attorney, CPA, banker, or securities dealer. These people often have a specific preference for the type of business in which they are willing to invest. In general, they prefer a business with which they are familiar.

### Trade Credit

Trade credit refers to the purchases of inventory, equipment, and supplies that are made on an open account in accordance with customary terms for this type of business. This source of credit should not be overlooked.

### Commercial and Industrial Financial Institutions

These institutions may provide you with funds. The proportion of funds such institutions make available may range from 25 to 60 percent of the value of the total assets. Usually, the cost of such financing is higher than that of other alternatives, but such funds may be the most accessible. These institutions may help you through:

1. Loans on your fixed assets.
2. Lease-purchase arrangements.
3. Accounts receivable financing.
4. Factoring arrangements on accounts receivable.

*Commercial Banks.*   In the past, commercial banks have been a good source of credit for business managers having funds of their own and with proven successful experience. More recently, because of the higher rate of return, banks have shifted a greater portion of their funds into consumer financing. The large demand for funds in recent years has pushed interest rates and terms of bank loans to higher levels and less favorable terms.

You should also consider the following services offered by commercial banks:

1. General accounting (demand deposit).
2. Payroll accounting.

3.  Income tax service.
4.  Various computerized services.
5.  Lockbox collections to expedite payments and cash flow.
6.  More individualized services.

**Investment Banks.** Investment banks bring together those who need funds and various sources of funds. Many of them are sound and have developed a reputation for integrity and for providing their clients with good service.

You should choose from investment bankers who specialize in regional business, for they are frequently more familiar with the geographic area and the economics of the region and are accustomed to servicing specialized needs. These investment bankers also maintain relationships with insurance companies, large individual investors, and investment managers of pension trusts.

The availability of an investment banker and the services provided are determined by your:

1.  Present financial requirements.
2.  Market potential.
3.  Projected status for two years in advance.

**Major Nonfinancial Corporation.** Major producing corporations, through their financial subsidiaries, often play a significant role in financing certain types of activities which are closely related to some phase of their operations. For instance:

> General Electric, Westinghouse, and others have been active in helping finance mobile homes and apartments. The mobile home manufacturers install the appliances of a specific supplier, who then helps finance the producer. In addition, the appliance-financing subsidiary often finances the sale of the home to the ultimate consumer.

> The Big Three auto firms operate through their subsidiaries to aid their dealers in financing dealerships, provide a "floor plan" arrangement for financing the dealers' new-car inventories, and finance the sales of cars (including used cars) to customers.

**Insurance Companies.** Insurance companies may be a source of funds for your firm. You can go directly to the company or contact its agent, an investment banker, or a mortgage banker. While insurance companies have traditionally engaged in debt financing, more recently they have demanded that equity purchase warrants be included as a part of the total package.

## Small Business Administration

One of the primary purposes of the SBA is to provide financial assistance.[1] The main difference between the SBA and a private lending agency is the terms of the loan. Though banks may be limited by regulation or law on the terms of their loans, the SBA tends to permit longer periods of repayment and make other concessions to smaller firms. Yet, as far as credit risks are concerned, the SBA has requisites very similar to those of banks. The borrower should be a good credit risk.

The SBA has been limited in its financial activities by the constraints imposed by Congress in allocating funds for loan purposes. The types of loans it can provide to you, and the manner of their utilization, are discussed in the following paragraphs.

*Direct Loans.* Direct loans usually fit into three categories:

1. Ethnic loans—significant interest has been shown in this type of loan, especially loans ranging up to $25,000.
2. Loans to women—up to $20,000.
3. Catastrophe or disaster loans—these loans are made in an area where some form of disaster has struck. Their terms are usually 3 percent interest and an amortization period of 20 years.
4. Small loans—made to business firms needing between $1,500 and $3,000.

Direct loans have been restricted because of the limited supply of funds.

*Participating Loans.* With participating loans, the SBA takes a portion of the total loan on a direct cash participation basis, and a bank or other lender provides the remainder. In this type of loan, the SBA assumes a subordinate position to the other lender in the event of liquidation. Because funds are limited, only a small number of these loans are made.

*Guaranteed Loans.* Guaranteed loans have been the most popular in recent years. The SBA guarantees the lender 90 percent of the loan up to a total of $500,000. The borrower may contact the SBA directly or through a bank whose policy is to make SBA-guaranteed loans. The practice of using the bank as an intermediary seems to produce more satisfactory results.

---

[1]Congress periodically enacts new legislation, and this determines the kind of assistance the Small Business Administration provides. We suggest, therefore, that you contact the nearest district office of the SBA to determine what type of assistance you may be able to obtain from this federal agency.

The SBA is now formalizing programs to help banks resell some of their guaranteed loans. This is creating an active secondary market in the loans guaranteed by the SBA.[2]

*Lease Guaranty Program.* The lease guaranty program was initially established to enable smaller businesses to locate in major shopping centers where a credit rating of AAA is required. Current regulations require:

1. Three months' rent must be placed in escrow at the outset.
2. The amount of lease that may be guaranteed is limited to $2.5 million.
3. A 2.8 percent single insurance premium is required, guaranteeing the total rent of the lease.

### Small Business Investment Corporations (SBICs)

SBICs are chartered by the SBA and make qualified SBA loans. The SBA matches each dollar an SBIC puts into a loan.

Loans are usually made for a period of 5–10 years. The SBIC may stipulate that it be given a certain portion of stock purchase warrants or stock options, or it may make a combination of a loan and a stock purchase. The latter combination has been preferred.

### Industrial Development Corporations

Industrial development corporations have freedom in the types of loans they are able to make. They make "501" or "503" loans.

*501 Loans.* These loans are granted from state-chartered industrial development corporations whose initial capital is provided by member commercial banks that also are members of the Federal Reserve system. These corporations make term loans, working-capital loans, mortgage loans, and contract performance loans, and they can borrow up to one half of the loan amount from the SBA.

*503 Loans.* These loans, made under the Certified Development Company program, are made to facilitate inner-city development, neighborhood revitalization, and so on. The loan procedure parallels that of the 501 loans. Loans are in the form of debenture bonds and are limited to $500,000.

---

[2]"A New Market for SBA Loans," *Business Week*, July 4, 1977, p. 54.

### Economic Development Administration (EDA)

The EDA makes a variety of direct loans to industries located in communities in areas classified as economically depressed or in communities that are declared as regional economic growth centers. This financial assistance usually starts where the SBA authority ends, at $500,000.

The direct loans made by the EDA may be used for fixed assets or working capital. In addition, the EDA may extend guarantees on loans to private borrowers from private lending institutions, as well as guarantees of rental payments of leases (from qualified lessors) for fixed assets.

The agency may lend up to 65 percent of the total cost of the assets for which the loans are made, but the agency prefers to remain in the 50 percent range. A rule of thumb in determining the amount of a loan is from an average of $5,200 to a maximum of $10,000 per employee for each new job the project will create. The rate of interest is reviewed quarterly. While the life of the loan may reach 25 years, the average maturity is 18 years.

It is suggested that you contact your local planning and development commission or chamber of commerce to determine your qualification for EDA financial assistance. Congressional authorization changes from time to time, so you should check to see what types of assistance are available at any given time. Recently, the tendency has been to liberalize the scope of EDA financial assistance.

### State Employment Agencies

Grants may be available through the local state employment agency for use in training and developing employees. Basis for this type of assistance may be the changing nature of work, training of new employees lacking the needed skills, or training employees for a new business for which the needed skills are lacking. Changes occur from time to time in the provisions of the authorizing legislation, and it is suggested that you check with the local state employment agency to determine what kinds of assistance may be available.

### Agricultural Loans

A number of sources of funds for agricultural loans are federally funded. The Cooperative Extension Service, or one of its local agents, may be checked for information concerning availability and procedures. Some sources of funds are:

1. Federal Land Bank Association.

2. Production Credit Corporation.
3. Farm Home Administration.
4. Cooperative Bank-Service Youth Area.

### Proposals for Loans

Two documents that can be of great benefit in obtaining money to begin operations are the miniproposal and the business plan. An example of each of these is shown in the appendix at the end of this chapter.

## Implementing the Plans

Now you are ready to take the plunge! It is time to obtain funds, get a charter, purchase facilities and supplies, hire and train people, and start operating.

### Capital Procurement

Using the capital structure plan and the sources of funds you have developed, obtain the funds, put them in a checking account, and start writing checks to pay for your business purchases.

### Corporate Charter and Permits

You should obtain the services of an attorney in acquiring a charter if you are incorporating. He or she can help obtain occupational licenses and permits.

*Contracting and Purchasing Facilities and Supplies.* After the funds, charter, and permits are obtained, you should refer to your timetable and start negotiating contracts and purchasing equipment, products, and supplies needed to run the business.

*Personnel Selection and Training.* As the time approaches for the beginning of operations, you should refer to your organization chart, job titles, and job specifications in order to determine personnel requirements. Methods of selecting and procuring personnel will be influenced by local conditions. The presence of a community college, liberal arts college, university, or vocational-technical school will influence your decision to use all full-time employees or to use some full-time and some part-time employees. You can receive assistance, in obtaining prospective employees, from institutional placement offices, state employment agencies, and private employment agencies. It may be necessary to use local advertising media to attract prospective employees, but this practice usually increases the amount of time required for screening. To attract capable people, you can emphasize the growth opportunities.

The nature of the business and the background of the newly hired employees will influence the amount of time needed and the methods to be used in employee training.

## Beginning Operations

You are now a business manager. You are operating your own firm, you have all the risks, and you hope to receive the benefits and rewards of being on your own. Some unforeseen problems should be anticipated, however, for they will surely occur during the "crank-up" period.

## Summary

The material in this chapter has outlined the steps to be followed in establishing a new business. By now you should have:

1. Developed and followed a realistic timetable.
2. Established your business goals and objectives.
3. Set up your organization structure, including the legal, financial, and administrative aspects.
4. Estimated, selected, and trained your people.
5. Determined your physical plant and facility needs, and contracted for or purchased them.
6. Planned your marketing activities, including advertising, channels of distribution, and pricing.
7. Prepared budgets.
8. Found sources of funds and obtained the money needed.
9. Secured your charter and the permits needed to begin operating your own business.

# Appendix: An Example of a Mini-proposal and a Business Plan[3]

## Miniproposal

The miniproposal is typically a three- or four-page summary of a business plan sent to potential investors to determine whether there is any interest in the venture. If investors are interested, they will request a complete business plan. Aspects covered in a miniproposal are:

1. Amount of capital required—a dollar range of investments is often preferred by investors.
2. Type of industry—investors often are interested, or uninterested, in certain industries.
3. Nature of the enterprise.
4. Sales and profit projections for three to five years.
5. Management—highlights of careers of each founder.

## Business Plan

A business plan is written by the individual(s) responsible for starting and operating a company. It covers the company objectives and describes the steps necessary to achieve them. It should provide information about the conditions in the industry and outline milestones—for example, completion of product development—against which progress can be determined.

When preparing your business plan, you should consider the information needs of bankers, suppliers, customers, investors, and employees.

Your managers should participate in developing the business plan. This participation should make the plan more salable to them, illustrate their interdependence, and build their commitment. You may desire to obtain the service of others—business consultants, lawyers, CPAs, bankers, stockbrokers, customers, suppliers, and government agencies—to aid in developing a plan.

The important aspects of a business plan are:

1. Brief description of business, including operating history if any.
2. Directors, including names and corporate affiliations.
3. Management team—brief resumes covering qualifications for attaining company objectives.
4. Management compensation and incentives.

---

[3]Donald M. Dible, *Winning the Money Game* (Santa Clara, Calif.: Entrepreneur Press, 1975), pp. 87–110.

5.  Outside professional assistance: attorney, CPA, etc.
6.  Organization chart.
7.  Capital required and its specific uses.
8.  Company's current financial condition.
9.  Major products.
    a.  Detailed description, including photographs and/or drawings.
    b.  Uses.
    c.  Unique characteristics.
    d.  Warranties.
    e.  Profit margins.
    f.  Costs.
    g.  Patent protection.
    h.  Technological advantages.
    i.  Research and development.
    j.  Product liability.
10. Market served:
    a.  Overall market.
    b.  Market studies.
    c.  Ease of entry.
    d.  Overall growth rate.
    e.  Names of potential customers.
    f.  Expectations concerning percentage of market share.
11. Market strategy:
    a.  Market segments.
    b.  Channels of distribution.
    c.  Advertising plan.
    d.  Methods of financing sales.
    e.  Pricing.
    f.  Sales organization.
12. Manufacturing:
    a.  Assembly characteristics.
    b.  Vertical integration.
    c.  Product cost breakdown.
    d.  Tooling cost.
    e.  Special or general-purpose equipment.
    f.  Economies of scale.
    g.  Supplier relationships.
    h.  Availability of raw materials.
13. Appendixes:
    a.  Pro forma projections for three to five years.
    b.  Legal structure of business.
    c.  Founders' resumes and financial statements.
    d.  Founders' compensation.
    e.  Market surveys.

# Chapter Twenty Four

## Planning the Legal and Financial Structure of the Business

Now that you have planned your strategies for the firm, you are about ready to start managing it. You have at least three more important decisions to make, however. First, you must determine what legal form to use for the enterprise. Second, you must decide your financial structure. Third, you must decide how to organize it for effective operations.

The material in this chapter should help you make these important choices. First, though, a word of caution is in order. While we will provide you with a summary of the most important basics in these areas, complete coverage is not feasible—or even desirable. Instead, we recommend that you seek the professional assistance of a lawyer specializing in business and corporate law, and a reputable CPA and/or banker familiar with local business conditions.

### Determining Legal Form

In many independent businesses, too little attention is paid to selecting objectively the legal form that best serves the owner's interests. There seems to be a lack of knowledge relating to the advantages and disadvantages of using the various forms of legal organization. Our intent is to provide you with a better understanding of the legal forms a business may have. The most popular of these legal forms are (1) proprietorship, (2) partnership, (3) corporation, (4) holding company, (5) trust, and (6) cooperative.[1]

### Proprietorship

A proprietorship is an enterprise owned by a single individual. It is the easiest and simplest form of business to organize. Many people prefer this type of organization because of its simplicity and their inherent preference for individual control. It provides for relative freedom of action and control, as well as being simple to enter or to leave. In these respects, you may find it an attractive form to use.

There are at least two negative factors though. First, as you and the business are one and the same, you and it cannot legally be distinguished and separated. Consequently, the legal life of the business terminates with your death; some legal action must be taken to reactivate and reinstate it. Second, you have unlimited liability for the debts of the firm. If the firm does not possess sufficient assets to pay for all of its obligations, you must use your personal assets to pay for them. Conversely, if you have unpaid personal debts, the creditors can use the assets of your business to satisfy their demands.

About four out of five of all businesses in the United States are proprietorships. The proportion is even higher for independent businesses.

### Partnership

A partnership is the joining together of two or more individuals to form an organization. Partnerships are quite popular because of their advantages, but they have many limitations.

*Advantages and Disadvantages.* The major advantages of a partnership are:

1. Pooling of the resources of more than one individual.
2. Specific specialized skills possessed by the individual partners.
3. Division of labor and management responsibility.

Partnerships are more effective than proprietorships in raising financial resources and in obtaining better management.

---

[1]If you wish further information on this subject without seeing a lawyer, refer to Harold F. Lusk, Charles M. Hewitt, John Donnell, and A. James Barnes, *Business Law and the Regulatory Environment: Concepts and Cases,* 5th ed. (Homewood, Ill.: Richard D. Irwin, 1982).

Yet, there are disadvantages inherent in the partnership arrangement, including:

1.  Death of any of the partners terminates the life of the partnership. This may be offset by an agreement that states that the remaining partner(s) will purchase the interest of the deceased partner from his or her estate. Frequently, the partnership itself carries insurance to cover this contingency.
2.  Members of a general partnership, or the general partners in a limited partnership, have unlimited liability for the debts of the firm.
3.  Partners are responsible for the acts of each and every partner.
4.  A partner cannot obtain bonding protection against the acts of the other partner(s).
5.  An impasse may develop if the partners should become incompatible.

Because of this last disadvantage, you should include in your partnership agreement a buy-sell arrangement to provide for the perpetuation of the business. This clause can be activated in the event of one or more of the following:

1.  An impasse develops between the partners in reaching an agreement on an important issue.
2.  One or more of the partners develops other interests and wishes to leave the partnership.
3.  A partner dies.
4.  A conflict of interest develops.

***Types of Partnerships.*** Partnerships may be general or limited. In a general partnership, each partner is held liable for the acts of the other partners. A limited partnership can be created only by compliance with a state's statutory requirements. Such a partnership is composed of one or more general partners and one or more limited partners. The firm is managed by the general partners, who have unlimited personal liability for the partnership's debts. The personal liability of the limited partners is limited to the amount of capital contributed by them.

Limited partners can be employees of the company but cannot participate in any way in its management. Unfortunately, legal decisions are not clear on the extent of advising or reviewing of management decisions that is allowed. Surnames cannot be used in the firm's name, and the limited partnership designation is not required in the firm's name or dealings.

In some states the law applied to limited partnerships permits a corporation to serve as a general partner. This arrangement, in recent years, has facilitated the procurement of capital funds through the sale of limited partnership shares.

*Tests of a Partnership.* It is sometimes difficult to tell whether an enterprise is a proprietorship, partnership, or corporation. There is no simple test for the existence of a partnership, but the major requirements are: the intent of the owners, co-ownership of the business, and carrying the business for a profit. Also, no formalities are required to create a partnership. You may form one and not realize it.

As a general rule, the sharing of profits and having a voice in the management of a business are sufficient evidence to imply the existence of a partnership.

*Rights of the Partners.* If there is no agreement to the contrary, each partner has an equal voice in the management of the business. Also, a majority of the partners has a legal right to make decisions pertaining to the daily operations of the business. All partners, however, must consent to the making of fundamental changes in the structure itself. Each partner's share of the profits is presumed to be his or her only compensation, and in the absence of any other agreement, the profits and losses are distributed equally.

## Corporation

A corporation is sometimes defined as a legal entity, or an artificial being, whose life exists at the pleasure of the courts of law. The formation of a corporation is more formal and complex than is required for the other legal forms. The minimum number of persons required as stockholders varies with individual state laws. Commonly, the number varies from three to five, and in many cases two of these may be "dummies" who serve as incorporators in name only and remain inactive as far as the activities of the firm are concerned. The procedure for formation is usually legally defined and requires the services of an attorney. Incorporation fees frequently amount to $300 to $1,000.

*Advantages and Disadvantages.* The primary advantages the corporate form offers you as an investor are:

1. It is a legal entity separate and distinct from you as an individual.
2. It offers permanence. If one of the owners dies, the shares can be transferred to others without affecting the legal life of the firm.
3. Your liability for the firm's debts is limited to the amount you invest in its stock. Your private resources cannot be touched.
4. You can have representative management.
5. Large amounts of capital can be raised relatively easily. (Some authorities would question the validity of this statement.)

Some offsetting disadvantages that might keep you from using this form of structure are:

1. Taxes and fees are high.
2. The procedures, reports, and statements required become cumbersome and burdensome.
3. Your powers are limited to those stated in the charter.
4. You may have difficulty doing business in another state.
5. The other stockholders may not be interested in the firm.
6. It tends to be a more impersonal form of business.

Because of the limited liability feature, the corporate form is considered superior to all other forms of organization.

**Other Considerations.** During the period when you and others are forming a corporation, but before incorporation is completed, a signed preincorporation agreement should be used to protect against any member or members of the group taking off on their own with the proprietary basis for establishing the organization. It at least provides you the restitution of damages that may be incurred.

In order to protect the parties involved, a buy-sell arrangement for the major stockholders should be included in the articles of incorporation. Also, if the success of the venture is dependent on your or certain other individuals' participation in the firm, key-person insurance should be carried on those persons. This type of insurance protects the resources of the firm in the event of loss of such a person and provides protection during the period of adjustment that follows.

Adequate bond and insurance coverage against losses that result from the acts of employees and others should be maintained. Also, liability and workers' compensation insurance coverage should be maintained.

**Subchapter S Corporation.** In addition to limited liability, corporations with 35* or fewer shareholders can reduce, under certain circumstances, the burden of taxes and their associated administrative expenses. A Subchapter S corporation is primarily established to eliminate multiple taxation of income and its attendant paperwork. It does not process certain taxes. For example, regular corporations must deduct social security taxes on income to the owner and pay the employer's share of the taxes. If an owner receives an outside salary above the maximum from which social security taxes are deducted, the Subchapter S corporation does not deduct or pay social security taxes on the owner's income.

---

*Husband and wife may count as one shareholder. This enables you to have 70 shareholders.

Also, income taxes are paid by the owners, as individuals, on income of the corporation. The payment process is similar to that of a partnership. The corporations must file a Subchapter S income tax return.

**Board of Directors.** Most states' incorporation statutes require that the stockholders elect a board of directors to represent their interests. Several important functions of a board are:

1. Appointing the company president and influencing the selection of other company officers, such as vice president, secretary, and treasurer.
2. Meeting regularly with the officers to review the company progress.
3. Assisting in the formulation of policy.
4. Establishing salaries of company officers.
5. Providing for management succession in the company.
6. Offering good management counseling services during board meetings and in private consultations outside the meetings.
7. Effecting changes in the management of the company.[2]

Company officers are responsible to the board of directors for day-to-day operatons.

Board members are often centers of influence and can assist in increasing company sales. The number of directors should be odd to ensure that a majority will exist when votes are taken on key decisions (as long as every member votes). The minimum number of directors specified in many statutes is five.

Sources of effective directors are diverse. Among the possibilities are: (1) experienced business people, (2) investors, (3) college professors representing disciplines relevant to the company's operations, (4) retired bankers and other professionals, such as attorneys, CPAs, or business consultants. The value of this group of professionals on the board is debatable. Their advice may be valuable. On the other hand, if company officers decide that their services are unsatisfactory, the problem of replacement can be troublesome.

Board members are generally compensated for their services by fixed payments for each meeting they attend.

Difficulties are experienced in obtaining outsiders to serve on the boards of small companies because liability suits may be filed against them by disgruntled stockholders, employees, customers, or suppliers.

---

[2]Donald M. Dible, *Up Your Own Organization!* (Santa Clara, Calif.: Enterpreneur Press, 1971), pp. 140–44.

## Holding Company

As your firm grows larger or you wish to expand your activities while conserving your own resources, you might consider it desirable to establish a parent corporation to serve as a holding company for your corporation. Under certain conditions, you may gain tax advantages from this arrangement. Furthermore, the assets of the parent company may be protected by limiting the liability.

## Trust

For estate and other reasons identified under the tax laws, the trust arrangement establishes a method of providing the owner of a business with certain tax advantages. A popular one in recent years has been the real estate investment trust, which gives certain income tax advantages to individuals in higher tax brackets.

A trust differs from a corporation in that it is established for a specific period of time—or until certain designated events have occurred. It is administered by a trustee or a board of trustees. The trust receives specific assets from the person or persons establishing it. The trust convenant defines the purpose of the trust, names the beneficiary or beneficiaries, and establishes a formula for the distribution of income and trust assets.

# Determining Financial Structure

The nature of the legal structure you choose for the firm will have a direct relationship with the nature of its financial structure. It should be emphasized that the methods of financing a business are varied, although certain patterns do seem to occur more frequently than others. Innovations that work are commonplace. In the material that follows, we attempt to discuss the more popular financial practices and structures.

## Proprietorship

Frequently, we think of the proprietorship as being financed from the personal funds of the proprietor. In many instances, however, only a small portion of the funds required is financed from personal sources. A bank loan, a loan from an individual, a loan from or guaranteed by a government agency, or a loan from a business may be obtained. The amount and percentage of money for a loan to a proprietor are determined by:

1. The "track record" of the individual proprietor—that is, a record of past performance.

2. The nature of the business venture itself, including the amount of fixed assets, size of inventory, the rate of inventory turnover, market potential, profit potential, and so forth.
3. The amount and quality of personal assets pledged for a loan by the proprietor.

## Partnership

In starting a partnership, one of the factors to be considered in selecting your partners is whether the individuals possess adequate financial resources to contribute. The capital contribution made by each partner goes into the paid-in capital account. Occasionally, one or more of the partners may make the partnership a loan after the business has started operating. In such instances, the loan will be evidenced by a note. The loan may be secured by fixed assets of the partnership or unsecured—that is, issued against the general credit of the partnership.

In some instances, additional funds may be obtained from outside sources such as banks, individuals, government agencies, and other businesses. Usually, this type of financing takes the form of short or intermediate-term loans.

## Limited Partnership

In recent times, one of the more popular forms of financial organizations has been the limited partnership, whose general partner is a corporation. The following example reveals how this arrangement may operate:

> Two friends wished to establish an existing "right-of-way clearing"[3] and "wire-stringing"[4] service company. They personally were only able to raise $200,000 toward a company whose capital requirement was $2 million plus. The project involved the purchase of existing firms with proven income records and a consistent track record of profitability. The attractiveness of the venture was facilitated by recent changes in the tax laws that made possible a rapid rate of depreciation of capital equipment. The fact that the operation involved the use of a sizable amount of capital equipment made the venture an interesting tax shelter for limited-partnership investors. The two principals capitalized their participation with a corporation that would act as the general partner.

---

[3]An operation that removes the vegetation growth from existing utilities' rights-of-way.

[4]An organization that erects and installs electrical transmission and distribution systems on a contractual basis for electrical utilities.

Before the organization could be completed, it was necessary to procure the service of an attorney and that of a certified public accountant to prepare the appropriate documents. These documents were necessary to satisfy the legal requirements involved in marketing the limited partnership shares. The marketing of the "limited partnership shares" was accomplished with the services of a regional investment banker.

A deterrent to this limited partnership arrangement is the amount of fees that must be paid to the lawyer and accountant for the preparation of the supportive documents. The inexperienced person finds it difficult to comprehend the amount of these fees or why it is necessary to have these documents prepared. For the independent business, this method (limited partnership whose general partner is a corporation) is one of the easier ways to raise capital. However, the fruition of this form of legal organizational structure and the marketing of the limited partnerships is dependent on the use of legal, accounting, and financial professionals.

## Corporation

In establishing a new business, the amount of equity capital required of the initial stockholders usually ranges from 40 to 100 percent. The amount is dependent upon such factors as the nature of the venture, abilities and past performance of the management group, kind of assets involved, and market potential.

*Equities.* Equity is the owners' share of the assets of a company. It is represented by stock, mainly common, and retained or undistributed earnings. Holders of common stock have voting power but are subordinate to nonvoting stock in receiving dividends and assets. Class B common and preferred stock are nonvoting (unless otherwise stated).

*Debt.* Financing a corporation, in addition to equity, is obtained from loans, as discussed for other legal forms of firms. Long-term loans can be obtained from the use of several types of bonds. Bonds can be secured by assets of a company (mortgage bonds) or based on its earning power (debentures).

Favorite financing instruments are the convertible debenture and, more recently, warrants which can be converted from debt into equity according to stated terms. These instruments receive fixed incomes until converted, which makes them attractive. The volume of debt (whether debentures, warrants, or mortgage bonds) is usually about 25–50 percent of the total capital structure.

*Other Considerations.* Under certain conditions, it may be advantageous for the incorporating investors to invest a portion of their funds in equity securities and the remainder in debt, because of tax advantages and a more favorable priority position in case the firm liquidates.

Sometimes, subordinated instruments such as second mortgages, junior notes, or bonds are used.

Preferred stock, which pays a stated dividend before the common stockholders receive any returns, may be desirable even though it tends to restrict the flexibility of the capital structure.

Warrants, as mentioned above, may be used or required by certain investors as part of the financial package. Examples of investors demanding these are SBICs (Small Business Investment Companies) and insurance companies.

Industrial revenue bonds provide a low-cost means of acquiring funds. They are available as inducements for business to locate in an industrial park, community, or region.

The use of debt in financing enables you to obtain leverage upon your equity investment; in other words, by using debt, you are able to expand your income relative to your equity—assuming that the firm's rate of income is greater than the interest it pays.

You should be careful that the indenture provisions of debt instruments are not so restrictive as to place undue limitations on actions.

*Section 1244 Stock.* Your corporation may be made more attractive to investors if you comply with the statutory concept of a small business corporation as defined in Section 1244 of the Small Business Tax Revision Act of 1958. For this to happen, (1) the total amount of stock offered under the plan, plus other contributions to capital and paid-in surplus, may not exceed $500,000; and (2) the total amount of the stock that may be offered, plus the equity capital of the corporation, must be less than $1 million.

Section 1244 stock is common stock (voting or nonvoting) in a domestic corporation. Losses on the sale, exchange, or worthlessness of this stock are treated as ordinary losses rather than capital losses sustained by an individual. Other provisions can provide considerable tax advantages, but stock issues are restricted to certain types of transactions and stock cannot be transferred.

## Summary

We have tried to show you how to set up your legal and financial structure. The usual progression is to determine what legal form you desire (or must have) for your business and to decide the source of your funds and your capital structure.

# Chapter Twenty-Five

## Planning the Administrative Structure of the Business

You must set up an administrative structure in order to run a business most effectively.

Organizing involves deciding what activities are necessary to attain your firm's objectives, dividing them into groups, and assigning each group to a manager possessing the necessary authority and expertise to carry out the activities properly. A major problem with many independent business managers is that they do not organize their activities properly. The material in this chapter, by helping you organize your firm better, should help you be more successful.

### Organizational Principles and Practices

An important principle of organization that you should follow is unity of command. Under this principle, each employee should have only one superior to whom he or she is directly responsible for certain matters. When subordinates must report to two bosses concerning the same assignment, they may become frustrated if they receive conflicting instructions from the two supervisors.

In assigning work to your subordinates, you should try to arrange for authority to be coequal with responsibility, although this is not always possible. Sometimes—in the short run—your managers must assume responsibilities greater than their authority.

However, try to give your subordinates sufficient authority to carry out their responsibilities. Otherwise, they lack the means of performing their duties. On the other hand, avoid delegating to your subordinates greater authority than they need to fulfill their responsibilities, or they may use that authority unwisely and encroach upon the decision-making power of someone else.

Delegating means placing responsibility and letting others take care of the details. It is perhaps the hardest thing owner-managers have to learn. Some never do; others pay lip service to the idea, but actually run everything themselves.

A written statement of duties, responsibilities, authority, and relationships should be provided for each employee. Inform each of them as to the limits of what they can and cannot—or should not—do. Remember, though, that if you delegate authority for certain duties, you relinquish the responsibility for how those duties are performed. Yet, you cannot relinquish responsibility for performance.

The owner-manager of a small factory established three departments—a production department, a sales department, and an administrative department—and appointed a manager for each. He specified the following responsibilities:

1. The production manager was responsible for manufacturing, packing, and shipping.
2. The sales manager was responsible for advertising, customer solicitation, and customer service.
3. The administrative manager was responsible for personnel, purchasing, and accounting.
4. The production manager also was designated assistant general manager and delegated authority to make all operational decisions in the owner's absence.

The owner gave each manager a detailed statement of the function of his department and the extent of his authority. Actions that the managers could take on their own initiative and actions that required approval by the owner-manager were enumerated.

Each department manager was instructed to designate and train an assistant who could manage the department when the need arose.

The owner coordinated the departments. The sales manager and production manager set customer delivery dates together.

Control was exercised by holding subordinates responsible for their actions and checking the results of those actions. The owner neither "breathed down his managers' necks," nor lost control of things. He relied upon reports and periodic staff meetings.

The owner kept his subordinates informed so that they would have the facts they needed for making their decisions. He tried to communicate effectively with them. He explained the "why" of his instructions.

His managers were given freedom to do things their way and he did not evaluate them upon whether they did a particular task exactly as he would have done it. He judged them by their results—not their methods.

If managers deviated too much from policy, the owner brought them back into line. He avoided second-guessing his managers. If subordinates did not run their department to the owner's satisfaction and if shortcomings could not be overcome, the owner replaced the managers.[1]

Another principle you should follow is that decisions are best made by the person closest to the spot. Also, authority should be exercised by a single person, usually the one responsible for performing the task. Time should not be wasted in unnecessary consultation and cross-checking before acting.

You should watch carefully the span of control of each supervisor or manager. By this span we mean the number of subordinates reporting to one superior. First-line supervisors may have 10, 15, 25, 30, or more employees reporting to them because of the similarity of their work. On the other hand, middle managers may have 5, 8, or 10 supervisors for whom they are responsible because of the diversity of their work. You should be especially careful of how many managers are reporting to you personally. If the number becomes too large, operations of your business could be severely hampered.

Division of labor, or specialization, should be used wherever feasible, as it leads to increased expertise.

## Forms of Organization, by Types of Authority

You should be familiar with the forms of organization, according to types of authority:

1. Line.
2. Line and staff.
3. Informal.

Your company may start with few people and such a variety of tasks that no one can specialize in one task. Almost everyone is engaged in some of the activities of producing the product or services of the firm. You have a direct line of command over producing and selling. This is a line organization.

As the firm grows, all employees become more specialized. Some specialists advise and perform services for those engaged in

---

[1]Stanley Wantola, "Delegating Work and Responsibility," *Management Aids for Small Manufacturers No. 191* (Washington, D.C.: Small Business Administration, 1972).

producing or purchasing and selling. Examples of these staff people are accountants, stockers, secretaries, and schedulers. This type of organization is called line and staff.

An informal organization will always exist within the formal structure of your business. This organization consists of many interpersonal relations that arise as a result of friendships that develop on and off the job. Two examples are the informal-leader and grapevine communication systems. You should determine who the informal leaders are, obtain their support for your programs, and encourage them to "sell" your programs to the rest of your employees.

## Ways of Organizing a Firm

With respect to a company's formal organization structure, you may choose to group the activities into manageable units by:

1. Function—like skills are grouped together to form an organizational unit such as production or marketing. The lowest level of the organization should probably be structured on this basis.
2. Product—production or sales activities may be grouped by product, such as menswear, ladieswear, and so forth.
3. Process—smaller companies often base their organizations upon manufacturing processes, such as welding and painting.
4. Geographic area—if your company requires a strong, local marketing effort, organizing the sales force by areas or territories can be appropriate.
5. Type of customers—a firm's customers may be classified as industrial, commercial, or another designation.
6. Project—to illustrate, a construction firm may be building on two projects, a store and an apartment complex. Each project needs management and workers.
7. Individual abilities of subordinates—you may assign work to people according to their particular talents. However, a limitation is that the organization structure tends to change whenever a key employee is replaced.

## Preparing an Organization Chart

You should recognize that there is no magical organizational structure, no one right organization. Instead, we recommend using whatever structure seems to make sense to you in your situation. The test is: Does it work at an acceptable cost? The people, not the form, should be concentrated on, because they are the key factor. While there is truth in these observations, the following discussion is also relevant.

You should set up a series of authority and responsibility relationships expressed in a formal organization chart. Even if you have a one-person business, a chart can be useful as a reminder of how your time might be most effectively utilized.

You may select a traditional, formal organization structure that may be described as a triangular pyramid (see Figure 25–1). This relationship provides for a tight and narrow span of control. It requires centralization of authority and detailed supervision.

**Figure 25–1**

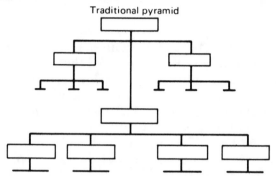

Traditional pyramid

On the other hand, you may select the flatter, broader span of control shown in Figure 25–2. If so, you will provide your subordinates with less centralized authority and less detailed supervision. A chart should not only be a useful tool for the present but also be an aid in planning for the future development of your organization and in projecting personnel requirements.

A list of job titles and job specifications should accompany the chart. Job specifications spell out the duties, responsibilities, and working conditions of the work assignment and the qualifications necessary to fulfill the jobs acceptably.

If you (or you and a partner) have an independent, unincorporated company, no one may have the title of president or any other management title. Instead, the organization structure might be similar to that shown in Figure 25–3. In fact, a tight, formal organizational structure should not be imposed, because it could stifle creativity and reduce initiative.

**Figure 25–2**

Flatter and broader

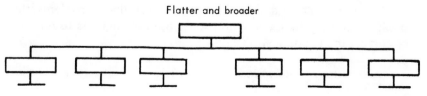

*Figure 25–3*
**Organization for a Small Manufacturing Firm**

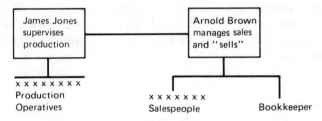

As the firm grows beyond a certain size, you will probably find that some specialized skills are required that you do not possess. You should first attempt to obtain outside part-time assistance to aid, say, the sales manager (who may lack advertising expertise) or the plant manager (who may lack industrial engineering training). You may also decide that you cannot manage the detailed operations any longer because the size and complexity of your operations are increasing too rapidly. Now seek people, preferably in your company, to designate as managers. Figure 25–4 portrays an organization in which several managers have been appointed to handle specialized functions.

*Figure 25–4*
**Organization Structure of a Small Manufacturing Firm**

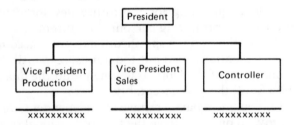

## Some Organizational Problems

If they exist in a company, organizational problems are the first, or at least among the first, types of problems that should be solved. To help you detect organizational problems—and to correct them— see Table 25–1. This table describes the symptoms of problems, the possible underlying causes, and some possible actions to remove or correct the problems.[2]

---

[2]Robert G. Murdick, et al., *Business Policy: A Framework for Analysis* (Columbus, Ohio: Grid, 1972).

**Table 25–1**
**Small Business Organizational Problems**

| Symptoms | Possible Problems | Needed Action |
|---|---|---|
| 1. Company seems to be drifting aimlessly or trying to go in several different directions. | The organization lacks an effective plan. | The board of directors should recognize these symptoms and formulate plans for one-three years. |
| 2. Conflicts occur among managers and key personnel. Confusion arises about current objectives and operations. | The manager is not working closely and personally with subordinates to develop unified objectives and a team approach. | Daily conferences should be held between the manager and the staff to build a working organization. |
| 3. When the manager is not available, the organization is paralyzed. | The manager may believe no one else can make a decision. | The manager should delegate authority. A committee of the more capable employees may suggest to the manager that they be given more responsibility in decison making. |
| 4. Supervisors make decisions that are reversed by the manager. | The manager has not developed a consistent set of policies. | Some policies and procedures should be put into writing to cover the major repetitive actions and areas of decision making. |
| 5. One activity, such as sales or production, cannot keep abreast of its work. | The manager is incompetent. Personality problems are present. | An immediate objective study is needed. A manager who cannot determine the cause of the problem should obtain a business consultant to study the situation and make recommendations. |
| 6. Administrative costs have grown more rapidly than sales. | Big-company organization structure is being imposed upon the small company. | The number of managers should be reduced and the remaining managers' responsibilities broadened. |

One of the most common weaknesses in the management of smaller businesses is that the owner is a "one-person show," doing everything and delegating nothing, and his or her people fail to develop.

An independent retailer was a jack-of-all-trades. He did all jobs in the store as the need arose. He assigned tasks to his employees on a random, unspecialized basis, and did not set up distinct functions or an organization structure.

*Problem:* Many organizational deficiencies existed.

*Solution:* The retailer introduced specialization of tasks and of people. Simple, repetitive routines were introduced. Each employee specialized in performing a major function and handling a certain grouping of merchandise.

The store was organized around the functions of merchandising, selling and adjustments, sales promotion, accounting and finance, store operations, merchandise handling, and personnel. Certain functions were combined and delegated to a specific employee.[3]

In some companies, organization structure tends to be loose for the first years of operations. The members of the management team apply their skills to the many jobs that are done. For example, one management member is concerned with overall internal and production management and mechanical engineering. Another deals with marketing, product development, company image, and systems engineering. A third member may interact with a certain type of customer. A fourth member may be the chief electronics engineer. Considerable overlap often exists between the functions of the management members; for example, the internal manager may sell equipment and develop new product ideas.[4]

## Summary

We have tried to show you how to set up your organizational administrative structure. We hope you have learned enough from this presentation to know when to call in an outside expert and to know what questions to ask when you do.

## Where to Look for Further Information

Barker, Phyllis A. "Budgeting in a Small Service Firm." *Small Marketers Aids No. 146.* Washington, D.C.: Small Business Administration, 1971.

Cornwell, Arthur W. "Sales Potential and Market Share." *Small Marketers Aids No. 112.* Washington, D.C.: Small Business Administration, 1972.

Golde, Roger A. "Breaking the Barriers to Small Business Planning." *Management Aids for Small Manufacturers No. 179.* Washington, D.C.: Small Business Administration, 1972, p. 2.

---

[3]Adapted from John W. Wingate and Seymour Helfort, *Small Store Planning for Growth* (Washington, D.C.: Small Business Administration, 1966), pp. 27–28.

[4]Jeffrey A. Timmons, Leonard F. Smollen, and Alexander L. M. Dingee, Jr., *New Venture Creation: A Guide to Small Business Development* (Homewood, Ill.: Richard D. Irwin, 1977), p. 508.

Sommer, Howard E. "How to Analyze Your Own Business." *Management Aids for Small Manufacturers No. 46.* Washington, D.C.: Small Business Administration, 1973.

Wantola, Stanley. "Delegating Work and Responsibility." *Management Aids for Small Manufacturers No. 191.* Washington, D.C.: Small Business Administration, 1972.

# EXHIBITS

*Exhibit 25–1*
## Developing Your Timetable

This questionnaire/form is intended to assist you in developing a plan for establishing your business in an orderly, rational manner, i.e., "What to do," "When to do it," and "Where to do it." This should enable you to move from the inception of the idea to the point at which you begin operation.

1. Definition of the business that seems best for me:

   _____
   _____
   _____
   _____
   _____

2. Dates for starting and completing the Economic Feasibility Study for the business:
   _____ to _____

3. Date for completing the legal organization of the business: _____

4. Date for determining the financial requirements for the business: _____

5. Date for completing the financial plan for the business: _____

6. Date for completing the financial arrangement for the business: _____

7. Date for completing the location requirements for the business: _____

8. Date for acquiring the location:
   a. Rent (lease) facilities: _____

   b. Purchase land or land and building: _____
   c. Contract for construction of building, driveways, parking, etc.: _____

9. Date for completing plans for equipment requirements: _____

10. Date for purchasing equipment: _____

11. Date for completing plans for organization structure (chart) and personnel requirements: _____

12. Date when location will be available for occupancy:
    _____

13. Date for receiving equipment and beginning installation: _____

14. Date for completion of equipment installation: _____

15. Date for completion of plans for inventory requirements (material, parts, supplies, etc.): _____

16. Date for acquiring inventory: _____

17. Date for decision on firm name: _____

18. Date for hiring personnel: _____

19. Date for personnel to begin work: _____

20. Date for receiving and placing inventory: _____

21. Date for completing plans for advertising campaign: _____

22. Date for launching advertising programs: _____

23. Date to obtain necessary business licenses and permits: _____

24. Date to begin business operation: _____

## Exhibit 25–2
## Locating Your Firm

Picking a good location of a plant or store can be very important to a company. This questionnaire is divided into area and site location analysis. Many of the figures and rankings will need to be your best estimates to avoid excessive time consumption. However, as you proceed through the checklist, be careful so that you select the best site and avoid a poor site.

### General

1. Have you made a location analysis for:
   a. Your present site?                          ☐Yes ☐No
      If no, you might use the simple "Rating Sheet on Sites," Worksheet 1, for your present location.
   b. For moving or expanding to a new site?
                                                   ☐Yes ☐No
   c. Your new business?                           ☐Yes ☐No
2. If you need more building (expansion), have you considered:
   a. Using space more efficiently?               ☐Yes ☐No
      Renovating?                                  ☐Yes ☐No

   b. Adding more space:
      (1) On the same floor?                       ☐Yes ☐No
      (2) By adding a floor?                       ☐Yes ☐No
   c. Moving selected operations to a new location and leaving others at the old location?
                                                   ☐Yes ☐No

      For example, have you considered:
      (1) Renting warehouse space?                 ☐Yes ☐No
      (2) Moving early operations nearer materials sources?                                 ☐Yes ☐No
      (3) Making office space convenient to customers?                                  ☐Yes ☐No
   d. Moving the entire company to a new location?
                                                   ☐Yes ☐No
3. Do you have a special feature in mind which will determine your company location, such as having it near your home?                              ☐Yes ☐No
   Have you exaggerated the importance of this feature so that it limits your opportunities?     ☐Yes ☐No
4. To obtain a basis for comparing locations, estimate items using the chart shown below.

| Item | Year | | | |
|---|---|---|---|---|
| | First | Second | Fifth | Tenth |
| Volume of sales ($) | | | | |
| Number of employees—total number with scarce skills | | | | |
| Volume of purchases ($) | | | | |
| Space needed (square feet) Plant or store | | | | |
| Expansion | | | | |
| Parking and drives | | | | |
| Other | | | | |
| Total acreage needed | | | | |
| Type of transportation needed | | | | |
| | | | | |
| | | | | |
| | | | | |
| Special ecological factors | | | | |
| | | | | |
| | | | | |
| Other | | | | |
| | | | | |

5. Have you talked to people in or received literature from:
   a. State industrial development departments?
                                                   ☐Yes ☐No

   b. Chambers of commerce?                        ☐Yes ☐No
   c. Utility companies, banks, etc.?              ☐Yes ☐No
   d. Location specialist firms?                   ☐Yes ☐No
   e. Friends?                                     ☐Yes ☐No

*Exhibit 25–3*
## Making a Franchisor Selection Analysis

Subject Company:_____

**Time**

1. How long before I can obtain a franchise? _____
2. After obtaining a franchise, how long will it be before I will be open for business? _____

    Some of the better franchises have a lengthy waiting period before a franchise is available; that is, the demand for their franchises is so great that the waiting line may be closed in some areas and lengthy in open areas. It should not deter you when you are told that you may have to wait two years. There may be locations that will enable you to jump the waiting order.

**Requirements for obtaining franchise**

3. Economic requirements
   a. Initial cost of franchise license    $_____
   b. Minimal facility cost    $_____
   c. Working capital requirement    $_____
   d. Total investment required    $_____
   e. Percent of equity required at outset $_____
   f. Debt amortization period in years    _____
   g. Financial assistance provided by franchisor?
             □ Yes □ No
      Percentage of total cost?    _____%
   h. Debt service cost (annual rate)    _____%
   i. Does debt contract provide for a penalty for pre-payment?    □ Yes □ No
      How much?    _____
   j. Will franchisor own building, equipment, and land?    □ Yes □ No
   k. Does the franchisor retain the right to purchase the franchise from the franchisee?    □ Yes □ No
      If yes, describe the arrangement briefly.

   _____
   _____
   _____
   _____
   _____

4. Service provided at outset by franchisor:
   a. Financial assistance?    □ Yes □ No
   b. Site location?    □ Yes □ No
   c. Architectural assistance?    □ Yes □ No
   d. Real estate procurement?    □ Yes □ No
   e. Franchisor-owned facility?    □ Yes □ No
   f. Lease-purchase?    □ Yes □ No
   g. Turnkey job?    □ Yes □ No
   h. Other services:

   _____
   _____
   _____

5. Criteria for selecting franchisee:
   a. Age:
      (1) Minimum    _____
      (2) Preferred age range   _____ to _____
      (3) Maximum    _____
   b. Education:
      (1) Minimum education required:
         □ Grade school
         □ High school 2 years
         □ High school 4 years
         □ College 2 years
         □ College 3 years
         □ College 4 years
      (2) Desired education:
         □ High school
         □ Technical school
         □ College 2 years
         □ College 4 years
         Degree: _____
         Comments: _____
         _____
         _____
   c. Marital status desired: _____
      _____
      _____
   d. Economic status preferred:
      (1) Cash/bank deposits/near cash $_____
      (2) Other investments    $_____
          Total net worth    $_____
      (3) Line of credit available at bank   $_____
   e. Indicate type of work experience franchisor prefers of its franchisees:

   _____
   _____
   _____
   _____
   _____
   _____
   _____
   _____
   _____

## Exhibit 25–3 *(continued)*

**Services provided by franchisor**

6. Buyer advantage:
   a. Sources of supply:
      (1) In-house (franchisor)?             ☐ Yes ☐ No
      (2) Does the franchisor have contracts with out-
          side suppliers to service needs of the fran-
          chisee?                            ☐ Yes ☐ No
      (3) Does the franchisor become involved with the
          franchisee's sources of supply?   ☐ Yes ☐ No
      (4) Explain the justification for depending on the
          franchisor for supply assistance.

          Economic: _____

          _____

          _____

          _____

          Quality:_____

          _____

          _____

          _____

      Difficulty in locating reliable sources of supply:
      _____

      _____

      _____

      _____

   b. Nature of contracts with supply sources.
      Explain: _____

      _____

      _____

      _____

      What items? _____

      _____

      _____

   c. Company logo?                          ☐ Yes ☐ No
   d. Parent organization managerial style?
                                             ☐ Yes ☐ No
   e. Franchisee supervision:
      (1) More centralized control?          ☐ Yes ☐ No
      (2) Less centralized control?          ☐ Yes ☐ No
   f. Management information systems:
      (1) More centralized?                  ☐ Yes ☐ No
      (2) Less centralized?                  ☐ Yes ☐ No
   g. Audit and inspection procedures?       ☐ Yes ☐ No
      Describe: _____

      _____

      _____

   h. Change in menu/parts/service offerings:
      (1) Expand number of items?            ☐ Yes ☐ No
      (2) Reduce number of items?            ☐ Yes ☐ No

      (3) Method in preparation?             ☐ Yes ☐ No
      How? _____

      _____

      _____

   i. Service system?                        ☐ Yes ☐ No
   j. Quality of product/service?            ☐ Yes ☐ No
   k. Kind of support service by franchisor?

      _____

      _____

   l. Management assistance?                 ☐ Yes ☐ No
      How? _____

      _____

      What? _____

      _____

   m. Buying assistance?                     ☐ Yes ☐ No

7. Advertising program offered by the franchisor:
   a. National?                              ☐ Yes ☐ No
   b. Regional?                              ☐ Yes ☐ No
   c. Local?                                 ☐ Yes ☐ No

8. Does the franchise provide a special advantage in the
   marketplace?                             ☐ Yes ☐ No
   What is it?_____

   _____

   _____

9. Management assistance:
   a. Technical assistance?                  ☐ Yes ☐ No
      What? _____

      _____

      _____

   b. Operation audit?                       ☐ Yes ☐ No
      How often?_____
   c. Market research?                       ☐ Yes ☐ No
      Describe: _____

      _____

      _____

      _____

      _____

      _____

      _____

   Frequency:
      ☐ Continuous?
      ☐ 3 months?
      ☐ 4 months?
      ☐ 6 months?
      ☐ 9 months?
      ☐ 12 months?
      ☐ Other? (specify) _____

      _____

## Exhibit 25–3 (continued)

d.  Performance evaluation?          ☐ Yes ☐ No
    Frequency:
        ☐ Monthly?
        ☐ 3 months?
        ☐ 4 months?
        ☐ 6 months?
        ☐ 9 months?
        ☐ 12 months?
        Other _____

Summarize what takes place in a performance
evaluation: _____
_____
_____
_____
_____
_____

e.  Nature of feedback from performance evaluation:
    (1) Graded response?          ☐ Yes ☐ No
    (2) Composite performance data comparison?
                                  ☐ Yes ☐ No
    (3) Suggested changes?        ☐ Yes ☐ No
    (4) Other comments:  _____
f.  Availability of management consultant service:
    (1) By request of franchisee?    ☐ Yes ☐ No
    (2) By request of franchisor?    ☐ Yes ☐ No
g.  Cost of management consultant service:
    (1) Covered by franchise fee?    ☐ Yes ☐ No
    (2) Shared by franchisor and franchisee?
                                  ☐ Yes ☐ No
    (3) Charged to franchisee by franchisor?
                                  ☐ Yes ☐ No
        ☐ Flat fee.
        ☐ Fee based on time spent by consultant.
g.  General statement concerning services provided
    by franchisor:_____
_____
_____
_____
_____
_____
_____
_____
_____
_____

**Future plans of the franchisor**

10. Status of company-owned units:
    a.  Increase in ownership:
        (1) New units?               ☐ Yes ☐ No
                                _____ % increase
        (2) Old units?               ☐ Yes ☐ No
                                _____ % increase
    b.  Decrease in ownership:
        (1) New units?               ☐ Yes ☐ No
                                _____ % decrease
        (2) Old units?               ☐ Yes ☐ No
                                _____ % decrease

11. Status of franchisee-owned units:
    a.  Increase in ownership:
        (1) New units?               ☐ Yes ☐ No
                                _____ % increase
        (2) Old units?               ☐ Yes ☐ No
                                _____ % increase
    b.  Decrease in ownership:
        (1) New units?               ☐ Yes ☐ No
                                _____ % decrease
        (2) Old units?               ☐ Yes ☐ No
                                _____ % decrease

12. Change in unit characteristics:
    a.  Expand size of units?        ☐ Yes ☐ No
                                _____ % increase
    b.  Eliminate small units?       ☐ Yes ☐ No
        Rate/year?              _____
    c.  Expand services and facilities?  ☐ Yes ☐ No
        Explain:
        _____
        _____
        _____
        _____
        _____
        _____
        _____

    d.  Establish classes of unit structures? ☐ Yes ☐ No
        Nature of structures:
        _____
        _____

13. Indicate planned changes:
    a.  Target markets?              ☐ Yes ☐ No
        Identify: _____
        _____
    b.  Identifying architectural design?  ☐ Yes ☐ No
        Why? _____
        _____

*Exhibit 25–3 (concluded)*

**What happens if this franchise is not successful?**

14. If this franchise does not prove successful, what will happen to the franchise facility?

_____
_____
_____
_____

15. What will happen to my investment?

_____
_____
_____
_____

16. What uses have been made of unsuccessful franchise properties?

_____
_____
_____
_____
_____
_____

17. Will I have the discretion to use the property as I choose?  ☐ Yes ☐ No

**In success, what may I anticipate?**

18. What kind of income may I reasonably expect from the franchise?

FIRST YEAR
(monthly)

| Salary | | Profit |
|---|---|---|
| $_____ | (1) | $_____ |
| $_____ | (2) | $_____ |
| $_____ | (3) | $_____ |
| $_____ | (4) | $_____ |
| $_____ | (5) | $_____ |
| $_____ | (6) | $_____ |
| $_____ | (7) | $_____ |
| $_____ | (8) | $_____ |
| $_____ | (9) | $_____ |
| $_____ | (10) | $_____ |
| $_____ | (11) | $_____ |
| $_____ | (12) | $_____ |

Average monthly salary after first 12 months:
$_____

Average monthly profit after first year: $_____

19. What kind of net worth projection may I anticipate?
  a. End of 1st year:  $_____
  b. End of 2d year:  $_____
  c. End of 3d year:  $_____
  d. End of 4th year:  $_____
  e. End of 5th year:  $_____

# Index